P9-DHR-895

Teach Yourself HOW TO BECOME A WEBMASTER

in 14 days

Teach Yourself
HOW TO BECOME
A WEBMASTER
in 14 days

James L. Mohler

201 West 103rd Street
Indianapolis, Indiana 46290

To Lisa, my wife and constant support, and Meisha,
my daughter and inspiration.

Copyright © 1997 by Sams.net Publishing

FIRST EDITION

All rights reserved. No part of this book shall be reproduced, stored in a retrieval system, or transmitted by any means, electronic, mechanical, photocopying, recording, or otherwise, without written permission from the publisher. No patent liability is assumed with respect to the use of the information contained herein. Although every precaution has been taken in the preparation of this book, the publisher and author assume no responsibility for errors or omissions. Neither is any liability assumed for damages resulting from the use of the information contained herein. For information, address Sams.net Publishing, 201 W. 103rd St., Indianapolis, IN 46290.

International Standard Book Number: 1-57521-228-5

Library of Congress Catalog Card Number: 96-71216

2000   99   98   97   4   3   2   1

Interpretation of the printing code: The rightmost double-digit number is the year of the book's printing; the rightmost single digit, the number of the book's printing. For example, a printing code of 97-1 shows that the first printing of the book occurred in 1997.

Composed in AGaramond and MCPdigital by Macmillan Computer Publishing

Printed in the United States of America

All terms mentioned in this book that are known to be trademarks or service marks have been appropriately capitalized. Sams.net Publishing cannot attest to the accuracy of this information. Use of a term in this book should not be regarded as affecting the validity of any trademark or service mark.

Publisher and President   Richard K. Swadley
Publishing Manager   Dean Miller
Director of Editorial Services   Cindy Morrow
Managing Editor   Jodi Jensen
Assistant Marketing Managers   Kristina Perry
Rachel Wolfe

Acquisitions Editor
Cari Skaggs

Development Editor
Jeff Koch

Software Development Specialist
Patty Brooks

Production Editor
Tonya Simpson

Copy Editors
Chuck Hutchinson
Marla Reece

Indexer
Benjamin Slen

Technical Reviewer
Sue Charlesworth

Editorial Coordinator
Katie Wise

Technical Edit Coordinator
Lynette Quinn

Resource Coordinator
Deborah Frisby

Editorial Assistants
Carol Ackerman
Andi Richter
Rhonda Tinch-Mize

Cover Designer
Tim Amrhein

Book Designer
Gary Adair

Copy Writer
Peter Fuller

Production Team Supervisors
Brad Chinn
Charlotte Clapp

Production
Jena Brandt
Mona Brown
Terri Edwards
Sonja Hart
Tim Osborn

Overview

Contents

Acknowledgments

There are many people to thank for getting me involved in this project. First, the editors at Sams.net: Cari Skaggs, Jeff Koch, and Tonya Simpson. I also would like to thank Sue Charlesworth, Technical Reviewer; Lynette Quinn, Tech Edit Coordinator; Patty Brooks, the Software Development Specialist; and Benjamin Slen, the Indexer.

Thanks also goes to the Department of Technical Graphics at Purdue University for giving me what I needed to write this book, as well as to all the students, to whom this book is written. Teaching you teaches me.

More than any other, I would like to thank my wife for the many hours she has sacrificed, allowing me to work on this project.

About the Author

James L. Mohler is Assistant Professor of Technical Graphics at Purdue University. He has produced interactive titles for national and international publishers and provides technical training and media services to various industries through Sunrise Productions. James can be reached at jlmohler@tech.purdue.edu.

Technical Graphics at Purdue University prepares graphics professionals for electronic publication, illustration, modeling, animation, and engineering documentation specialties. You can visit the department at http://www.tech.purdue.edu/tg/.

Tell Us What You Think!

As a reader, you are the most important critic and commentator of our books. We value your opinion and want to know what we're doing right, what we could do better, what areas you'd like to see us publish in, and any other words of wisdom you're willing to pass our way. You can help us make strong books that meet your needs and give you the computer guidance you require.

Do you have access to CompuServe or the World Wide Web? Then check out our CompuServe forum by typing GO SAMS at any prompt. If you prefer the World Wide Web, check out our site at http://www.mcp.com.

 NOTE

> If you have a technical question about this book, call the technical support line at (800) 571-5840, ext. 3668.

As the publishing manager of the group that created this book, I welcome your comments. You can fax, e-mail, or write me directly to let me know what you did or didn't like about this book—as well as what we can do to make our books stronger. Here's the information:

Fax: 317/581-4669

E-mail: opsys_mgr@sams.mcp.com

Mail: Dean Miller
         Sams.net Publishing
         201 W. 103rd Street
         Indianapolis, IN 46290

Introduction

Those of us who are part of the Information Age, involved with Web development and its expansion, are lucky to have experienced the birth and growth of this transient communication media. Much like early pioneers, we are continuing to push to the limit the hardware, software, and any other technological resources we can get our hands on; seeing just how much we can do with it, and how much it'll handle. Often in both corporations and educational institutions, it means seeing how much we can do with how little intervention and resources.

Although the rate of change can be alarming to some, we should consider ourselves lucky to have been able to be a part of one of the largest explosions of technology in the 20th century. Many would say, "Heck, I've been using the Net for 20 or so years," but let's put this into perspective. There's a big difference between a couple hundred universities and organizations using the Internet versus the vast millions using it today. In addition, communicating via the Net "back then" (as little as 10 years ago) was very cryptic and difficult. Sure communication occurred, but oh, was it ugly! Today things are more standardized and easier than 10 years ago, but there is still a significant amount of technical skill that is required.

The largest amount of growth and development of the Internet has occurred within the last 10 years. Sources state that today nearly 2,000 new users get on the Internet each month. Aside from the number of surfers on the Web, the number of Web sites alone has increased from just over 1,000 in the early '80s to close to 10 million today. Ten years ago, who would have imagined Internet access and services available to virtually every in-home user, not to mention tagging an Internet feeder line onto your incoming television cable line or through a satellite link? It is extremely exciting to be a part of the rapidly evolving world of the Internet.

With every new and lasting technology comes the development of specialists who learn to master and utilize it. With the Internet, the Webmaster is the one who is assumed to know the technology, its implications, and its limitations. From Day 1 you'll see that the Webmaster must be the jack of all trades when it comes to the implementation and use of Web technology. I can think of no other job in which both technical and artistic skills are more important. The Webmaster's livelihood is based on knowledge of both. The tasks of the Webmaster usually involve both a knowledge of how to solve a technical problem and how to make the solution aesthetically pleasing. With these two major categories of skills, preparing yourself for a career as a Webmaster will require many hours of preparation. It might look like an unattainable task, but it is not. The skills, knowledge, and artistic eye can be learned; the hardest part is catching up to the current level of knowledge. From then on, it is simply maintaining your edge. Most individuals who are successful in any computer career acknowledge that to be successful you must attain the current knowledge base, and then keep up with advancements in technology.

Although it is exhilarating to be involved with the beginnings of the Information Superhighway, using new technologies carries a significant amount of cognitive overhead. Preparing to involve yourself with any technical field requires preparation, but the implications of Web technology are astounding. Futuristic books and movies propose what it will be like in the future: telecommuting, teleconferencing, instant access to full-blown, full-screen interactive multimedia, and online resources all delivered via a single cable to the home, office, or mobile computer at the click of an input device. At the extreme end, even implications of a submersive, completely visual and virtual Web navigable via head-mounted displays and data gloves are possibilities. But those who are familiar with current virtual reality and Web technologies realize that we are a long way off from being able to support such environments. However, look well young soldier; it is a possibility.

Today the technology has limitations. To support many of these futuristic features requires significant advances to overcome the limitations of the media and the communications channel. Even some of the simple things we'd like to accomplish today require ingenious and creative solutions. Our Net, today's Net, has limitations that we all must learn to overcome. I believe that, much like the advances in personal computer technology, Internet technologies will advance to enable us to do what we want to do.

Look at the personal computer. As what we wanted to do got more complex, through human ingenuity, the hardware progressed to allow more and more to be accomplished. Who would have thought 20 years ago that a 70MB application suite such as Microsoft Office would be widely used or even possible on a personal computer? Who had a 70MB hard drive back then? Advancements in technology created hardware to support task-oriented software. Pushing the envelope, the hardware expanded to allow more complex software. Human intervention and ingenuity will again advance technology for an applied task. The Internet will undoubtedly expand to give us the ability, as well as the capability, to do what we want to do.

Who Should Read This Book

Ultimately, this book is designed to equip you with the skills of a Webmaster. Therefore, its purpose is two-fold. First, this book is designed to help you engage in the current state of the Internet technology knowledge base. Being a Webmaster first requires technical knowledge of the systems, networks, resources, and software of the Net. Second, this book focuses on the actual information that is delivered over the Web. This includes information that is visual by nature and can include any multimedia element such as text, graphics, sound, animation, and video. In addition, you also learn the development of these individual elements; often, the Webmaster must have the skills to develop the individual elements as well as the site's global environment.

Most individuals who become interested in the evolving Webmaster field usually have experience in either the technical or visual communication aspects. This book, however, starts at ground zero in both; striving to equip you with the necessary skills no matter what your background. This book is designed for you if

☐ You have used the Web and have content that you would like to develop and distribute in cyberspace.

☐ You would like to develop your own personal Web site without having to pay to have it done.

☐ Your company or institution would like to develop its Web presence but doesn't know where to start.

☐ You have been designated to manage or create your company or institution Web site.

☐ You have a sincere desire to pursue a career as a Webmaster.

☐ You are a freelance developer and want to consult with companies and institutions as a Webmaster.

What This Book Contains

This book is divided into two distinct sections. In the first seven days you look at the various hats the Webmaster wears. The Webmaster must be competent in several areas because of the range of skills needed. Specifically, the Webmaster can be expected to serve as an Internet specialist, information design specialist, media designer, technical designer, technical manager, and a professional consultant.

☐ Day 1, "The Webmaster: Jack of All Trades," focuses on how each of these "hats" contributes to the global skills of the Webmaster in more detail. You also briefly take a look at the history of the Web to help you understand from where it has come.

☐ Day 2, "The Internet Specialist," concentrates on the real power of the Web: the browser and how it functions. You also examine the types of network hardware that are the backbone of the physical Internet architecture.

☐ Day 3, "The Information Design Specialist," gives you an in-depth look at the development process: how to develop the content, media elements, and pages at your site, and how to plan for implementation.

☐ After looking at the development process as a whole, Day 4, "The Media Designer," leads you into media design. How do you lay out pages so they look good? What about fonts, color, and graphics? You see how to design and implement all of the building blocks to create a "cool" site.

☐ Day 5, "The Technical Designer," is techno-weenie day; you look at the various technical aspects of site development. From Internet server standards to function and accessibility, you'll look through the eyes of a system administrator to get a feel for technical design and management.

☐ So all there is to being a Webmaster is production, right? Wrong! You'll also have to have some managerial skills. Most often you'll have to know not only how to manage your pages, but also your equipment and any other people you work with. Thus, Day 6, "The Technical Manager," is for you!

☐ The first week concludes with one of the most difficult topics: professional consulting issues. How do you establish good consulting relationships? Even more important, how do you keep them? Day 7, "The Professional Consultant," looks at protecting your ideas, professional conduct, support, proposals, and of course, pricing and payment.

The second half of this book focuses on the particulars of developing Web pages and coding in HTML. Undoubtedly, this is what most people think of when they hear the term Webmaster: someone who knows HTML. As you will have already seen, there is much more to the proverbial Webmaster, but HTML programming and utilization of other Web languages and features are important as well.

☐ To get you up and running in HTML land, you start with the basics of the language. On Day 8, "Introduction to HTML and Block Tags," you see how HTML differs from SGML, as well as the various editors you can use to crank your code. You see how basic block tags work within the HTML language.

☐ After you get a grip on the block tags, on Day 9, "Text-Level Tags," you begin taking a look at the text-level tags, which include physical and logical text tags as well as several other important tags.

☐ Life would be pretty boring with just the HTML language, so on Day 10, "Utilizing Graphics and Image Maps," you look at how to incorporate graphics and image maps at your Web site.

☐ Now that you know HTML and some of the other nifty features available on the Web, it's time to start getting down to business. On Day 11, "Using Tables To Format Pages," you learn one of the niftiest features of the HTML language called tables. You see how to use tables to format data as well as how to use them to format pages.

☐ On Day 11 you laid the framework to lay out pages using tables. On Day 12, "Using Frames To Format Pages," you see another way to lay out pages using frames.

☐ On Day 13, "Using Forms To Gather Data," you see another advanced capability of Web development and how you can get feedback from your audience using forms.

☐ All work and no play makes Jack a dull boy! On Day 14, "Advanced Web Components," you take a look at some of the newest technologies that are available for Web developers and how each can be utilized at your site.

With this book, you will become the jack of all trades, I mean, Webmaster. No matter the task, with experiences from this book you should be able to comfortably say, "Why, yes, I am a Webmaster!"

What You Need Before You Begin

Undoubtedly, because this book is about Webmastering, I assume that you have a sincere interest in the Web and already have a hook to the Internet. Concerning development of Web pages and graphics, really any computer of 486 class or higher should be sufficient. I say this with tongue in cheek however, because I am sure there are some people who do much more with much less. Most of the references and exercises in this book can be performed with a simple text editor, paint program, and the utilities supplied on the CD-ROM. I use a Pentium class machine with PhotoShop, Word, Netscape 3.0, and Microsoft Internet Explorer 3.0. This does not mean, however, that your setup must be exactly like mine. Where I can, I will make it as neutral as possible. Heck, you might even be working on a Mac or UNIX machine. Along the way, I'll point out some of the differences you might see if you're working on a platform other than a basic Windows system.

Now it's time to buckle up and take off for your journey through the Web. Let's get started by taking a look at this position you so much want to attain (drum-roll please)—the Webmaster!

Conventions Used in This Book

This book uses different typefaces to differentiate between code and regular English, and also to help you identify important concepts.

☐ Actual code is typeset in a special monospace font.

☐ Placeholders are set in a special *italic monospace* font. You should replace the placeholder with a specific filename or value that it represents.

☐ *Italics* highlight terms when they first appear in the text and are sometimes used to emphasize important points.

☐ ➥This arrow at the beginning of a line of code means that a single line of code requires multiple lines on the printed page. Continue typing all characters after ➥ as though they were part of the previous line.

NOTE

Note boxes highlight information that can make your Web programming more efficient and effective.

New term boxes provide clear definitions of new, essential terms.

TIP

Tips offer insight or shortcuts to becoming a Webmaster.

Warnings help you avoid Webmastering pitfalls.

WARNING

HTML Tags

Special sidebars like this one highlight and explain new HTML tags as they are introduced.

At a Glance

The first seven days you will be looking at the various hats the Webmaster wears. The Webmaster must be competent in several areas because of the range of skills needed. Specifically, the Webmaster can be expected to serve as an Internet specialist, information design specialist, media designer, technical designer, technical manager, and a professional consultant.

This week you learn all about those different roles and how to prepare yourself for them.

1

2

3

4

5

6

7

Day 1

The Webmaster: Jack of All Trades

Many careers that have emerged over the past century have evolved as a direct result of new technologies. The positions of system analyst, network specialist, computer graphics specialist, virtual reality technologist, and so on all were created as a result of technological advancements. Technology is a wonderful thing if you have it and you know how to use it, but one of the most demanding parts of a career in any computer field is having the vast number of skills required to get up to speed, not to mention staying there.

Some call technology a cutting edge. To others, technology is a bleeding edge; it is relentless in its continually changing nature. Great are the demands on the Webmaster due to the rate at which the Web is evolving—no other arena seems to be expanding and changing as quickly as the Web. It seems that every day there is something new that can be done on, with, or to the Web. This presents a significant hurdle for those who want to be knighted as Webmaster. If you are relatively new to the Web, you might need some "sink time," or time for the information to take root. During this first day you will become familiar with all the various hats that the Webmaster is often required to wear (see Figure 1.1).

The Webmaster usually is the person who creates, develops, and maintains a Web site, but as you'll see there is often more involved than just creating pages and posting them to a Web site. Because Webmastering is based on technology, its definition can vary from company to company or from person to person. Most often the Webmaster is classified as someone who can create Web pages, but in most instances, the job requires much more than a knowledge of posting pages to a site.

Figure 1.1.
Roles of the Webmaster.

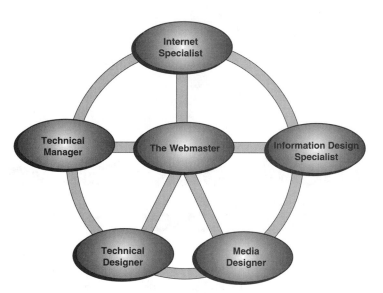

Today, you also look at the history of the Internet. Where'd this thing come from? Did it crop up overnight? And how does the infamous Information Superhighway tie into it all? These are some of the questions that this first day will answer. Finally, the day concludes with a description of the various services that are available via the Net and how you can use them to garnish the vast information resources that are connected to your backyard.

NOTE

Keep in mind that throughout this book you'll see terms such as the Net, the Web, and cyberspace. To most people, these terms all refer to the World Wide Web (WWW) or the Internet. To others there's a difference between the World Wide Web and the Internet. This distinction is highlighted later in the chapter in the section titled, "The History of the Web."

The Different Roles of the Webmaster

The next few sections describe the various roles that a Webmaster can be expected to play. This does not mean that in every company or in every situation a single individual will be ultimately responsible for all these tasks. In large corporate settings there often are several individuals involved in web development, but there will always be a coordinating leader for the group. This leader, the lead Webmaster, will undoubtedly have knowledge in all these areas and be able to guide, direct, and coach the other individuals in their tasks. This book really tries to prepare you to be that lead individual in your group. If you are a Webmaster for a small company with no other individuals involved with this process, you are the lead Webmaster already.

The Internet Specialist

First and foremost, the Webmaster is an Internet specialist. An Internet specialist is one who understands what the Net is, from where it came, and where it might be going. Understand that the Web didn't develop overnight, although current newspaper and broadcast media would like to suggest otherwise. The Internet has been in use since the early 1960s and has grown drastically over the past 10 years. The latest media hype is predominantly due to the large-scale swing of corporate America onto the Web, not to mention the fastest growing section of connected users: the in-home user.

NOTE

> Although an Internet specialist is someone who knows about the Internet as a whole, this book focuses on the specifics of which the Webmaster must be aware. Many aspects of the Internet are not covered here. What we are interested in are the portions that directly relate to the Webmaster.

An *Internet specialist* is an individual who understands what the Internet is, from where it has come, and where it might be going. The Internet specialist also understands how to connect to the Internet and how to utilize it.

Again, you might wonder, what do you mean "where it (the Web) might be going?" You must understand that the future of the Web is still relatively unclear. Today the Net is a mass of computing power connected together, enabling many different types of communication to occur. Corporations, businesses, and institutions all are scrambling to establish their presence on the Web (which is good for you!). This gives you many opportunities to get involved with companies that are beginning to establish their Web presence. But the future of the Web is unclear due to advancements we have yet to discover, not to mention an extremely accelerated period of growth. As the hardware and software advance, so will the capabilities of the Web. Much like a business that is bursting at the seams, the Web is growing so fast that it is difficult to determine what effect the growth has on performance. Will performance break down as the user base expands? Will it create new advancements in technology? Will the hardware naturally expand to enable growth or will the infrastructure collapse under the increasing load?

As an Internet specialist, you must be aware of these rising issues. More than likely, you will be posed with questions like these if you serve as an institutional Webmaster or corporate Web consultant. Many corporations are rushing headlong to throw their information on the Web, working from a paradigm in which the fear of being left behind is greater than the fear of losing money in a Web investment. Yet, most have sincere concerns about the longevity and commercial validity of the Web. As an Internet specialist, you must educate yourself on the latest technologies so that you can present logical and technological answers to these types of questions and concerns. Having ESP wouldn't hurt, either!

Additionally, the Webmaster must know how to use the Web and how to connect to it. What are the best resources on the Web? Where the heck are they, and how do you get connected? From machines to cables to software, you must know how to get yourself and your company latched on to this beast. Today, you'll start at ground zero and look at being both a consumer and provider of content on the Web. When you're surfing the Web, how do you do it with efficiency? In other words, how do you know a good wave? When you're making waves (providing content), how do you make the "Big Kahuna?" You take a look at both these issues when you focus on being an Internet specialist.

Information Design Specialist

The main purpose of the Web is to entertain, inform, or persuade your audience; it is a new way of communicating. To effectively communicate in each of these ways, you must know how to put together several different elements in a logical and effective manner. Most often the Webmaster is given content, such as information that describes a company or product, to put on the Web. This makes the task a little easier. Sometimes he or she will need to develop the content or coordinate content development among a group of individuals. In either case, the main purpose behind providing content is to communicate.

NEW TERM An *information design specialist* is an individual who understands the communication process and how to design products that inform, persuade, educate, or entertain efficiently and effectively.

As most developers know, rule number one in multimedia and hypermedia development is that content is king. Poorly designed content can never be masked. No matter how many slick graphics, dancing bullets, or animated elements are added, poor content is still poor. It is like dressing up the exterior or interior of a house that has a cracked foundation with the intent of selling it. It won't sell because the footing on which everything else rests is unstable. The same is true of poor content. The content is the foundation from which communication occurs and to which all supporting elements enhance and clarify.

Communication is a process that can be described graphically, as shown in Figure 1.2. For communication to occur, by definition, a sender must send a message and a receiver must receive and comprehend the message. Also involved in the communication process is the issue of environmental noise.

Figure 1.2.
The communication model.

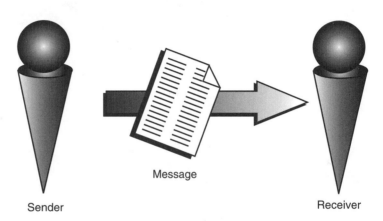

Message

Sender   Receiver

In Web communication, noise is something with which you should be most concerned. As shown in Figure 1.3, noise disrupts communication. Noise is comprised of those things that distract the receiver and inhibit the reception of the message. Noise can occur from the sender in the form of poor content. It can occur in the communication channel in the form of a hefty page that takes an eternity to download. It also can occur on the receiver's end in the form of an incompatible browser. You see a lot of this on the Web. Many people on the Web have things to say; however, due to noise, their messages are not received. In the information age, you must understand that people are inundated with information. When a message is blocked or surrounded with noise, it can be misunderstood, misinterpreted, or ignored outright. A site must communicate clearly, effectively, and precisely for maximum impact.

Figure 1.3.
Noise disrupts communi-
cation.

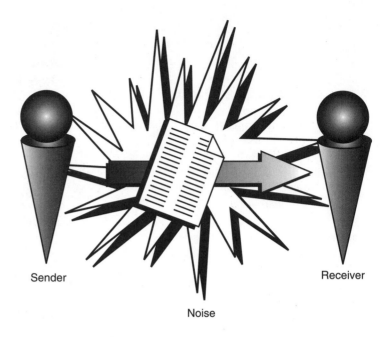

Sender   Receiver

Noise

NOTE

Noise disrupts effective communication. Noise on the Web could be a graphically unappealing page, poorly written text, typographical errors, poor grammar, or a page that takes 20 minutes to download.

In reality, creating a product that communicates effectively, whether it be a book, an article, a CD-ROM, or a Web site, requires the use of careful planning so that the product itself is successful. The success of such a product is determined by how well the message is received and interpreted by the audience. So how do you ensure that a product communicates well? Look for a product that has been deemed successful and see how it was developed.

For the most part, creating a good Web site can be summed up in one word: *planning*. Most sites fail because issues arise that were not considered during the site's conception. People instantly jump behind a computer and start pushing pixels and spewing code, inevitably creating, in most cases, a horrid site. Problems with browsers, platforms, fonts, downloading, and so on will snafu this quick method of creating a Web site, which you'll see later. There is no replacement for time spent planning a site.

As you develop a site, you must be concerned with providing good content. You also must ascertain whether you can adequately provide what your audience wants. Can your equipment support the number of people or hits made to your site? Do you have the resources

in-house to support a site, or should you look for outside vendors for help? Questions, questions, questions, but they are ones that need to be considered.

 A *hit* occurs when a browser from a remote location requests information from a Web server. Each time a new or different page is loaded from the site, a hit is recorded.

Undoubtedly, most of the things with which the Webmaster deals are technical issues such as connecting to the Net, finding resources, and using those resources. However, to some extent the Webmaster must have some inclination as to the whole purpose of the World Wide Web: communication. The criterion for a good Web site is its communicative value and how efficiently and effectively communication occurs.

Media Designer

Some of the biggest inhibitors of Web communication are poorly designed graphics, animations, and multimedia elements. To be an effective Webmaster you must develop an artistic eye, an understanding of the communicative power of graphics, and a designer's imagination. The hypermedia world is filled with many different additive elements that can be used to help a site or page communicate. You should use graphical elements to help communicate more effectively; this is their goal and purpose. One of the first steps is to develop an understanding of page layout and composition and how it affects readability and visual appeal. Web documents become much better communication tools when they are formatted and include graphics. As shown in Figure 1.4, they also become more interesting.

Figure 1.4.

Graphics help to enhance communication.

A *media designer* is an individual who understands computer graphics, animation, video, and sound, and can effectively use these media elements to enhance communication.

Technical Designer

When the word Webmaster is mentioned, most often it implies a individual who is a Web "techno-weenie." Undoubtedly one of the supreme tasks of the Webmaster is to understand the technical implications, advantages, and limitations of the Web.

 A *technical designer* is an individual who understands the standards, hardware, and software of a Web network and how to fit them together to make a working site.

Part of being a technical designer is to first understand the technology behind the Web. This includes having an understanding of the hardware—networks, machines, and connections—and the client and server software. Fortunately, today's Net is somewhat more standardized than in days gone by. However, there are many standards. The various parts of the Web use several terms for which the Webmaster must have definitions and understanding. This is the first step in being technically "Web adept."

When you're putting a puzzle together, there's much more than just having the pieces and understanding that the pieces interlock to create a picture. Therefore, much like a puzzle, being Webmaster will require you to understand how to connect all the pieces of your corner of the Internet world so that it will function correctly.

The last two concerns of technical design are issues of accessibility and management. Really this has more to do with the layout of your Web site's files than anything else. It also is an issue of control. Who is in control of your site and, more important, who has access? The adage, "Too many cooks spoils the broth," applies here. Too many individuals having access to a site can create chaos in developing and managing a Web site. Without a doubt, as Webmaster you will need to define the terms of accessibility for all individuals involved with your Web site and development process. Doing so will reduce many future headaches.

Technical Manager

Today, the role of the Webmaster is continually changing and evolving. This is natural because the item on which the Webmaster's livelihood depends—the Web—also is evolving. In days gone by, a single individual was designated as Webmaster, but in many companies today there is often a team of people working to assist and support the tasks of the Webmaster.

The Webmaster still must manage and maintain hardware and software, but often managerial skills extend beyond these two items to one of the hardest things to manage: people.

 A *technical manager* is an individual who manages the hardware, software, resources, and people involved in the Web development process.

In reality, you do not manage people. People are not machines and therefore cannot be treated or "managed" as such. Most managers who approach people as machines have no end of trouble, but those who support, provide, and coach subordinates find that management is easy. You'll find that in many larger companies and institutions that have a dedicated Web development group, Webmastering can include individuals representing each of the skills outlined in the previous role descriptions. Articles from several magazines and other resources show this as a trend that is occurring in many firms. Most firms have too much information for a single individual to create and manage. For example, Adobe, one of the leaders in computer illustration software—makers of Photo Shop and Illustrator—has a Web site with an estimated 10,000 pages, much more than one individual could maintain. Managerial and people skills are very important in institutions of this magnitude.

Preparing To Be a Webmaster

If you're still reading, I assume I have not scared you off with the long list of skills or hats that a Webmaster must wear. These skills often take time to develop, and as you read about them in more depth, they will appear more attainable. For the most part, the largest portion of the Webmaster's skills deals with the technology itself. However, as in many careers, the broader your range of skills, the more successful you'll be as a Webmaster. The skills presented also can be viewed in a different light. The skills themselves deal with three areas: technology, technique, and maintenance and management.

Mastering the Technology

To master the technology, you must put into practice what you learn in this book. Reading about it brings theoretical knowledge, doing it brings applied and practical knowledge. You can read many books, on subjects well beyond what you learn in this one, but until you actually start tinkering with the technology it's only head knowledge. Hopefully, you'll have the opportunity as you read this book to put into action what you learn by trying examples, looking at the technology you currently have, or even to the ultimate, setting up your Web system using this book as a guide. Regardless, you will have to put into action the things you read in this book for it to actually take root and be applied knowledge. The best teacher is the technology.

Mastering the Technique

To develop a technique or style in Web development, you must take action and begin developing your own pages and sites. The predominate knowledge base on techniques comes both in page design and information design. To help you develop the eye for design and the understanding of good content, you hopefully already have one of the best applied teachers right at your fingertips: your Web connection. One of the best ways to see what I am talking about is to spend time surfing. In this book you see examples, and even the Web addresses, but you'll have to link to the Web yourself—somehow I am sure that black-and-white pages won't do some of the sites and pages justice. So be prepared to do a lot of surfing over the next 14 days. Consider it a "course requirement." For more information on page layout techniques check out *Laura Lemay's Web WorkShop: Graphics and Web Page Design* by Sams.net Publishing.

NOTE

As you surf the Web, you must understand how it works. Many times Web addresses change, sometimes daily at some sites. I am going to do my best to provide accurate Web site addresses in the examples. However, by the time this book is printed, some addresses might have changed or even been nullified. This is natural on the Web due to its fluidic nature; it's just one of those wonderful things we have to deal with, but we'll do our best to work around it.

Mastering Maintenance and Management

As you read earlier, many companies and corporations are struggling just to get their presence established on the Web. Many throw information on the Web and let it sit for several months before updating or modifying it. This is not a way to get "repeat customers." One of the most important things to a successful Web presence is change. Customers of your site, your audience, like to know that you are current, consistently updating the information on your pages. They like to see activity on the Web. Planning to invest in the Web, only to let information stagnate at your site, is not recommended. Optimally, you want that repeat customer. Heck, you want them to have a bookmark straight to your page, and one of the best ways to accomplish this is to consistently and frequently update your pages with something new.

NOTE

> One of the things you must note about Web surfers is that most are used to quick information bursts and rapidly changing information. Suffice to say that the attention span and patience level for information is much lower. Most are used to the quick-changing nature of TV, video games, and multimedia information delivery. More than likely they'll expect similar things from the Web sites they visit.

To enable this, the Webmaster must lay out and enable a maintenance and management strategy. Much of this can be accomplished in the design; you should design a site for easy management and maintenance. Creating a site on which pages are scattered from here to kingdom come will make your job more a task of memory than of management or maintenance. Managing all of the links and pages in a site are important, too. As you proceed through this book, you'll find ways in which you can make managing and maintaining your site easier.

The History of the Web

The idea of platform-independent, computer-independent communications systems actually has existed for a long time. Heck, we don't want to be limited in our communications system. For example, it probably wouldn't be very profitable to have only a point-to-point telephone system. In other words, it wouldn't be advantageous if we had to connect a single cable from our house to everyone we wanted to call. If it were so, we'd have a mess. However, our phone communication system is designed so that we can connect to any user who is properly connected to the phone architecture. It is natural that computer communication support the same paradigm and structure—enabling global communication rather than proprietary, geographically limited communication.

The idea of a nonproprietary computer communication system was first conceived in 1965. An individual by the name of Ted Nelson helped to define two of the basic precepts of the Web we enjoy today; he defined both hypertext and hypermedia. Although to some they are the same, there is a distinction.

Hypertext is text that is nonsequential or nonlinear in nature. The reader is actually able to choose a path to delve deeper into the information.

The idea of nonsequential text was not really a new idea; however, in relationship to computer documents and communication, it was a drastic departure from the things that people were used to. A traditional document such as a book is a linear document—you read from beginning to end. However, a hypertext document enables you to go deeper into a particular subject before proceeding (see Figure 1.5).

Figure 1.5.

Linear text and nonlinear text (hypertext).

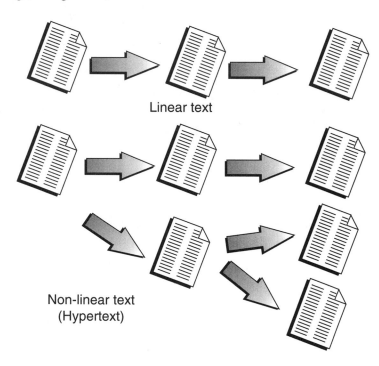

Linear text

Non-linear text
(Hypertext)

NEW TERM   *Hypermedia* is nonlinear, nonsequential media elements that can be viewed independently of one another. Hypermedia is media-based communication that is not strictly limited to text.

Hypermedia extended the idea of hypertext beyond just text, as shown in Figure 1.6. The idea that communications can occur not only beyond static text but also in a nonlinear fashion has significant implications in education, training, and marketing. Hypermedia connotated the use of multiple forms of media elements into a single document. Hypermedia documents draw their resources (media elements) from many locations or storage devices.

1

Figure 1.6.
*The concept of
hypermedia.*

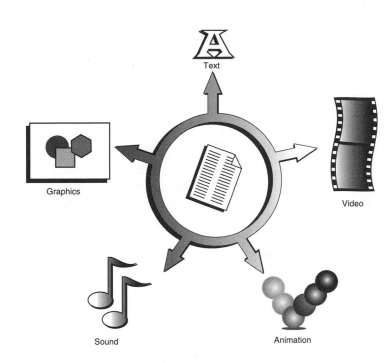

By defining the new computer communication paradigm, Ted Nelson's ideas had a significant impact in many areas of computer communication. One of the first attempts at a more rational computer network design, one that was a precursor to what we know today as the Internet, was started by the U.S. Department of Defense in the 1970s. This work focused not only on an uninterruptable network but also on a means of a universal communication protocol.

NEW TERM A *protocol* is a set of standards that define how data is transmitted and received between computers. A protocol ensures that data is transmitted in a defined way so that it also can be received.

The U.S. Department of Defense network, called the Advanced Research Projects Agency Network, or ARPAnet, was designed to support military research. The objective of ARPAnet was to create a computer network that could withstand partial network outages and still function properly. For example, in networks of that day, a computer that shut down or died in the network caused the network to fail. No more data could be transferred because the network was dependent on every computer. In ARPAnet, if a computer malfunctioned or was disconnected, the network would still function because all of the computers could pass the data to the destination. The computers themselves were responsible for transferring the data, not the network. ARPAnet led to the development of the Internet Protocol (IP). You learn more about IP and TCP/IP on Day 5, "The Technical Designer."

 The *Internet Protocol* (IP) transfers data using small packets or chunks of data. Data being transferred is broken into packets, sent through the network, and then reassembled on the receiving end.

Throughout the 1980s, several networks were developed and helped lead networking technology to that which would support the Internet of today. Most networks at the time were UNIX-based and were focused in academia. Organizations such as the National Science Foundation (NSF) built upon the discoveries of ARPAnet and continued to develop the technology. NSF was responsible for setting up regional supercomputer centers, using the fastest computers in the world for high-end research. Because financial resources were limited, only five supercomputer centers were established, but they had a tremendous impact on the development of the Internet. Throughout the 1980s, the Internet was primarily used for military research purposes but quickly began extending beyond government and politics into academia.

In 1989, using Nelson's paradigm of a global, nonproprietary computer communications system and newer networking hardware technologies, Tim Berners-Lee proposed a computer-based communication network that would enable physics researchers to share information. As a researcher for the Conseil European pour la Recherche Nucleaire (CERN) in Switzerland, Berners-Lee proposed a system that defined a consistent, cross-platform interface that would enable universal access to a variety of document types. The proposal also defined the use of multiple protocols to access the information. The most astounding part of his work was that it focused on a universal method of distributing information. Networks that existed at that time didn't provide a significant means of enabling computers to communicate across platforms and across systems.

The next major development was a contribution from the academic community in 1993. Working for the National Center for Supercomputing Applications (NCSA) at the University of Illinois Champagne-Urbana, a young graduate student named Marc Andreessen began working on one of the biggest advancements in Web technology: the first browser. Developing the software for the X Window platform, which is a Windows interface running on a UNIX workstation, Andreessen worked on Mosaic, a graphics- and text-based browser that semantically used the HTML language. Although the number of Web servers in 1993 was significantly small, Mosaic quickly captured the attention of many people. The ability to view hypertext and hypermedia from remote sites was a significant advancement. (Giving the browser away for free also helped!) This development, more than any other, is attributed to starting the wildfire called the World Wide Web.

In 1994, the number of Web servers drastically increased. Realizing that the Web would eventually become commercialized, several universities and private companies began writing a list of standards for Web communications using the Web. This group became known as the World Wide Web Consortium, or W3C. The various elements specified by the group included not only content standards but also hardware and software standards to be followed by individuals.

In addition to the work by the World Wide Web Consortium, many companies announced commercial versions of Web browsers; the most significant company was Netscape. Marc Andreessen, who left NCSA, and Jim Clark, formerly an employee of Silicon Graphics, founded Netscape Communications Corporation and created the browser of the same name.

Following the W3C committee's set of standards and the introduction of Netscape came exactly what many believed would happen: Web commercialization. With commercialization also came many new and exciting things, but especially, technological change. Many companies, now aware of the real-time possibilities on the Web—predominantly due to Mosaic and its wide user base—began setting aside a vast number of resources for provisional Web development. By mid-1995 there were more than 15,000 HTTP servers, a huge increase from the previous year.

New Term   An *HTTP server* is a Web server and is an acronym for HyperText Transfer Protocol. HTTP is a set of standards for providing content and media elements on the Web.

From 1995 to today, the Web has grown and expanded more than any of the individuals involved with its evolution could have known, and it shows no signs of stopping soon. Many developments have occurred throughout its lifetime. The Java language introduced by Sun Microsystems, ActiveX from Microsoft, and the myriad of plug-ins and resources make almost anything possible on the Web. Today the number of Web servers is nearing 10 million, and the number of users is well over 30 million. Online commerce, banking, travel, and other resources make the Web a continually expanding marketplace.

The Development of Technology

The wonderful technological advancements that have been made over the last 10 years have been predominantly sparked by computer users wanting to do more. The advancements can be seen in two major areas: hardware and software. Luckily, the hardware architecture that is the backbone of the Web has, up to this point, been strong enough to uphold the software traffic that occurs on the Web. However, if the hardware technology ever stops advancing or reaches a point where no further advancement can be made, the Web will die.

The hardware advancements that have contributed to the Web are basically focused on making the hardware faster. On the Web, everything is an issue of speed. Talk to users who can view the Web only via modem and their likely impression of the Web is that it is slow and often cumbersome. They probably will prefer a magazine or newspaper to Web-based communication. A user directly connected to the Internet through a university or corporate Web system will say the biggest problem is content quality.

Regardless of which one of these scenarios typifies you, advances in the hardware have predominately focused on making the Web faster, and indeed, it is faster than in times past. The newer multimedia elements, including video, demand a greater transmission speed simply because these elements require more data. As we want to do more, we need faster communications. Advances in network wiring from unshielded copper wire to coaxial cable to fiber optics have enabled data to be transferred faster and with greater accuracy. Improvement in internal computer processing speed also has helped.

Program Development

Aside from hardware, browsers too have led the way to program development. As you read earlier, many would argue that Internet communication occurred many years before the Web developed, which is true. However, most technological developments have occurred in a stair-step fashion. If you look at the various ways in which to communicate via the Web or the various Web services available, you see a natural progression. Each program was developed to be a modification or a better rendition of the previous communication method. From e-mail to Gopher to FTP and WWW, each type of communication occurred as an advancement of a prior technology, enabling something new to be done. Even today, plug-ins and add-on scripting and programming languages are being added to the technology of yesterday: the browser. Note that the word *yesterday* implies technology that is only a year old, but technology always develops this way. Technology is applying and adapting what has been learned yesterday to do something new today.

The Browser

Marc Andreesson probably had no idea that Mosaic would have the impact that it did—he probably wouldn't have just given it away had he known. However, the act of giving it away is partially responsible for the rapid development of the Web. Many browsers quickly followed on the heels of Mosaic, but Mosaic ruled supreme for quite a while. Today the two biggest players in the browser market are Netscape Communications and Microsoft. These two browsers look a little different than the Mosaic of yesterday. Over time, many new and exciting features have been added to the basic Mosaic look and function; however, all the current browsers still basically function the same.

NEW TERM *Browser software* is a software program that enables the user to view Web-based documents. All browsers retrieve semantically described information from remote computers and then compose or lay out text, graphics, and multimedia elements on the user's machine.

As you begin flipping from one site to another you'll see that your browser is quite busy. The prompt line at the bottom of the browser shows the various elements that are downloading for the page to be displayed. But how does the whole thing work? Each and every Web site has an address, or Uniform Resource Locator (URL). Much like your home mailing address, the URL is unique to the site. Clicking links or using bookmarks causes the browser to try to access the respective site's address or URL.

NEW TERM A *Uniform Resource Locator* (URL) is the specific address of a Web site or Web resource.

When you are simply surfing the Web, you really don't have to know too much about URLs. That is what's nice about the Web. You can just click items in the page to go where you want to go rather than having to enter information with the keyboard. However, many times you might know the address (URL), so you also can enter it by typing in the browser's address field as shown in Figure 1.7.

Figure 1.7.

Using the browser's address field.

The address field

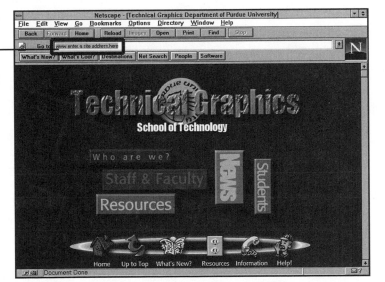

NOTE

> If you want to enter an address into the browser's address field, make sure you enter it exactly as you see it. Web addresses are case sensitive, and browsers don't like extra characters or backslashes (\) for foreslashes (/). A site at www.somesite.com is a different site than www.Somesite.com. Also be careful when you're writing it down for future reference.

As you're surfing the Web, keep in mind that it is not unusual for a Web site's pages to get shuffled around. If you try to enter a Web address and get an error—Page not Found—try accessing another part of the site first. For example, if you try to access a page with http://www.somesite.com/home/page.html and cannot access it, try http://www.somesite.com/home/. If that still doesn't work, try http://www.somesite/. Trying the addresses in this fashion will help you find what you are looking for.

Internet Services

Although this book is predominantly focused on creating World Wide Web sites and pages, you also must be aware of many other Web-based communication methods and services. Some of these services might not be available to you; it depends upon your service provider or Net hook-up. Most provide access to at least news, e-mail, and the Web. As is the case with FTP and Telnet, you simply must have the application software and connection to the Internet to use the services.

WWW

The first and foremost item you should have is a Web browser and a connection to the Internet. Beyond that, you need nothing to be able to surf the Web. More than likely you will already have either Netscape Communication's Navigator or Microsoft's Internet Explorer. There are some differences between these two browsers, both in speed and functionality. If you don't have them yet you can download the latest versions from http://www.netscape.com (Netscape Navigator) or http://www.microsoft.com (Internet Explorer).

Many call Navigator, shown in Figure 1.8, the "original" browser. If you've seen Mosaic, Navigator should look very familiar. Many sources state that Navigator is faster than Explorer (shown in Figure 1.9), and I tend to agree. However, Navigator doesn't have the robust formatting features that Explorer does. For the most part, pages loaded in either will appear similar but not exactly the same. Keep in mind that HTML is a semantic language, not a page layout language. This means that the layout of pages is loosely defined by HTML. Some things might shift and look a little different from one browser to another. In most instances the differences are quite small and really affect only how text is laid out on the page.

Figure 1.8.

Netscape Navigator.

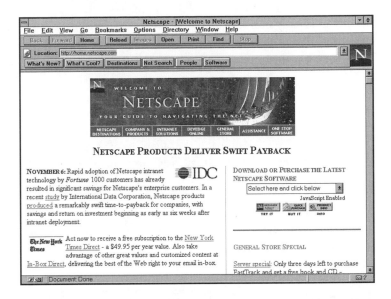

Figure 1.9.

Microsoft Internet Explorer.

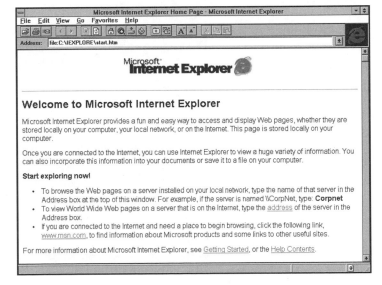

  HTML is an acronym for HyperText Markup Language. HTML uses style "tags" to define how text, graphics, and other elements should be arranged on a Web page.

As you are working in this book, keep in mind the vast number of resources available via the Web. When you read about different subjects, don't ignore the information that is on the

Web. Many sites such as Yahoo! (www.yahoo.com) have in-depth information about technological subjects such as HTML. At some point, check out the many different HTML subjects available on the Web, including the discussion of various HTML versions.

Mail

Send about five letters and you'll appreciate the nonexistent cost of e-mail, not to mention its speed. E-mail is probably the oldest use of the Internet. Early days of the Internet revolved around e-mail. Today, e-mail is as common as snail mail (regular U.S. post office mail).

 Electronic mail, or *e-mail*, enables you to send electronic messages and attached files to remote users via the Internet.

Sending e-mail using your browser is quite easy; however, you must have a valid e-mail account. Netscape Navigator will enable you to receive and send e-mail right from the browser using the small envelope icon in the lower-right corner, as shown in Figure 1.10.

Figure 1.10.

Using mail in Netscape Navigator.

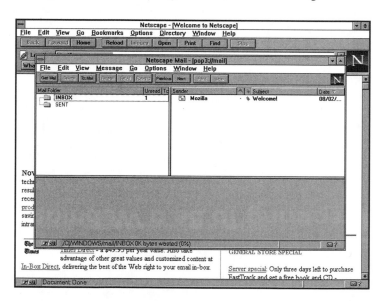

If you are a Microsoft Internet Explorer user you cannot send and receive mail directly from your Web browser. However, you can use Microsoft Exchange, which is installed with Microsoft Internet Explorer (see Figure 1.11).

Figure 1.11.

Using Microsoft
Exchange.

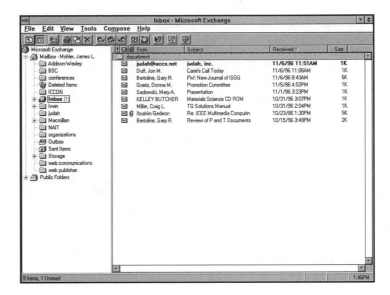

In addition to using your browser, you also can use an external mail program such as Eudora to view mail. *External* programs are applications that are separate from the browser and operate independently. Some people prefer external mail programs because they often enable better integration with other software resources.

NOTE

No matter what e-mail program you choose, pick one and stick with it. Often people will try to utilize many different programs for mail. Unfortunately, address books, which automatically remember the e-mail addresses and other information about various people, are not compatible from program to program.

News

Do you ever wish you could talk to people about a specific computer software problem? Using newsgroups enables you to do just that.

A *newsgroup* is an electronic message board on which you can post messages, read messages, and exchange files.

Today there are approximately 10,000 different newsgroups concerning subjects from computer vendors to fans of the Goo Goo Dolls. Anything you want to talk about or read about can be found on the Internet's newsgroups (see Figure 1.12).

Figure 1.12.

Using a news program to read messages that are posted to newsgroups.

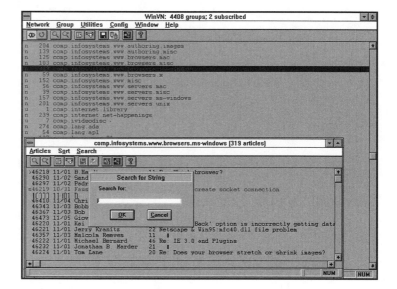

Both Navigator and Explorer support newsgroups right in the browser. To be able to use the newsgroups, you must tell the browser where your news server is located, assuming your Internet Service Provider has one. Both browsers enable you to establish this information through the *preferences*, which are settings that are specific to your browser—in other words, how your program is set up. After you tell the browser where to find the news server, you can choose which newsgroups you would like to subscribe to.

NOTE   Instead of using the Web browser, you might want to use an external newsreader program, which will run much quicker than a browser news reader. You can download one of the most popular newsreader programs, WinVN, from `http://www.winsite.com`.

FTP

FTP was one of the first methods for distributing information over the Internet. The whole purpose of the Internet is to distribute files and data to remote users. An FTP program is a program that enables you to send files (upload) or retrieve files (download) from an FTP server, as shown in Figure 1.13.

 FTP or *File Transfer Protocol* is a set of standards for the transmission of files across the Internet.

Figure 1.13.

Using file transfer protocol (FTP) to connect to a remote FTP server.

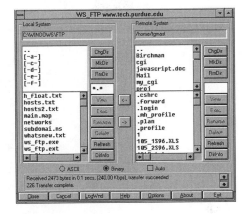

 FTP servers are usually private, secure servers, meaning that you must have an account—a login ID and a password—to gain access to the server. Depending on your account setup, you might be able only to read files, or you might have full read-write access. You will need to talk to the system administrator of the FTP site to gain access if it is a private FTP server. For most public servers, ones where you can download shareware and freeware programs, you can use anonymous for the login and guest for the password. This will often give you read-only access, enabling you to download but not upload.

Most browsers can be used to access FTP sites, assuming you have a login and password. To do so you simply need the address of the site. Remember that World Wide Web communication was designed to support multiple protocols, FTP being one of them. You enter an FTP address into the browser's address field in the form ftp.*somesite*.com. Notice that the www is replaced by ftp, denoting an FTP server.

As is the case with newsreaders, using an external FTP program independent of the browser is much faster. Many shareware and freeware versions of FTP clients are available via the Net. The one I use, WS_FTP by John A. Jonad, can be downloaded from http://www.winsite.com.

Gopher

Gopher was an early, pre-Mosaic Internet tool. Before the graphics and text-based browsers we enjoy today, many people wanted an easier way to search for information on the Internet. Seeing the need, a group of students and professors from the University of Minnesota created a text menu-based Internet browsing tool called Gopher, shown in Figure 1.14.

Figure 1.14.
Using Gopher.

```
┌──────────────── Winsock 3270 Telnet - ssinfo.purdue.edu ──────────────────┐
│ Connect   Close   Exit   Edit   Print Screen   Setup   Help                │
│      PURDUE UNIVERSITY                                                      │
│      West Lafayette, IN, USA                          h=help--h=help       │
│      SSINFO MAIN MENU                                                       │
│                                                    h   IF You Can't   h     │
│  1. Academic Life/                                 =   FIND IT, ASK   =     │
│  2. Campus Life/    SOMETHING NEW IN HERE!         h     FOR HELP!!    h     │
│  3. Student Life/                                  e                   e     │
│  4. STUDENT PERSONAL INFORMATION ACCESS (PAC)/     l       PRESS      l     │
│  5. School News/                                   p       h          p     │
│  6. Admission to Purdue/                           -     FOR HELP!    -     │
│  7. Employment Opportunities & Info/                                        │
│  8. International Students & Scholars/              h=help--h=help           │
│  9. WWW via lynx/Gopher                                                     │
│ 10. Phone/addr/e-mail Student/Staff Directories                            │
│ 11. Where Do I Go For ... ???                                              │
│ 12. About SSINFO/                                                          │
│ 13. This and That/                                                         │
│ 14. FIND YOUR ALIAS to access PUCC/Res Hall Lab machines                   │
│ 15. Voting/Validation                                                      │
│ ========================================================================== │
│ More Options: <h/?>=Help, <l>=Logout, <c>=Change Terminal Type             │
│ Select Option: Terminal IBM-3278-2 is unknown.                            │
│ Connection closed by host ssinfo.purdue.edu                               │
└────────────────────────────────────────────────────────────────────────┘
```

> **NEW TERM**   *Gopher* is a menu- and text-based Internet browsing program that can be used to download files and information from remote computers.

When Gopher was created and conceived it was a striking innovation, but today Gopher servers are becoming less common. Most Web browsers, including Navigator and Explorer, support Gopher menus. Much like an FTP address, a Gopher address exchanges the www of a regular Web address with gopher. A sample Gopher address might look like gopher.*somesite*.com.

Telnet

The last of the Internet services is Telnet. Using a Telnet program enables you to connect and use a remote computer as if you were actually sitting at it. Purdue uses Telnet to link to an online referencing system for its libraries (hey, it's always good to put in a plug for your university). Using Telnet, I can link to a remote computer, maybe 400 or 500 yards from my office, and use it just as if I were right there (see Figure 1.15).

Figure 1.15.

Using Telnet to connect to a remote computer.

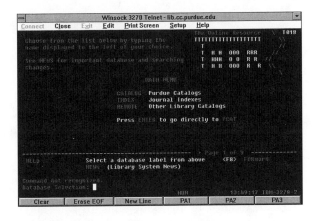

NEW TERM *Telnet* is an application that enables you to connect to and use a remote computer and its applications.

The biggest problem with Telnet is that each remote computer behaves a little differently from the others. Some might be using UNIX or some other operating system. The applications running on the remote system can be different as well. Telnet applications must be set up to run a specific way for each machine to which you connect. In addition, how the Telnet application's interface looks will change depending on the machine to which you connect.

Summary

Over the past 10 years, Internet communication and services have greatly improved and developed into more useful tools; ones that work the way we do. The Internet has had several major contributors that have helped to make possible what we call the World Wide Web. In addition, the services and things we can do all have become easier to use and more efficient. The various services including the Web, e-mail, FTP, and Telnet make us more efficient and effective communicators.

Q&A

Q What are the main roles of the Webmaster and what do these roles entail?

A The Webmaster serves as

Internet specialist, who understands what the Internet is, from where it has come, and where it might be going. The Internet specialist also understands how to connect to the Internet and how to utilize it.

Information design specialist, who understands the communication process and how to design products that efficiently and effectively entertain, inform, or persuade.

Media designer, who understands computer graphics, animation, video, and sound, and can effectively use these media elements to enhance communication.

Technical designer, who understands the standards, hardware, and software of a Web network and how to fit them together to make a working site.

Technical manager, who understands how to manage the hardware, software, resources, and people involved in the Web development process.

Q Being a Webmaster also can be viewed as mastering what three things?

A Technology, technique, and maintenance and management.

Q What is the difference between hypertext and hypermedia?

A Hypertext is nonlinear, nonsequential text. Hypermedia is nonlinear, nonsequential media elements that can be viewed independently of one another. Hypermedia can include hypertext.

Q What are the various services that can be used over the Internet and what are they for?

A The Internet services described in this chapter include

> The World Wide Web: Viewing graphics and text documents.
> E-mail: Sending electronic messages and files.
> News: Reading and posting electronic bulletin board messages.
> FTP: Uploading and downloading files and programs.
> Gopher: Browsing the Web using text menus.
> Telnet: Using a remote computer and its applications.

Workshop

The purpose of this workshop is to get you up and running with some of the various services on the Internet. Depending on how you are connected to the Internet, you might not be able to do all of the exercises. Today, you predominantly want to get your connection and services established so that you can use them through the remainder of this book. You can find the answers to the quiz questions in Appendix A, "Quiz Answers."

Quiz

1. What is HTML and how is it used on the Web?

2. What is an HTTP server?

3. What is a Web address and what does it look like? How does it change when you access an FTP or Gopher site?

4. What effect did Marc Andreessen's Mosaic browser have on the development and expansion of the Web?

Exercises

Focus on acquiring and setting up your client software such as a Web browser, newsreader, and e-mail program. Also download an FTP program. Throughout the remainder of this book, references, addresses, and sites will be mentioned using these Web services.

Day 2

The Internet Specialist

As you learned yesterday, the Internet specialist is an individual who understands what the Internet is, from where it has come, and where it might be going. Day 1 touched on the implications of the Web and what the future might hold for the Webmaster and included a quick overview of the many hats you'll have to wear. You also learned many of the Internet services that are available as well as a brief history. The most important skill of the Internet specialist, however, is an understanding of how to connect to the Internet and how to utilize it. Today you'll learn how the Internet functions and how the browser actually works.

First, you'll look closely at the browser software. Because both Netscape Navigator and Microsoft Internet Explorer function similarly, you learn in general how they access pages and how they function internally. You then examine the browser's preferences, cache, and how the browser utilizes plug-ins, scripting, and embedded applications.

The Browser

The *browser* is a relatively small piece of software; however, it is quite diverse in the various types of data that it can read. I find it fascinating that this small piece of software gives access to such a large domain of data. All browsers use Berners-Lee's idea of a singular interface that can handle multiple data types, such as pages that combine both text and graphics. The browser also handles various protocols such as WWW, Gopher, and FTP. This capability is part of Berners-Lee's original proposal specifications for the universal computer communication system.

So how does this intertwined mass of computing power work? To find out, begin by taking a look at what happens as you surf the Internet. When you access any site, the browser requests information from the remote site, downloads the data, and then arranges and displays that data in the work area of the browser, as shown in Figure 2.1.

Figure 2.1.

The work area of the browser.

The browser work area

To better understand how you use the browser to surf through pages, look at the graphical representation of a simple Web site shown in Figure 2.2. Here you see the contents of the Web site mysite.com. Notice the main page of the site, labeled A, in the graphic. You want the audience to start here when the users come to the site. This page is typically called the *home page* or *splash page*. On this page, most developers usually list a table of contents for the site. This list can be either a bulleted list or a graphic that denotes the various areas of information found at the site. Clicking the text or graphics takes you into the information for that area.

2

Figure 2.2.

A graphical representa-tion of a typical Web site.

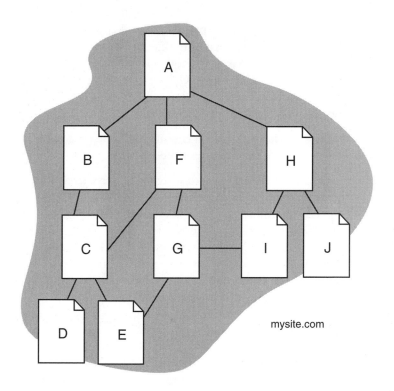

mysite.com

NEW TERM A *home* or *splash page* is the main or first page that is loaded from a site. It usually gives the audience an overview of the contents of the site.

As you look at Figure 2.2, keep in mind that the site here is quite small. Many corporate sites can grow to be well over 1,000 pages with complex and intertwined series of links between them, not to mention all the graphics and elements associated with the pages. Adobe's Web site, for example, has well over 10,000 pages.

The second thing you should notice about Figure 2.2 is the relationship of the pages to one another. The lines drawn from page to page show the *hyperlinks* or *hotlinks* from one page to the next. You use these links to navigate through the information.

NEW TERM A *link*, *hotlink*, or *hyperlink* is an area on a Web page that, when clicked, takes you to another site or page.

The lines connecting the pages show the hyperlinks within the site. These types of links are called *intrasite links*, meaning the internal links within the site. Clicking an intrasite hyperlink takes you from one page to another in the site. In Figure 2.2, you see that from page F you can jump to page C or page G. This graphic representation not only shows what links are, but it also shows what I mean when I say that hypermedia is *nonlinear* and *nonsequential* information. Throughout the site, you have a choice of what you view and where you go.

NEW TERM An *intrasite link* is a hotlink that is referenced to other pages within the current Web site or on the current Web server.

Even though the example from Figure 2.2 is relatively simple, it shows the basic concepts of site development. In the figure, note that the main links from the home page (page A) lead to the subordinate pages. These subordinate pages are generally grouped in a logical arrangement. If this were a corporate Web site, page B might be Products, F might be History, and H might be Customer Services. Web sites are normally set up so that the deeper you go into a Web site's pages, the more specific the information. Also, subordinate pages are usually related in some way. In Figure 2.2, all the pages that you can get to from page B (C, D, and E) probably relate to the same type of information—Products.

NEW TERM An *external link* is a hotlink that jumps you to a page at a different site.

Now look at one more example. Figure 2.3 shows a graphical representation of an external link. In this figure, you see the original site plus another site somewhere in cyberspace, labeled anothersite.com. This site could actually reside anywhere geographically—across town or across the world. It really doesn't matter as long as it is properly connected to the Internet. Note that from the original site, you can see an external link from page H to this new Web site's home page.

Figure 2.3.

A graphical representation of two Web sites.

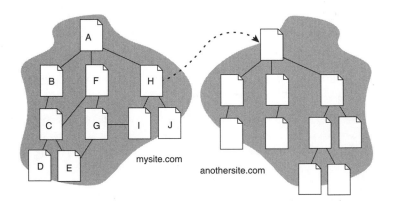

mysite.com

anothersite.com

NOTE

> Often, creating links from your site to another site's home page is best rather than creating links to some page deeper in the site's structure. The names of pages inside a site's structure often change; creating a link directly to them might not work after a period of time. The site's home page, however, is not likely to change (in name). This is more a matter of netiquette and logic than anything else.

For Figure 2.2, you learned that an intrasite link jumps within a single site. Figure 2.3 shows an external link to another site. Clicking the external link jumps you to the new site's home page (anothersite.com).

I've presented a very simplistic view of the Web in the preceding examples. The Web itself is composed of thousands of Web servers that each can contain several different Web sites, several thousand pages, and millions of intrasite and external links. To see what I mean, link to the Web and check out Yahoo!'s site (www.yahoo.com), which contains a master link-list of various sites of information. You won't see a hierarchical structure as shown in the preceding figures, but you will find several thousand links to sites all over the world and on almost every conceivable subject. Visiting this site will give you a realistic view of how many pages are actually available via the Web.

Browser as Real-Time Interpreter

As you're working with Web documents, you must keep in mind that HyperText Markup Language, or HTML, is a *semantic* language. This means that the HTML code loosely defines the way in which the elements on the screen—text and graphics—should be laid out. The browser, however, actually does the compositing of the text and graphics after downloading. Each browser therefore might present the contents of a Web page differently, as shown in Figures 2.4 and 2.5. These different representations are caused by the differences in how the HTML coding is interpreted by the browsers, differences in the operating systems, and differences in the features the browsers support. Predominantly, the look of the page is affected by both the browser and platform on which the browser is running.

Figure 2.4.

The Netscape home page as seen through Netscape's browser.

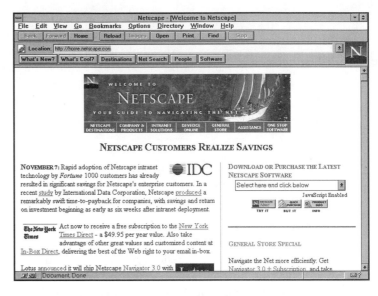

Figure 2.5.

The Netscape home page as seen through the NCSA Mosaic browser.

Because every Web page is composed on-the-fly, you can think of the browser as a real-time HTML interpreter. It works like older BASIC program interpreters that executed programming code a line at a time. The code itself, unlike an executable application, is read and executed on-the-fly. Problems or bugs don't appear when the user is entering code. Errors appear when the code is interpreted or executed. In the case of HTML, errors, or undesirable formatting, appear after the HTML code is loaded into the browser.

Another similarity between BASIC code and HTML is that both files are nothing more than ASCII text, as you can see in Figure 2.6. ASCII text is a plain, unformatted text file. You can create HTML code in any text editor, as long as it stores the recorded file as simple or plain text. You can use a simple text editor such as WordPad (Windows 95) or Simple Text (Macintosh) to create HTML files.

Figure 2.6.

HTML code is nothing more than a plain text file.

```
                              Notepad - 217_ASN.HTM
 File  Edit  Search  Help
<html>
<head>
    <title>Technical Graphics 217 Lab Assignments</title>
    <meta name="GENERATOR" content="Mozilla/2.01Gold (Win32)">
</head>
<body text="#000000" bgcolor="#FFFFFF" vlink="#FF0000" alink="#FF0000" -->
<!-- Created J.L.Mohler 7/5/96 -->
<hr><img src="gear.gif" border=0 height=247 width=256 align=right>
<h4>Department of Technical Graphics</h4>

<h1>TG 217 Drawing Systems</h1>

<h3>Lab Assignments</h3>

<ul>
<li><a href="index.html">Course Description</a></li>

<li><a href="217_lay.html">Weekly Layout </a></li>

<li><a href="217_ske.html">Sketching Assignments</a></li>

<li><a href="http://www.tech.purdue.edu/tg/faculty/mohler/moh_scd.html">Professor Mohler's
Schedule</a></li>

<li><a href="http://www.tech.purdue.edu/tg/faculty/mohler/mohler.html">Professor Mohler's Home
Page</a></li>
</ul>
<hr>
<p>
<b>Hey these links work now!!</b>
</p>

<p><b>Weekly Lab Assignments</b>
<br></p>

<table border=3>
```

After you enter the HTML code into a simple text file, you then can load the code into an interpreter (a browser) to actually see how the file works and how it is displayed. Because different browsers interpret HTML code differently, and because you can see the differences only in the browser, testing your HTML code on various browsers is always a good idea; this way, you get a feel for how it appears when the user loads it.

Multiple Interpreters (Browsers)

Although browsers are a big part of the whole process that makes the Web function, to many, they are a troublesome foe to work with. Because of the wide variety of browsers used on the Net, coding a Web page so that it looks exactly the same from every browser is difficult. Actually, making a page look exactly the same across all browsers is nearly impossible.

One source states that 58 percent of the Web population use Netscape, whereas 24.8 percent uses Internet Explorer. These two browsers compose documents with slight differences, as you can see in Figures 2.7 and 2.8. The remaining 17.2 percent of the Web population, however, uses other browsers such as Spry Mosaic, NCSA Mosaic, and others. The "Others" category shows the biggest formatting differences. These browsers can create a wide variety of variations for a single HTML document.

Figure 2.7.

A view of the Web through Navigator.

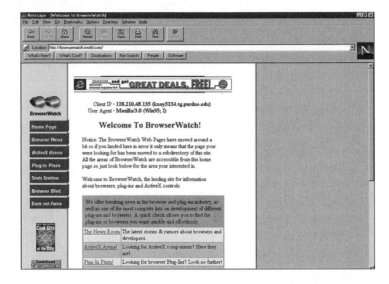

Figure 2.8.

A view of the Web through Explorer.

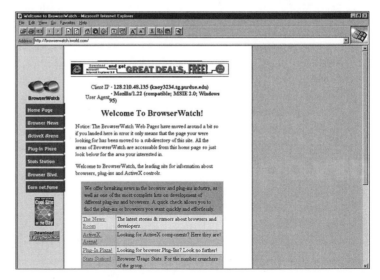

For the most part, the differences from browser to browser are subtle but noticeable, particularly if you're trying to get a specific formatted document every time. In many instances, getting a relatively standard look across browsers is important. For now, realize that HTML code is interpreted with minor differences from browser to browser.

Another issue that you should be cautious of is the speed at which the browser brings up a Web page. When you look at the technical design side of Webmastering, you'll see how the type of network connection also greatly influences this speed, but the type of browser you're using also affects how quickly the page is laid out before your eyes. In general, Microsoft Explorer is more robust than Navigator in its text formatting capabilities, but it also is slower than Netscape Navigator when it comes to compositing Web pages.

Operating Environment Implications

In addition to the browser, the operating system or platform also can affect the way in which the browser combines text and graphics. The operating system affects Web pages in two specific ways, which include color and font issues.

If you could set two computers with different operating systems side by side and view the same graphic image, you would notice a perceivable difference in the colors between the two computers. In general, colors from one platform to another appear different in *value* and *saturation*.

NEW TERM The *value* is the lightness or darkness of a particular color, such as light blue versus dark blue.

NEW TERM The *saturation* is the pureness of the color, such as a fluorescent blue compared to a subdued blue.

You might notice some of the apparent color shifting in the example just because of differences in the way computer hardware is manufactured. Variability and manufacturing errors are natural, but how the operating system creates color is also a factor in this color shift. If you set a PC and Mac side by side, you would notice that the colors on the Macintosh are desaturated (not as pure) and lighter in value than the colors on a PC. The colors on the PC would appear more saturated (more fluorescent) and somewhat darker in value. And if you throw a UNIX box in, it could be anywhere in between. As you move into Day 4, "The Media Designer," you'll see how you can design for the optimum effect no matter on what type of box you're viewing your site.

Typefonts or *fonts* are the second operating system attribute that can affect how a page is displayed. Due to differences in the types, styles, widths, and heights of various typefaces, the text can shift significantly from platform to platform. This difference presents a problem if you're trying to align text and graphics tightly on a Web page. On one platform, the page might look good, but on another text might have an undesirable appearance as it flows around inline graphics.

 A *typefont* or *font* is a set of characters with similar attributes, such as similar height, width, and spacing. Examples of typefonts include Arial, Helvetica, and Times.

 An *inline graphic* is a graphic that is embedded or inserted into a Web page shown in a browser. An inline graphic is displayed without the aid of external viewers or helper applications.

As you look at a typefont, the actual differences in size and spacing can be imperceptible, but the additive differences cause the text and graphics to shift as shown in Figures 2.9 and 2.10. Suppose the difference between text heights across platforms is approximately $1/_8$ of an inch, and you have 64 lines of text flowing around some graphics. Multiplying the $1/_8$ inch by 64 lines causes the text to shift by 1 inch at the end of the page, which definitely is a noticeable shift. Right now, don't worry about how to control this difference, but be aware of its overall effect. You learn about designing around this situation on Day 8, "Introduction to HTML and Block Tags."

Figure 2.9.

Navigator as seen on a Windows 3.x platform.

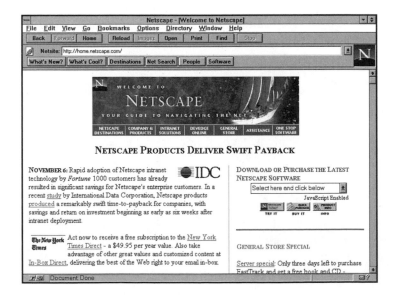

Figure 2.10.

Navigator as seen on a Windows 95 platform.

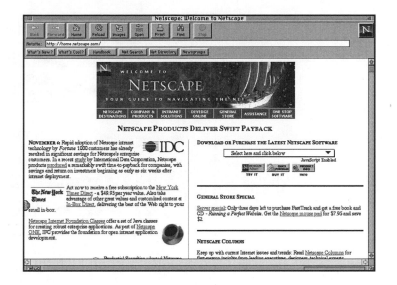

How the Browser Functions

In the preceding examples, you looked at what happens externally when you surf the Web, but what do you actually see in the browser as you're surfing? How are links to remote sites represented?

A page that is loaded into a browser can contain several items that you can use to navigate the particular site. Navigation is the most important thing in a hypertext environment. Most sites are designed so that you can delve deeper into an information thread by clicking blue, text-based links, as shown in Figure 2.11. These links textually represent another site or page, and clicking the link takes you to that site or page.

Aside from text-based links, you also can use graphics as links. Graphics are used for buttons, button bars, and icons to help you navigate through the site, as you can see in Figure 2.12. On Day 8 and Day 9, "Text-Level Tags," you'll learn how to create both text- and graphics-based links in your Web pages using the HTML language.

Before I begin discussing networking basics, take a look at some of the ways you can customize your browser as well as how you set up the browser on your computer. The next few sections talk about some of the specific aspects of the Web browser.

Figure 2.11.
Clicking a hypertext link takes you to another site or page.

Figure 2.12.
Graphics also can represent links.

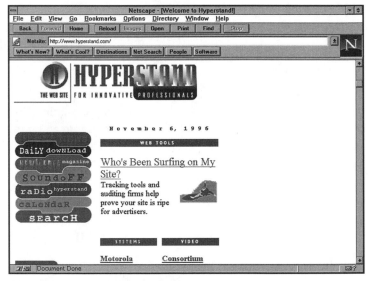

Preferences

As you use your browser, you might want to adjust several specific preferences or settings. If you just recently installed Navigator or Explorer, you should make sure that you have set up your mail and news server preferences so that you can use them in your browser. Remember that Explorer has no mail viewer in the browser. To set the news and mail preferences in

Netscape, choose Options | Mail and News Preferences to point the browser to your mail and news server. In Explorer, you can set your news preferences using Go | Read News. You'll be prompted the first time you use this to enter the location of your news server.

In addition to these services, you might want to set your browser so that it does not automatically load inline images. If you turn off this option, the browser substitutes a small icon for the graphic instead of taking the time to download it and display it. Normally, when I am at home with a 14.4 Kbps modem, I turn off inline images so that pages download more quickly. In my office at the university, where the network is directly connected to the Internet, I leave inline images turned on. In Netscape, you can set this option by choosing Options | Auto Load Images; in Explorer, you can set it by choosing View | Options | Multimedia | Show Pictures. Become familiar with this option. By using it, you can cut your surfing time when you're looking for something specific or when you're in a hurry.

The Cache

Not too long ago, a friend of mine installed Netscape on his computer, and he was very excited to be able to surf the Web to see what all the talk was about. He was very satisfied with his Web connection and the vast array of information that was at his fingertips. Soon he noticed that he was quickly running out of hard drive space, and he couldn't figure out why. Knowing that he had recently installed a browser was an indicator of the problem for me.

As you've already learned, Web browsers download the HTML code from a remote site and then composite graphics and text in real time on the recipient's computer. To understand what was happening to my friend's computer, examine this situation a little closer.

The HTML code that is downloaded contains *tags*, or descriptions of what should be shown in the browser's work area. HTML is really nothing more than a text-based code description of what is shown on the page and how it is shown. Again, the HTML file itself is just a simple text file and is usually small. Within this text file, tags describe the browser text that is to be laid out on the page. The file might also include references to graphic files that are to be a part of the page. When you access a Web page, the browser first downloads the HTML code to the local hard drive to see what needs to be done. The file is stored in a special location called the *cache* (pronounced "cash").

 The browser *cache* is a special location, usually a folder or directory, on the user's hard drive where HTML files, graphics, and resource files are stored during the browser work session.

After it downloads the HTML file, the browser then downloads and saves the graphics that are needed for the Web page. These graphics also are stored in the cache. Each time you access a new Web page or site, HTML files and the associated graphics files are saved in the cache. Unfortunately, browsers don't automatically empty the files that are in the cache. With my friend's computer, the accumulation of the files in the cache folder was eating up space on his hard drive.

Although the cache folder tends to get "meaty" at times, it does have a good quality. Suppose you visit a particular site frequently. The first time you visit it, the site's HTML code and graphics are stored in your cache directory. On subsequent visits to the same site, the HTML file is, again, loaded from the site. The graphics are loaded from the cache, however, instead of from the Web site, thus making the page load more quickly. Without a cache folder, each time you visit the site you would have to wait for the HTML code and graphics to download. The cache, then, holds residual data to enable the browser to work faster and decrease wait times. The first place the browser checks for graphics and resource files is the cache. If the browser does not find the items it needs in the cache, it downloads them from the site.

Undoubtedly, you should keep an eye on the number (and size) of the files in your cache directory, as my friend now does. Both Navigator and Explorer enable you to empty the cache from within the browser; however, I find it much easier to do from the operating system. You can find the cache folder for either browser in the same location as the browser executable file (`netscape.exe` or `iexplore.exe`). Deleting all the files in the cache "cleans it" and does not cause any problems for the browser.

NOTE

> Both Navigator and Explorer can empty the cache inside the application if you tell them to. To empty the cache in Netscape, choose Options | Network Preferences | Cache | Clear Disk Cache Now. To empty the cache in Explorer, choose View | Options | Advanced | Settings | Empty Folder.

Plug-Ins

Probably one of the biggest improvements and advancements in the last two years is the addition of *plug-ins* for Web browsers. Even in the early days of HTML, it was obvious that HTML alone couldn't support the wide variety of features and media elements that users wanted to utilize and distribute on the Web. Being a derivative of the Standard Generalized Markup Language (SGML), a precursory coding scheme used for general electronic publishing, HTML is predominantly focused around static Web documents—text and graphics. It does not directly support multimedia element execution in a document—it doesn't know how to view the element.

NEW TERM   A *plug-in* is an add-on program that acts as an interpreter and viewer for multimedia elements distributed over the Web. The plug-in interprets and executes the sound, video, or program, enabling the user to listen, watch, or interact with the multimedia element.

Before plug-ins, developers who wanted to distribute video, sound, or other nontraditional Web items had to let the user download it and view it with an external application called a *helper application*. With the addition of the <embed> tag, browsers can now tap into the multimedia resources that were once limited to CD-ROMs by using plug-ins. The browsers are "multimedia enabled" by the plug-ins.

Today several hundred plug-ins exist for Web browsers. Some of the most widely known plug-ins include Shockwave, RealAudio, QuickTime, Video for Windows, VRML, and others. Each plug-in is a separate program that executes when a respective media element is accessed through the browser, as shown in Figure 2.13.

Figure 2.13.

Plug-ins for multimedia elements.

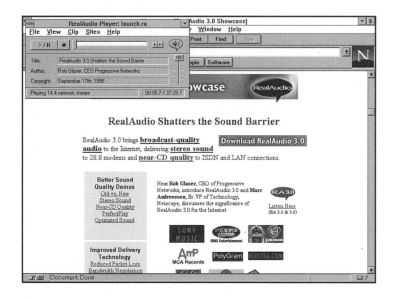

WARNING

Be cautious about installing plug-ins because they can sometimes corrupt your browser. I suggest installing only plug-ins that you know have been tested and used with your particular browser. Several plug-ins that are still in beta form have been distributed over the Net—generally meaning that they are still "buggy." Also, downloading a plug-in created by Country Bob's Discount Plug-in Resources and Software might not be a good idea. Check out the plug-in before installing it.

Acquiring and installing plug-ins is relatively easy. Because most plug-ins use professional setup programs, you can easily install the files after you download the plug-ins. Unfortunately, not all plug-ins support all platforms. The following is a list of some of the most frequently used client-side plug-ins. Client-side means that they install onto your machine and coordinate with your browser at runtime. You might want to download and install them so that you can automatically view multimedia elements with your browser. If you access a page that requires a plug-in that you don't have, the page will load but you cannot view the multimedia element.

NOTE

> Some of these plug-ins are included on the CD-ROM in the back of this book. Look there for more information on the resources on the CD-ROM.

Shockwave	`www.macromedia.com`
RealAudio	`www.realaudio.com`
QuickTime	`www.apple.com`
Video for Windows	`www.microsoft.com`

TIP

> When you're installing plug-ins, storing them in a common folder is a good idea. Windows 95 automatically tries to store them in the `Program Files/Netscape` or the `Program Files/Iexplorer` directory. If you use Windows 3.1 or 3.11 or the Macintosh, storing plug-ins in a single folder is a good practice; this way, you can easily delete them if necessary.

Scripting

In addition to the various plug-in capabilities, many browsers also support custom scripting languages that enable a Web page to contain special functions. Netscape browsers, for example, support a special scripting language called JavaScript. Using JavaScript, the Web developer can add special application-type programming into a Web page. Microsoft Internet Explorer supports ActiveX and VBScript, special languages created by Microsoft that enable the same type of programming capability as JavaScript.

NOTE

> As you're surfing the Web, determining if the page you're accessing uses scripting or plug-ins for multimedia effects is often difficult. Don't forget that you can use the View Source option in the browser to look at the code behind the page. Looking at the code is also a good way to learn HTML programming skills.

Embedded Programs

In 1995, Sun Microsystems introduced a revolutionary new concept to the Web world. Through the use of a new application programming language called *Java*, small applications (called *applets*) could be created and embedded into Web pages. When the user accessed the Web page, the application would be downloaded and executed. Originally intended as a new programming language for electronic devices such as household consumer devices, Java has turned the possibilities in cyberspace upside down.

NEW TERM   *Java* is an object-oriented programming language used to create executable applications that are commonly distributed over the Internet.

Many people see Java as having a tremendous impact in the software industry, and indeed it has. Aside from small trinkets and nifty animated effects, Java offers the capability to create entire online programs that are downloaded to your machine only as needed (rather than installing them permanently on your computer)—a definite paradigm shift. The biggest limitation today is that to view Java programs you must have a Java-enabled browser (Netscape) and either Windows 95 or Window NT. You can do almost anything with Java's robust capabilities, as you can see in Figure 2.14. This particular Java application is a Java-based calculator that is embedded within a Web page. After the Java applet is downloaded, it runs entirely on the client machine. This would be next to impossible in a Web page without the Java programming language.

Figure 2.14.

Java programs via the Web.

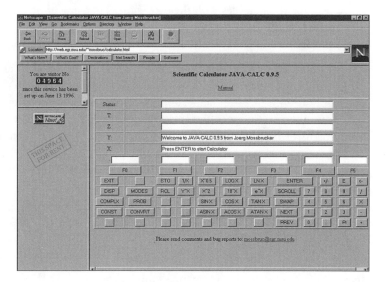

Helper Applications

Last but not least in this discussion are helper applications. Originally, helper applications were designed to aid Web surfers in viewing almost any digital file that could be passed over the Internet. Today helper applications are quickly being replaced by internal browser plug-ins.

So how does a helper application work? Well, really, a helper application is just that, an external application that helps the browser view almost any type of digital file found on the Internet. From shareware applications to commercial applications such as Microsoft Word, almost any application can be set up as a helper application. When the user commands the browser to download or access a file, the browser checks its list of MIME file types to see what to do with it.

NEW TERM *MIME*, which is short for *Multipurpose Internet Mail Extensions*, is a definition scheme that associates a specific file extension with a respective application.

When the browser checks the MIME file types list, it looks for the three-letter extension of the file in the list. After it finds the extension, the list tells it what to do with the file. The file types list can tell the browser to save the file or open it with an external application. For example, you cannot open TIF files, a type of bitmap graphic file, directly using Netscape. Netscape can open only GIF or JPEG images; therefore, you need a helper application to open TIF images from the Net. In this case, you need to create a MIME setting that tells Netscape to open files with the extension .TIF using another application on your machine such as a commercial product like Microsoft Imager or Adobe PhotoShop or with a shareware product such as JASC Paint Shop Pro.

In times past, the only way to open a digital video clip such as a QuickTime or Video for Windows file or a sound clip such as a MIDI file was through a MIME definition and a helper application. The use of helper applications is basically being replaced with browser plug-ins. You might still need to use some helper applications, however, as you surf the Web. You establish MIME definitions within the browser and set them up just like mail and news preferences. In Netscape, you set up MIME types by choosing Options | General Preferences | Helpers. In Microsoft Internet Explorer, you define them by choosing View | Options | Programs | File Types.

Now add a MIME association in Netscape for the TIF file type that was introduced earlier so that you know how to do it.

NOTE In the following example, you enter a MIME entry for the TIF file format. Scroll down your list of MIME types, and make sure that you don't already have an entry for the TIF file format. If a MIME type is already entered for TIF, click the entry and start from step 7.

1. Start Netscape and choose Options | General Preferences to open the Preferences dialog box.
2. Click the Helpers tab.
3. Click the Create New File Type button.
4. In the Mime Type field, type `image`.
5. In the Mime Subtype field, type `tiff`.
6. In the lower part of the screen, type `tiff, tif` in the File Extensions field.
7. Select what you want done with the file: Save to Disk, Unknown: Prompt User, or Launch the Application. If you choose Save to Disk, Netscape prompts you to provide a location to put the TIF file upon downloading. The Unknown option gives you these same three options when a TIF file is encountered. You can use the last option to define a graphic application that can open TIF files. When a TIF file is accessed in the browser, it is automatically opened in the application specified here.

NOTE

> As you start setting up various MIME types in your browser, you might want to test them to make sure that they are set up correctly. Fortunately, you can use a single page at `http://www-dsed.llnl.gov/documents/WWWtest.html` to test all your MIME types instead of having to surf to find each file type on a page.

Assuming that you can download the file from the Net, you can set up any file type in the same fashion as the TIF extension you just entered. All you need to know is the extension and an application that you would like to use to open the file.

Surfing the Web

As you're surfing the Web, you'll undoubtedly run across a lot of information that will help you in your Webmastering tasks. Use all the wonderful digital resources you have at your fingertips. Don't think of yourself as an island—not needing anything but this book and your technological resources. Many people, just like yourself, are out there and are willing to share the information and timesaving techniques they've learned. Some digitally publish that information on the Net, others post it to newsgroups, and still others are willing to communicate via electronic mail. Don't reinvent the wheel when you can almost instantaneously research and find out about the work of others on the Web, in newsgroups, or via e-mail.

WWW

As you're beginning your trek through the World Wide Web, you will undoubtedly begin compiling the all-important list of Web sites as *bookmarks* (Netscape) or *favorites* (Explorer) for easy reference. A few sites are well worth mentioning at this point.

 Bookmarks, used in Netscape, or *favorites*, used in Explorer, enable you to save the address of a particular site or page in a menu of the same name.

One of the most valuable reference sites that you should have in your address list is Yahoo! (www.yahoo.com), shown in Figure 2.15. I will make many references to this site because I visit it on a daily basis. The site contains a huge list of sites dealing with subjects from bald eagles to the top ten deadly mistakes when creating Web sites. Yahoo! is the encyclopedia site of all sites.

Figure 2.15.

Yahoo!, the never-ending list of sites.

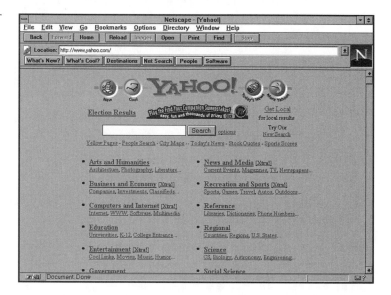

A second site worth visiting is the Index to Multimedia Resources at viswiz.gmd.de/ MultimediaInfo/, which contains a large listing of sites that contain information about Web and CD-based hypermedia. This index site contains a listing of standards, resources, conferences, and information related to multimedia and hypermedia.

The following are other sites that you might want to stock in your bookmarks or favorites:

Macromedia Web site	www.macromedia.com
Microsoft's Web site	www.microsoft.com-2
The World Wide Web Consortium	www.w3.org

Adobe's site	www.adobe.com
Web software	www.w3.org/hypertext/WWW/Status.html
Web accessories	www.stroud.com/web.html
Web development information	www.webreference.com

Finally, be aware of the various online search engines that you can use to find information on the Web, as shown in Figure 2.16. You can use search engines such as AltaVista, Magellan, Infoseek, Lycos, and Yahoo! to find almost anything on the Web.

Figure 2.16.

Search engines.

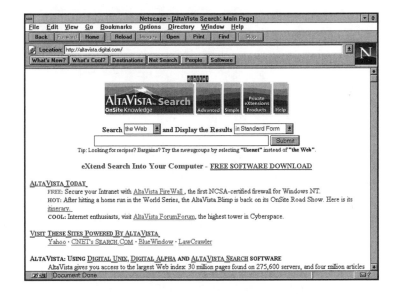

NEW TERM   A *search engine* is a Web software mechanism that compares the keyword you enter to words in the HTML files that exist in cyberspace, giving you a list of sites that might relate to your keyword.

After you give the search engine a keyword, the engine returns a listing of documents in which the keyword appears. Many not only give you a list but also show the frequency of the search word or words in the particular document, giving you a better idea of whether the page relates to what you want. Many engines also enable you to customize and limit your search parameters so that your search is more accurate.

The following are some of the most common search engines and sites:

Infoseek	`guide.infoseek.com/`
Lycos	`www.lycos.com/`
Magellan	`www.mckinley.com/`
AltaVista	`altavista.digital.com/`
Excite	`www.excite.com/`

Tutorials

One of the most valuable resources on the Web is online tutorials. Earlier I suggested that many individuals post their information on the Web—things they are doing and techniques they have learned. Check out some of these tutorial sites for further information. You can find out how many in-depth, specific techniques are done using a wide variety of the current and up-to-date technologies.

NOTE

> As a side note to my suggesting tutorial pages, keep in mind that some of the tutorials on the Web are wanting, if not bogus—meaning they flat out don't work. In addition, not everyone posts information onto the Web in a way that is easy to follow either, but that's the beauty of the Web, I guess. No one moderates what is delivered.

Tips for Effective Browsing

You will find that browsing the Web can be both a pleasurable and frustrating experience. You'll find a fine line between the two. Most often you'll be faced with finding mission-critical information right now. Few people find time to surf leisurely, although being able to do so would be nice once in a while. The two most effective means of browsing efficiently are to turn off inline images and to use the wide variety of search engines available on the Web. Also, be careful to trace your steps using your bookmarks or favorites.

News

In addition to World Wide Web sites, you can find many newsgroups that directly relate to Webmastering. After you have a news client such as WinVN, setting it up requires knowing your access provider's news server address. Simply point the newsreader to the server to access the newsgroups. From that point on, you can easily subscribe to the various newsgroups. Again, you can use your browser to access newsgroups, but using it isn't as quick as using an external newsreader program.

NOTE

> Keep in mind that most notes posted to newsgroups are intended to be short comments and brief discussions. Often it is appropriate to discuss more lengthy items and specific details via e-mail rather than post them through a newsgroup. Newsgroups are generally unmediated, meaning that you can run across some pretty strange things.

You can find several newsgroups that deal with both software and hardware issues as well as HTML code specifics. Some that might interest you include

- [ ] `comp.infosystems.authoring.cgi`
- [ ] `comp.infosystems.authoring.html`
- [ ] `comp.infosystems.browsers.mac`
- [ ] `comp.infosystems.browsers.misc`
- [ ] `comp.infosystems.servers.mac`
- [ ] `comp.infosystems.servers.ms-windows`

Because the list of newsgroups exceeds 4,000, I have included only a brief listing here. Several other lists include discussions about HTML, Java, and VRML. If you want to talk or find out information about something, you can probably find a newsgroup to post to easily.

Online Services

As a prior CompuServe subscriber, I am aware that several other sources of information are also available via online services such as CompuServe and America Online. Many offer additional services not available over the Internet such as discussion groups and proprietary chat rooms. If you have an account on one of these services, check it out for additional resources that can help you.

Summary

Throughout this lesson, you took a closer look at the World Wide Web and the browser and saw how they actually work. You learned how the Internet, intrasite, and external site links work and help you navigate information on the Internet.

Aside from more global issues, the browser, as small as it is, plays a very important role in how Web pages are both composed and delivered. You saw how different browsers and different platforms affect the display of Web pages in the browser. All the various parts of the browser also contribute to the hypermedia communication capability. The browser's preferences are used to define the operational parameters for the browser, although the cache helps the browser operate faster and with greater efficiency.

Plug-ins and helper applications assist the browser in opening digital files that are not directly interpretable by the browser alone. Using MIME file type associations, the browser can associate external applications with specific file types. You also read about the various online resources available through sites such as Yahoo! and other Internet services such as newsgroups.

Q&A

Q Does the type of browser affect what is viewed on the Web? Does it affect how pages are viewed on the Web?

A Yes. Each browser interprets the HTML code a little bit differently. Because some browsers support special features, such as Microsoft Internet Explorer's robust text formatting features, pages might look different from one browser to another. HTML is a semantic language that gives a loose definition of how to lay out a page but does not give specific page composition positions. Because the definition is loose, pages might be interpreted loosely and universally rather than as fixed by proprietary software.

Q How does the platform or operating system affect pages shown in a browser?

A Because the HTML language is designed to be used on multiple operating systems, certain parameters of a page might change slightly from platform to platform because the individual elements that make up the page change. Because typefont differences in size and height exist across platforms, for example, shifting of the laid-out page text occurs. Also, graphic colors can appear slightly different from one platform to another. Colors on a PC appear more saturated and darker than those on a Macintosh. Colors on the Macintosh appear desaturated and lighter than on a PC. A UNIX machine might show a range anywhere in between. Color variations might also be due to manufacturing variabilities.

Q What is the difference between a helper application and a plug-in?

A Helper applications and plug-ins both extend the capabilities of the browser, enabling the browser to view an almost unlimited array of files via the Internet

2

including text, graphics, sound, video, and animation files. The major difference is that helper applications are external applications that can include shareware and freeware programs as well as commercial applications. When a particular file type is accessed, the browser uses the external helper application to open the file. On the other hand, a plug-in is an internal program that runs from within the browser when it is needed to open a particular type of file.

Q For what is a scripting language used? What are some examples of scripting languages?

A A scripting language is a programming-type language that is used within an HTML file to extend the capability of the common Web page. Examples of scripting languages include JavaScript, VBScript, and ActiveX.

Workshop

The Workshop provides quiz questions to help you solidify your understanding of the material covered and exercises to give you experience in using what you've learned. The quiz answers are provided in Appendix A, "Quiz Answers." Try to understand the quiz answers before you go on to tomorrow's lesson.

Quiz

1. What is MIME and how is it used in the browser?
2. What is the difference between an intrasite link and an external link?
3. What is the browser cache and how can it affect the hardware resources on your computer?
4. What is an embedded program? Give an example of what it would be used for.
5. What is the first page of a Web site commonly called?

Exercise

For today's exercise, focus on setting up all your helper applications. Use the page at http://www-dsed.llnl.gov/documents/WWWtest.html to make sure that you've set up your MIME types properly. You might also want to download and install plug-ins for your browser so that you can view multimedia elements via the Web, but be careful of "generic" plug-ins.

Day 3

The Information Design Specialist

More than anything else, the Web is a communication medium. Just as with the development of any other communication media, you can follow a defined process to create Web documents that effectively communicate. Whenever a document, book, or other published product is created, the people involved painstakingly follow a living process, most often developed through trial and error.

When you're creating a document such as a brochure or flyer, you look at the audience and what you want to communicate. Then you determine how best to fit the content to that audience. If you were writing a book, again, you would center upon the audience and cater your information to that audience. Web-based delivery is no different. With hypermedia and multimedia, however, you have many more options, many more elements, and often a wider audience. Adapting the wide variety of media elements such as text, graphics, sound, and video so that they effectively communicate can be challenging. This is where the information design specialist is important.

An *information design specialist* is an individual who understands the communication process and how to design products that inform, persuade, educate, or entertain efficiently and effectively.

Today you'll read about a development process that you can use to help you develop your site. As the Webmaster, you will be presented with content that is to be distributed over the Internet. Sometimes your job will be as simple as posting predeveloped pages to your site and making the connecting links so that the pages work properly. Other times, you might be responsible for creating the content, generating graphics, and acquiring multimedia elements that support the pages. What happens if the content and the pages are not already developed? How do you go about massaging the content, planning the pages, and developing the site so that it communicates well? How do you develop it so that it pleases the audience? And how do you know that the content is appropriate for Web-based delivery? That's what you'll focus on today: establishing a development process for the delivery of Web content.

Much of what you'll read here has its roots in educational design and verbal and visual communication principles. The model described in this lesson was originally intended for multimedia development, but it is easily adapted to developing content and pages for a Web site. In fact, you can adapt this development process to the development of almost any communication media.

Note

As you're reading through today's lesson, remember that the development process presented here is not an absolute method of development. Often budget or personnel constraints compress the amount of planning that can be done. Implement the method described here to the level that your constraints allow.

The Nature of Information

So what is your Web site really trying to convey? Yep, you guessed it, a message. On Day 1, "The Webmaster: Jack of All Trades," you were presented with the communication model and the effect of noise in the communication process. Communication is the essence of what a Web site is all about. Whether the goal is to inform, persuade, educate, or entertain, the intent in delivering content via the Web is to present the audience with information and for that information to be comprehended, encoded, and acted upon by the audience.

One of the main goals in planning a Web site is to reduce or completely eliminate the noise that can hinder the communicability of a Web site. If the audience misinterprets what you present or if the users don't understand what was presented, your Web site has failed.

Next question: How do you get the message to be comprehended and encoded by the audience? How do you get the users to remember or act upon it? Well, the first step is to make your information relevant to your audience as shown in Figure 3.1. The site shown in the figure is focused on giving the user direct access to events and conferences relating to computers up to the year 2000 (this is one of my frequently used bookmarks). The site is straightforward and centers upon the audience, giving them quick access to the content.

Really, any content you provide should be audience-centered; it must be relevant and pertinent to the users. The content must attract and hold their attention while also completely communicating your message. This is the first law of Web communication.

Figure 3.1.

*Communicating with a
Web-based medium.*

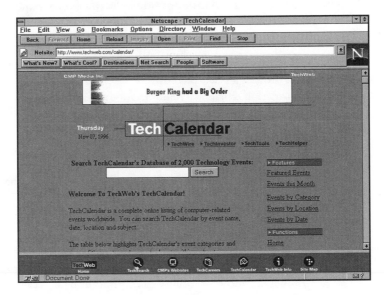

In addition to relating to the audience, your content should also be presented logically. Any communication media should show a logical progression or thought process that can be identified. Sites that are poorly planned often fail due to illogical arrangement of content. Arrangement of your content should be intuitive—like the audience would expect to see it. Again, ESP wouldn't hurt, but you can solve most of these problems with ample planning.

With traditional documents, logical order is created in the presentation of paragraphs, sentences, and words, as well as in the flow of the text passages. Hypermedia is a little different because you can arrange pages in a variety of ways, and you can insert text, graphics, sound, and so on in any way you want. With Web-based media, you must also deal with its nonsequential nature. You must be careful that your content follows a logical progression throughout your site and throughout the pages contained within it.

I'm sure that by now you've seen some horrid sites on the Web. They're all over the place. Dancing elements, prancing around your screen, huge graphics that communicate poorly, content that is presented in an awkward fashion—you should be leery of these things. Logical progression within your pages stems from how and how well you use graphics and multimedia elements and navigation items.

You should use graphics and other media elements only to enhance, complement, clarify, or complete what you say with words. Often people use graphics to fill space, cramming every nook and cranny with something visual. The overall effect of such a page is less than stimulating and often confusing. To help present your site's information in a logical order, you should utilize graphic design principles to help your audience assimilate your information. You look at these principles in more depth in the lesson for Day 4, "The Media Designer."

Finally, the nature of Web-based information centers around navigability and nonlinearity. You must provide an easy navigation scheme for your site. Being able to dive deeper into a site's information efficiently is important to the audience, as is easily being able to get back out. Navigation should never overshadow the information being presented. As you're developing your site, be attentive to the issue of navigation. Many users are turned off by the difficulty of navigating through a site that is difficult to use. The users leave the site still looking for the answers they came to the site to find. When you begin developing your site, use navigation items such as buttons, icons, and button bars that are obvious, almost exaggerated. Remember: The users didn't just come to surf; it's your content they want.

Nontransient

As you learned on the first day, the tremendous evolution of computers and computer networks has advanced the ability to communicate. It has also greatly affected the types of media you can use to communicate and how quickly you can make changes to the delivery medium. In these next two brief sections, you examine the media you use to communicate and look at how your choice of media is actually dependent on the nature of the information.

Before the advent of the Web, all physical information distribution media (such as books, CDs, and so on) had a relatively stable and nontransient life cycle. People therefore could accept the time needed to develop them. Textbooks, for example, usually contain information that remains relatively stable for a period of six months to a year, so writers can accept a three-month cycle to create a book. Information such as this—information that remains stable—can be classified as *nontransient information*.

New Term *Nontransient information* is information that changes or becomes outdated on a 9- to 12-month cycle.

3

Today, most developers still deliver nontransient information using static media—media that cannot be changed. This is no new revelation. Almost all communication media, including print-based media, CD-ROMs, and laser discs, fall into this category. Looking at these media, you see that up to this day stable information could be easily delivered on one of these media. But what if that information suddenly changed? What if you wanted to use one of these media to communicate information that changed on a day-to-day basis? Could you accept that the product is entirely outdated at the time it is released? No, the delivery method must be dynamic rather than static for information that rapidly changes.

Transient

Today, you see an exponential rate of change in the information you deal with on a day-to-day basis. As it relates to computers, the information changes daily (almost hourly); thus, it is *transient information*. At this point, Web development and delivery excel. World Wide Web-based delivery is dynamic. It can be quickly changed or adapted and can support the demands of transient information. It is fluid and can be developed in real time.

NEW TERM *Transient information* is information that has a short life cycle, changing or becoming outdated within nine months or less.

So why bring up the issue of transient and nontransient information? Who cares? Because you're a Webmaster, this issue is vitally important because it reveals a trend that is occurring both in industry and education.

Most institutions are beginning to distinguish between transient and nontransient information in how they distribute it. Institutions are focusing their development efforts based on how quickly the information changes. If the information has a relatively long life cycle, the information supports distribution in a book or on a CD. If the information has a short life cycle, it is distributed via the Web. Many publishers and other traditionally based businesses are focusing on providing information rather than a physical, tangible product. As the Web develops to the point of supporting full-blown multimedia capabilities (full-screen video, CD-quality audio, and so on), it will be vital that companies shift their focus from being product producers to information facilitators and providers. Information provision is becoming increasingly more dependent on the Web as a communication medium due to the increasingly fluid nature of the information.

The Development Process

So your boss comes into your office one day and says, "We'd like for you to spearhead our Web development team as Webmaster. We don't really know what we should put on the site. We just know we need to establish our presence on the Web for our clients." Now that he's told you this, he begins to walk out of your office. He concludes by saying, "By the way, we have a major conference in a month and would like to showcase our new Web site." What do you do? Where do you start? How do you know where you're going? One thing is for sure, your job (and credibility) is riding on successfully establishing your company's Web presence.

Never fear, the entire Web development process can be laid out procedurally. You can take a step-by-step approach to developing a Web site successfully, as shown in Figure 3.2. This approach is not necessarily the end-all to developing sites, but it should help you in planning and looking at all the variables involved in Web site production. Most sites fail simply due to poor planning and design.

Figure 3.2.

The development process.

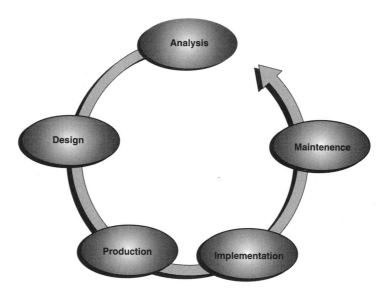

Content Analysis

As people say in the multimedia development field, "content is king." Successful Web development is centered on how successfully the content and graphics communicate to the users. A precarious balance exists between these two elements. Poor content can never be dressed up, even with great graphics. The content is still poor. Also, good content can never communicate effectively with poor graphics. Visual appeal is an important aspect of any communication medium. The first step in developing a good communication tool is analysis of the content you intend to provide.

To begin looking for the content for your site, the first thing you must have is a general goal, as you can see in Figure 3.3. What's your site going to be about? What are you providing to your audience?

3

Figure 3.3.

Analyzing the content.

Most Web sites are established to inform, persuade, educate, or entertain the audience. Depending on which of these tasks you're trying to perform, your site might look different. Most sites focus on the first of these tasks: informing and persuading. More than likely, if you're developing a site for your company, your job will also be categorized as either informing or persuading. Do you want to present information about your company or its products? Are you trying to persuade the audience to buy your product, or are you just presenting information? Establish what you're trying to do at your site, and then try to state your goal in a single sentence. This way, you are forced to focus on the main purpose of your site rather than all the little extras you'd like to provide.

Authorship

The next decision you must make concerns authorship of the content. Often you might want to provide information that has been developed by someone in the company. Most of the time, the company owns content of this nature. Let me be honest—most Web sites being developed are transformations of information that already exists. They can be online versions of traditional brochures or other corporate documents. Nonetheless, even if you believe your company owns the content, you still must ascertain whether the information you want to present via your Web site belongs to the company. Establishing authorship in writing is always a good idea.

In addition to the text provided on your pages, the graphic elements and any multimedia elements are also concerns. Due to the legal aspects of ownership and copyrights, you cannot just throw anything on your Web site. You must consider who owns or who has created any and all items you want to present at your Web site. You also must get permission from the owners before using them.

In this respect, creating a Web site is just like creating a book. You wouldn't begin writing a book by simply copying illustrations or text from another book. So it is also with Web content. You must establish who owns the copyright for the material you want to present and obtain the proper permissions to use it.

Copyrights

Copyrights fall into a gray area on the Web, even though the lines defining copyrights in the United States are in black and white. Most of the information that is put on the Web is assumed to be in the *public domain*. Many of the graphics, text, and other items, however, are actually copyrighted and could be determined as such in court.

 The *public domain* refers to any work that is not protected under copyright (patent or trademark) or media that is not considered a creative work. An item also can be considered public domain if the copyright for the item expires.

What is a copyright? From the date of creation, any text, graphic, sound, video clip, or animation belongs to and is the property of the individual who created it. To use any of these items requires permission from the copyright holder. Unauthorized use of copyrighted material can carry significant financial repercussions, regardless of whether the item has been officially copyrighted through the Library of Congress. Anything you create that is deemed a creative work can be copyrighted. This work includes graphics you create, text you write, or even Web pages in some cases. To protect your work, you can simply add a copyright signature to it (Copyright, 1999 John Doe). Under current copyright laws, this signature protects your work, even if you do not officially copyright it. In legalese, this act is known as "Intent to Copyright." To use any item carrying a copyright signature requires permission from the holder of the copyright.

On the Web, however, tracking infringement—who is using what—is a problem. Finding or prosecuting individuals for copyright infringement is very difficult. For the most part, the same rules that apply to traditional documents also apply to Web-based documents. Concerning copyrights, you must be cautious of what you use at your site, including not only what you create, but also what you use from the "public domain."

Whenever you create something for Web distribution, realize that, literally, the whole world has access to your information. In addition, U.S. copyrights do not apply outside the U.S., nor do many people outside the United States respect them. Do not put information on your site that you want to protect through a copyright. Although copyright laws are established and you could pursue litigation (in the U.S.), proving or prosecuting for copyright infringement is very difficult. It is also very costly. I say this because many people mistakenly believe that anything on the Web is in the public domain. Nothing could be further from the truth! That's like saying anything I find in a magazine I can reprint. Things on the Web can be copyrighted, and just because they appear on the Web does not mean they are public domain. Be cautious about what you provide on your Web site.

On the flip side of this issue is the assumption that I just mentioned. Before you begin cranking out pages, verify, in writing, that you have permission to use the media elements you want to provide, including all the media elements: text, graphics, sound, animation, and video. Even some specialized scripting and programming can be copyrighted. Note: Even if everyone says it was developed in-house or says it's okay to use, you should obtain permission in writing. This path is the safest to follow.

Licenses and Releases

Obtaining permission to use a copyrighted element can be as simple as a permission letter. It might, however, require a *license* or release.

 A *license* is a fee that is paid to use a copyrighted item in another publication.

In the digital publishing arena, licenses are the most common way of obtaining permission. Most often, licenses are required when the media element such as a graphic or sound clip is used in a salable, corporate product. Often the licensing fee is based on the price of the new product that uses the copyrighted item, the level at which the product is distributed (regional, national, international), and the number of copies of the product being created. Say that you want to use a stock image from ABC Images, Inc., in a brochure you're designing. Also say that this brochure is to market your product internationally and that you're going to print 500,000 of them. In this instance, you will pay more to use the image than you would if you were marketing regionally with a small print run of about 1,000. Licensing fees are often subjective and based on the assumed value of the item to the licensee.

The second type of permission that can be obtained for copyrighted items is a *release*.

NEW TERM A *release* is a formal agreement that enables an individual to use a copyrighted item at no charge. A release usually defines specific parameters in which the item can be used.

A release is frequently associated with the development of products for which no price is set or in which the price or distribution is quite small. This often includes Web site development. Although releases are free, restrictions of use are also associated with them. Some releases, for example, state that you cannot use the copyrighted element for public display (like a presentation), whereas others can have restrictions specific to the type of media element. For Web development, even for those things that are created "in-house," securing a release before using those items at least is always a good idea.

Graphics and Media Elements

Here are a few final words about protecting your graphics and media elements. Keep your eyes open for emerging technologies designed to help you protect your work. One prime example is a new graphics encoding technology that embeds copyright information right within the graphic image. The copyright information, however, cannot be seen without the aid of special decoder software. Because I'm a graphic animal myself, this capability is something of a godsend to people like me in the graphics industry. I believe that you will be seeing more software innovations like this in the very near future, innovations designed to protect creative work digitally.

Audience Analysis

One of the most promising aspects of Web development is the ability to customize your site to your audience. All good Web sites are audience-centered. What does your audience expect to see at your site? What will attract users? What will repel them? The whole point in identifying and analyzing the audience is to custom-tailor the Web site around the users' needs.

Whether you're communicating through a book, a live presentation, or a Web site, it is imperative that you build a profile of your prospective or target users like the one shown in Figure 3.4. You might find that you have a very diverse audience due to the global nature of the Web. However, try to target a single population for which you are providing content. What is the age of these users? What is their background? What skills do they have? As any good communicator knows, successful communication occurs only when the text, graphics, and any other aids transfer a message from sender to receiver in its entirety. To do so requires knowledge about the audience. A measure of whether communication has occurred successfully can be seen in how much of the message the audience receives and in the accuracy of the audience's interpretation. Many factors contribute to the way the audience receives and interprets your message.

Figure 3.4.

Audience attributes.

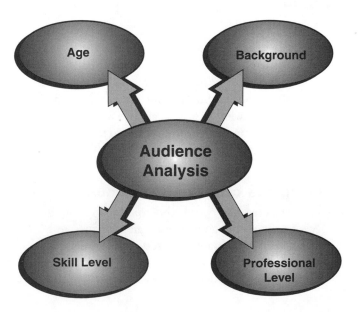

Age

One of the first factors to consider as you look at the audience is age. The age of your users greatly affects how you present your content. If the age of your audience is younger than 20 years, for example, you might want to use some attention-getting device. Also keeping this age group's attention requires some ingenuity. If your audience is older than 20 years of age, however, an attention-getting device might repel if not offend the audience. So age plays a large role in how you present your information.

Background

You also must consider your audience's background when developing your site. A technical discussion on some complex concept, for example, might be good for some of your audience members, but are you excluding those who don't have the background needed to assimilate the information you're presenting? Does the audience need to have some prerequisite knowledge before your content makes sense? If so, you might want either to provide links to sites on the Web where your audience can get the prerequisite knowledge or prepare your content for a lower level. I prefer the former to the latter.

Skill Level

Another consideration is the skill level of your audience. If you're planning to create content that requires a specific plug-in or helper application, for example, will your audience have the skills necessary to find the plug-in or helper and install it? Will the audience need to know how to download files or understand compression programs like Pkware's PKZIP or Aladdin's Stuffit Expander? To you these tasks might seem simple, but to an audience member, they can be significant hurdles. If necessary, provide links to get plug-ins and helpers and even instructions for installation if you believe your audience members need them. To overcome skill limitations in your audience, use a customer service approach. Give the audience members everything they need to be able to use your site efficiently and effectively.

Professional Level

Finally, you also must consider the professional level of the individuals who will be accessing your site. This factor really has to do with the tone of your site, but it also can be related to age level. Do business professionals predominantly make up your audience? If so, you'll definitely want to take a reserved approach to both navigability and content presentation. When you're questioning at what professional level you should aim, erring on the side of conservatism is always better than on the avant-garde. Even in avant-garde (far out, techno-punk, artsy, flamboyant, and so on) sites I create, I still attempt to present the sites with professional overtones.

Development System

To some people, the idea of the development system being a variable involved in Web development seems strange; however, I see it as an important consideration. As you learned the first day, more and more corporations are creating Web development groups rather than having a single individual create all the Web site information. In addition, often the Webmastering group is made up of individuals from several different departments who are often oblivious to the collaborative resources.

The primary aspects of concern for the development system are the applications, platform, tools, and other resources that can be utilized. Looking at these items in a group session makes everyone aware of the collaborative resources. Figure 3.5 graphically shows the major points of development system analysis.

Figure 3.5.

The development system.

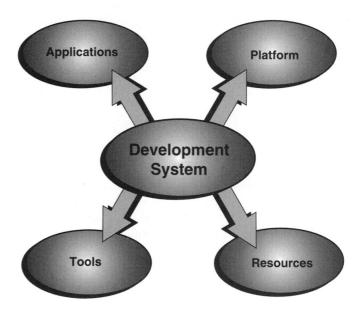

Applications

As you begin planning your Web site, you really need nothing more than a simple text editor and a paint application for graphics. You'll find, however, that many tools have been developed to make Web page creation and maintenance more efficient. Each person in your group probably has at least one of them. If you're part of a Web development group, consider discussing the various software applications you have between yourselves. The following are some of the most useful tools for Web development:

☐ A Web creation tool such as Microsoft FrontPage, Adobe Page Mill, or Macromedia Backstage

3

- ☐ A raster editor such as Adobe PhotoShop or Fractal Design Painter
- ☐ A vector drawing program such as Macromedia FreeHand or Adobe Illustrator

Platform

You also should verify the platform on which you or your Web group will be developing the Web site. Before you upload it to the Web server, developing a site on a local hard drive or storage device is common. Some developers prefer UNIX, others Windows, and still others prefer the Macintosh. Any platform will do, but you must be aware of the differences across the various platforms as you begin working. Also, you must address file format differences across platforms. Aside from the issues of colors and fonts discussed earlier, if you're a PC user, you might want to invest in a utility program that enables you to read Macintosh disks. If you're a Macintosh user, you should be able to read cross-platform disks, assuming that you have System 7.5 or later installed.

If you're working across platforms for Web development, you might want to consider purchasing the following:

- ☐ File transfer software such as Pacific Micro's Mac-In-DOS or MacOpener to enable cross-platform capability (PC users) and file transfer
- ☐ A graphic converter such as Hijaak95 (Windows) or Debablizer (Macintosh)

Tools

In addition to specific development applications, you also might need some other specific tools to add special capabilities. If you want to add internal multimedia elements, for example, you might want to consider adding other applications to your list of development tools. If you want to deliver a wide range of multimedia elements through your Web site, you might want to include the following:

- ☐ Authoring software such as Macromedia Director or Macromedia Authorware
- ☐ Digital video software such as Adobe Premiere or AutoDesk Animator Studio
- ☐ Animation software such as Kinetix 3D Studio Max or Rio Topas
- ☐ Audio software such as Sound Forge or Sound Edit Pro

Other Resources

Beyond the hardware and software resources you will be using, you must also establish what skills each of the group members has. Often a Web development group consists of individuals who have a wide variety of skills. At the same time you're looking at the development system, you can discuss the skills that each person has and how each one can contribute to the development of the Web site.

Delivery System

Earlier you analyzed the audience and considered what the users would be looking for at your site. Now you must also look at the hardware that they will be using to access your site. This part of the development process is the most frequently overlooked.

The main concerns in the delivery system are what types of network access the users have, what platforms they're using, and what types of typical machine configurations they will be using (see Figure 3.6).

Figure 3.6.

The delivery system.

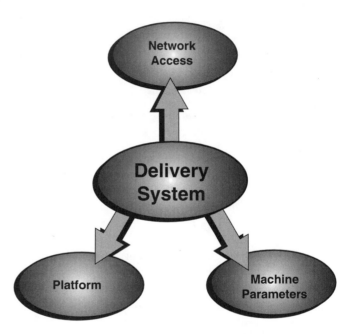

Network Access

The most important aspect of the users' delivery systems is their connection to the Internet. Earlier in this book, I said that many people's opinions of the Web are based on how fast their connections to the Internet are, and indeed most opinions are based here. As you're planning to deliver specific elements to your audience, you need to consider from where they will be logging onto the Internet. Is your audience predominantly composed of users logging in from home using dial-up connections? If so, you should carefully choose how much and how many multimedia elements you deliver due to the amount of time these elements take to download via a modem (see Day 5, "The Technical Designer").

Aside from multimedia elements, even inline graphics can cause users significant problems. Providing too many inline images can result in frustration for the users and their immediate exit of your site. If your audience is mostly dial-up users, consider providing a "lightweight" site that they can quickly and easily access. Your content plan should reflect any limitations that your audience might have.

Platform

On Day 2, "The Internet Specialist," you looked at how the operating system affected the pages that are loaded into the browser. You read how both fonts and color change from platform to platform. One of the things you will invariably do is create a profile of a typical user's machine. Much like a profile of the audience for content guidelines, a profile of a user's machine helps you create content that can be effectively displayed on a user's machine. Undoubtedly, this profile will keep you from creating what cannot be utilized by your audience.

Machine Parameters

Last but not least are the individualized parameters of the users' machines. This factor is more than just the platform or network connection. You must consider the various aspects of the users' computers so that you know what type of multimedia they can utilize. Do they have sound cards? Do their computers play downloaded video? Do the computers have enough RAM to support multimedia plug-ins such as Shockwave, VRML, or QuickTimeVR? Discuss these types of questions with the development team members. Try to put together a typical audience member's computer configuration much like the audience profile.

Functional Analysis

After looking at the content, audience, development, and delivery systems, you must summarize the information you have. Up to this point, you've been defining the parameters under which communication should occur. At the beginning of this process, you developed a general goal in a single sentence. Now you must take that goal and create objectives and an abstract to summarize and describe your site. The objectives and the abstract should give more definition to your overall goal. To do a functional analysis like the one shown in Figure 3.7, you need to document your goal, create objectives, and create an abstract that describes your site.

Figure 3.7.
Functional analysis.

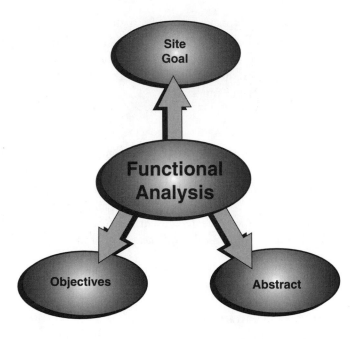

NOTE

Through the functional analysis, I want to emphasize that written documentation of the information found during analysis is vitally important. For this reason, the functional analysis is really nothing more than a concluding document describing the factors that the group has found. Consider that you or one of your group members might not always be involved with Web development. Some might move on to other jobs, become ill, or for some other reason be removed from the Web development group. Documenting the parameters for your site helps any newcomers to your group. It also helps keep everyone on track with the original purpose of the site. The document becomes an abbreviated summary that can be used to brief a new member quickly on the focus and purpose of the Web site you're creating. It also can be used to explain to your boss or a consulting client what the Web site is about and what it will communicate.

Site Goal: Inform, Persuade, Educate, Entertain?

In the functional analysis, you refine and develop the information you have found during analysis into concise statements that describe your site. As you're creating objectives and the abstract, make sure that these items culminate, complete, and support your overall goal of informing, persuading, educating, or entertaining. The objectives should supplement yet complement your goal. They should all contribute to accomplishing the main goal of the site. Alternatively, the abstract should give the background necessary to establish your rationale for the way in which you plan to create your Web site.

Objectives

Objectives are generally short statements that give definitions to the way the overall goal will be accomplished. Each statement can deal with a specific area. An example objective might be "The Web site's product area will inform the reader of our current and new product lines." Also, the objectives can be used to not only describe a feature, but also to indicate how that feature will be executed—for example, "The Web site's product area will inform the reader of our current and new product lines using descriptive 3D animations that the user can download."

Typically, the objectives deal with each of the various aspects that are to be included in the Web site. You can have fewer than 10 objectives or as many as 20 or more, depending on the size of the Web site you're planning.

Abstract

After defining the objectives, you should describe your rationale for what has been included in the site. This description generally explains why certain features are included and why certain features are not included. All the information is based on the conclusions made from the analysis performed by the Web design group.

The abstract should be written with sufficient length that an individual outside the company can read the document to get a description of the site as well as the rationale for its existence. Use the parameters that you found during the analysis as your basis for the decisions made.

Graphic Design

As I have hinted throughout the first few days' lessons, graphics and graphic design play a large role in the communicability of a site, as you can see in Figure 3.8. The communicability of the site portrayed in the figure is a result of how well the page is laid out. The graphical layout of the pages and the graphics themselves largely contribute to the audience's opinion of your site in addition to the site's communicative value.

Figure 3.8.

Evaluation of your site begins with the graphics.

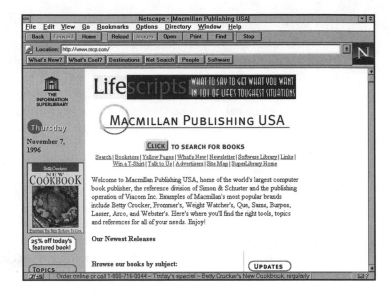

The "Look"

Designing appealing graphical pages is not rocket science. Indeed, the biggest difficulty is in developing an "artist's eye." What looks good to some would be rather unappealing to others. The "artist's eye" is somewhat subjective; however, there is a general range that most people will agree looks good. To develop an artist's eye simply requires training yourself so that you can tell what looks good and what looks bad. With regards to that skill, you will continue to develop it throughout the remainder of this book.

At this point, simply realize that the graphical content of a page should contribute to the content that is being provided. Don't use graphics just to take up space. You can use graphics to set the mood as well as the tone for a site. Figure 3.9 shows an example of a site that utilizes graphics to set a technical overtone.

Graphics also help in the aesthetic dimension by providing visual appeal. Static text becomes more interesting as you add related graphics to a page, as shown in Figure 3.10. The content of the page also becomes clearer because you can visually describe what is being communicated with text. In the center of the figure you see a graphic being used to represent information about digital cameras.

Figure 3.9.

Graphics set the mood of the site.

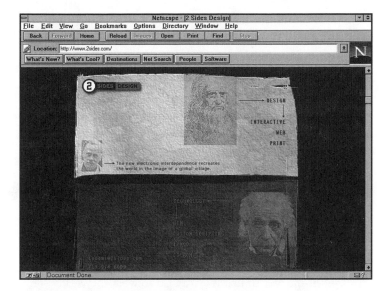

3

Figure 3.10.

The power of graphical communication.

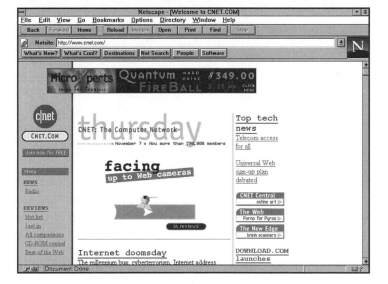

NOTE Many people discredit the power of graphics. I feel that they hold much more communicative power than static text. I would much rather have an image presented to me than three pages of text describing the image. As you know, "a picture is worth a thousand words."

Images communicate more quickly than text and more vividly as well. As you continue to develop your Webmastering skills, you will learn to develop an artist's eye and an appreciation for the power of graphics.

Metaphor

In the multimedia world, a common buzzword creeps up as you begin discussing multimedia and hypermedia; it is *metaphor*.

NEW TERM   A *metaphor* is a theme, motif, or storyline that attempts to familiarize the audience with something new using association. Metaphors are intended to decrease user apprehension when presented with a new environment by drawing on the user's past knowledge.

One of the most difficult items to tackle when dealing with communication tools is the comfort level of the users. How do you get the users comfortable with navigating or using a new informational environment such as a Web site? How do you get the navigation issues out of the way so that they can get to what they really came for—your content?

By using a metaphor, you can attempt to handle this situation. By drawing on a user's previous experience, a metaphor links something the user is familiar with to the workings of a new informational environment. For example, you might create a Web site that works like a book—which would be blasé, but nonetheless it is a metaphor. By using a book metaphor for your pages, you would assume that a user could more quickly and easily begin navigating your site. Using the book metaphor means that users don't have to learn how to navigate the site. They use it just like a book—something they assumably already know how to use. This is the primary goal of a metaphor: to get the users past navigational issues and environment control so that they can get to the content quickly and easily.

Many different metaphors have been used for Web sites. Figure 3.11 shows an example of a digital device metaphor. Note that this site uses an interface analogous to a handheld device. The developers are assuming that you are comfortable and can use such a device. Using this site therefore draws on your past experience and makes using the site easier.

As you begin considering how the users will navigate your site, consider using a metaphor like the one shown in Figure 3.12 to draw on their past knowledge. Sites using metaphors are more successful, aiding the users in overcoming the new environment. If a metaphor is designed with the users' knowledge and skills in mind, it can be fun, both in design and execution.

Figure 3.11.
An example of a metaphor.

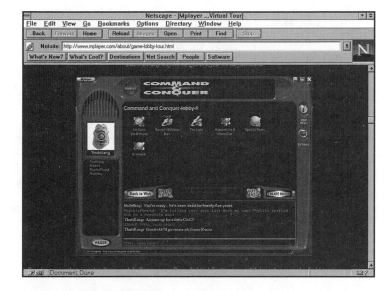

Figure 3.12.
Using a metaphor to draw upon past knowledge and skills.

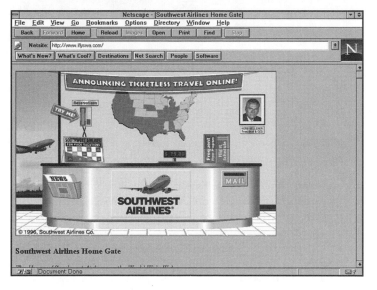

NOTE

If you decide to use a metaphor, make sure that it is somewhat obvious to your audience. Use something that is relevant to the users. If the metaphor you use is too abstract, it will become counterproductive. The best metaphors are the ones with which the audience quickly associates.

Interface

In addition to the use of a metaphor is the issue of the *interface* itself. The interface that you present to the users is the communication channel between the users and the content of the site. The interface contains all the navigation controls for the site, as you can see in Figure 3.13. It is the point of communication and interaction whereby the users interact with the computer and vice versa.

Figure 3.13.

The interface presents the navigational controls for the site.

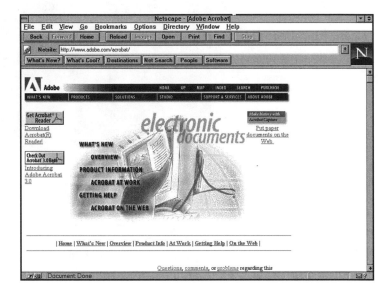

An *interface* is the point of interaction between the computer and the user. It must provide for input and output from both parties.

NEW TERM

Often the interface is part of the metaphor—the two can overlap. The metaphor is the association; the interface is the place of physical interaction, as shown in Figure 3.14. As you proceed through this book, you will invariably see many sites that sport good and bad examples of metaphors and interfaces.

Functionality

Developing the interface and a metaphor for the information at your site can be the most difficult parts of creating a good Web site. The biggest problems with most interfaces is that they are unnatural and difficult to use, or they have little relevance to the audience. When you're developing your site, approach interface design in a utilitarian way. Look at the various functions you must support (from your objectives), and design buttons, icons, and button bars based on those functions.

3

Figure 3.14.

The interface: a point of interaction.

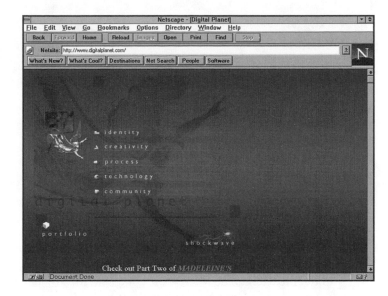

NOTE

One final note about interfaces and metaphors is that the two should be consistent. I have seen Web sites and multimedia CD-ROMs alike that lose the connection between the metaphor and the interface. In some, I can find no connection. Make sure that you are attentive to the consistency between your metaphor and your interface.

Technical Design

After you address the content and graphical issues, the next step is to begin laying out the technical structure for your Web site. When Web sites are conceived, often they are designed with shortsightedness. Often the site is developed on a small scale, and then the site quickly mushrooms into a very large site almost overnight. When this situation happens, the technical design of the site can be either a help or a hindrance.

Developing a technical plan for your site is really a continuation of all the planning you have done thus far. At this point, you should have the various areas of your site defined and a good idea of the pages in each area. You should have the various graphics and multimedia elements you want to include identified, complete with releases or licenses secured or in process. The focus of technical design, as it relates to developing the site's pages and media elements, is to develop a visual, hierarchical structure for your pages. To do so often requires some basic sketches of how your site will be laid out. The main concerns in technical design are the site layout, server structure (see Figure 3.15), and the actual directories and files.

Figure 3.15.
The aspects of technical design.

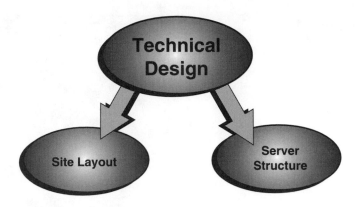

Site Layout

How often do you leave for a trip without a map? For me, rarely. I hate to wander aimlessly, hoping I'll find my destination. Oh sure, sometimes my wife and I just go on a short vacation without predetermining where we're going, but time is not an issue on trips like that. Most often when I travel, at least for business purposes, I don't have time to waste. I cannot leave anything to chance when I'm on a time schedule. I must reach a destination accurately and in a timely manner.

Creating a Web site is much like a business trip. You've done your homework, and you know where you want to go. Now all you need is a map to lay out the physical pages and structure for your site. You could just start cranking pages and leave the arrangement to chance, but why would you? Leaving without a map can leave you aimlessly wandering, hoping you'll hit your destination.

Now that you know what your site will contain as far as the content is concerned, you need to develop a site map. Although the site map is usually a sketch, Figure 3.16 shows a Web site that uses the map in its pages. A site map shows all the various pages at your site and is most often a sketch. The site map lays out all the links from one page to the next as well as the various media elements that will be a part of the pages. The site map becomes an invaluable tool as you start creating the pages and uploading them to your HTTP server.

NOTE

Most of the designing and planning that you will be doing throughout this process requires sketches. Don't try to jump behind a computer before you know where you're going. I am amazed that one of the most powerful planning tools for Web development is still paper and pencil. No software required!

3

Figure 3.16.

Creating a site map.

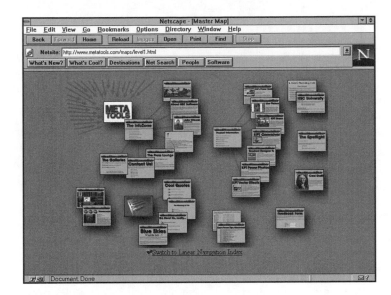

Server Structure: Directories and Files

In addition to being an aid for page development, the site map also shows you the relative and absolute file structure for your server. This structure will become very important as your site grows and as you begin adding more content and pages to your site. Just like the abstract and the objectives, the site map is a living document. As you expand your site, your map, abstract, and objectives also expand.

One of the things you need to focus on when developing a site map is how you will set up the file structure on your server. You should create a structure that is logical and easy to manage. All the pages for a particular area, for example, should probably reside in the same folder or directory on the server. Subsequent divisions of each area can have their own directories. Try to group your files logically so that managing your site is not a memory exercise. As you add pages and content to your site, make sure that you also frequently update your map. I hate using a highway map or a site map that's not up-to-date. You will, too, so make sure that you update.

In addition to developing a logical directory structure, you also should adopt some type of file-naming convention for your HTML and other files that are on the server. If you're working in an environment that supports long filenames, use this fact to your advantage. If you have PC users in your group, however, you might have to adopt the eight-letter naming convention of the DOS environment for those who might still be using Windows 3.*x*.

Production

As you've seen already, a great deal of work and planning is put into a site before a single page is ever created. It might seem like a lot of up-front work, and it is. Successful sites don't just happen. A tremendous amount of planning is involved in creating any good communication medium.

The production phase is the part in which everything seems to come together. If you're working as a freelance Web consultant, at this phase the client will see most of the physical product, but don't be afraid to justify the tremendous amount of work that has been done already. The planning that goes into Web site development is a long-term investment that will pay off after the site is completed.

Putting Together the Site

Most of the work performed during production is performed offline. In fact, I suggest setting up the entire site on a machine other than the server as you're working. This way, you can ensure that your work is left untouched by any other personnel. Second, it gives you full control of what you're creating and saves the "unveiling" of the site until you're ready.

NOTE

During the production phase, I cannot emphasize enough about how important it is to back up your work. As you're developing your site, make sure that you keep incremental versions of both your HTML files and any other media elements that you're incorporating.

Managing Production

If you're working in a group setting, communication and coordination among group members is vitally important. As Webmaster, you are ultimately responsible for seeing that work is being completed on the various elements for the Web site. Make a habit of frequently reviewing the work that is being done by others. Secure accurate deadlines of when elements will be completed and ready for inclusion into the Web site pages.

NOTE

During the production phase, remember to test the pages and site frequently as it is being completed. Remember the discussion concerning browsers and platforms. Test the pages using the hardware and software that the target audience will be using. Test, retest, and then test again to ensure that the pages appear as intended.

Client or Corporate Check-Offs

If you're working as a freelance Web consultant, you definitely should establish a system of client check-offs or approvals. By doing so, you give the client the opportunity to review the work being done rather than get surprises at the end of the project. Using written approvals also gives you, as a consultant, documentation that the client signed off on what you're doing. You can run into no end of trouble if you don't use a system of approvals with your clientele.

Implementation

After all the pages are completed offline, the last part of setting up the site is moving it to the server. Some of the software mentioned earlier, such as Microsoft FrontPage, provides an easy way to upload pages. If you manually upload the pages to your server using FTP, you will undoubtedly have to do some fine-tuning. Regardless, you should rigorously test all the pages and elements to ensure that the site works as intended.

Maintenance

Because the Web is a fluid medium, updates and maintenance will be required over time. The hardest part is over—planning and getting your site online. If you've followed the planning steps presented in this lesson, you should find that managing your site is easier. You will find, no doubt, that your Web site will be a continually evolving creature, and as long as you continually adapt your objectives, abstract, site map, and pages concurrently, managing your site will be easier.

Summary

Today, you looked extensively at the development process for Web sites. Beginning with an analysis of the content, the developer reviews all the necessary items to be included in the Web site, including all text, graphics, sound, animation, and video. Prior to delivering these elements over to the Web, the developer must secure licenses or releases for their use. As you read, you must be cautious of what you place on the Web both as a provider and developer.

By analyzing the audience, you can establish an audience profile that describes the audience's age, background, and skills so that the content can be audience-centered. There is a correlation between analyzing the content and audience and having successful Web communication media.

You also looked at the development and delivery systems to determine collaborative capabilities and developmental constraints. Concluding the analysis is the documentation of the site goal, objectives, and abstract, which describe, define, and validate the site and its content.

Following analysis is production—the phase in which most of the physical product is created. Most sites are developed offline and include client check-offs for work that is done. During the production process, frequent testing should be done to ensure operability of the site with the target browser, platform, and machine. Implementing the created site requires uploading the site pages and materials to the server with ample testing of the finished product. Finally, site diagrams, the goal, objectives, and the abstract should be updated as frequently as the site itself. Maintaining up-to-date documentation ensures manageability.

Q&A

Q What is the difference between transient and nontransient information, and why is it important in communication media?

A The main difference between these two types of information is the rate of change. Transient information changes or becomes out-of-date in less than nine months, whereas nontransient information remains stable for longer than nine months. The comparison of these two types of information is important because of the media that you use to distribute each.

Q What are the main variables to look at during the planning of a Web site?

A The variables are content, audience, the development system, and the delivery system.

Q What are the main pieces of documentation that you should create after analysis?

A Concluding documentation should record the main goal of the Web site, the objectives of the Web site, a site map, and an abstract describing a rationale for decisions made during development.

Workshop

The Workshop provides quiz questions to help you solidify your understanding of the material covered and exercises to give you experience in using what you've learned. The quiz answers are provided in Appendix A, "Quiz Answers." Try to understand the quiz answers before you go on to tomorrow's lesson.

Quiz

1. What is a site map, and why is it important?
2. What is a metaphor, and what is its purpose?
3. What is an interface?

4. How is a license different from a release?

5. How do items become public domain? Isn't everything on the Web public domain?

Exercise

Search the World Wide Web for metaphor and interface examples. Hypothesize the assumptions the developers have made about the audience on which they are basing their metaphors. Take a look at various site interfaces, and describe why some are more easy to use than others.

3

Day 4

The Media Designer

What is the value of a graphic that communicates well? Is it more valuable than a page of text? Does it replace the need for text? For many people, graphics play a very important role in the presentation of information. This should not surprise you. You've probably been to a bored, I mean, board meeting or other presentation in which the presenter used overheads or screens composed entirely of text. Ho, hum. We want—we need—graphics to help us decode what people are saying as well as to motivate us to listen. Communication occurs more effectively and more efficiently when graphics and multimedia elements are used. Why should computer communication be any different? Part of being a Webmaster means being a media designer.

 A *media designer* is an individual who understands computer graphics, animation, video, and sound, and can effectively use these media elements to enhance communication.

It is amazing to see the dramatic explosion in the field of graphics. For many years, graphics and publishing changed only moderately. Sure there was new hardware and software that came along, but in the last five years there has been an explosion in the field of graphics like there's never been before. It is predominantly due to the computer and the Internet.

NOTE

As I'm writing I am reminded of what happened with the advent of computer desktop publishing in the mid- to late '80s. When the first Macintosh desktop publishing software came out, many people became "desktop publishers." With no apparent background in design, writing, or graphics, individuals began cranking out flyers, brochures, and pamphlets that had the design and finesse of Conan the Barbarian. The overwhelming belief was that all you needed was technology, not skills. It's funny how history repeats itself.

The same trend has appeared in the Web world, which is why there is so much noise on the Web. Much like the realization that came to the overnight desktop publishing crowd, individuals are realizing that you need skills and not just technology. We are in the weeding out process where the real Web designers come forth—those who are busily gaining the background skills necessary to be good Web developers and Webmasters.

You easily can see the growth as the number of people creating computer-generated graphics continues to multiply exponentially. From *Toy Story* to the local mall kiosk, graphics have infiltrated many parts of society. If you've been to one of the latest SIGGRAPH confer-ences—the conference of conferences for computer graphics jocks—you know what I mean.

A proliferation of graphics has invaded many aspects of the world. We are finding that static and dynamic graphics can aid and enhance many areas of our lives. However, how do you create graphics, particularly Web graphics, if you're not a "graphics animal?" What does it take to create a graphic that communicates well and that inspires, captures, or motivates the audience to dig deeper into your site?

Today's lesson focuses on how to create Web graphics and how to design pages using those graphics. Note from the size of this chapter the important role that I believe graphics play in the overall presentation of a Web site. To be blunt, I believe that the graphics and multimedia elements presented at a Web site are as important, if not more important, than anything else. I say that with tongue in cheek—remember the precarious balance between graphics, content, and the audience.

Graphics that appear on Web pages are generally used for three main purposes:

- ☐ To enhance, complement, and supplement content that cannot be adequately described or explained with text
- ☐ To present navigational items such as buttons, button bars, and icons to enable the user to navigate within your site

☐ To aid in creating a visual flow by laying out information through the use of directional, helper, and "filler" graphics

As you are laying out your pages and making decisions about what the page will include and how the content will be presented, keep in mind that graphics are a vital part of Web page design. Aside from the purposes for graphics, note these important things that a graphic should always do:

☐ Graphics used for content purposes should always aid in communication. Graphics used this way should always add more clarity to the text or display something that cannot be adequately communicated with text.

☐ Graphics should never overshadow or distract the audience from what you are presenting.

☐ Graphics should contribute to the overall tone of the site. Graphics at a site for business professionals should contribute to a professional tone or look.

☐ The audience's impression of your graphics will not be based only on what is being shown in the graphic, but also on its size, placement, and orientation.

☐ Graphics displayed on a page must be designed around the target audience's browser, platform, and machine.

Aside from traditional graphics issues, today you also examine some of the other wonderful media elements you can use at your site. How do various sizes and styles of fonts aid in communication? What about video, audio, and animation? In addition to graphics, you'll look at some of the specifics of designing many different types of media elements for inclusion on Web pages.

Page Layout

One of the first and foremost concerns about Web pages is the physical layout of the information on the page. How do you present your information so that it is easily readable and visually stimulating? Each page you create must be designed so that the audience can easily read it, as shown in Figure 4.1. Graphical elements that you use should not hinder the text information that is being presented; instead, it should complement and complete it.

NOTE

As you have undoubtedly noticed, there are many pages on the Web that do not communicate well. Some of the authors of the pages don't know what they are communicating. Others know what they want to communicate, but they do it poorly. Strive to pick up the key elements in this chapter on the proper use of media elements in Web page design and communication.

Figure 4.1.

Pages must be easily readable.

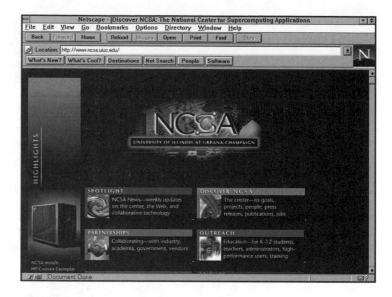

What is it about the page layout that makes it effective? Is it simply the look, the content, or is it all subjective? When you browse the Web, you'll predominantly find that there are three main attributes on which most objective criticisms focus: tone, visual appeal, and consistency. These three areas create the legs for supporting communication and helping to enhance the content. When you look at the page layout and design—the visual aspect—if any one of these items is weak, the overall appeal of the page is lessened.

Tone

Earlier in this book, you learned that the tone of a site is created from the layout of the pages and graphics. Now take a closer look at how tone is created by the layout of the page. As you look at the overall layout of Web pages, keep in mind that there are several subordinate things that build toward this overall tone as well.

NEW TERM The *tone* of a site refers the manner in which the Web document is presented to the audience.

NOTE

Undoubtedly, if you are the designer sort, some of the things in this chapter might be information of which you are already aware. If you fit the designer category, probably one of the most difficult things you will have to contend with is the HTML language. As a designer, you're probably used to a page layout program such as Adobe PageMaker.

> Keep in mind that HTML is a semantic language, and laying out pages so that they look the way you want using the HTML code structure probably will be your biggest hurdle. The people that often have the most difficulty with the HTML language are those who are accustomed to page layout programs.

Figure 4.2 shows a Web page that presents a very professional tone; in other words, it looks like a formal business page. Let's examine why. First, notice the overall layout of the page. Notice how many of the elements are aligned and create a very formatted look. This is one way to create the tone of a site: through the balance of the items on the page.

Figure 4.2.

Building a site's tone using page layout.

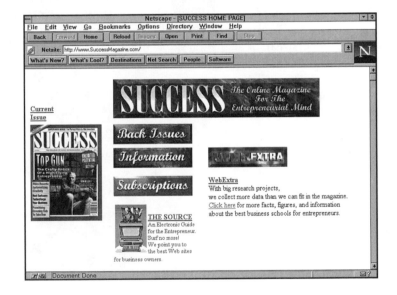

NEW TERM   *Balance* describes how the page elements are arranged visually; comparing one half to another.

A page that has an equal number of elements on each side of the page is said to have *symmetrical balance*. A page with unequal elements on each side would be said to have *asymmetrical balance*, as shown in Figure 4.3. In general, symmetrical balance presents a more professional, formal tone whereas asymmetrical balance is more informal or aesthetic.

As you'll note from Figure 4.2, the page does not strictly adhere to a completely formal balance definition, yet it still gives the site a professional tone. Overall, the page would be classified as formally balanced, but the alignment of elements helps to create this formal look even though it does not explicitly adhere to the definition.

Figure 4.3.

Symmetrical and asymmetrical balance.

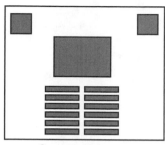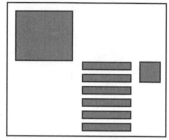

Symmetrical balance   Asymmetrical balance

Now look at another site with a professional tone. Figure 4.4 exactly follows the traditional idea of a formal balance. Notice the balance of all the elements equally on either side of the screen, which presents a very formal presentation of the information. The highly structured and formal look is often required by professional organizations. However, a formal look doesn't have to be aesthetically unappealing to the artistic crowd. As you'll see shortly, you can reach a middle ground.

Figure 4.4.

Another site with formal balance.

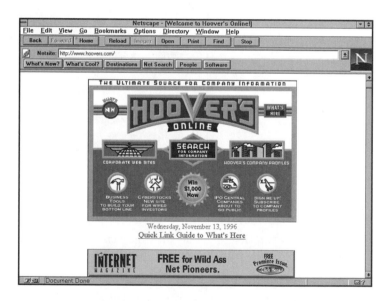

In all of the preceding examples, you can see how the actual layout of the elements on the Web page contributes to the tone of the site. The tone also is formed by the look of the individual elements. For example, a specific typefont or graphic can help present the site professionally. In any site, the tone becomes stronger as more of the elements are presented in a similar manner. If all the elements on the page are presented the same way and with the same look and feel, the tone of the page becomes very strong and consistent. If there are conflicting elements, elements with varying styles, the page loses its tonal coherency.

Aside from formally balanced sites, you also can present an avant-garde or nontraditional look to your site by using more of an artistic flair in your pages. As you learned earlier, the whole idea of what tone is needed centers on your audience. What do they expect to see? How do they expect it to be presented? If your audience is business professionals, use symmetrical balance in your page. If you're flavoring your site for the artsy type, use an informal balance as shown in Figure 4.5.

Figure 4.5.

Providing an artistic look.

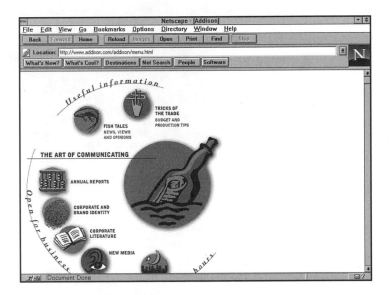

What makes something look avant-garde? As you learned, first notice in Figure 4.6 the asymmetrical look of the Web page. This is the first thing that contributes to the artistic look. Second, all the individual elements such as text and graphics also provide a flair for the dramatic. The elements flow together and intersect, creating a piece of art within the page itself. Finally, the fonts that you use also contribute to making a piece that screams "I am avant-garde!"

NOTE

When you see the term *avant-garde*, you often will find that the term is subjective. It is based on your past experiences—what you are expecting versus what you have experienced in the past. Some sites that might be avant-garde to you might not be avant-garde to me, and vice versa. Really, the term avant-garde describes a paradigm shift—a change from what we really expected. As you're surfing the Web, be conscious of things people incorporate into their Web pages that attract your attention. Be conscious also of why it attracts your attention in either a positive or negative way.

Figure 4.6.

Hinging on aesthetic qualities.

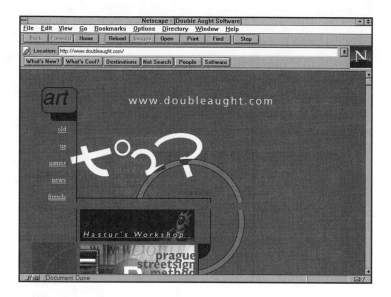

In the previous figures, you have seen the opposing ends of the tonal spectrum. More than likely, most of your pages will be a combination of the aesthetic and professional, as shown in Figure 4.7. Carefully designed pages, centered around the audience, will increase the satisfaction of your audience and guarantee a return visit or the all-important bookmark.

Figure 4.7.

Combining the aesthetic and the professional.

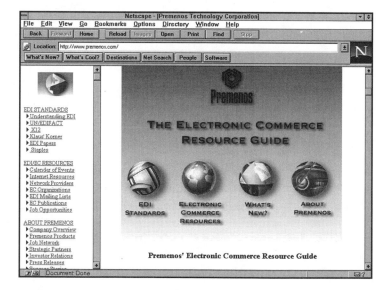

Visual Appeal

A second leg that contributes to communication is visual appeal. Face it, this is what the Web is really about: enabling you to browse the myriad of information in a graphically pleasing way. Being able to look through the hundreds of pages of information without the graphics wouldn't be very exciting; it wouldn't be much more than a glorified Gopher menu. Strip a page of its graphics and it will likely appear on Yahoo!'s Worst Top Ten list.

The visual appeal of a page is focused around several things. All the elements contribute to visual effectiveness, none more than graphics, as shown in Figure 4.8. A well-designed, sharp-looking graphic will always attract attention, but only when it is relevant to the content being provided.

Figure 4.8.

Appealing to your audience through graphics.

The visual appeal of a page can be significantly hampered without design savvy. As you are designing, look for ways to intelligently incorporate graphics to enhance, support, or complement your site's content. You might want to use a graphic to show your site structure, as shown in Figure 4.9, which is a very good use of a graphic. The graphic helps you see a complete picture of what the site is about. The home page shown in Figure 4.9 is well designed and quickly gives you an idea of what is at the site and where you can go. However, what makes the graphic alone good? Negative space, visual clarity of the buttons, and the typefont all contribute to the effectiveness of this splash page graphic.

Figure 4.9.

A splash page graphic that shows the site's structure in an appealing way.

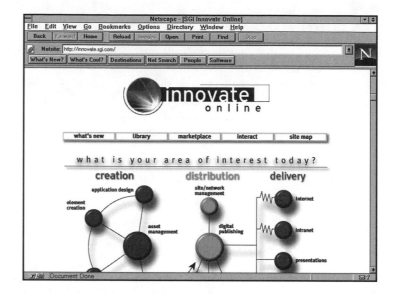

The are many different ways to effectively use graphics. Figure 4.10 shows a very effective, yet very artistic way to present the site's structure using graphics. You can see the same characteristic threads running through this graphic. It is effective because of negative space, visual clarity, and fonts. The next couple of sections examine the common threads that can be found in all well-designed Web pages.

Figure 4.10.

An effective, yet artistic home page.

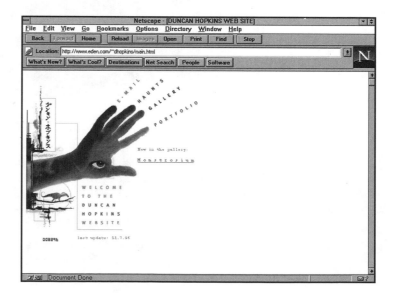

4

Positive and Negative Space

As you have seen, some of the best Web pages are created not only using positive space, areas with graphics and text, but also using negative space. It seems absurd to some, but what you do with blank space is just as important as what you do with the areas in which you insert graphics and text.

 Negative space or *white space* is an area on a page where no graphical or textual elements appear. Alternatively, *positive space* is an area on a Web page that contains a media element such as text or graphics.

When you are creating pages, it is vitally important that you don't chock every nook and cranny with a visual element. Have you ever tried to read a badly designed brochure? You know the one—a horrendous looking brochure with graphics, lines, and text elements strewn all over the place, not to mention fonts that make your eyes sore. When you are designing, leave ample breathing room around the various text and graphic elements. Our eyes need the blank space around these elements to help us process the text or graphics. The white space around text helps us cognitively differentiate between paragraphs, columns, and text bodies. The negative space around graphics aids us in visually interpreting the graphic being presented.

You've seen several examples of Web pages that have effectively used graphics. Figure 4.11 shows another well-designed Web page. In this page, the negative space surrounding the graphic helps direct your eyes through the page. In design terms, this is called *eyeflow*.

4

Figure 4.11.
Directing the audience's eyes using positive and negative space.

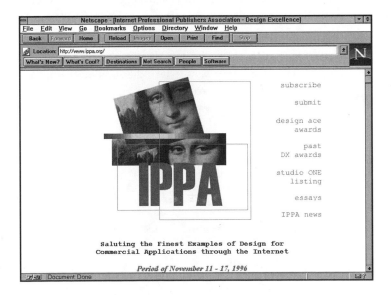

Eyeflow is the pattern or direction in which your eye flows across a page of information. Designers use text and graphics to direct the audience's eyes across the page, drawing attention to specific elements in the document.

You were taught to read normal text from left to right, top to bottom, so your eyes flow through a normal page of text as they have been taught. However, with a Web page composed of graphics and text, your eyes need to be directed in the way to read the page. Using positive and negative space helps direct your eyes and focus your attention.

In Figure 4.11, the first thing that probably grabs your attention is the image in the middle of the screen, but then what do your eyes do? Note the white space on the left side of the screen, counterbalanced by the text on the right side. The absence of a balancing element on the left side (the negative space) causes your eyes to shift to the right side, drawing your attention to the text menu. In this way, the designer has indirectly pointed you to the navigational controls for the site. Quite clever, eh? But not many people actually notice when this is happening. As a media designer, however, focus on using your page elements to direct the audience's eyes.

The previous example displays the whole purpose of designing pages. To design an effective page, you must control the audience's eyes. As is the case in the previous example, often you must first start by getting the audience's attention (the center image in Figure 4.11). Then, using negative and positive space, you'll draw their attention to a specific item. In the example, your eyes are drawn to the menu. In most Web pages, you want to eventually lead the audience's attention to your navigation items. In a scrolling environment, where pages extend beyond a single screen, this might be difficult to achieve at all times.

While you design your pages, be conscientious of what the user's eyes will do as they view your page. On poorly designed pages, the user's eyes are often drawn off the page or left staring in one place. You really want to lead the audience's eyes, not just let them wander aimlessly until they figure out how to navigate your site. Use graphics, rules, and text elements to help the user find his or her way around by providing ample positive and negative space.

Typefonts and Styles

As I've hinted earlier, typefonts and typefont styles (such as bold and italics) play a key role in how a Web page looks. Much of the tone of the page or site depends upon the use of fonts.

As you look at the various typefonts in Figure 4.12, you can see that how the font actually looks can determine the look and feel of the page. The thickness, style, weight, and height all contribute to presenting a feel of the font.

Figure 4.12.
Various fonts can be used to connote tone.

Bold & Beefy
TECHNOPUNK
Technical Graphics
LEGAL BEAGLE
ELEGANT NIGHTS
Old West

4

What would happen if the size of the word "Why" were made smaller in Figure 4.13? The overall effect of the presented image would probably be lessened, right? As you design Web pages, keep in mind that you can create or support a page's tone with fonts that you decide to use. How you present titles, subtitles, bylines, and so on can change how effective your Web page is.

Figure 4.13.
Various styles, colors, and sizes can affect the presentation of the site.

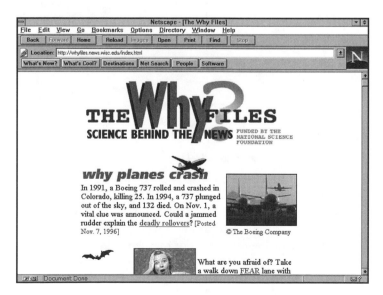

Graphics

The graphics you present at your site can have varying degrees of effectiveness on the tone of your site. Again, as displayed in Figure 4.8, graphics often are used to get the attention of the audience. Whether or not your graphics are effective depends upon the realism of your graphics and the graphic prowess of your audience. The audience's impression of a photo-realistic rendering might be quite low if they are used to such images. However, if the audience is used to lower quality graphics they might be quite impressed with such an image. Consider your audience's expectations.

As you are designing graphics, focus on what your audience expects and design the quality of the graphics for them. For example, in Figure 4.14, the main navigation graphic has been designed as a cartoon. You can use the entire range of graphics, from photo-realistic images to cartoons. It all depends upon your audience.

Figure 4.14.

All qualities of images can be effective.

Multimedia Elements

Probably one of the most exciting ways to get and direct attention on a Web page is through the use of multimedia elements. However, these elements are often overused and poorly used. When you are trying to get and direct attention, remember that multimedia elements shouldn't overpower the content being provided at the site. Often, too many dancing bullets and animated items distract or irritate the user.

If you decide to use multimedia elements on your page, make sure they complement your content as shown in Figure 4.15. Notice that the layout and the multimedia elements (which you cannot see in a static page) complete the content. Obviously, multimedia elements will not be appropriate for all the content you might be delivering. However, you frequently can add small multimedia effects that will not distract your readers from the content. For example, you might want to use a rollover effect for interactive portions of the screen, where the color of the item changes as you drag the mouse over it. Small things like this can be used with almost any content and will make your site easier to use.

Figure 4.15.

Make sure your multimedia elements complement your content.

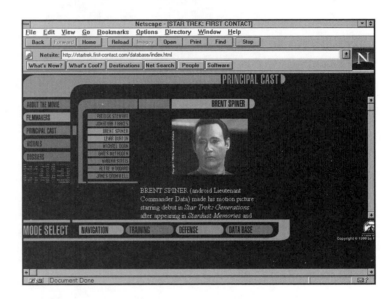

Consistency

The last leg that enhances communication is consistency. Above all else there should be some commonality between all the pages you deliver at your site. A site on which navigation items shift from one location to another across pages frequently disorients the user.

You can create and maintain consistency at your site by using common elements on your pages, as shown in Figure 4.16. For example, you can use a common title bar or navigation bar on all your pages. As you read earlier, one of the main things you must do is familiarize your audience with your site's environment. If the audience continually has to search your pages to learn how to navigate them, they will become disassociated with the content and be more concerned with navigation than acquiring information. Strive to create common elements that appear in the same location on every page. This will help to create consistency across your pages.

Figure 4.16.
Common elements across pages create consistency.

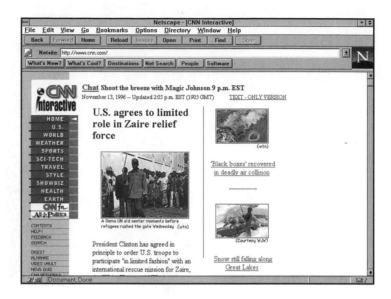

Often, the elements that you use for navigation and eyeflow will be the items that you want to present in the same place on every page. For example, a navigation bar at the top of the page tells the user that he or she can expect it to be there on every page. As you are surfing, notice how often you yourself see an element such as a navigation bar on one page, and then expect to see it in the same place on the other pages. What happens if the location of the bar changes on another page? You have to search for the darn thing, right? Consequently, you become separated from the information—the thing on which you where focused—to search for the silly navigation bar. Small things like this become significant hurdles for users. Some will exit stage left. As you are designing, design for consistency as shown in Figure 4.17.

Fonts

Now that you have learned the various elements that can be used to help communicate, you need to look at some more general concepts concerning fonts and colors. You briefly have seen how fonts affect the tone of a page. Fonts that you use on your pages can be incorporated in two different ways. HTML pages can actually present fonts as either postscript or bitmap. Postscript fonts, often called vector fonts, describe every character in the font via a vector description, whereas a bitmap font describes the font with pixels, as shown in Figure 4.18. You begin by learning the characteristics of postscript fonts and conclude with a lesson on fonts displayed as bitmaps.

Figure 4.17.
Navigation and eyeflow elements are often prime choices to appear across pages.

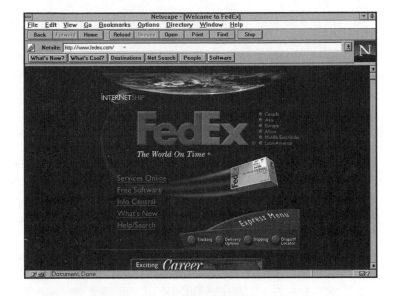

Figure 4.18.
Bitmap versus vector fonts in Web pages.

The fonts that are used as part of the HTML code are created and laid out by the user's machine. As you learned on Day 2, "The Internet Specialist," (when you learned about the browser's cache) when you access a site, the HTML file is loaded to your machine's cache directory. Within the code file, HTML tags describe text that is to be fluidly laid out on the Web page for the user to view. The browser calls for the font, and the font is created in the browser per the definition on the client machine. These fonts are called postscript fonts.

The postscript description of the font itself is resident on the user's machine; it is part of the operating system. This description tells how the font looks—how tall it is, how wide it is, and so on—by defining the outline of every character in the font. The font description is a vector description of every character, so it can be created at any size. This is why you can specify various sizes in the HTML code. However, with postscript fonts, you are also limited to the fonts that are on the user's machine; basically, you are limited to the fonts that come with the user's operating system.

So what happens if you want to use a font that the user's machine doesn't have? In this case, you create a graphic of the font using the text tool in an image editor. After you have created the graphic of the font, you incorporate the graphic into the Web page as an inline image.

There are advantages and disadvantages to using each type of font. Font bitmaps enable you to incorporate any type of font into a Web page; however, bitmaps take longer to download because they are graphics rather than code. You'll also notice that bitmap fonts appear much smoother than vector fonts, as shown in Figure 4.19. Compare the text that says, "Search the Database." Notice the jaggy edges that are characteristic of a vector font created by the browser. It uses a standard font description from the client machine. The text that says, "the internet movie database" appears smoother and uses a unique font. This is a bitmap or graphic font inserted as an inline image.

Figure 4.19.

Bitmap fonts appear much smoother than vector fonts.

Font Characteristics

In general, there are two different types of fonts, serif fonts and sans serif fonts (see Figure 4.20). The biggest distinguishing characteristic is the presence or absence of serifs.

Figure 4.20.
Serif versus sans serif typefonts.

Serif Fonts
Sans Serif Fonts

 Serifs are the small feet and tails that appear on the characters of a font to increase readability. Fonts with serifs are called *serif fonts*. Fonts without serifs are called *sans serif.*

Aside from the global distinction between serif and sans serif, there are several other font characteristics. These include the following:

☐ The overall size of the font is called the *point size*, which is measured in points (see Figure 4.21).

Figure 4.21.
The point size of a font.

This is 8 point text.

This is 12 point text.

This is 14 point text.

This is 16 point text.

☐ The *weight* of a font is the width of the strokes composing the lines and curves of the letters (see Figure 4.22).

Figure 4.22.
The weight of a font.

4

☐ The *horizontal space* of a font is the relative width of the letter M in the font (see Figure 4.23).

Figure 4.23.
*The horizontal space
of a font.*

☐ *Letter spacing* is the defined spacing between letters (see Figure 4.24).

Figure 4.24.
*The letter spacing
of a font.*

Letter spacing
Letter spacing
Letter spacing
Letter spacing
Letter spacing

☐ *Leading* is the spacing between multiple lines of text (see Figure 4.25).

Figure 4.25.
*The leading of a font
shown with equal leading
between lines.*

Leading is spacing between lines.
Leading is spacing between lines.
Leading is spacing between lines.
Leading is spacing between lines.
Leading is spacing between lines.
Leading is spacing between lines.
Leading is spacing between lines.

☐ *Alignment* is the physical arrangement of a body of text (see Figure 4.26).

Many of these characteristics are the very things that cause problems on Web pages across browsers and platforms. As you saw earlier, postscript text that is laid out on a Web page can shift significantly from browser to browser as well as across platforms. This is something you cannot control because it depends upon the user's machine and not on how you lay out your HTML code. If you need precise placement of text elements, particularly for a composed graphics and text element, I suggest using a bitmap of the font, about which you learn shortly.

Figure 4.26.

The alignment a body of text.

This is right justified text.
This is right justified text.
This is right justified text.
This is right justified text.

This is left justified text.
This is left justified text.
This is left justified text.
This is left justified text.

This is center justified text.
This is center justified text.
This is center justified text.
This is center justified text.

Readability

The types of fonts you use in your Web pages can either significantly increase or decrease communicability. In general, designers most often will strive to use serif fonts for large bodies of text and sans serif fonts for titles or headlines. A lot of sans serif text used for body text becomes difficult to read due to the absence of feet and tails. Alternatively, the serifs get in the way when serif fonts are used at large sizes. Keep in mind that serif fonts are good for small text or body text because of the feet and tails (serifs), but those same serifs get in the way when the text is very large.

A second thing to keep in mind as you are designing pages is not to go font happy. Using five different fonts on one page can be aesthetically disastrous, so strive to use only one or two different fonts on a single page. Using many different fonts on a single page can have adverse effects on the user; the text can become difficult to read and be visually unappealing.

A final note about fonts is that although creating italic, bold, and underlined fonts in HTML code is quite easy, you should use these type treatments sparingly. Entire bodies of italic or bold text are extremely difficult to read. Special type treatments, including script or decorative fonts, should be used only in special places such as headings and headlines. Choose your fonts and font treatments carefully.

Bitmaps

You might want to use a specific font such as an ornate or decorative font that you cannot be assured is on the user's machine. In this case, you will need to create a bitmap image of the font to include it on the Web page. This means that you must make the font an inline image rather than a text tag. You'll find that getting the font on the page just right might require some adjustment, but after you've adjusted it, it will be foolproof.

Color

When you are designing graphics, there are several things that you should be aware of concerning color in graphics. When you see a graphic that is effective, certainly the colors that were used in the image are not there by accident. Much planning goes into creating effective graphics. As you are designing, you must be conscientious about both the psychological and visual aspects of the colors you use.

Psychological Aspects

Much research has been done concerning colors and what they evoke in people. Many sources state that specific colors elicit certain feelings, thoughts, and actions. For example, the color red often connotes danger or stop, whereas green can represent money or go. The colors that you choose for your Web pages can be used to represent different things. For example, you might use green text for the financial section of a particular corporation's Web site. You might use red to attract attention to information vital to the audience. Colors can be used representatively at a Web site to mean many different things.

The one thing that is for certain, however, is that color representation depends on a person's culture and experience. We in the United States connote green with money because our money is green. In another culture green might mean the exact opposite; in fact, green might be a negative color. All the color research that has been done suggests that colors evoke feelings, thoughts, and actions in people, but that these things are relative to the viewer's experience, background, and culture.

You need to be conscious of the genre of the Web because it is accessible worldwide. On the Web, most links are displayed in blue, while other colors can represent other actions or things. When you're designing your page, be careful not to use strange colors with which people are unfamiliar.

Also, if your target audience crosses cultural boundaries, do some research on the cultural representations of colors and graphical elements. Don't assume that the audience will automatically know what something is by an abstraction based on your own experience.

4

Visual Aspects

Colors are also known to have specific effects concerning the way we view them. It is known that certain properties of colors are implicitly responsible for the way we see depth and size relationships. In general, colors that are cool, such as blue, violet, and green, appear to recede in graphic images. Colors that are warm, such as red, orange, and yellow, appear to come toward us in graphic images. Even variations within a single color cause us to visually interpret a three-dimensional effect from that color. For example, in nature, things closer to us seem to be darker in value and somewhat saturated (more pure). Colors toward the horizon appear to be desaturated and lighter. Keep this in mind when you are creating graphics. You can create three-dimensional effects by lightening and darkening colors. In addition, using cool versus warm colors also can change your audience's depth perception.

Defining Colors

In Web graphics, the definition of colors in the image is a function of the raster or paint program that you use. With bitmap graphics included on Web pages, there is no direct color definition in the HTML file. All colors are inherent to the bitmap itself and are defined when you create them in the paint program. However, with text elements, backgrounds, and horizontal rules defined by the HTML coding, you must work with something called hexadecimal color.

NEW TERM *Hexadecimal color* is a base-16 mathematical numbering system used to define and describe HTML colors. Each color is defined by a string of six numbers such as FFFFFF or 000000. The possible values for each numeral are 0, 1, 2, 3, 4, 5, 6, 7, 8, 9, A, B, C, D, E, and F. The lowest numeral is 0 and the highest is F.

As you will find, working with colors in a bitmap editor is much easier than working with colors in HTML coding. In a raster editor, you define colors simply by choosing them with the mouse. In HTML, however, you must mathematically define colors using abstract letters and numbers such as FFFFFF for white or 000000 for black. You'll take a closer look at defining hexadecimal color a little later in this chapter, in the section "Hexadecimal Color." Just realize that it is easier to use a paint editor to create bitmaps than it is to define hexadecimal colors in HTML code.

Graphics

Being a graphics animal, I love working with graphics. Hopefully, you do too. As you begin creating graphics, you will find that there are basically two different ways to create them, each with its own advantages and disadvantages. In fact, you've been indirectly dealing with them through the first parts of this book. As you've learned, the two main types of graphic images are raster (bitmap) graphics and postscript (vector) graphics.

NEW TERM *Bitmap graphics* are graphics in which the smallest drawing element is the pixel or picture element. *Vector graphics*, on the other hand, are graphics in which the smallest drawing elements are points, lines, and circles.

Vector and Raster

Most of the graphics found on the Web are raster-based, although new technologies exist and are being developed that enable the developer to distribute vector-based illustrations as well. These two illustration technologies have some significant differences between them. By definition, you can see that raster and vector drawings are different due to the way the image is created and defined, but there are other differences as well.

The first major difference between these types of graphics is how they display on-screen. Raster images are characterized by a more photo-realistic representation of the image, as shown in Figure 4.27. Because raster images use anti-aliasing (blurring of edges), elements within them appear much smoother, as shown on the left of Figure 4.27. The blurring of the edges gives the raster image a more photo-realistic quality. Alternatively, vector images are characterized by jagged or stair-stepped edges on the elements in the image.

Figure 4.27.

Raster versus vector graphics.

Although raster images present images in a more photo-realistic way, there is a price to pay for this characteristic. Because the smallest element in a raster image is the pixel, each pixel must be defined. A single raster image can contain thousands of pixels, and each pixel has color data associated with it. This makes the raster image's file size quite large. A single 640×480 raster GIF image can require up to 40KB of hard disk space. This file would then require approximately seven seconds to download over a 28.8 Kbps modem, which doesn't seem too bad until you compare it to a vector version of the same file.

Although vector files are marked by "jaggies," they define each and every element in the image through mathematical code (postscript) rather than by pixel color definition. This significantly reduces the size of the vector graphic. If the 40KB GIF image were instead a vector file, it might require only 8KB or 9KB of space, which would download within a second. This is a considerable difference when you are waiting for a Web page to download.

As you design Web graphics, you'll find that the majority of images you create will be bitmap graphics simply because no vector formats are directly supported by Web browsers. Vector formats are pretty much dependent upon plug-ins such as Shockwave for FreeHand. However, even when vector images are used, they often don't show up very well on-screen due to their stair-step (jaggy) nature. Throughout the remaining sections of today's lesson you'll continue to learn the terms related to bitmap graphics.

Imaging Attributes

Undoubtedly, the biggest hurdle with which you'll have to contend is designing your bitmap graphics so that they download quickly for your audience. Many of the following defined attributes directly affect download speed: image resolution, image size, and image bit depth. Optimally, you want to design your graphics so that your audience can view them without waiting for long periods of time for your pages to download.

Image Resolution (dpi)

The first term to learn is dots per inch, or dpi. This term is commonly associated with graphics and desktop publishing output.

 Dots per inch or *dpi* is a measurement used to describe the number of physical, printable dots per square inch of an image.

When you are dealing with Web development, dpi is not as big of a concern as it is with printed media. The image resolution that you need for a graphic image depends basically upon your output device. Understand that for most Web development tasks, all you need are 72 dpi images because that is the maximum number of dpi that a monitor has. Anything more and you're just wasting bandwidth on the Net. Alternatively, if you want a graphic to print out very cleanly from the Web, the dpi must be higher. Figure 4.28 shows a 72 dpi graphic image on the left printed at 300 dpi and a 300 dpi graphic image on the right printed at 300 dpi. Notice the significant difference between the clarity of the two images.

Another difference, one you can't see in the displayed image, is the file size. Creating raster images at a high resolution exponentially increases the file size. In Figure 4.28, the file size of the high-resolution image (right) is about four times the size of the low-resolution file (left). When you're designing Web graphics, design for the lowest common denominator.

Figure 4.28.
A 72 dpi image versus a
300 dpi image.

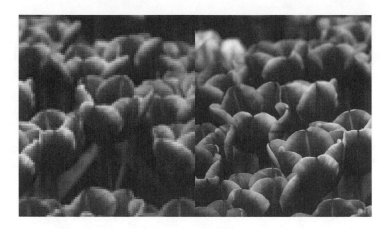

Now, an enterprising person might say, "Just increase the dpi on the low-resolution image so it will print correctly." Unfortunately, that won't work. Bitmap graphics are device-dependent graphic files, which means that after the graphic is created at a certain resolution you cannot increase the dpi. The image is dependent upon the device for which it was originally created. Figure 4.29 shows what I mean. The image on the left was created at the proper dpi and the image on the right was created at a lower dpi and then increased. Notice the blurring that occurs on the right due to the increased dpi.

Figure 4.29.
Increasing the dpi on a
low-resolution file doesn't
increase the output
clarity.

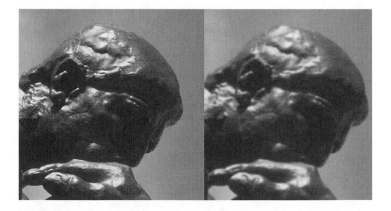

 NOTE

It seems appropriate to mention here that the device dependency of bitmap graphics is the biggest single problem with using them. This is why vector images are so appealing. Vector graphics are device-independent, which means that the dpi can be increased or decreased based upon the output device. This makes sense because vector files are based upon mathematics rather than absolute pixel definitions.

Because most Web developers design for screen use only, dpi might not be a concern. However, some readers might want to design for multiple devices. In any case, you should develop all bitmap graphics at 300 dpi. This will give you flexibility in case you want printable versions in the future. Again, you will notice increased file storage requirements as well as processing speed, but you give yourself more future options to reuse the graphics later by designing at a higher dpi.

Image Size (Physical)

The image size is directly related to dpi. There is a fixed relationship between the image size and the image dpi after the image is created. As you learned in the previous section, the device dependency of raster images forces you to plan your raster image size before you create the graphic.

NEW TERM   *Image size* is the physical height and width dimensions for the image.

For example, in Figure 4.30, you see a graphic image whose image resolution is 72 dpi and whose image size is 2 inches by 2 inches. The first image is printed at true size and looks pretty clear. Suppose you decided to print the image at that scale. Everything would be OK. However, suppose that someone wants a print that is larger than 2 inches by 2 inches, say about 4 inches by 4 inches. Simply scaling the image up should do the trick, right? Wrong! Scaling a bitmap image up will almost always break up the image, as shown in the Figure 4.30.

Figure 4.30.

A 72 dpi, 2-inch by 2-inch image printed at true size and scaled size.

Why does scaling it do this? Remember, a bitmap image is device-dependent, or in other words, fixed. Figure 4.31 shows why. At the 2-inch by 2-inch layout, the dots appear as they are supposed to. The original fixed relationship is 1:1. In the second image, scaling or stretching the image causes the dots to separate, and the resulting image becomes blurry. Stretching or scaling a bitmap image to a larger size causes the fixed dots to separate, and the image becomes blurry. Alternatively, shrinking or scaling the image down causes the dots to become more condensed, and the resulting image becomes sharper and clearer. Bitmaps always work this way.

Figure 4.31.

Scaling a bitmap up spreads out the dots, scaling a bitmap down compresses the dots.

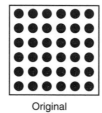  

Original   Scale Down   Scale Up

 NOTE

I just couldn't resist another note concerning the advantage of vector graphics. Again, because vector graphics are device-independent, you can scale them without being concerned about the dots separating or the image blurring. Being based on mathematics makes vector graphics fluid both in image size and resolution.

A final comment related to bitmap image size is just a statement of the obvious. As either dpi or image size increases, so does the size of the file due to an increase in the number of dots (pixels). Often, you will want to create your bitmap images at true size—the size that they will appear in your Web pages. You also might want to create them larger than needed for those just-in-case print purposes.

Image Bit Depth (Descriptiveness)

The final concern with bitmap images is an issue totally unrelated to vector graphics, the issue of bit depth. For most people, bit depth is a confusing topic. Hopefully, any misconceptions can be cleared up through a somewhat lengthy explanation.

First, understand that bit depth concerns much more than just graphics, although that's what you are dealing with right now. Bit depth also is an issue in digital video and audio.

NEW TERM *Bit depth* defines the physical number of bits that can be used to describe an image.

Before you begin, look at the underlying reason why bit depth is an issue when you are dealing with digital data. Everything the computer deals with must be digital data. However, everything that our natural senses can interpret, such as sound, video, and graphics, must be presented to us as analog data. What is the difference between these data types?

NEW TERM *Digital data* is data that is represented mathematically as a series of zeroes and ones. *Analog data* is data that is defined by a series of frequency variations. Color, sound, and even smell are a result of varying waveforms that are detected by our natural senses.

Binary data doesn't mean much to us because our physical senses can't interpret it as it really is. Our senses interpret analog data such as sound or visual imagery. For example, color is the effect of a specific waveform being reflected back at us. Sound, too, is a result of wave frequencies that our senses can detect. Therefore, much of what the computer does revolves around the conversion between analog data, which is what we can interpret, and digital data, which is what the computer can understand. Computing is not just processing data, it also is managing the digital-to-analog and analog-to-digital conversion process.

What does this have to do with bit depth? Well, it really is a prelude to understanding bit depth and its relationship to imaging. Any time you want to represent analog data digitally, you must sample the analog data into the computer. For example, digitizing audio into the computer requires sampling the audio. The sampling process requires taking small chunks of that data at specific intervals and converting it to digitally represent the analog data. These chunks are called samples. The more frequent the chunks or samples, the more the digital audio is like its analog counterpart. The frequency with which you take those samples is called the *sampling rate*. The higher the sampling rate, the more accurate the finished audio clip.

Now, down to the bit-depth issue. After you have a sample or chunk, you must digitally describe the sample regardless of whether it is a graphic, audio, or video clip. Bit depth relates to the number of physical computer bits you can use to describe the sample. The more bits you can use to describe the sample the more representative that sample is. The higher the bit depth, the better the digital representation. This is true not only with graphics but also with audio and video. The overall conversion of analog to digital data is dependent upon the sampling rate and the bit depth.

Now that you understand what bit depth is, look at it in relationship to imaging. Most images with which you will be working will be either 24-bit or 8-bit images. In a 24-bit (true-color) image, each pixel in the image can be any one of 16.7 million colors; there are 16.7 million color possibilities for any pixel. In an 8-bit (indexed) image, each pixel can be any one of 256 colors. Notice that a 24-bit image allows for a better representation of an image because it has more bits to describe the image (see Figure 4.32). It's like the difference between coloring an image with a set of 12 crayons versus a set of 72 crayons. The more crayons, the more representative is the image.

Figure 4.32.
The higher the bit depth, the more descriptive the image.

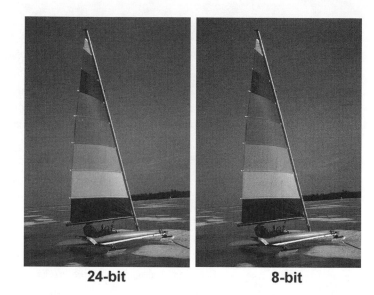

24-bit   **8-bit**

Throughout the previous section you learned that bitmap images are device-dependent: Their resolution and image size are fixed. Bit depth, too, is a one-way street. If you reduce the bit depth of an image, you decrease the amount of data that can be described, which in turn reduces the amount of data in the file. For example, if you have a 24-bit image and you convert it to 8-bit, you are decreasing the quality of the image. If you try to convert it back to a 24-bit image, in effect you have 8-bit data in a 24-bit file (see Figure 4.33). Even though both parts of Figure 4.33 are 24-bit images, the left part contains original 24-bit image data. The right portion, however, contains data created at 24-bit, reduced to 8-bit (which loses some of the 24-bit image data), and then was changed back to 24-bit. In essence, the right portion of the figure is a 24-bit image file that contains 8-bit data. You will want to make sure that you always keep a version of your graphics in high bit-depth mode.

Image File Size

The three primary attributes of raster images that you have looked at all contribute to how big your graphic files are. On the Web, this is your primary concern. The smaller the graphic file size, the quicker it will download to your audience. As image resolution, size, or bit depth increases, so does the file size. Shrink any one of these image variables, and the file size also will shrink.

Figure 4.33.
Reducing the bit depth decreases the descriptiveness of the image.

Browser Color

As you have learned, creating colors in HTML code is much more difficult than using the visual point-and-click environment of most image editors. To define colors in a Web page, you must use hexadecimal code (base-16) to define the colors; something that you probably didn't even know existed until you started designing Web pages. Probably one of the least favorite tasks of the Webmaster is dealing with hexadecimal color. Or, at least it is for me.

All browser colors are defined using hex. Colored text, colored links, colored outlines, anything that is not a graphic and that you want to be a color on the Web page must be defined using hex.

Hexadecimal Color

If you have ever used an image editor, you've probably seen how the raster environment defines colors. Using RGB (Red, Blue, Green) or CYMK (Cyan, Yellow, Magenta, and Black) sliders, you combine additive or subtractive primaries to create a single color. In hexadecimal, however, each color requires a hexadecimal code to define it. For example, in RGB, white is defined as R:255, B:255, G:255. The hexadecimal representation is FFFFFF. For black, the RGB definition is R:0, G:0, B:0. The hexadecimal representation is 000000. You'll find that hex is a pretty abstract way to represent color, and it is one that many people despise. Probably the only ones that you will remember from memory are black, white, and Netscape Gray (CCCCCC). Never fear, though! As a definite hex-hater myself, there is a method that you can use with a calculator that will give you accurate results every time. Note that it won't make it any more fun, though.

Calculating Hex

To calculate hexadecimal values, you'll need two things. The first thing you'll need to know is the RGB definition of the color you want to convert to hex. For this, you can use PhotoShop or another comparable raster imaging software that will show you RGB color values. The second thing you'll need is a scientific calculator. If you have a PC, you have it already (look in the Accessories group). Unfortunately for Macintosh users, there is no system calculator that can work in scientific mode. There are, however, several shareware and freeware calculators that have this capability.

To convert an RGB color to a hexadecimal color you would do the following:

1. Begin by finding the red, green, and blue values for the color in your image editor as shown in Figure 4.34. I have chosen an RGB color defined by R:222, G:39, and B:151.

Figure 4.34.

Finding the RGB red, green, and blue values for the color conversion.

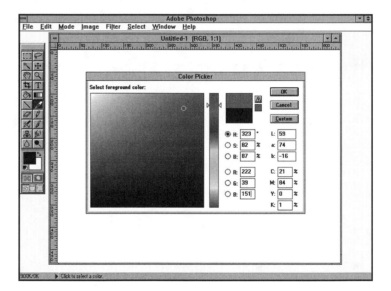

2. Next, open the calculator from the Window's Accessories group.
3. Select Scientific from the View menu.
4. Make sure you are in DEC mode and enter the red value into the calculator. From the color in Figure 4.34, you would use the red value of 222.
5. Next, click on HEX in the calculator, which will show you the hex value of the red decimal value. The red value of 222 gives you a hex value of DE. Jot this hex value down.

4

6. Repeat steps 4 and 5 with the green and blue values. My green value of 39 gives me a hex value of 27. My blue value of 151 gives me a hex value of 97.

7. After you have converted the red, green, and blue values to hex, write your results as a single string. This is the hex value of the color. In this example, an RGB color of R:222, G:39, and B:151 is represented in hexadecimal code as DE3997.

As you begin to create HTML code in the latter half of this book, you actually will begin using hex values to define colors on your page.

NOTE

> If you're a Post-it Notes type of person, this is probably a good page to bookmark, dog-ear, or put a Post-it Note in because you will be dealing directly with hex again in many of the later chapters of the book!

Web Resources

In addition to the calculator method, there are several sites on the Web that have online RGB-to-hex converters that you can use to calculate hex values from RGB values. Check out these sites to help you calculate hex values:

- ☐ `http://www.bga.com/~rlp/dwp/palette/palette.html`
- ☐ `http://www.echonyc.com/~xixax/Mediarama/hex.html`

Bandwidth and Graphics

Of the things you must be concerned with when you are designing graphics, the two most important are the speed at which the graphics download and how visually appealing the graphics are.

When you create graphics for Web pages, you must be aware of how your audience will be connecting to the Web. If most are connected via modems, be careful about how many graphics you use. A good rule of thumb is that it will take approximately 10 seconds to download 50KB of data via a 28.8Kbps modem; double that figure for a 14.4Kbps modem. If users have to wait too long, odds are that they will dodge your site.

Visual Appeal

Your second concern when you are creating graphics is the visual appeal of your graphics. Again, the audience is central to decisions about how photo-realistic your graphics need to be. As the Web is used more often, people will become accustomed to higher quality graphics, and it will require extremely impressive images to evoke the ooh and ahh factor. Strive to meet exactly what the audience is looking for, but note that it always is nice to visit a site and get a surprise once in a while.

Formats

No discussion of graphics would be complete without a discussion of the various file formats you'll run across on the Web. Undoubtedly, there are a myriad of file formats that you can use to distribute your files; however, it's not guaranteed that your audience will be able to view those files unless you stick with one of the more standard graphics file formats. Now look at some of the various computer graphic file formats and their positive and negative aspects.

Graphics Interchange Format (GIF)

Without a doubt, the most widely used file format on the Web is the Graphics Interchange Format (GIF, pronounced "jif "). It's no wonder that this format has become a Web standard because it was developed by CompuServe to deliver graphics over its online service, which was one of the earliest of its type. The GIF file format is a computer graphic file format that enables up to 8-bit (256-color) image data to be distributed. Almost all browsers directly support the GIF format, meaning the browser can display them in its work area directly.

Flavors

The GIF file format comes in several different variations. The most widely used version is the GIF 87a version, which is standard raster image data. A later version of the format, called GIF 89a, supports a special function called *transparency*.

The special GIF 89a format was developed to enable users to create bitmap images in which certain elements can be transparent, as shown in Figure 4.35. In the figure, the title at the top as well as the guy on the trashcan are transparent GIFs.

To create a transparent GIF, the user can assign a particular color in the bitmap to be transparent, enabling the background color or tiled image in the browser to show through the inline graphic. It's really a pretty cool feature of this little format. Even with transparency data, GIF files generally remain small due to the low bit-depth data that they contain.

Figure 4.35.
*Using the GIF 89a
format to deliver
transparent bitmaps.*

Joint Picture Experts Group (JPEG)

The second most widely used format on the Web is the Joint Pictures Experts Group (JPEG, pronounced "j-peg") format. This format is much more robust than the GIF format, enabling near-24-bit quality, as well as compression—about which you learn in the section titled "Compression." The JPEG format alone enables you to create high-quality images that can be integrated as inline images and can be interpreted by the browser.

A relatively new type of JPEG image is now appearing on the Web as well. These new JPEG files, called Progressive JPEGs, enable the browser to create low-resolution representations of the graphics that become clearer as the browser downloads more of the file. Much like focusing the lens on a camera, the image is blurry at first and then becomes clear when it is completely downloaded. JPEG files themselves can contain both 8- and 24-bit information, which makes them a good candidate for delivering graphics at greater than 256 colors.

Encapsulated Postscript

An early file format that appeared in Web pages was the Postscript format. Yes, a vector format on the Web. This format required the use of an external helper application and is decreasing in use. Most people have focused their efforts on new Postscript plug-ins such as Macromedia FreeHand to deliver vector graphics on the Web, but the plug-ins still do not get rid of the vector jaggies—in other words, they still look like vector images.

Other File Formats

Although GIF and JPEG images are the most common formats found on the Web, there are many others that you can run across as you are surfing. You'll find that each has its own quirks and advantages. They are mentioned here just as an overview.

BMP

The BMP, or Windows Bitmap graphic file format, enables you to store up to 24-bit image data. This image format, originally designed for Windows graphic images, is widely used on the PC for raster images. This particular image format can also incorporate a special internal compression scheme called Run-Length Encoding (RLE).

TIFF

Tagged Image File Format (TIFF) is a special computer graphic file format that was designed to support the output of high-resolution images. This particular file format will enable up to 32-bit images and is a very robust format. It is not uncommon for TIFF files to be quite large. Because it is designed to hold images for printing, the TIFF format uses a special internal compression scheme called Lepel-ZivWelch (LZW) compression.

PICT

Most of the formats mentioned so far are raster formats, which means they hold only pixel data. The PICT format, used predominantly on the Macintosh, is a special type of file format called a *metafile* format. Metafile formats enable either raster or vector data within them. In fact, they can store both simultaneously. PICT files are very popular in both vector and raster imaging on the Macintosh due to their very small file size. However, take PICT to the PC and you'll be lucky if you can find software that is able to open it. If you are working cross-platform, PICT is not a good choice for a file format.

Compression

Throughout the previous discussion of file formats, you learned many that use compression. Actually, you'll find that for Web-based graphics and files, there are two different types of compression that you can use: lossy and lossless. These terms describe how the compression scheme works. Before you learn specifics, look at the generalities of compression.

As you learned, one of the biggest problems with raster images is their size. To overcome this hurdle, compression schemes have been developed to help reduce the file size of raster images. Almost every raster image has redundant data. For example, an image with a lot of blue hues in it has redundant data in it due to the repeated definition of the blue pixels. Compression schemes take the redundant or repeating data and substitute tokens or representative characters for the repeating data, thus reducing the file size. Every compression algorithm works this way.

Compression schemes use an algorithm, or codec, to compress and decompress the image file.

New Term   A *codec* stands for Compressor/Decompressor, which is an algorithm used to compress and expand the file.

Most compression schemes, such as the ones used in BMP and TIFF files, are transparent to the user. Many times you don't even know that the compression is occurring, but the compression can significantly reduce the size of the file.

How does it do it? Again, the whole thing occurs due to the redundant data in the file. However, the compressibility of a file is dependent upon how much redundant data there actually is in the file. A file with a lot of similar hues will compress more than an image with a wide variety of colors. Compression is dependent upon the amount of redundant data.

Compression schemes are judged by the amount that they compress the file or their compression ratio.

New Term   The *compression ratio* is the ratio of the uncompressed file's size to the compressed file's size.

Many of the compression schemes claim a ratio of 2:1. Others can perform only 1.25:1. You must be careful, however, of these fantastic claims. Look at the difference between lossy and lossless compression and you'll see why.

Lossy Compression

When files are compressed, not all codecs reproduce an exact copy of the original file when they are uncompressed. Some data is lost to attain smaller file sizes. This is the case with lossy compression.

New Term   *Lossy compression* is a compression scheme in which certain amounts of data are sacrificed to attain smaller file sizes.

Lossy compression schemes, such as those used with JPEG images and many of the video formats, do not create an exact replica of the original file after decompression—they lose some of the original data. This might alarm you at first, but lossy compression schemes are typically used when the files that are being compressed don't need the extra data. For example, an image that you display on-screen requires less data than a file that you're going to print. Therefore, you can sacrifice some of the data for the sake of a smaller file size. This is also true in the digital video realm. Again, a certain amount of data can be sacrificed without significantly hurting the playback performance.

If you decide to use a lossy compression scheme, you do have a choice about how much data is lost. Most of these schemes enable you to choose a loss rate or ratio. For example, when you create a JPEG file you can adjust how much data is lost. The same is true if you are creating video snippets. Of the file formats mentioned, only JPEG uses lossy compression.

If you decide to use JPEG images, keep two things in mind. First, if you try to print the JPEG file after compression it probably will look bad. Second, you should keep a backup of your JPEG images in a format that either doesn't use compression or that uses lossless compression.

Lossless Compression

As its name implies, lossless compression can be used for image files that you want to print and use in situations in which loss of data is detrimental.

 Lossless compression is a compression scheme in which a decompressed file creates an exact replica of the original file.

Lossless compression schemes do not sacrifice data. In fact, they create an exact copy of the original file when they are decompressed. Lossless compression schemes are often used with files that need to maintain the highest level of data. Often they are used in the desktop publishing field for printing purposes, where loss of data would be unacceptable. Lossless compression schemes include the TIFF's LZW and the BMP's RLE compression schemes.

Internal File Compression

In addition to looking at compression from a data point of view, you also can examine compression at the file level. All the schemes about which you have learned thus far have been internal compression schemes. These internal compression schemes generally occur within commercial packages and in effect are part of the file format itself. Internal file compression occurs at the data level. It understands the contents of the file and compresses the data based on redundancy within the data.

External File Compression

External file compression is a second type of compression scheme that you might run into on the Web. Have you ever seen a .ZIP file? How about an .HQX, .SIT, or .BIN file? These compression files have been created using an external compression program.

External file compression means that the compression algorithm knows nothing about the data itself. It simply looks at the file level to see how the file can be further decreased in size. External file compression is lossless, so you don't need to worry about data loss.

You actually can take a file that has been internally compressed and compress it even more using an external compression program. However, after they are externally compressed, the contents cannot be opened by any other program until it is uncompressed. For example, suppose you created an internally compressed JPEG file and you compress it using something like PKWARE's PKZIP. So now it is a zip file. You cannot link the file to an HTML file as an inline image because HTML cannot read zip files. So you lose one degree of freedom by externally compressing files. However, you end up with a more highly compressed, smaller file.

If you want to use external compression programs in your file delivery there are several from which to choose. First and foremost on the PC is PKWARE's PKZIP, which probably is the oldest of the bunch or Nico Mak Computing's WinZip. For the Macintosh, there are several that you can choose from, but I would suggest Aladdin's Stuffit Expander. For less than $100 it beats all the others. Of course there are others, but these three are the most widely used software on the PC and Macintosh operating systems.

Sound

Now that you've looked at everything you wanted to know about computer graphics, take a cursory look at the concerns about digital sound files being distributed over the Web. CD-quality sound isn't being used over the Web just yet, but steps to that end are progressing quite nicely. When you are dealing with digital audio or digital video, your biggest constraint is bandwidth. Both of these types of files require large amounts of bandwidth for downloading high-quality audio or video. Today, the audio and video you deliver must be designed around today's limitations.

Most of the sound files you'll find on the Web are Musical Instrument Device Interface (MIDI) and RealAudio sound files. You'll also find common formats such as .WAV and .AIFF. In general, the files themselves can be divided into two groups: those that mathematically define the music clip and those that define the sound clip in terms of waveforms.

The first type of audio file mathematically defines the notes in the music and the instruments that play them. MIDI files are an example of these types of audio files. MIDI files are like vector sound files in that they use mathematical representations to define the notes and instruments that play in the piece. On the other hand, sound files such as RealAudio, .WAV, and .AIFF files are digital descriptions of variations or frequencies, also know as waveforms. The difference between these two Web audio formats is a lot like the difference between vector and raster files. The most prominent difference is in file size.

Analog and Digital Data

As noted in the discussion of bit depth, audio deals with a conversion or sampling process in which analog data is converted to digital data. The analog data is what you actually can hear. On the computer it is represented as digital bits. It's amazing that almost any user today who has a sound card, the appropriate software, and a radio can create digital audio. However, knowledge of bit depth and sampling rate is needed to do it well.

Bit Depth

When you are dealing with audio on the Web, you basically are limited to 8-bit audio. To give you a frame of reference, audio CDs are 16-bit, so there is a much lower quality of music over the Internet. Like raster files, most high-quality sound files are quite large. Ten seconds of high-quality digitized sound can require over a megabyte of storage space, much more than what can be adequately delivered over the Web. For the most part, this is due to the limited transmission speed that you have over the Web. A vast majority of users connect to the Internet using a modem. More than likely, part of your audience will fit this category. Current network bandwidth will not support the highest quality bit depth that you can use for audio because you are only as strong as your weakest link, the modem.

If you are planning to sample audio for Web distribution, as with graphics, you must save your audio at the highest quality possible as you are working with it. Even though you can't deliver the highest quality output, you must start with the cleanest source possible. The entire process of creating good Web-based audio is focused upon the quality of the source audio. Most sound packages will enable you to sample or record your audio and then downgrade it to a lower bit depth so it can be distributed over the Web, but you must start with a high-quality source for your Web audio to be effective.

Sampling Rate

Earlier in the chapter you learned what sampling rate is, and there are several sampling rates for digital audio. Most digital audio comes in 11kHZ, 22kHz, and 44kHz. These sampling rates signify how big the chunks are that are taken during the sampling process. Again, you want to sample your audio at the highest possible rate, which is 44kHz. This gives you the highest quality source. You then can downgrade it to that which is acceptable for the Web. Most Web-based audio is distributed at 11kHz or 22kHz. The lower of these begins to get quite scratchy, but it also can be downloaded more quickly.

One other issue that you must deal with concerning audio is stereo versus mono audio clips. Stereo clips actually maintain two clips within the sample—one clip is for the left speaker, and the other is for the right speaker. You will find that stereo audio files are much too large for Web distribution. All audio that is delivered over the Web must be mono—single-channel sound—to play effectively.

Streaming and Compression

Audio files that are distributed over the Web predominantly are distributed using one of two techniques. The first of these is a relatively new technology but holds promising things for the future.

The first technique for audio on the Web is the use of streaming technology such as RealAudio. Most streaming technologies require the use of a plug-in for the browser.

NEW TERM *Streaming* is a technology where data files are sent to the client in chunks. These chunks begin playing or executing before the entire file is downloaded.

Currently there are many limitations to using streaming technologies effectively. Your audio files must be low-quality as compared to CD-quality audio. Most streaming technologies will support only 8-bit, 11kHz, mono audio files. This means that often the audio file will be somewhat scratchy and not completely crystal clear. I believe that the technology will continue to improve and eventually will support CD-quality audio, but today you must work around the limitations of the current technology.

The second way to distribute Web audio is through the use of a helper application or through embedded MIDI files. The first of these is the traditional approach, in which the file is completely downloaded and then opened into a helper application for playback. Streaming technologies are beginning to catch on, but the predominant method still is the use of helper applications.

MIDI files, on the other hand, are very compact files (because they are mathematically defined) and will play as long as the user has a sound card that is MIDI-compatible. The biggest problem with MIDI files is that they often sound like artificial or replicate sound. Often they lack good bass and high tones.

To effectively design audio files for Web distribution you must work around limitations. Today's lesson takes only a cursory look at the state of the technology. On Day 14, "Advanced Web Components," you actually sample some audio and prepare it for Web distribution. Web audio still is in its infancy but is rapidly advancing.

Animation

Probably one of the most sought-after effects on the Web is animation due to the complementary effects it can have on the content that is delivered. Some sites pull it off very well, whereas others need a lot of help. There are several ways to accomplish Web animation. Some are very crude and others are quickly making a name for themselves. With all of the various techniques for creating Web animations, choosing which is the best can be difficult. Just keep in mind that animation should be used only to enhance and complement your content. I've seen several sites that animated so many elements on the screen that they looked more like a carnival than a Web page. Stay focused on your main task (communication) as you begin deciding whether or not to add animation.

Constraints

As with Web audio, the biggest hurdle that you are up against is the issue of network bandwidth and the deliverability of your Web pages. Animation requires a tremendous amount of Web resources. Because animation is an effect caused by multiple images, each image must be delivered from the server to the client, which can significantly increase the number of hits made to your server.

Several new technologies, such as Shockwave, help to reduce the number of hits made to the server. By downloading a single file that contains all the elements for the animation, you can increase the speed at which the user receives your page. Even still, with a modem connection, animation can severely tax both the users' modem and their patience. Again, conservatism is key.

Browser Tricks

You can deliver animations to your audience using one of several methods. Probably the oldest, client pull, is a function of the browser. Others such as Shockwave are a result of plug-ins that assist the browser with playback capability. The last method, and at the time this book was written, probably the best, is the use of external helper applications where the user downloads the file and then views it externally. This still is the most widely used technique for delivering animations.

Client Pull

Client pull is an HTML technique that can be used quite effectively, although it is often criticized. Through the programming in an HTML file, the developer can instruct the browser to succinctly download a series of images from the server. Most often the HTML file is programmed to download a series of small images. The only time the client pull is ineffective is when the images themselves are quite large. I've used client pull in the past, but I would say that many of the newer scripting technologies such as JavaScript or ActiveX are beginning to take the place of client pull. I doubt that we'll see this effect used for very much longer due to the wealth of newer capabilities found in HTML and other Web technologies.

Animation Files

The last and most frequently used method for delivering animations at a Web site is through the use of normal digital animation formats. The most frequent is AutoDesk's FLI or FLC (pronounced "flic") format. Animations often are also delivered using some of the digital video formats about which you learn shortly.

Due to the tremendous amount of resources required to deliver animations over the Web, the best way to deliver them quickly and efficiently is to allow the user to use an external helper application. By providing animations to the user in a single file, you let your audience choose whether to download them or not. Of course, if you're animating only a small portion of your screen, use one of the other technologies such as Shockwave, but if you are trying to deliver animations that require one-quarter or one-half of the screen don't expect your audience to wait for the animation to download. A user connected via modem probably won't wait for it. Choose the technology that best supports what you are trying to do.

Digital Video

The last of the media elements that you learn today are digital video formats. Notice that there is a distinction between animation and video. Most often video is considered to be audio and video data. Animation, however, is usually video data only. However, you can use the same formats to distribute both animation and video. All digital video formats will support audio only, or audio and video movies.

Constraints

As with all the other high-density files delivered over the Web, video files are limited by bandwidth restrictions. Today, the Web is a somewhat small road compared to the large amount of data that users want to push over it. Many strides are taking place to both reduce the size of the data being pushed (through compression technologies) as well as to increase the size of the roads (making data channels wider). However, there still is a long way to go to reach full-screen video distribution capability.

Video files, much more than animation files, are severely taxing the Web. Animation files contain only video information. With audio files all you have to push is the sound, but with video files you must deliver both—not to mention the fact that the video and audio must be coordinated. Again, designing around the limitations is your biggest task.

4

Streaming

One of the ways in which you can overcome bandwidth limitations is to use streaming technologies. As you have learned, streaming data sends to the user's machine portions of a file that are immediately executed or played. However, with video, the amount of data that is being pushed is twice as much. Streaming technologies used today, such as QuickTimeVR, are still in their infancy. When you deliver files using these technologies you must use a very small portion of the screen to deliver the video. This means that the files are much less than full-screen. Often the audio is miss-timed if it plays at all. Much development needs to take place for this technology to become widely used, even by users who have fast Internet connections. However, you spend some time later in this chapter looking at ways to implement this technology as it currently exists.

Formats

Although you can use plug-ins such as QuickTimeVR to deliver animation files, the easiest and most common practice is to let the user employ helper applications to view the animation files. You don't have to make sure the user has a plug-in, and you can almost guarantee that the file will play back as you have created it. If you want to deliver animation files from your site, I suggest delivering the files through hotlinks; enabling users to download the file at their leisure. Often they will download it on some off-peak time for later viewing. If you decide to do this you'll need to be aware of some of the commonly used formats for video files.

AVI

On the PC, the video format of choice is the Video for Windows or AVI format. This video format enables you to create compressed video files that use lossy compression. You can control the amount of data loss when you create the file from a video editor such as Adobe Premiere.

QuickTime

The video format of choice for the Macintosh is the QuickTime format. This video format also enables you to distribute video files that are compressed using a lossy compression. Which format you use (QuickTime or AVI) depends on what platform your users are on. Each format touts that it is better than the other. The QuickTime format has players for both the Macintosh and PC platforms whereas the AVI format supports only the Macintosh. There are many players that will play on both platforms. Focus your development on the audience's platform.

4

MPEG

The last format that you learn today is the Motion Picture Experts Group (MPEG) format. This format has some amazing possibilities. Currently it probably is the most widely used digital video format in the digital video industry and also is used in several digital satellite technologies. It boasts a very good compression ratio without significant data loss. However, to create MPEG movies, you need a special adapter board in your computer, and unfortunately they can be quite expensive—more than $2,500. Nonetheless, this is a format to watch in the near future.

Summary

Whew, what a day! You've covered a lot of ground, and as you can see, a significant amount of what you deliver over the Web depends on you being able to create all the various media elements you've learned. Remember that to use any of the media elements you must use them effectively. The biggest struggle will be to deliver them in a timely manner so that your audience isn't waiting a long time for a page to download. One way you can ensure this doesn't happen is by making sure all the elements you use contribute to communication. Most pages that are very large contain too many multimedia and graphical elements. Designing graphics, sounds, animations, and video for your Web site must be centered on the user.

4

Q&A

Q What are the three purposes for graphics on Web pages?

A Graphics should be used to enhance, complement, and supplement the content, present navigational items, and aid in creating visual flow.

Q How is tone created at a Web site? What elements contribute to creating this tone?

A Tone is created from the layout of the pages and graphics through the use of balance, fonts, graphics, and multimedia elements.

Q What is visual appeal? How do you make your pages visually appealing?

A A page that is visually appealing interests and communicates to the audience through the use of negative and positive space, clarity of buttons, and varying typefonts.

Q **What is the difference between lossy and lossless compression? Give an example of each.**

A Lossy compression is a compression scheme in which certain amounts of data are sacrificed to accommodate smaller file sizes. Lossless compression is a compression scheme in which the compressed file creates an exact replica of the original file after decompression. An example of lossy compression is JPEG compression and an example of lossless compression is the TIFF's LZW compression.

Q **What are the two main types of fonts? How do they affect readability?**

A The two main types of fonts are fonts with serifs, called serif fonts, and fonts without serifs, called sans serif fonts. Serif fonts are most readable when they are used for body text or small text. Sans serif fonts are most readable when they are used for headlines or large text.

Workshop

The Workshop provides quiz questions to help you solidify your understanding of the material covered and exercises to give you experience in using what you've learned. The quiz answers are provided in Appendix A, "Quiz Answers." Try to understand the quiz answers before you go on to tomorrow's lesson.

Quiz

1. What are the three legs discussed in this chapter that support communication?
2. How is consistency implemented at a Web site?
3. What is the difference between internal and external compression?
4. What is hexadecimal color and how do you calculate it?
5. How does color affect the way we interpret Web pages and graphics?
6. What are the differences between vector and raster graphics?
7. What are the three main raster image attributes? Define them.
8. What are the two most widely used Web graphics formats?
9. When dealing with the distribution of sound, animation, and video files over the Web, what should be your biggest concern? Why?

Exercise

Surf the Web and find examples of well-designed pages. Why do these pages attract your attention? Why are they appealing to you? Also, find examples of the various media elements that you learned today.

Day **5**

The Technical Designer

Aside from the content, graphics, and actual pages that you deliver at your site, as a Webmaster, you must also have knowledge of the various networking and communications hardware and software involved with the Web delivery process. This aspect, like the rapid development of browsers, scripting languages, and plug-ins, is an area that is exploding with new technologies. It seems that every day there is a new breakthrough in networking technologies. Undoubtedly, by the time this book hits the shelf, there will be more new advances. Today's lesson, however, focuses on the state of the technology today and the technical design considerations associated with Webmastering.

NEW TERM A *technical designer* is an individual who understands the standards, hardware, and software of a Web network and how to fit them together to make a working site.

NOTE

Although I acknowledge that new advances are likely, if you pick up the basic concepts presented today, you'll find that learning the new advances in hardware and software should be somewhat easy. Technological advances are almost always based on previous technologies.

To begin looking at technical design, today's lesson begins with an overview of how networking works. You need to examine not only the basic models around which networking revolves, but also connections, protocols, servers, and standards. You also will look at how you can work to lay out your own networking schemata.

Networking Basics

As was stated, the Internet is based on a multiprotocol, universal environment. Any computer correctly connected to the Internet, either through a direct connection or a modem connection, can access information on the Web. The entire communication system is set up so that any user with a browser or appropriate client software can connect to the myriad of Internet services.

To connect to the Internet you must have both the correct hardware and software. The hardware that is required is either a modem or a network interface card. The software that is required can include network device drivers and access provider software. It also includes client software such as a Web browser, FTP client, or other Internet service software.

The entire Web structure is composed of interconnected networks of computers. The various networks can include local-area networks (LANs) as well as wide-area networks (WANs). The distinguishing characteristic between LANs and WANs is geographically based.

 A *local-area network* (LAN) is a computer network that spans a very short distance, such as a network of computers in a single office.

 A *wide-area network* (WAN) is a network that includes a much wider region, such as networked computers that span an entire city or the entire world.

The Internet is the compilation and connection of several million smaller networks that work in conjunction to provide Web, mail, news, and FTP capability. All of these various computer networks are connected through many gateways and bridges.

 A *gateway* is the point of interconnection between two dissimilar networks that handles routing functions and can translate information between the two networks.

 A *bridge* connects two or more similar networks that use the same protocol.

As its name implies, the gateway serves as a means for information to be passed between two computer networks that use different protocols. Bridges are used to connect similar networks. As you see in Figure 5.1, many major networks are interconnected. This is what enables the mass of computing power to communicate. Networks such as Bitnet, CompuServe, and America Online, as well as a wealth of personal and corporate networks, are also connected, providing a very complex matrix of computer networking. Underlying all of the hardware involved in the physical connections is the protocol and the addressing scheme for all of these computers.

Figure 5.1.

The connection of major computing networks.

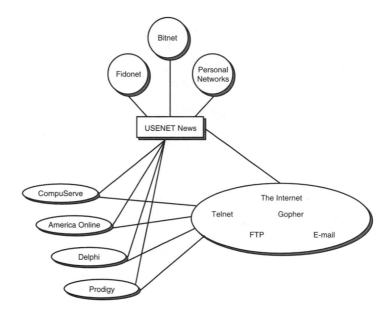

First, each computer that is connected to the Internet must be uniquely defined or addressed. On Day 1, "The Webmaster: Jack of All Trades," you learned the WWW-based method for identifying Web servers through the use of the Uniform Resource Locator (URL), but this addresses only Web servers. It does not uniquely define all the computers connected to the Internet, only those that serve up Web pages. All computers addressed on the Internet use Internet Protocol (IP) addresses. In reality, there are two predominant addressing schemes used on the Internet:

- ☐ The Internet Protocol (IP) address uniquely defines every computer connection to the Internet through the use of a numerical sequence.

- ☐ The Uniform Resource Locator (URL), which is based upon a domain name, is established for computers to provide information on the Web. Domain names are verbal descriptions of Web site addresses.

In both addressing schemes, the addresses define the location of the computer, and not the computer itself. Internet protocol addresses are set up using a 32-bit numerical sequence. A typical IP address will contain four numbers separated by periods. An IP address can look like 128.49.245.10. These numbers basically identify the location of the parent network to which the computer belongs (usually the first set of numbers) and then the network hierarchy that must be used to locate the computer. In essence, the address tells where the computer is located and directs information to and from it through the network hierarchy. Whenever a machine's location on a network changes, so does its IP address. The domain name, however, can remain constant no matter where the computer is on the network.

The domain name service (DNS), used for textually representing Web sites through URL addresses, is set up using words separated by periods rather than the numerical IP addressing scheme. The words that are used in the domain name are somewhat arbitrary, although there must be some way of linking the name representation (DNS) with the numerical IP address. This is done through the use of special computers that look up the names of URLs on the Web. When a user types a URL in the address field of his or her browser, such as www.someserver.com, the computer goes to a domain name server further up in the user's network to resolve, or find out where to look for, the information.

I won't get into the process that it uses to resolve it, but you do need to know that each server's domain name must be unique and that domain names are the method used for Web servers. This is how your audience finds your Web server and your pages when they are browsing. If your server's location in the network changes, the IP address will change, but the domain name will not. Notifying the domain name server of the new IP address associated with the domain name enables the domain name to remain constant even if you change the server's location.

NOTE

> If you are setting up a Web site, you'll definitely want to create a domain name for your company or the company for which you are consulting. When you choose a name, choose one that is easily recognizable as your company, and one that also is easy to remember.

As you can see, having an Internet Protocol address to even access the Web, mail, or any of the other Internet services is mandatory. However, you need a domain name or URL only to provide World Wide Web-based information, not to simply access these services.

5

NOTE

> The relationship between the IP address and domain name is arbitrary. No specific set of IP numbers determines the domain name. However, domains are referenced to IP numbers. The IP address is numerical and therefore more difficult for humans to use, which is why the domain name was created—so humans could more easily use the Internet and Web-based browsers.

The protocol that enables all of this computing horsepower to be connected is the TCP/IP protocol.

 TCP/IP is the protocol used on the Internet that consists of the Transmission Control Protocol and the Internet Protocol. This protocol is a packet-based protocol in which packets of information are transferred to the client machine from a server machine.

In general, the TCP/IP protocol is a set of rules and standards by which information is able to be sent out over the network, as well as be received by a requesting client. TCP/IP is a combination of two specific protocols, TCP, which handles transport, and IP, which takes care of routing. Much like protocols in many other areas of life, such as rules concerning verbal or written communication, the TCP/IP protocol ensures that communication can occur over the network. Again, for communication to occur, a sender must send a message and, most important, someone must receive that message. Use of the TCP/IP protocol ensures that the message can be sent and received.

Before you examine protocols and standards further, you need to get a basic understanding of networking models so you know how the whole thing works in general. Take a look at the networking models and how your audience can become connected to the Internet.

5

Network Models

Networking models are used to describe how a network works. This is not necessarily an examination of the hardware or software; it is a look at how communication occurs and how resources are managed. Does one computer on the network serve as a mediator or master of information on the network, or do all equally share this responsibility with no one computer dominating the network? This is what you want to look at. All networks follow one of the two models: client/server or peer-to-peer networks.

Client/Server

The first of the networking models is the client/server model. This is probably the most widely used method of networking, and it is the method used for World Wide Web information delivery.

The *client/server* networking model describes a network in which all information is provided and managed by a single computer in the network, called the *server*. Information from the server is requested by client computers.

The client/server networking model describes the process of information distribution over the Internet as shown in Figure 5.2. A client computer's browser makes a request to a remote HTTP server for a particular Web page or piece of information. The Web server then sends the information to the client computer. All requests for information are made to the server, which puts much of the burden of network transmission on the server itself.

Figure 5.2.

The client/server networking model.

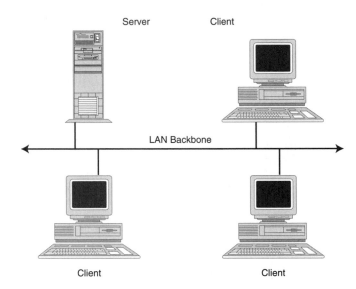

In computing networks based on the client/server model, the server itself must be a very fast computer. Because all information depends on this computer, a slow server can cause a bottleneck in the network. If the server is too slow, many users can be left waiting for long periods of time to retrieve information. This is the negative aspect of the client/server model. Often, network traffic will exceed that which the server can handle or maintain, which bogs down the network to a slow crawl. This is why the pages at some sites load so slowly; there might be hundreds of other users trying to access pages on the server. The server must give all the users the information they need.

Peer-to-Peer

The second type of networking model is the peer-to-peer networking model. This particular model is used most often in smaller networks.

NEW TERM The *peer-to-peer* networking model describes a network on which all computers on the network share equal responsibility for managing and providing information.

Because the peer-to-peer networking model does not use a central computer or server, communication in smaller networks is quite fast (see Figure 5.3). In the peer-to-peer networking environment, network resources are managed and maintained by several computers. However, if a network that follows this model grows to be very large, network performance can decrease significantly due to the lack of a centralized controlling computer. The mass of communication becomes too great for such a distributed management style. The large number of computers exceeds that which can be managed by the computers on that network. Peer-to-peer networking is used most often with less than ten computers and in small office situations.

Figure 5.3.

The peer-to-peer networking model.

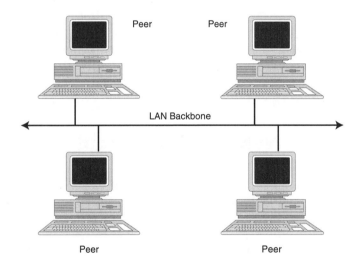

In general, you will find that most LANs and WANs use the client/server networking model. The entire World Wide Web is based on the client/server model. Often these networks will utilize multiple distributed servers that each manage certain aspects or regions of the network.

In recent years, there has been a trend away from centralized, client/server computing—in other words, to one huge, very fast computer that manages a very large network. We are verging onto a cross between the two models to overcome the limitations of each. Today, most institutions are vying for multiple, interspersed, powerful servers that aid in managing and serving special divisions of the network.

5

Connections

Because the Internet is based on the client/server model, in the rest of today's lesson you learn about the server-side considerations of providing pages on the Internet. However, before you do so, look at the main client-side consideration: how your audience will be connecting to the Internet.

Connection is extremely important. As you learned in previous lessons, how the user gains access to the Internet is vitally important, for it will determine how quickly data flows to his or her computer after it is released from your server. Connection is also important to you. How are you connecting your server to the Net? The speed of your connection will also contribute to how fast your pages will be served up.

As you look at this, try to examine the audience you will be serving in relationship to these various methods of connection. Put yourself in their situation. Much of what you design and provide will hinge upon the user's connection. Obviously, the faster the audience's connection, the more graphics and multimedia elements you can provide. However, if you provide a significant number of these elements on your pages, you'll probably lose some of your clients who are connected through a modem due to significant download times.

Direct Network Connection

The first and best method for connecting to the Internet is through a direct network connection. Unfortunately, if you have to pay for it, direct network connection is also the most expensive type of Internet connection. In this scenario, users have a network adapter inserted into their computer. Undoubtedly, they are either connected to a LAN or WAN, which in turn is connected to the Internet. Single users can also be connected through the use of ISDN, T1, or T3 lines described later in this chapter. Yet for most, this is too expensive.

In a direct network connection, the users connected to the network each have a static IP address as shown in Figure 5.4. A static IP address is one that does not change and remains fixed. With a direct network connection, full-screen graphics and tremendously large multimedia elements download very quickly. Most direct connections tout a download speed of 1.5 megabytes per second or faster, which means a full-screen graphic can load within one second or less.

5

Figure 5.4.

A direct network connection uses static IP addresses.

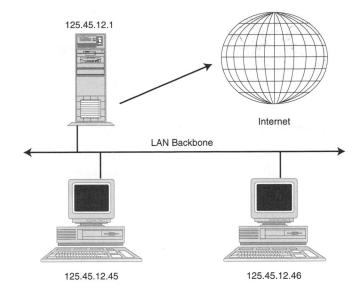

If you are not yet connected to the Internet and think you are interested in establishing a direct network connection, there are several options from which you can choose. You probably will lease a line from a local telecommunications company (Telco). To lease a line, you must pay for the line and the hardware needed to connect to the Internet. Even with leased lines there are several speeds or bandwidths from which you can choose. You will find that the price that you must pay is based on speed and your distance from the Telco company. The biggest decision you must make is how much you want to pay. Depending on the size of your organization, you can choose from the following:

- ☐ 56 Kbps, which will cost under $500 per month and can transfer approximately 1,000 pages of text (equivalent to the Bible) in 15 seconds

- ☐ 1,540 Kbps, which will cost around $1,000 per month and can transfer approximately 1,000 pages of text in about five seconds

- ☐ 15,000 Kbps, which will cost around $10,000 per month and can transfer approximately 3,000 pages of text in one second

Note that most of these prices are much more than a single individual can afford for a home connection. However, leased lines are really only one type of connection. In the section titled "Protocols and Transport Layers," you look at some other alternatives that are quickly gaining momentum and could provide some very promising things for the in-home user in the near future.

However, wouldn't it be wonderful to attain speeds like these out of your home? To be honest, to support many of the things that we'd like to do on the much-talked-about Information Superhighway will require these types of speeds and greater. Full-screen video, CD-ROM multimedia, and real-time communication (both video and audio) will require the common user to have this type of connection, but it's still a long way off.

Dial-Up Connection

The second type of Internet connection is a dial-up connection. Except for the blessed few who have a direct connection, most home access is provided via either dial-up connection or dial-up access. Dial-up connection is the faster of the two.

With a dial-up connection, the user dials up a remote computer with a modem to gain access to the Internet, as shown in Figure 5.5. Information that is downloaded from the Net is downloaded directly to the user's machine through the modem.

Figure 5.5.

A dial-up connection to the Internet.

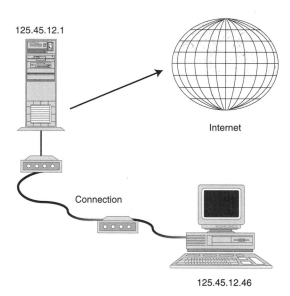

125.45.12.1

Internet

Connection

125.45.12.46

Using a dial-up connection requires the use of an Internet service provider (ISP) or access provider. Both are for-fee services or companies that provide access to the Internet. Often, the fee pays for access to the Web, mail, news, and FTP services. It might also include leased server space, on which the user can provide Web pages and other information. After logging into the access provider's computer, the client has direct network access, through the modem, to most of the services on the Internet.

5

ISPs also provide leased space for companies to enable them to distribute their content as well. This is a very attractive option for those companies that don't want to purchase and maintain their own server. This option provides one big advantage. All maintenance and setup is handled by the ISP, which can significantly reduce the amount of start-up expenses associated with establishing a Web presence. It is very helpful for the mid-size to small business that wants to utilize the World Wide Web without purchasing and maintaining a server.

 NOTE

> One of the things you might be concerned about is that your domain name might not represent your company if you use an ISP for leased space. For example, maybe your ISP's site is www.isp.com, and you don't want your clients to enter the ISP's domain name to access your pages. You want your clients to use a domain name that represents your company. Most ISPs can use *domain aliasing* to create a domain name for your company even if it resides on their server. Domain aliasing creates a special domain name for a site residing on someone else's server. For example, your pages located on www.isp.com could be accessed by your audience using your own domain name rather than your ISP's domain name. Nifty!

As you have learned, an Internet connection via modem is much slower than the speeds with a direct network connection. Using a dial-up connection, you'll see download and upload speeds of about 20 to 40 seconds per 100 to 200KB of information using a 28.8 Kbps modem. This is significantly slower than a direct network connection predominantly due to the modem itself. In addition, the speed of your computer, the amount of noise in your phone line, and the number of users logged into your ISP's server can affect how quickly this type of access works.

Before you move on to learn dial-up access, you must also be aware of a few other concerns when dealing with an ISP. First, one of the decisions you will have to make is whether you want a static or dynamic IP address. As you have seen, the address is a defined path to your computer. Most ISPs will charge a higher fee for you to have a static IP address on their machine. A static IP address enables easier FTP access to a site. A dynamic IP address, which is a fluctuating IP address, can cause problems if you want to be able to directly access your space on the ISP's server. If you are establishing this relationship for business purposes, you probably will want a static IP. Space provided for personal pages and Web data might not need a static IP address.

The second concern about which you must be aware is the type of software the ISP requires for you to connect to its service. The two predominant software connectors used are Serial Line Internet Protocol (SLIP) and Point-to-Point Protocol (PPP). To gain access to the

5

provider's server via a modem requires one of these two protocols. These two protocols are discussed in more detail later in this chapter under the "Dial-Up Access" section, but note that services using these protocols are more expensive.

Finally, for those users who simply want access to the Internet and its services, there are two predominant ways that ISPs charge for access. The first of these is a simple flat-rate charge. For example, my service provider allows unlimited access to the Web, mail, news, and FTP for a flat monthly rate of $20. This is pretty nice because there are no time limits. The biggest thing you must consider is whether a phone call is local or long-distance. Long-distance charges on top of a flat rate add up quickly when you are surfing the Net.

The second type of fee is based on hourly usage. For example, a service provider might charge $20 an hour or $40 for four hours. Usually you are required to specify which you want. Any hour over your allotted time is $1. This method of calculating is widely used because it is more profitable for the ISP.

Dial-Up Access

The least desirable type of Internet connection is dial-up access. In this scenario, the user dials into a computer that is connected to the Internet (see Figure 5.6). When the user downloads information it is first downloaded to the host computer and then is transferred to the user's computer via the modem. Most downloads using this method require approximately 180 to 300 seconds per 100 to 200KB of information via a 28.8 Kbps modem. You can see that accessing a single page using this type of Internet access could easily take up to five minutes. It definitely is not the best type of access. As Web pages and the information delivered over the Web have increased in the last year, this type of access has been dying out due to tremendous download times.

Figure 5.6.
Dial-up access to the Internet.

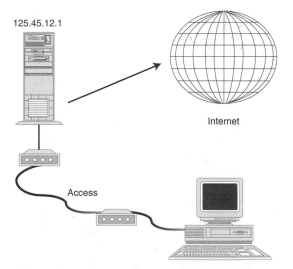

Protocols and Transport Layers

Protocols on the Internet are simply a way of defining the standards for communication. The Internet as a whole is based upon TCP/IP. Being able to connect to the Internet requires the use of this protocol in some way.

Direct

To access the Web using a direct network connection you must have a network adapter board inside your computer. If your computer is connected to a local-area network or wide-area network already, then you have an adapter board.

If you are getting ready to purchase one of these boards, you will find there are many to choose from. As you prepare to choose, make sure that the adapter board uses the same bus connector that you have inside your computer. Many of the network adapter boards are ISAs, the standard PC bus connector. However, these connectors are only 16-bit channels, meaning that they are much slower than the more modern PCI connectors found in most Pentiums. The PCI bus inside your computer runs much faster than the older ISA-type slots. For the fastest internal speed, choose a PCI-based adapter. Above all else, make sure the connector type of the card matches what you have free inside your computer.

TCP/IP

Another concern in choosing a network adapter is making sure the card you choose supports the TCP/IP protocol. I have friends who bought adapter boards only to be disappointed to find that the network card didn't support the TCP/IP protocol. Some of these boards do not provide drivers for TCP/IP. If you're lucky, Windows 95 or NT will provide general system drivers that will work, but tracking down the proper driver can be difficult. The best bet is to ensure that the board supports and comes with TCP/IP device drivers.

ISDN

Aside from the normal Telco leased line options discussed earlier, there are also several other new technologies that are emerging for direct network connection for companies and institutions using transport layers. These technologies utilize the TCP/IP protocol over special, dedicated lines.

Integrated Services Digital Network (ISDN) enables a user to access a digital phone line via dial-up using a codec rather than a modem. Much like the codecs discussed concerning graphics and video, codecs used for ISDN handle the real-time compression and decompression of the information coming over the digital phone line. ISDN lines can range in speeds from 56 Kbps up to 1,544 Kbps. ISDN is slowly gaining in popularity and use.

NOTE
> Many sources are talking about new ISDN modems that will be coming out early in 1997 focused on the in-home user. Estimated retail prices for these modems will be approximately $400.

T1 and T3

A T1 connection, another type of transport layer, is one of the most widely used corporate Internet connections. This type of connection supports a bandwidth of 1,544 Kbps; however, the cost ranges from $1,000 to $3,000 per month on top of the cost of the leased phone line. Often, a T1 connection can be leased in portions or increments called fractional T1. Fractional T1 generally is divided into multiples of 256 Kbps.

A T3 connection is much wider and faster than the T1. A T3 line is only used to connect major Internet service providers. T3 lines can support hundreds of LAN networks and boast a 44,736 Kbps bandwidth. T3 is also what forms the Internet backbone's major network connections.

Frame Relay and Switched Multimegabit Data Service (SMDS)

SMDS enables the company or institution to access the Internet based on time or services. As a function of Telco, the line or service is leased only for a portion of time. For example, services required only at a certain time of day can be set up using a frame relay or SMDS. These options give the users bandwidths that range from 56 Kbps to 512 Kbps and 56 Kbps to 10,000 Kbps.

Other Connections

Other connection services include cable TV, Asynchronous Transfer Mode (ATM), and satellite link-ups. These other connections are rapidly advancing and are currently being tested with Internet-based information services.

The following shows the relative speeds of the various transport layers:

Speeds of Direct Lines

Frame Relay	56–512 Kbps
ISDN	56–1,544 Kbps
SMDS	56–10,000 Kbps
T1	256–1,544 Kbps
T3	44,736 Kbps

Dial-Up

In dial-up connection and access, the communication that occurs between the dial-up or host computer and the Internet uses the TCP/IP protocol. However, the communication that occurs between the user's computer and the host must use either a SLIP or PPP interfacing protocol. This type of software is a client-side communication software that lets the user's computer communicate with the host computer. All of this is done through the modem.

SLIP

To connect to an ISP's remote server via a modem you must have additional software. Most often a service provider will provide necessary SLIP or PPP drivers on a floppy disk for installation on the user's computer.

SLIP, or Serial Line Internet Protocol, operates over a serial (modem) connection. Basically, SLIP software is a device driver that operates over and above any normal modem device drivers. To install a SLIP you must point the software to the modem and identify the baud rate of the modem. SLIP connections support only asynchronous communication.

 Asynchronous communication is communication that occurs without any basis on time. It requires the use of extraneous bits to encode and decode the data for transmission.

In order for data to be transferred over a modem, computers on both ends of the line must know when breaks occur in the information—when a file or data string starts and ends. To do this requires some sort of identification in the data. Asynchronous communication causes the software to add start and stop points, called *stop bits*, in the data being transferred so that the computer on the other end of the line can then decode the information. Asynchronous communication is generally slower than synchronous communication due to the extraneous data bits that are added for encoding and decoding.

PPP

The second type of service provider software is Point-to-Point Protocol (PPP). Like SLIP, PPP is used to communicate via a modem; however, PPP is more versatile and enables synchronous or asynchronous communication. PPP also enables the phone line to be used for more than one purpose. For example, the same phone line could be used or interrupted for voice service. SLIP does not enable other services to interrupt the line. In general, you will find more and more service providers using PPP over SLIP due to its advantages; however, PPP cannot run on all operating systems.

5

Servers

Now the moment of truth. You've chosen not to use leased space on an ISP's server and you must choose a machine for your server. You'll find that most decisions are based upon the hardware that the company has used in the past. Often, corporations have a dedicated company that they will go with. If you're consulting, make sure you check to see if the company for which you are working has a service agreement with a specific computer manufacturer.

Internal Servers

When you are choosing a machine for your server, you'll find a myriad of choices. In fact, any computer can actually be used as a server, but the speed of the machine will directly affect how many people can access your server and how quickly the pages are delivered to them. In addition, the machine you choose will determine the server software you can run as well as the security options that you have.

When you are looking at computers to be used as a server, there are four things with which you will need to be concerned. These concerns include the speed of the computer, the server software that you want to run, the security features of the server software, and the associated price tag.

Workstations

Web servers usually are workstation-class computers. Workstations are the fastest way to provide your information to the Web, but they also are the most costly. Workstations excel at Web delivery due to the faster processor (of which there can be more than one) and the generally abundant amount of RAM. Often these types of computers also provide a significant amount of hard disk space and extremely fast graphics processing. All in all, workstations provide the fastest performance available and also give a wide variety of options for future expandability.

If you choose to use a workstation as your server, the software should be UNIX-based. Several flavors of Web server software are available for the UNIX platform. These include NCSA httpd, CERN httpd, and Netscape Communications Netsite Communication Server. Each of these Web server software packages gives you various features. Because UNIX comes in different flavors, probably the best suggestion is to refer to your UNIX OS developer to see which he or she recommends. All of these software packages support various versions of UNIX, but you still should check with the developer.

Because UNIX is designed as a multiuser and multitasking system, it is the best choice for complete security. With UNIX, you can limit access to files, folders, or groups of either one. UNIX is a true multiuser environment, so it supports robust security features not available with some other operating systems.

Finally, if you are looking at purchasing a workstation you'll find that the price tag can vary quite drastically. Workstations can range in price from $5,000 all the way up to (and beyond) $30,000. The price inevitably will be determined by how many processors, how much RAM, and how much hard drive space you need. Even on a low-end workstation, pages can be delivered to many users without a significant drop-off in performance.

The following shows the characteristics of using a workstation:

Characteristics of Workstations

Expensive
Multiple RISC processing
Multitasking environment
Abundant amounts of RAM
Secure operating system
Fast graphics processing

Personal Computers

The second choice for a Web server is the use of a beefed-up PC or Macintosh. You'll find the price tag of either of these systems much lower than that of a workstation. However, there are some limitations to choosing a PC or Mac over a workstation. Part of this is due to the processor. Part of it is also due to the nature of the operating systems running on these machines.

The first thing you must note with a PC or Macintosh is the variety and nature of the operating system. You can use several operating systems on a PC, including Windows 95, Windows NT, and UNIX. With the Mac, you are basically limited to System 7.0 or higher. A Windows machine running any of the three primary operating systems will be able to adequately function as a Web server. The biggest advantage to using a PC is price.

PCs and Macs have a slower processing speed compared to a workstation due to the difference in the processor itself; the PC processor is based on a more complex instruction set than the workstation processor. Generally speaking, all other things are equal. PCs and Macs alike support multiple processors, SCSI-based communications, and abundant amounts of RAM. Therefore, the only real difference is the processor and how the operating system works.

5

Until lately, the standard PC operating system (Windows 3.1 and 3.11) did not support a true multiuser or multitasking environment, in which information could be securely protected. However, with the creation of Windows 95 and more importantly Windows NT, users of these systems now have true security and can provide extremely secure sites. Through the use of software products such as Windows NT Server, users can provide a lot of secure information at their sites using Windows httpd.

Price is probably the most attractive feature of choosing a PC or Mac as a Web server. A maximized PC or Mac running 128 to 256MB of RAM, several gigabytes of storage space, and a quick CISC processor will cost approximately $5,000 to $10,000. A comparable workstation would run $15,000 to $25,000—a definite savings.

The following shows some of the characteristics to using a PC for a Web server:

PC Characteristics
Low price
Multiple CISC processors
Abundant amounts of RAM
Can be SCSI-based
Secure operating systems
Multitasking environment

Intranets

Probably one of the most talked about networks is the intranet. Aside from its exclusive nature, it's not really any different from a normal Web server except that it is for internal use only. Items that can be included on an intranet include human resources information, internal systems information, training, scheduling, and other miscellaneous business information. Often intranets are established separately from the Internet, but they also can have access to the outside world.

 An *intranet* is an internal, exclusive, and secure Web server that gives employees and staff inside an institution or company the ability to share information without releasing it to the Web community at large.

The whole issue of the intranet is security. Individuals and institutions want to be able to use the accessibility and real-time delivery capabilities of the Web to distribute their information internally. However, the information must be stable and secure. Newer Web server software is beginning to make this a reality, but in many server software packages, there are still loopholes—ways for intelligent crackers to get through.

Predominantly there are two ways to develop security in a Web system. The first is to maintain two separate and distinct Web sites on a single server. To the extreme, some companies will even create two separate physical networks to avoid any chance of intermingling between the two. This might seem excessive, but often more critical data requires this type of measure.

Setting up two Web sites on a single server requires maintaining two individual sites, which doubles the workload of the Webmaster. Maintaining two separate sites requires as much work as maintaining two separate servers. There really is no difference. In addition, you must be certain that the two sites are not embedded in each other. The two sites must reside side by side on the server directory structure, at the same directory level, so that access to one does not provide access to the other.

Firewalls

A second way to establish Web site security is via a firewall. Much like the origin of the term, a firewall prevents or limits access to network resources.

 A *firewall* is a software application that is used to limit or prevent access to network resources; it restricts outsider access while enabling internal users to see the outside world.

Most firewalls are set up so that all data going in or coming out of the network must pass through a very restrictive gate, as shown in Figure 5.7. Often there will be several gates constructed, one for each type of service being provided. For example, e-mail would be quite useless if it were limited to the confines of your four walls or the limits of your building. Using a guarded gate—a firewall—you can provide access in and out of the organization in a protected way. E-mail seldom uses a firewall; however, in this example it is something we can all relate to and understand. There are institutions that must use a firewall not only on Web access but also on e-mail and all services due to the highly sensitive nature of their data.

Figure 5.7.
Limiting access with a firewall.

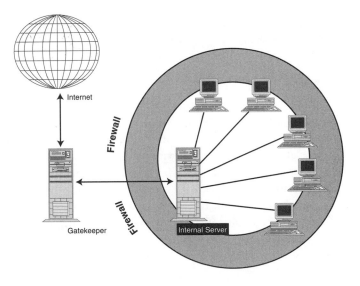

In real terms, most firewalls enable users on the inside to view the outside world, but don't enable the outside world to come in. In most cases, institutions are not trying to keep people in, they are trying to keep people out. Believe it or not, there are many people who just want to invade your site and screw it up—they might not really be interested in your data. This is what the firewall is for: to prevent intruders, viruses, and other mischievous software from corrupting or destroying your corporate or institutional data.

External Servers

For many institutions not considering an intranet or providing secure information, simply creating a Web site is a less time-intensive task. Often, the first steps toward creating a Web site should be aimed at providing information to the public domain even if an intrasite is part of your future plans. Often, Web sites will develop and expand to include sensitive data and secure information at a later date. If you are developing a site from scratch, focus on starting small and planning for future expansion.

Internet Service Providers

A final note about ISPs and intranets. Many companies with which I have consulted have chosen to utilize ISPs for their external information while using their own servers for their intranets. Many of these companies have been very successful in maintaining internal networks and don't want to have to deal with maintaining and providing bandwidth for an external site. Utilizing the ISP's mass-market capability has enabled these companies to provide and maintain their own internal servers while letting the ISP maintain the external server. This doesn't mean the ISP is developing the content for the external server. It just manages the hardware, Internet connection, and Web server software.

Other Gateways

In addition to ISPs, you or your company can choose to use a commercial online service such as CompuServe or America Online to provide Web site space or access. Although they do provide such services, you might find that certain services don't work like having your own server or using an Internet service provider. Because these commercial online services were originally developed as proprietary systems, they still have some difficulty dealing with certain Internet services. For example, sending e-mail messages with attachments generally will not work from the Internet to a CompuServe account or vice versa. Often the receiving CompuServe account will be unable to read the e-mail, even with the use of certain conversion tools. In addition, pages provided on these sites often are limited in size and scope. They also are generally slow to load due to the number of users on the online service.

Internet Standards

To support the universal access of information there must be standards. There must be something that enables communication no matter what platform, protocol, or browser a person uses. As you look at the Web, you see a communication media in which the messages delivered and presented change, on a daily basis. However, there are several aspects of the Web that do not fluctuate even though the Web, its protocols, its domain names, files, and MIME extension are expanding.

HTTP

Although HyperText Transfer Protocol (HTTP) is rapidly advancing, you must note that the protocol remains relatively stable. Many new advances are taking place to improve the way that it works, its portability, and its security. A vast number of individuals are continually striving to improve this protocol; however, its basic workings remain the same.

Domains

As noted earlier, domain names are the English version of the IP address. One thing I did not address is the standardization of the extension, or last three letters, of the domain name. This information gives you vital information about the organization, institution, or corporation to which the domain name belongs. The standard endings, such as `.com` (corporate), `.edu` (educational institution), and `.org` (non-profit organization) are standards set by various governing bodies such as the W3C (see the following list). Currently, discussion is proposing the addition of more extensions to allow for the exponential growth occurring on the Web. Undoubtedly, we'll continue to see additions to the domain extension as the Web continues to expand.

The following shows some of the most frequently used endings for domain names:

Common Domain Name Extensions

`.com`	A corporation or business
`.edu`	An educational institution
`.org`	A non-profit organization
`.gov`	A government organization
`.mil`	A military organization
`.net`	A network access provider

5

Files

The various types of files that you see on the Web are also evolving. The standard GIF and JPEG images are now being accompanied by various other formats that are focused for use with plug-ins. Browsers continue to support a wider array of file formats. Multimedia formats also are claiming new ground and require specific file formats to be recognized by both servers and client software.

MIME Types

As a reaction to the variety of new file formats on the Web, the number of MIME types recognized by server software and browser software is rapidly increasing. To enable distribution of files, a server must be told to release the information to the public. To receive and view a particular file, assuming it is not directly supported by the browser, requires setting up MIME types in the browser and an external plug-in or helper application. The list of file extensions found on the Web is requiring drastic additions to the MIME lists of both browsers and servers.

Layout

Now that you've taken a look at your server and how you're going to provide your pages to the Web, you must begin looking at your site's layout. Many people have an idea of what they want to provide, but never draw a map of where they are going. I am the type who must have a map to know where I am going. I don't like to just "have an idea of where I am going." I want to know for sure, particularly because I'm not fond of asking for directions. This is why site maps and pre-computer planning are important. Two of the best tools for designing pages and sites are paper and pencil—no software required.

Site Design

Recall some information that you learned earlier. I cannot emphasize how important planning is in the Web development process. Although many claim that achievement is in execution, I would argue and say that without proper planning, execution is impossible. Using the various planning tools already described, you create a plan of action that you can act upon and execute.

Site Maps

Do you have a daily planner? I do, and I know I would be lost without it. I use my planner to schedule my daily tasks, my life's major events, and things that are months away. Site maps are much like daily planners; they help you get a visual picture of the Web site. They can even be used to aid in scheduling work to be done as well as work in progress. In the latter part of this book you will develop several sites and see how to use the site map to help lay out the files on the server.

Server Implications

The size of your server's hard drive could ultimately affect what can be delivered at your site. The speed of your server could ultimately affect how many satisfied users can download at a single time. All the various parts of your server will ultimately affect the performance of your server and your Web site.

If you are planning to purchase a server, as with any computer purchase, buy the best you can get with the resources you have. Changing a Web server after it has been designed can be a significantly time-consuming task. I suggest buying a server that will more than adequately support what you want to do for at least a year. Outgrowing a server in less than a year can add a significant amount of file management time to your schedule. Good Web server software, like a good operating system, will require as little attention as possible. Again, you want to focus on developing content to be delivered to your audience, not technical details of the operating system or the Web server software.

Accessibility

One of the chief concerns with Web site development, particularly on internal servers, is the issue of accessibility. As you or your Web development group are busily working on the Web site, you must be aware of who has access and who is updating files. There must also be a logical structure to the documents that reside on the server. In a large institution, as many as 5,000 to 10,000 people will need to put information on the server. They also might need to be able to transfer data through the server. So how do you satisfy this need?

Who Has Access?

When it comes to creating, updating, and managing a Web site there are several ways to determine who has access. In general, you will need to develop a scheme that works for you and your company. Any one method might be too limiting or not limiting enough. The method you choose will be based upon the number of individuals who need access, how critical the information is, and the size of your network.

The first way to provide access to the server is an open access policy as shown in Figure 5.8. Using this scheme simply opens the entire server to the individuals of the company. However, managing a site in this way can be very dangerous in situations in which the technical skills of the involved individuals are low or where the information on the server is critical. Often, open server access is easy to implement, but it can have chaotic results because of the number of individuals adding, revising, and deleting information from the server.

Figure 5.8.

Open server access.

Open Server Access

The second method of access, and probably the best in sites that are less than 100 pages, is the use of a centralized individual to handle additions to and deletions from the server, as shown in Figure 5.9. In this scenario, the individual receives pages, change orders, and deletions from the various individuals in the company and then executes them. Although this access method is used quite often, the centralized individual can become overworked trying to keep up with the large number of revisions and deletions if the site grows very large.

Figure 5.9.

A centralized individual makes all additions to and deletions from the server.

Centralized Individual

The last method of controlling access is used most often in settings where a group of individuals is responsible for maintaining the Web site, as shown in Figure 5.10. In a decentralized access situation, the centralized individual (most often the lead or primary Webmaster) receives instructions for revisions from company personnel. The lead Webmaster then instructs the rest of the group members to make the revisions that have been requested. Most often, each person in the group is responsible for a specific area or portion of the Web server.

Figure 5.10.

Decentralized access.

Who Has Authority?

Resolving issues of control and access are of the utmost importance for efficiently and effectively maintaining a Web site. Redundant changes or misplaced pages and graphics result from a lack of organization in the revision and editing process.

Summary

Today you have looked at the various hardware, software, and networking concepts involved in Web development. You've seen that the Web is based on the client/server model and that it is composed of thousands of computer networks. The two major addressing schemes used on the Internet—the Domain Name Service (DNS) and the Internet Protocol (IP) address—also were discussed. Remember that the entire Internet is based upon the TCP/IP protocol even though the Internet is a multiprotocol environment.

Highlighted throughout this chapter is the importance of connection, both the server's connection to the Internet and the client's connection to the Internet. You've taken a brief look at both connections and the implications that each type of connection has for the user browsing the Net, and the serving of pages to the Net.

Q&A

Q What are the three types of client access to the Web? How do they differ in the hardware required and speed?

A The three types of client-side access to the Internet are direct connection, dial-up connection, and dial-up access. The direct connection requires a network adapter card, whereas dial-up connection or access requires a modem. In a direct connection the user has direct access to the Internet via the network adapter board. Direct access is the fastest type of client-side Internet connection. Dial-up connection requires the use of a modem to dial into a host computer connected to the Internet. In a dial-up connection, the user has direct access to the Internet through the host computer and modem channel. Dial-up access is the slowest type of client-side connection. In a dial-up access scenario, the user dials into a host computer for access to the Internet; however, files must be downloaded to the host computer and then downloaded to the client's machine via a modem.

Q What are the main differences between using workstations and PCs for a server?

A Workstations used as Web servers are generally faster than PCs, predominantly due to a RISC-based processor and the UNIX operating system. However, workstations are much more expensive that PCs.

Q Upon what protocol is the entire Internet system based? What makes up this protocol?

A The undergirding protocol for the Internet is the TCP/IP or Transmission Control Protocol/Internet Protocol. TCP/IP is the combination of two separate protocols. TCP handles transmission and IP handles the routing of data over the Internet.

Q **What is the difference between the domain name service and the Internet Protocol address?**

A The domain name service, or DNS, is a textual description of a Web page location. Generally, DNS names conform to a sequence of logical words separated by periods. The Internet Protocol (IP) address is a 32-bit numerical address that identifies a Web page location. The DNS name was designed to be used easily by humans, whereas the IP address is the standard method that the computer uses to identify a Web site or computer node on the Internet.

Workshop

The Workshop provides quiz questions to help you solidify your understanding of the material covered and exercises to give you experience in using what you've learned. The answers are provided in Appendix A, "Quiz Answers." Try to understand the quiz answers before you go on to tomorrow's lesson.

Quiz

1. Name the two networking models. How do they differ?
2. What are the types of connections (or services) that can be used to connect a corporate server to the Internet? For what is each type used, and how do they differ from one another?
3. What is the difference between a LAN and a WAN?
4. What is a T1 line? What is a T3 line? How do they differ?
5. What is the difference between synchronous and asynchronous communication? Which is faster?
6. What is an intranet, and how is it used?
7. What is a firewall? How does it work?
8. What are the three methods of controlling server access?

Exercise

Begin examining how you will get your server onto the Web. Look at the various line options available in your area. Begin getting actual quotes for monthly charges in your area, and then decide how you will implement your server. What type of computer will you need? What will your budget allow? What about software? Begin making plans for designing and establishing your server on your local network.

Day 6

The Technical Manager

One of the aspects of being a Webmaster that is not often addressed is that of being a manager. Regardless of whether you are the only person working in Web development or whether there are several people in your Web development group, managing all the various aspects, not to mention your time, is vitally important. To be efficient requires the ability to accurately and precisely manage your work time. You must focus on those things that are important but not immediate.

A *technical manager* is an individual who manages the hardware, software, resources, and people involved in the Web development process.

All the tasks with which you are concerned can be divided into several groups or classes. All the things you must do on a day-to-day basis can be divided into a four-area matrix as shown in Figure 6.1. These include important and not important, and immediate and not immediate. In reality, you want to focus on the tasks that are important but not immediate. Many Webmasters continually find themselves putting out fires. Unfortunately, working continually in this mode is detrimental to most development projects as well as exhausting for the developer. So how do you escape this mode of operation? The key is to work in a preventative mode, always looking for ways to reduce the amount of work you have to do in the future. Most of these tasks are simple management and maintenance strategies that can help you to globally maintain your site, pages, and people.

Figure 6.1.

A matrix of time management.

Important/ Immediate	Not Important/ Immediate
Important/ Not Immediate	Not Important/ Not Immediate

Today's lesson focuses on some management tips and tricks that you can use to help yourself farther down the road. Many of these things might seem obvious, and at times they are. However, I mention them to aid you in your Webmastering tasks. Implementation of any and all of these things can save you a significant amount of time. However, they might not all be applicable in your situation. Take what is presented and apply it to your situation. Leave behind those things that are impossible or self-defeating for your situation.

Maintenance

Probably 50 percent of the work that goes into a Web site will be revised, changed, or deleted from the Web server over a period of a year. In addition, there might be new individuals joining your Web group, or you might find that in a little less than a year you have moved from being the only Webmaster to being the leader of a group of individuals responsible for developing your corporate Web site. You must, from the beginning, develop a scheme for tracking changes, additions, revisions, and any other modifications of your Web site. To do any less will cause no end of trouble with maintenance and management later.

To provide a means of easily managing the day-to-day tasks requires a documentation strategy. You must develop a scheme for tracking changes to your site or pages. This gives you a paper trail that you can follow if you need to reinstate a page or revert to a previous version of your Web site.

Pages

As you learned on Day 3, "The Information Design Specialist," it is important to create a site map, not only for planning, but also for maintaining your site. A site map is usually a sketch that describes the various pages in your Web site. If you love graphics, you might want to create it in a drawing program as shown in Figure 6.2.

Figure 6.2.

An example of a site map.

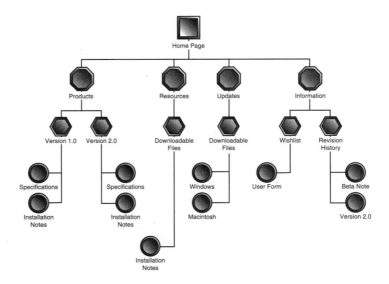

A site map should be designed so that it can be updated easily as your Web site begins to expand and evolve. If you originally created a hand-drawn sketch of your site layout, I would suggest transferring it to the computer to make it more easily editable for the future. One individual I know constantly creates huge sketches that he pastes on the wall to visually plan things such as a Web site. Some of his "sketches" have been as large as 36 inches by four or five feet! This is an acceptable method; however, the drawings get a little messy at times, and it is difficult to edit. Site maps drawn on the computer are much easier to manipulate, edit, and read. There are several good programs on the market that will enable you to create a site diagram or map quickly. Programs such as Visio Corporation's Visio or Micrographx's ABC FlowCharter are prime examples. Of course, you also could use any Postscript drawing tool such as Macromedia's FreeHand or Adobe's Illustrator.

6

Now look at a site map and learn how you should lay it all out. Figure 6.3 shows an example of my department's Web site. In this example, you see that there are five main branches from the home page and that the site has a three-tier structure. Also note that the site is relatively linear.

Figure 6.3.

My department's site map.

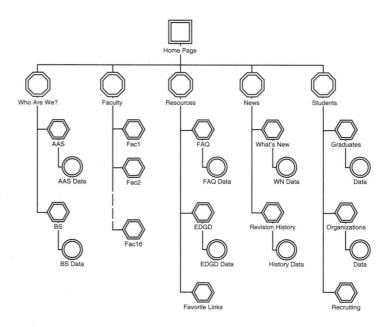

Site maps are very explanatory. They can quickly give you an idea of the size and scope of the Web site as well as the links between the data. For simplicity's sake, the image does not show every hotlink or connecting link between every page on the map. There are actually links on every individual page to each of the main divisions.

Tools

Now one of the things you need to be aware of is the wealth of new Web development tools on the market. A quick glance through a Microwarehouse or PC Mall catalog shows many new tools are available for this purpose. Many of the Web development tools, such as Microsoft FrontPage, enable you to visually arrange pages much like the site map. For example, Microsoft FrontPage enables you to arrange pages easily much like drawing a site map. This makes creating Web sites an easy task for just about anybody. However, it does not negate the need to learn the fundamentals of the language or how the entire Web process works.

Files

Continuing with the site map example, you can add a few things to the map to make it more descriptive of the Web site as shown in Figure 6.4. By adding files and filenames to the site map, you can better represent the current state of your site.

Figure 6.4.

Adding filenames to the site map makes it more representative of the actual site.

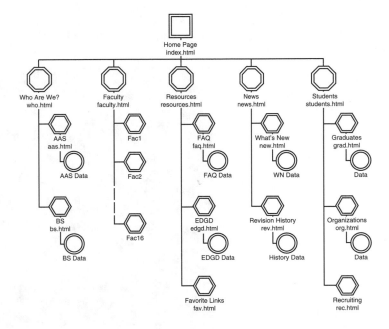

One other helpful item that can be gleaned from the site map is a file structure for the site. Notice in the sample site map that the root document, or lowest-level document, is the home page. This home page probably resides at the root level of your server. Then, each major division (that is, Who Are We?, Faculty, and so on) is another folder or directory. Looking at the site map in Figure 6.4, notice that in the "Who Are We?" branch there are two subdivisions. Those subdivisions would probably each also have a directory throughout the rest of the site. Eventually, the folders would contain the actual pages of the site. For example, inside the AAS directory would be all the pages or data relating to AAS. Using this approach makes multiple uses of the site map and creates a coherency for managing the site.

Tracking Changes

One of the major concerns with developing Web material is tracking the changes that have been made and when they were made. You can use the site map to help you do this, yet it does not show actual edit dates and descriptions of the revisions. Along with a site map, it is common to keep a revision history file where all changes made to a site are logged.

The revision history for a Web site is much like a revision history document found with many commercial and shareware software products as shown in Figure 6.5. A revision history is a simple text file that lists changes made to the site or site's pages. The revision history file usually gives the date the revision was made, as well as a short description of the changes made. Often a separate revision history document is kept in the same directory as the major division directory. For example, in my department's site, a revision history document would be stored for changes made in each major division. The revision history documents would be stored in the directory where each division starts.

Figure 6.5.

A revision history document.

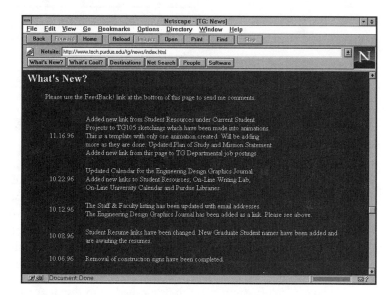

NOTE

In addition to an external revision history, you can put comments right inside the HTML files to help you track when additions or changes were made. You'll take a look at this on Day 8, "Introduction to HTML and Block Tags."

Graphics

Aside from managing the pages and your overall site structure, you must also manage all the various graphics at your site. Assuming you agree with the visual paradigm of the Web, you will undoubtedly have many different graphics in use on your site. However, as you have learned, the graphics that are distributed over the Web are usually low-end versions. For future editing ability, you'll want to keep the high-resolution, high-color versions so they can be used and reused later.

One of the best ways to keep track of your graphics resources is to maintain a portion of your server for a Web graphics archive. If you have the local resources, such as those in your own machine, you might want to keep a backup copy there also. As you are working with the computer to create graphics, HTML, and script resources, nothing is more frustrating than to have to re-create something you've done in the past. Losing a code string, a graphic image, or a custom script on which you worked for days will undoubtedly cause frustration. Losing work that you've done on the computer is part of life. Many people have lost valuable creations due to file corruption, file deletion, or simple negligence. I, too, have lost work that I created several years ago and still kick myself for misplacing or losing it. The best way to avoid this is by backing up your work and documenting it. For those who are in the consulting business, this is a must. I suggest creating backup space on your server and your local computer and storing copies of all your documents in both places.

NOTE

This might sound absurd, but after working with more than several hundred students a semester, I don't leave anything to chance. Let's define a backup.

Backing up a file does not mean making two copies of the file on the same diskette, hard drive, CD-ROM, or honestly, even two copies on the same computer. A backup of a file must reside on two separate storage media or on two separate computers. If a disk becomes corrupt, both files are trash. If the hard drive is corrupted, more than likely, both files are corrupted. If a machine goes belly-up, how will you get either copy off the machine? A true backup is one in which the files are on two (or three) separate diskettes, hard drives, CD-ROMs, or computers.

People

Most tangible things are manageable, that is, except for people. With people, you support, encourage, coach, and guide. That does not mean, however, that you don't have realistic expectations for their performance. Those expectations must be apparent, spoken, and rewarded. It is amazing to me that many managers, both in graphics and in other industries, expect things from their employees that they never voice or communicate. How do you take a test without knowing what the questions are? To be effective with people, you must voice your expectations. Then it is their responsibility to perform with your coaching and guidance.

6

What does this have to do with Web development? Well, I will bet if you are working for a company, at some time, you have been expected to do things that were never outwardly spoken to you. However, you probably started doing them after you were aware of the expectation. If you are working in a group of people, or even if you are a single Webmaster for a company, you must find out the realistic expectations of what you will be doing. If you are a lead Webmaster you must also be able to voice your expectations to those working in your development group. You'll find that when expectations are laid out, most individuals will exceed your expectations. When expectations are hidden, people will barely meet your expectations, if at all.

Managing Internal Human Resources

Aside from communicating your expectations, you must also be concerned with group dynamics whenever more than one individual is involved with development. When all of the people developing the site are employees of the institution, most often group dynamics and authority structure are predefined. The biggest issue with which you'll have to contend is the issue of control mentioned on Day 5, "The Technical Designer." Establish early on who is in control of the Web site's additions and revisions. Furthermore, establish who has ultimate authority on what goes into the site and what stays out.

If you are using a site map and a revision history list, establish who will be responsible for maintaining these items. Often it will be a good idea to make each individual in a group responsible for a portion of each of the Web site sections. This makes dividing the workload much easier. However, you might want to use a method of rollover where each person is responsible for a specific amount of the site for a limited period of time (six to nine months). Using a rollover method keeps the morale and interest of the involved individuals much higher than if the individual is responsible for a particular Web site section for an indefinable period of time.

Using External Resources

Using external consulting services is often a method of establishing a Web site. For those who are using external resources or are consultants, communication is imperative. Most of the trouble with external consultants is the lack of communication. I look at my own consulting work and see that in areas where communication broke down, there were misconceptions about particular features or sections. Miscommunication or lack of communication always— I repeat, *always*—results in either more money paid to or lost from the consulting body.

One of the ways in which the lines of communication can be forced open is through legal documents that ensure communication. Often work-for-hire agreements and other contracts specify that communication must occur in writing. If you are a consultant, it is vital that you use this clause to get as much information as possible when you have committed to a contract or project. As you'll see in tomorrow's lesson, much of this responsibility is on you. Tomorrow, you'll also learn how you can use a proposal to list your expectations for communication to occur between yourself and the company with which you are consulting.

Resources

When most people think about management, concerns focus on hardware, software, and the physical connections of the network. This book hasn't focused significantly on the minute details of hooking up your network or establishing software due to the wide variety of variables that depend on your situation. However, there are several things that you can do to make your Webmastering tasks more efficient, effective, and enjoyable.

Hardware

In general, after you have a Web site set up, very little must be done to the hardware for maintenance. Most maintenance tasks will be focused toward expanding the capabilities or speed of the machine. Most additions such as additional processors, more RAM, or more hard drive space can be added quite easily.

Regardless of whether you have chosen a workstation or a personal computer, you will always want to keep up with the technologies to know what things can be added to your machine to make access and internal processing faster.

Software

To maintain the software that is on your machine you should follow the documentation scheme mentioned earlier. In addition, you will want to keep your server software up-to-date to ensure that it supports the latest features and functions. It is not uncommon to have quarterly updates that need to be added to various server software. You'll also want to check to see what kind of software support your server software manufacturer supports. Commercial server software generally offers the purchaser the option of buying a certain amount of technical support in addition to the default technical support time period. Most often, support of this type is a good investment but will depend on your budget constraints.

6

Connections

Finally, if you are using an ISP or a Telco company, strive to make your business relationship a partnership. Before choosing either one, look for a company that will give you a long-term relationship and one that is genuinely concerned for the welfare of the information you plan to provide. There are many, many startup ISPs that go out of business as quickly as they start. Be cautious of choosing an ISP or Telco for your business that has not been in business very long. A sudden change in Internet service providers or telecommunications companies can be detrimental to your site's establishment and development.

Summary

In today's lesson you have taken a look at the various aspects of technical management. You learned that one of the aspects of a good manager is the ability to manage time. In this respect, you must focus on those items that are not immediate, but are important. This forces you to take a proactive stance on what you do on a day-to-day basis, instead of working in a reactive position. In today's lesson you have also seen ways in which you can make maintenance on your site easier through a site map, various supplemental development tools, and good file management. Likely, you'll find the hardest part is tracking the changes that occur in your site on a daily basis. The revision history is also vital in maintaining your site. Keep in mind as you are managing these various things that you must not try to manage your people. Be a coach and a motivator while also being a technical manager.

Q&A

Q The most important aspect of managing a Web site is documentation. What type of documentation should a Webmaster create to improve maintenance efficiency?

A A Webmaster should have and maintain two major documents that describe the Web site. The first is a site map that visually describes the structure, files, pages, and filenames of the site. The site map also shows the layout of the files on the server. The second document is a revision history document for each major part of the Web site.

Q How should files be organized on the Web server? Does the way they're organized affect site maintenance?

A Files should be arranged according to the site map that has been created. By following the site map for arrangement, maintenance and management of the pages, files, and directories is easier.

Q What is a backup?

A A backup of a digital file is a duplicate copy of the file that resides on two separate storage media.

6

Workshop

The Workshop provides quiz questions to help you solidify your understanding of the material covered and exercises to give you experience in using what you've learned. The quiz answers are provided in Appendix A, "Quiz Answers." Try to understand the quiz answers before you go on to tomorrow's lesson.

Quiz

1. What is a revision history? What should it include?
2. To be effective at time management, on what types of things should you focus?
3. What is the most important aspect of effective consulting?

Exercise

Begin to create a site map of your Web. Do you see any inconsistencies in the way the files should be laid out versus what appears on your server? Do you see any ways that you could improve the efficiency of your site based on your site map?

6

Day **7**

The Professional Consultant

Many individuals, in pursuit of the American dream, are working for themselves by consulting with business and industry. The current trend in technology allows for individuals with specialized skills who work outside industry to provide services to corporations of all sizes. Many corporations find it more feasible to pay for external services rather than to devote employees to certain tasks. Often, individuals, including myself, work from their homes providing computer graphics, computer and networking services, video and audio services, as well as a wide range of other computer-related services. For most, this type of career appears to be the "perfect" job, allowing them to work when they want and how they want. But, being a successful consultant requires a significant amount of self-discipline and a wide variety of skills.

NOTE

> Much of what is presented in this lesson is really a paradigm, or way of doing business. It is based on my success as a consultant. Although specific situations call for specific actions and decisions, in general the key to success as a consultant lies in how business is conducted as much as it does in producing products.

The biggest reason that most people can consult at all is due to low-cost, powerful desktop systems. Let's face it, with a capable Pentium computer stocked with the proper software, a skilled operator can create many of the things that only a few years ago were created by large publishing or media houses. Who would have thought that a single individual could run a multimedia development company out of his or her home with as little as a $5,000 investment? Or a desktop publishing house from a one-room home office? You're seeing a trend that enables the small businessperson—the individual—to produce very sophisticated products and projects using desktop computers. So why has the computer drastically affected the number of consultants? Because the consultant can underbid the large corporation due to low, and sometimes nonexistent, overhead, providing products that perform equally well for less money. The lack of significant overhead makes consulting possible and advantageous for the consultant and the corporation.

You must note one thing about consulting, however. There is a flip-side to the freedom enjoyed by the full-time consultant. The responsibility that is divided among the individuals in an established business must be shouldered by the consultant. A single individual must perform (or pay for) all the business functions. The consultant is responsible for financial records, production, marketing, support, and all other business functions related to his or her self-made business. Most of the time, however, a single individual is not capable in all the areas related to running a successful business. The consultant does not have access to the human resources available in a larger company, unless of course he or she wants to pay for it. Therefore, the consultant must have or attain business savvy in deficient areas. Lacking sufficient skills in any of these business areas will either limit the consultant's capability or increase overhead.

A second negative attribute of consulting, particularly in the early years of the business, is that it most often follows a sporadic pay cycle. One month can be a time of feasting, whereas the next can be a time of famine. In business, this cycle is natural. Almost all businesses' profits fluctuate in this manner. For the individual not wary of this situation, however, the news can be completely devastating. Suddenly quitting your job to pursue a consulting career can be detrimental if you're not aware of the monetary fluctuations associated with consulting. You must have a means of stabilizing income so that it is distributed over time.

A third issue in consulting concerns motivation. Most individuals believe that having the freedom to work when you want would be wonderful. The negative side, however, is that you are your own boss and you often have to force yourself to work. For some, this discipline is not difficult; for others, though, self-discipline does not come easy. Being a successful consultant requires the utmost in self-discipline; no one pressures you to get the job done—except maybe your client.

In addition, if your office is in your home, you never leave your office, so to speak. Many consultants begin their businesses only to burn out quickly because they cannot physically get away from their work. Successfully running a home business requires managing your time but also clearly defining personal work guidelines so that a home-based business does not consume the consultant or his or her family.

Today's lesson focuses on the various aspects of consulting. Many Webmasters serve as external consultants to various businesses and industries. As a side note, I have served as a consultant, creating Web-based material for many regional and national institutions over the past several years. I have worked with many companies in both a development and review role. Although my consulting business predominantly focuses on computer graphics and interactive media, Web-based development is well within my scope of delivery. Through this lesson, I hope that you'll pick up some of the information that I have learned over the past seven years as a consultant with many different corporations.

NOTE

I want to conclude this lesson opener with a side note and an encouraging word toward consulting as a "real job." Many people begin a consulting career with family members constantly asking, "When are you going to go out and get a real job?" I don't know; maybe I'm the only one who was presented with this question.

Indeed, the first years of consulting can be quite trying. Building a personal network, business relationships, and a portfolio of successful projects requires vast amounts of your time. However, I believe that, if you persevere and follow the points outlined in this lesson, you can be a successful consultant.

Not to sound conceited or to boast, but rather to build credibility, as of my third year of consulting I made a modest $32,000. The first two years were slow, but today's ends are better than yesterday's means. Since my second year, my consulting business has doubled every year to the point that I now can pick and choose the projects on which I want to work. And I live in the heart of the Midwest! If you want to pursue a career as a Web consultant, be encouraged, be patient, persevere, and you can succeed—as well as say, "I do have a real job!" to those family members.

7

Establishing Relationships

If you're planning to begin consulting, probably one of the most difficult tasks is building lasting consulting relationships with companies and corporations. A majority of this lesson is devoted to ideas and methods you can follow to ensure that you keep a long list of satisfied customers. It is important that you not only learn how to get contacts, but also how to keep them. Your best marketing is the words of a satisfied customer.

How do you establish freelance contacts? In the business field, who you know is important. No matter where you meet people or how you meet people, who you know is important. Let me say again, who you know is important.

The first few years of a consulting business must be devoted to establishing relationships with individuals who could be possible clientele. However, even people who might not directly be possible clients are important also. Often you might have to get acquainted with three or four people before you actually are able to talk to someone who makes decisions and has the authority to look at you as a possible consultant. You must do so graciously and professionally. Many a brash young opportunist has offended people trying to get a business going. I'm sure that at one time or another you've had a friend with a heavy marketing overtone, trying to get you to buy this or that. If you don't go about this task effectively, you can push people away rather than persuade them. Making contacts must be done subtly but with a definite point. Treat everyone with respect and honor.

What can you do to get your foot in the door? The most important thing to have in any product-oriented field is an example of something you've created. If you're a multimedia consultant, you need an example. If you're a programmer, you need an example. If you're a desktop publisher, you need an example. Humans are creatures that require proof of performance for consideration. You must show that you have the capable skills by providing a convincing example.

When should you focus on creating the example? Well, to be honest, far before you need it. You might already have examples of a Web site or other product you've created, but many new consultants hold off on creating marketing pieces until they need them. Not a good idea. Projects you create as examples don't have to be "real" projects. You can design them around fictitious or certain types of companies. If you don't begin early, often you'll be rushed to throw something together to show a possible client, and this rush can result in a poor piece on which to sell yourself. Begin now, well before you need the example!

Networking

As you begin making contacts and establishing relationships, you should track the people you know. Remember, as the consultant, you are responsible for all aspects of the business. You

7

should keep and maintain a database of names, numbers, and other information. To do so, you can use many commercial software packages that make the task easier. Software products such as Janna Contact or Commence Corporation's Commence enable you to track networking information easily. Many of these software products also allow for easy integration with commercial application suites such as Microsoft Office or Lotus SmartSuite.

One of the biggest jobs you need to do as a consultant is to find ways of reducing the amount of time you have to spend on tasks that don't make money, such as creating invoices, tracking projects, billing, accounting, and so on. When you're a consultant, the time spent performing these tasks is the only overhead you have (aside from any computer resources you have to purchase). If you're comfortable doing these tasks, find a software product that enables you to decrease the time you spend. Many software products that enable you to significantly reduce the labor involved with accounting and marketing functions are now available.

If you're looking for business software, you should ask yourself the following questions:

- ☐ Does the software have multifunction capability? How many tasks can you perform with it? Software that can perform many business tasks is better than a program that can track only names, addresses, and phone numbers.

- ☐ Does the software allow for your business to expand? Some software has a limit to the amount of data it can hold.

- ☐ How well does the package integrate with other desktop software packages that you have? Can data in it be used in a suite product such as Microsoft Word, or is the data proprietary, thus unable to be extracted or reused?

- ☐ What kind of hardware do you need to run the program efficiently? Some database-type programs require hefty amounts of RAM or hard drive space.

- ☐ Does the software come on a CD-ROM? Can you install a minimum configuration on your machine to help reserve hard disk space?

- ☐ Who's the publisher? Often, cheap software packages are created by companies such as Joe's Software Pub and sold on a local CD-ROM stand for $5. Be wary of staking the reliability of your financial data on a product produced by an "unknown" publisher or a shareware program.

Resources

While I'm on the subject of networking and making contacts, remember that you have one of the best networking resources right at your fingertips—the Internet. Many newsgroups and Web sites provide free bulletin boards where consulting opportunities are readily available. You can find several thousand news postings or several thousand Web postings to funnel through. The following are some of the sites you might want to check out:

☐ http://www.careermosaic.com/cm/

☐ http://www.cweb.com/

☐ http://espan2.espan.com/cgi-bin/gate2?espan~simple/

☐ http://www.netline.com//Career/career.html

☐ http://www.techni-source.com/

☐ http://www.ceweekly.wa.com/

☐ http://www.mmwire.com/classifieds.html

☐ http://www.occ.com/

☐ http://www.careerexpo.com/

☐ http://www.zdnet.com/zdi/jobs/jobs.html

In addition, online services such as CompuServe and America Online provide additional postings that are not accessible via the Web. If you have an account on one of these commercial services, be sure to check it out as well.

NOTE

> Keep in mind that, as you're searching for leads, you might make 20 contacts with only one reply showing interest. As you're starting your business, this rate of return is common. Do not be discouraged. Networking takes time.

Protecting Your Ideas

As a consultant, you must always be concerned with the issue of ownership. As you learned in previous lessons, any creative work can be copyrighted from the day of creation by the author or creator. As per the Copyright Act of 1976, however, an employer who hires a consultant as work-for-hire owns the copyright if the copyright is within the scope of the project. All derivative works, compilations, and reuse of a copyrighted piece, in whole and often in part, require the permission of the author or copyright holder. You must protect what you create and be cautious of giving away copyrights for what you create.

Up to this point, I have not really defined what a consultant is. Defining whether you are "consulting" with a company is really what determines the authorship, and ultimately right of copyright, of a particular creative work. The outer fringes of the "consultant" definition can become quite gray. In fact, the Supreme Court has stated that no single rule determines whether you are a consultant or employee. In general, anyone who is not a consultant is an employee. You are either one or the other.

In a case of precedence, the Supreme Court established a list of 14 questions that can be used to help determine this issue. Defining what is not consulting is easier than defining what is. I am not a legal expert; I have no law degree, but you can use some simple guidelines to determine whether you are legally considered a consultant or an employee.

You are not consulting if

- [ ] The person hiring you has the right to control the means and the manner in which the product is created.
- [ ] Work performed on the product is conducted at the hiring party's premises, office, or location.
- [ ] Work performed on the product is conducted using the hiring party's software, computers, or equipment.
- [ ] Work performed on the product is required to occur during work hours set by the hiring party.

Ultimately, deciphering whether you are an employee of the hiring party is what determines copyright issues. If you are an employee, all copyrights of creative work generated in the natural course of business belong to the hiring body. No formal documentation is required between an employee and an employer for this to occur. A consultant creating something for a company, however, has much more power over the issue of copyrights. For transfer of copyrights to occur, the scope of the employment must include a description of this transfer in the contract between the consultant and hiring body.

By definition, three rules concern authorship. An author can be defined as

- [ ] The creator of a work
- [ ] The hiring body of the creator of a work when the work is created in the normal course and scope of employment
- [ ] The hiring body who hires an independent contractor by commission or special order

First and foremost, a copyright is held by the person who created the work, so the first type of author who can hold a copyright is the creator of the work. This is not true only when the author of a work is hired by a company with the scope of the project including the copyright to the work. Ownership can also be nullified if the individual is hired as a subcontractor with the scope of the project including the copyright to the work. Both of these cases require the author to sign a work-for-hire agreement. In such an agreement, normally an entire section deals with the scope of the project, defining any and all boundaries and limitations concerning copyrights and use of the work. The work-for-hire agreement also defines other parameters such as pricing, deliverables, and tax issues. I discuss these issues later in this lesson.

7

What defines works that can be copyrighted? Nine different types of commissioned works are specified in the Copyright Act of 1976; they include contributions to collective works, audiovisual works, compilations, supplementary works, translations, instructional text, tests, answer material for tests, and atlases. As a Web developer, you'll most often be faced with the first two.

Individuals contracted to create Web pages or sites must carefully define the scope of any work-for-hire agreements made. A scope of a work-for-hire can include copyright transfer for the graphics on the page as well as the pages themselves. The degree to which copyrights are transferred either increases or decreases cost. If you develop a page or site, giving the copyrights for all associated elements to the hiring body, the price you charge should be higher than if you maintain the copyrights for those elements.

 Note

> If you want to copyright a graphic, page, or other item that can be copyrighted, contact the Copyright Office, Library of Congress, Washington DC 20559 and ask for Form VA.

After a copyright has been established, affixed with a copyright symbol or registered by the author, the copyright lasts for the life of the author plus 50 years. If multiple authors work on a project, the copyright lasts for the life of the last survivor plus 50 years.

Ideas Cannot Be Copyrighted

People sometimes mistakenly believe that they can copyright their ideas. An idea cannot be copyrighted. The only way that you can protect your ideas is through a nondisclosure statement or a patent. A *nondisclosure statement* is a written document that both parties sign recognizing the idea and that the hiring (or consulting) party cannot capitalize on the idea. A patent, on the other hand, is much more detailed and costly.

Professional Conduct

As a consultant, you must always strive to present yourself in a professional manner. Even if you're working out of a home-based office, you must conduct business like any other company or institution. Aside from the most common required business elements such as business cards, stationery, letterheads and such, how can you present your business professionally?

In reality, you can present your company professionally in many ways. In most cases, though, if you boil it all down, the little things kill most consulting businesses. It's not always how well you do the big things such as building Web sites, being able to create graphics, or coding Web pages that count. Realize that I am not belittling technical competence. Your business hinges on these tasks, and likely you can do them well. In most instances, however, how well you do the little things impresses your clientele, makes them want to do business with you, and keeps a good working relationship between consultant and company.

"What little things?" you may be asking. The small things to which I am referring include professional correspondence, organization, and identity. Developing a professional consultancy requires excellence in everything, shown in everything you do—all the way down to e-mail messages and traditional correspondence. In these areas, most consultancies are weak. The individual is the core of the consultancy. Weaknesses in the individual are then inherent in the consultancy. Quick letters that are sent out, that e-mail you just flamed, and the support of a product or project are often done hastily because they are overhead. Consequently, they are often done unprofessionally. Appearance, too, can either help or hinder the consultant's future with a particular company.

For a prime example, look at e-mail, which is an area that most consultants use frequently and don't give much thought to using. As a consultant, you must remember that you are everything in the business. You must write the e-mail, review the e-mail, spell-check the e-mail. More than one e-mail I've received in the professional setting has been filled with spelling errors, atrocious grammar, and the occasional emotional-flame letter. These examples will kill a consultancy. You must strive for excellence in the smallest of things. Even a quick e-mail note you send to a company is judged and contributes to the opinion of your services. Always spell-check your e-mail. Always read it several times before you send it. Critically analyze the tone. You may hastily write e-mail that can present an offensive tone, even when you don't mean to. Sarcasm kills when it comes to e-mail. To help in this area, don't send an e-mail until you've read it at least twice. Reading it three times is even better.

As a professor at a major university, I have read over a hundred résumés, cover letters, and other correspondence written by students and faculty alike. I am amazed at some of the things people put in writing that spoken verbally shock even the writer. Any correspondence you send out should be professional, void of sarcasm, and grammatically correct. Writing may not be your forte; however, you can save yourself much grief by finding someone to review your materials before you send them. If you know no such individual, read your work out loud to yourself. This procedure is incredibly simple, but how many people actually do it? Unfortunately, very few. Nine times out of ten, even if you are a deficient writer, you can catch grammatical errors and unintended tone problems just by simply reading it out loud. Many students and faculty members have entered my office hearing me read materials out loud. It is simple, and to many silly, but it works.

A final statement I have concerning professional conduct is that of organization. Keeping track of materials for your business is vitally important. As your consultancy grows, you must develop a system to maintain not only all the digital elements associated with a project, but

7

also all the various paper documents that go along with it. If you have one or two projects that you are managing or developing, keeping track is pretty easy. But what do you do when you have five, six, even nine projects to manage and maintain? Develop a system for keeping all the materials for a particular project together.

I simply use file folders. When I receive a document related to a project, the first thing I do is place it in the folder. Having to ask a company you're consulting with to resend you something because you lost it is extremely unprofessional. Often frustration is shown just in the asking. Begin organization at the beginning. Bad habits die hard, but so do good ones. Often people who are disorganized with materials get less accomplished. You must do everything you can today to decrease overhead tomorrow.

Getting Clients

The first step to getting clients is creating your promotional piece. You might already have several examples of work that you've done. In actuality, having three or four examples of your work to show a prospective client is good. The key here is to pick only the best examples of what you've done.

To deal with clients who are looking for Web-based materials you must present your promotional piece or pieces in one of two ways. The best way is to show your examples directly online. If you've done work for another company or created a site for them, use some of these materials to sell yourself. Keep in mind, however, that if you did not create the whole site or page, be honest and tell what you actually did in the project. If you created the graphics, claim them. If you did the layout, claim it. If you did the coding, claim it. Be up front about your abilities. You can get around the subject of what you did and what you didn't do by simply saying, "No, I didn't do that part, but I could if given the chance." Honesty goes a long way. I have often run into people who lay claim to work that they really did not take part in, and eventually it shows. The truth often prevails in situations because the proof will eventually be in the resulting product. Just be honest.

The second way of displaying your work is to have it loaded onto a laptop or storage device that you can port with you as you make presentations. Web sites that you design can be run offline with a little tweaking. The optimum is to have a laptop that you can take with you. This way, you are not dependent upon setting up your materials on a prospective client's hardware, which the client will always be leery of on that first meeting. In addition, those first meetings are tense enough without having to troubleshoot why your presentation won't run. It is always best to be in control of your own technical goods rather than to be at the mercy of someone else's.

In meetings with clients, you may not have a link to the Net. Few conference rooms have direct network connections for presentational use. Most of the time, I present my promotional pieces with them running off a laptop. I always take my laptop to do presentations because I can never be assured that the presentation room has a connection to the Internet. Using a laptop also speeds along my presentation because I don't have to wait for the pages to download off the Net. Make a decision beforehand how you will present your materials to the prospective client. First meetings can be taxing enough without having to worry about the technical details of presentation.

When you're presenting to a prospective client, make sure that you specifically define what you do want and do not want to do as a consultant. In other words, don't show examples or describe the things that you don't want to provide for the company. If you don't feel comfortable developing content, such as the text or structure of a company's Web site, acknowledge that fact. If your graphics skills are weak, acknowledge. Sell yourself on your strengths, and acknowledge that you will need assistance in other areas.

As I have performed consulting over the past seven years, I have always strived to do a lot of different things. I have gotten jobs in areas that I knew I could learn but knew I didn't have the skills right at the time. I feel comfortable enough to say that if I cannot do something, I can learn it. As a result, I have done various things in my consultancy, learned a lot, and still made money doing it. If you're starting out and want to be a consultant but don't have a lot of experience, consider taking this approach. When I started my consultancy, I was still an undergraduate student. I approached every job openly and honestly, acknowledging what I could and couldn't do. The prices that I charged reflected how much I knew concerning the project. I was up front with the clients by saying that I had not directly done that type of project before, but I believed I could do it. In addition, I charged less because I knew learning would be involved. Almost every time, the clients accepted my proposals, prices, and honesty. Needless to say, some of the those clients are still my best customers.

My point? If you're starting out, focus on small projects. Take small steps to build your consultancy. Look for projects that you can do, and do them. If you come across a project that requires you to do some learning, take the challenge but let your price reflect the fact that you are a newbie. Be open and honest and acknowledge that you have not done that type of project before, but that you will learn how to do it. Most hiring bodies look at three areas when making consultancy decisions: performance, price, and attitude. You can use the many available jobs as stepping stones to build your consultancy. Remember that a positive attitude goes a long way to help you get these jobs.

Keeping Clients

As your consultancy grows, you must continually strive to satisfy your clients. Often a single-person consultancy can quickly grow to the point of overworking the individual. You have to learn your own limitations and how much work you can feasibly and physically do. Don't bite off more than you can chew. Committing yourself to many different projects is tempting, particularly when word-of-mouth begins to spread about your work. As your consultancy grows, you must manage your time and be careful not to overcommit yourself.

7

At the beginning of your consulting business, you should define where you want to go. How big do you want your business to be? How much do you want to work? If your business grows too fast, you'll find yourself continually behind the eight ball, and your clients will probably begin finding others who aren't so busy. If your business grows too slowly, you might have to begin working for someone else to get a stable income. Take some time early on to decide what you want your consultancy to be, where you want it to go, and how you will know when you get there. Establish a plan of action so that you can grow your consultancy and most important, keep the clients that you have.

The Customer Is ALWAYS Right

One of the quickest ways I know to get rid of clients is by being disagreeable. Again, attitude is everything. Often you'll find that the companies and corporations you consult with do not have a clearly defined solution in mind. Often they know only that they want to create a product with a specific goal. How that goal is reached is often partially based in technical aspects and partially based in opinion. It is the opinion side that often causes problems.

In regards to Web development, the client wants to provide something on the Web. Often, as a consultant, you have to help the client define what he or she will deliver on the Web. In discussions, however, keep in mind that the customer is ultimately right. After a client makes up his or her mind about something that he or she wants, your job is to deliver it. You don't have to agree, but you do have to deliver.

In these situations, you must find a precarious balance between providing your technical expertise and satisfying the customer. The goal in situations in which you, as the consultant, don't agree with particular decisions that are made is to try to get the company to see things your way. Often disagreements or differences of opinion are with a single individual. Proceed cautiously in these situations, and realize that the client is paying. Don't take your clients for granted. There is a point of no return—discussions turn into arguments. Graciously present your point, but allow your client to make the ultimate decision. Then, don't go back and rehash your point of view. After a decision has been made, don't revisit it.

One of the hardest things to learn in any business, particularly in consulting, is that even if you believe the customer is wrong, try to get him or her to come to the conclusion you have made. Present your rationale, but again the ultimate decision is the customer's. Arguments and sarcasm do very little except decrease your creditability and the opportunity for future business.

Payment and Support

Probably one of the most difficult aspects of consulting is pricing the products that you produce. The lines of what to charge for and what not to charge for are sometimes blurry. In general, the only tangible that you can charge a client for is time spent developing a product. But what about resources such as hardware and software you need? And how do you make a reasonable explanation of what you're charging?

The first and foremost concern with payment is being able to come to an agreeable price. You're looking for the client's margin of value. How valuable is the product to the consumer? You must set your prices so that the final product falls into the range the client wants to pay.

Today you can charge for Web development in many different ways. When you're developing pages, you can charge by the page, the hour, or by the project. You may also include support fees for changes requested by that client as well as charges for transfer of copyrights. Ultimately, the prices you charge are determined by the following:

- [ ] The number of pages
- [ ] The number of graphics on those pages
- [ ] The amount of special programming, such as forms, frames, or scripts
- [ ] Multimedia or other special elements
- [ ] Copyrights
- [ ] Turn-around time
- [ ] Maintenance

You also need to be realistic in saying that the price you charge also deals with the current demand on your time and how much you want to do the project. All these factors are used to determine the price for a prospective client.

To establish a price for a client requires you to know accurately what the client wants. Does the client want graphics on every page? Does he or she want special elements that require huge amounts of your time? Does he or she want things for which you don't have skills? Does a structure already exist for the pages, or are you creating the site from scratch? To find out the answers to these questions requires you to listen to the client and to develop a unique solution for his or her problem. Notice the key words here, "to listen."

One of the keys to satisfying a customer is to listen first. Before spewing ideas, making suggestions, or providing inadequate solutions, listen first to understand the client's unique problem. Develop a complete understanding of what he or she wants to do and provide. Develop an understanding for the client's business and how the things you are to create fit into his or her plans. Take a complete and wholehearted interest in the business. Then, you can suggest a solution as well as a price that accurately reflects the situation.

7

Pricing: The Difficult Part

After you understand the client's unique problem, then you can begin providing possible solutions. Providing several solutions that all come to the same end is best. Take the time to discuss the solution with the client. Also, take the time to discuss pricing with the client. Get feedback of whether the solution and price satisfy the customer.

In this situation, you also can be flexible both with the solution and the price. Your client may not know what takes the most work and what takes little work to create. He or she may not know the technical aspects of creating a Web site, page, or media element. That's why the client wants you. If you provide an explanation, you can work with the client to come to some acceptable solution and price.

For example, I had a client who wanted a Web site with several multimedia elements—animations and so on. I quoted a price that was about twice what he wanted (or was able) to pay. But by talking with the client, I was able to explain the technical aspects of creating the Web animations and why the price was higher than expected. Ultimately, we were able to reduce the number of media elements and come to a price that he wanted to pay while still satisfying his problem with a unique solution.

Being an individual consultant, you have the means to be flexible. You don't have a mass of overhead to deal with, so you can much more readily adjust your prices compared to a large business. Be ready to work with the client. Again, your attitude is what provides this malleability. I know some companies that have lost possible clients because they presented one fixed solution and a fixed price. Usually, the client interprets this thinking as "Here's the only solution we'll give you, and this is the price. Take it or leave it." After you show, by example, that you can create a product, the next step is usually a matter of coming to an agreeable price and solution. Doing so requires flexibility. Most clients want to work with you. Do you want to work with the client? Or do you simply say, "Here's my solution and price. Take it or leave it."

I'm not saying that you should simply drop your price just to get a job or that you should work for free. There is a minimum amount that you can do any job for and still come away making money. You must approach a possible job, however, by trying to make a win-win situation. If the price is too low for you to make money, you lose and the company wins; plus you'll probably end up creating something you (and the company) won't like. If you quote a price that is too high and have no flexibility, the company loses in the sense that it cannot pay what you're asking. Again, you lose because you don't get the job. If, however, you strive to work out an arrangement that is win for you (you make money) and win for the company (the price is acceptable), the business arrangement will work out to the advantage of both.

Consistency

In addition to flexibility, consistency is also important. You need to establish a pricing structure according to your strengths and weaknesses. If you're a good code junkie, pricing in this area may be higher. If you're a graphics animal, pricing may be higher in this area. In addition, the jobs that you hate to do may require your learning or subcontracting another individual. All these elements contribute and should remain fairly consistent as you develop a pricing structure for your consultancy.

NOTE

> I have met many young consultants who, for the sake of getting freelance jobs, have done work for free or for such a low amount of money that they were in a losing situation. I never suggest doing a job for free. Due to expectations of consistency, any subsequent jobs done after a "freebie" or low-ball quote can almost be guaranteed to be low-ball as well. Not undercutting yourself is as important as not quoting a job too high.

Long-Term and Short-Term Gains

One thing that many people don't think about when they are pricing is long-term versus short-term gains. Often they overprice the first product proposal for a particular company and lose the opportunity to do work for that company in the future. In actuality, these individuals are losing more than this one-time job. What about all the future projects they could have worked on?

Although you can't really predict these future opportunities, you need to consider this point when you're making quotes on projects. Particularly with Web sites, considering maintenance is important. If you get a job developing a Web site for a company, more than likely it will mean future business from the company, assuming the client is satisfied with your unique solution and wants to continue to invest in the Web site.

You can usually make up short-term losses over a period of time if you do so in a conscientious manner. Ballooning all make-up costs into a second project doesn't work, but distributing the costs over the life of a project does. As you're discussing pricing with clients, keep these points in mind.

7

Support Structures

I've taken a complete lesson in this book to discuss my "methodology" of consulting. I believe that many of you reading this book probably are consultants or want to be consultants in the area of Web development; therefore, I wanted to show you the things that have made me a successful consultant. You can find many books that go into more detail concerning consultancies and small businesses. Many government agencies are set up to help you get started. I have not focused on these elements because resources are out there for you already. Don't hesitate to use the resources that are readily available. Use the information that others have learned instead of reinventing the wheel or learning the hard way.

Growing a Company

Many strong Web development companies are born from consulting ventures. The expansion that is occurring with the Web is creating an entirely new market for those people who want to pursue it as a career. Keep in mind that starting a personal consulting business requires as much effort, time, and energy as starting any other business. In essence, you are growing a business.

Growing Beyond Your Own Abilities

One thing you have to watch as your consulting business grows is overextending yourself. As I discussed previously, you must not bite off more than you can chew. Doing so hurts your reputation and damages your professional relationships. It is best to establish how big you want to grow, how many projects you want to take, and how many hours you want to work prior to reaching that point. Begin with the end in mind. Know where you want to go and how you can get there. You must be able to acknowledge your own limitations and know when and with what you need help.

Dealing with Subcontractors

Dealing with subcontractors can be a touchy issue. Sometimes you may need to hire help on particular parts of a project. Realize that if you do, you must make sure that the scope of your contract with a subcontractor has the same scope as your contract with the main hiring body. If your contract with the hiring body includes copyrights, so must your contract with the subcontractor.

A second issue is that of payment and taxes. If you pay a subcontractor more than $600 in a given year, you are required to file a Form 1099 with the Internal Revenue Service at the end of the year. You send one copy of the form to the government and the other to the subcontractor. Make sure that the subcontractor knows up front that you're reporting this income and that he or she is responsible for his or her own income taxes. You should explicitly state this fact in the contract between you and the subcontractor.

NOTE

> If you're considering hiring subcontractors on an ongoing basis, you may want to consider registering your business and obtaining a federal tax ID number. Doing so often causes the IRS to look very closely at your income taxes. If you use subcontractors only on an as-needed basis, you do not have to get a federal ID number. I suggest acquiring professional accounting or legal advice concerning these matters before proceeding in either direction.

Finally, when you hire subcontractors, you are ultimately responsible to the hiring body for all work you plan to do plus what you hire the subcontractor to do. You must maintain quality control yourself and ensure that the subcontractor is meeting deadlines and the quality expected by the hiring body. For this reason, in addition to the extraneous paperwork, many people stray away from using subcontractors. If you need something specific done, however, and don't have the necessary skills, you may find that subcontracting can be a blessing.

Tax Issues

As a consultant, you should become familiar with the tax laws concerning your consultancy. You must make sure that you protect yourself by paying enough taxes throughout the year so that you don't accrue penalties. Most consultants pay quarterly taxes to satisfy current tax laws. The general rule is that you must pay (during the year) either 90 percent of what you owe for the current year or 100 percent of what you paid the previous year. If you had a return last year, more than likely you can easily match the 100 percent rule. However, I suggest seeking counsel during the first couple of years of your consultancy.

In addition to seeking an accountant's advice, you can find many good software tools that will enable you to maintain and record your tax information easily throughout the year so that you don't get in trouble at the end. I do my own taxes and use an off-the-shelf software package. Many packages not only support small businesses, but also allow for expandability if you decide to incorporate or add partners to your business.

Proposals

Undoubtedly, the most demanding part of getting your first project is writing the proposal. Creating a good proposal requires a great deal of thought and excellent writing skills. After you have a good idea about what the client needs, you can create your proposal, which

7

describes your unique solution to the client's problems and documents how you will create that solution. For this reason, listening to the client is very important. Much of what the client says in the first meetings should end up being part of your proposal.

Most proposals contain clearly defined sections that describe the proposed project solution. A proposal generally contains an abstract, an introduction, a project plan, a budget, and any other related limitations or assumptions for the project to be executed. You also may add miscellaneous sections per a particular solution. You may want to ask the company whether specific formatting guidelines are established for vendor proposals submitted to the company.

Abstract

The first part of the proposal is the abstract. The *abstract* is generally a condensed, to-the-point description of the project. Most often, the abstract highlights all the main points of the project excluding the project price. The abstract should be written concisely. It is often the only portion, aside from the budget, that is read by business executives who are reviewing many proposals for a particular project. When you're writing a proposal, you may find it helpful to write the abstract last so that you know it truly covers the main points of the proposal.

Introduction

The second part of most proposals is an introduction to the project. The *introduction* serves to provide background on why the project is being proposed at all. This section might include information about why the company wants to pursue the particular project and why it is beneficial to do so. Plan to use some of the information that the company representatives used to describe what they wanted to you. The introduction can also briefly establish your interest in providing the company with a solution.

In addition to the background, the introduction is also used to establish your creditability. Several paragraphs can be devoted to describing your prior experience in such matters. In addition, this section may also include references to real examples with samples attached as appendixes to the proposal. Through these paragraphs, you should sell yourself and establish a basis of why you are different, unique, or more qualified to do the project than other proposing companies.

Project Description

The third part of a consulting proposal is the project description. This part of the proposal explicitly describes the solution you want to create for the company. You can set up this part in several ways, but a bulleted list or paragraph form is used most often.

Defining Boundaries

Through the project description, you must define the boundaries for the project. The more descriptive this section is, the better. You should describe what the deliverables are as accurately as possible. Define what will be included in the project and what will not. Also describe whether copyrights will be held by the developer or by the hiring company.

Establishing Support

In the project description, you also should describe the type of support you plan to provide for the product. For a Web site, you should describe what kind of editing, changes, additions, or deletions you will allow during the project's creation. Clients often want to use some type of control or check-off procedure so that they have control over the look and feel of the Web site. You should not disallow changes. However, you do want to limit changes so that you don't get stuck in an endless revision cycle.

Project Plan

After you describe the background for the project and the details concerning the project, you should then describe your methodology for executing the project. Generally, you develop a timeline showing the work to be completed with the deadlines. The timeline can show a weekly or monthly completion schedule. You should probably allow for some flexibility within your timeline—for edits or changes—so plan liberally. It is extremely frustrating to get into the middle of a project and have a client request changes when no time is available. You must appropriate some time for instances in which the client wants specific changes or edits to be made.

Establishing Client Control Mechanisms

To save yourself time, make sure that you define how the company will sign off on what you've done. Requiring a company to approve what you're doing is very important. Most of the time, this approval simply requires your showing a company representative what you're doing and then requesting a signature that he or she likes what you're doing. Again, communication is very important in consulting work. By requiring a company representative to approve your work, you make sure that communication occurs.

Defining Procedures

When you're formalizing the project timeline, make sure that you specify turn-around times on tasks that require a corporate check-off. Generally, turn-around times are set at approximately a week or a little more. The proposal should not only define what the company can expect from you, but also what you expect from the company.

Budget

The final part of the proposal is the budget. Often the budget is broken up into segments based on the timeline. Try to divide the project into logical pieces so that the budget accurately reflects work being done in the time period.

Usually in the budget section, the proposal specifies any money that is required up front to begin working on the project. Requiring approximately one-fourth to one-third of the total project budget up front is customary. This money signifies that the company is genuinely interested in the project. If the project is later canceled, which happens from time to time, you usually keep money provided up front. If more work has been done, worth greater than the advance, the company usually compensates you for the difference.

One of the things you may want to add into your budget is a contingency. A *contingency* is money set aside for any unforeseen costs. Without it, as the consultant, you would bear the burden of the costs. At the end of the project, contingency money that you don't use remains the property of the hiring body. Most contingencies are set as a percentage of the total project budget. Requiring a 10 percent contingency is customary.

Contracts

The last item for discussion concerning professional consulting is contracts. Most of the contracts you will sign and review as a consultant will be a work-for-hire agreements. Most companies use standard work-for-hire agreements. In reality, these types of documents have many parts, so I'll highlight them here. As with any legal documents, you may want to have an attorney review the documents. You must carefully review work-for-hire agreements to know both your requirements and the requirements placed on the hiring body.

Although work-for-hire agreements may have varying sections from company to company and from project to project, you should look for six basic elements: the contracting bodies, length of term, pricing, timeline, description of deliverables, and limitations and scope of the employment.

Contracting Bodies

The contracting bodies are usually established within the opening segments of the contract. Often this part of the contract establishes not only names but also places of business. Contracts commonly note specific individuals who will be the point of contact for each party.

7

Length of Term

A contract often includes a limit or length of term that describes the current date versus the preferable length of the employment. If you're planning to provide ongoing service to a company's Web site or pages, this section should describe how long the contract is valid and how long services will be rendered.

Pricing

Pricing within a contract is normally stated in regards to the timeline and check-off dates. Often milestone submissions mark times in which you are paid. At other times, an entirely different structure may be established according to corporate guidelines or precedence.

Timeline and Check-Off Dates

The timeline and check-off dates are established in conjunction with those established within the consultant's proposal. Aside from simply listing these dates, the document normally specifies what happens if the target dates are not met.

Deliverables

Sometimes attached as a schedule on the end of the contract, an entire section of the contract is devoted to describing the project at length. The deliverables section should be as constricting and defined as possible. A vague deliverables section can hurt both the consultant and the hiring body.

Limitations and Scope

The last part of a contract or work-for-hire agreement is the limitations and scope of the project. Here assumptions, copyright issues, and other related matters are defined in writing. Any peculiar or situational items are noted for the contracting bodies.

Summary

In this lesson, you looked at many of the various aspects of professional consulting. I focused on a philosophy of consulting as well as related issues. You saw both the positive and negative aspects of being your own boss. Many people may believe that consulting is easy; however, being the accountant, marketer, producer, production specialist, and human services specialist all wrapped into one person is very demanding. You must become versed in all these areas to be an effective consultant, but many tools and resources are available to help you accomplish these goals.

7

Today you also looked at copyright issues as well as the fine line between distinguishing an employee from a consultant. You learned how to effectively begin creating networks of business relationships that will ultimately help your professional consultancy. As I said, networking is everything. In addition to finding those contacts, you learned ways in which you can keep those contacts, which is much more difficult than finding them. Keep in mind that the client is always right. Present the client with your technical expertise and let him or her make the decisions. I concluded this lesson with a discussion of both proposals and contracts and what you should be looking for in each.

Q&A

Q **As a consultant, I want to find software tools that will decrease the time I spend managing my business and taking care of overhead items. What are the main things I should look for in this type of software?**

A In general, you should be looking for the following in financial or accountant-type software:

- ☐ Multifunction capability
- ☐ Expandability
- ☐ Compatibility with other software programs
- ☐ Cross-platform compatibility
- ☐ Hardware requirements
- ☐ Whether it is CD-ROM based
- ☐ Who the publisher is

Q **I have an idea for a new way of distributing Web pages. Should I copyright my idea?**

A Ideas cannot be copyrighted. The only way to protect your ideas is through the use of nondisclosure agreements or a patent.

Q **Concerning copyrights, the main thing I need to determine is whether I am an employee or a consultant to a particular company. How do I determine this?**

A The U.S. Supreme Court established a precedence that states that a single measure does not determine whether you are an employee or a consultant. However, the court established a series of questions that you can use to help determine the answer. The following are some of the questions:

- ☐ Does the company control the manner in which the product is created? Does the company control the means that are used to create it?
- ☐ Does the work have to be done at the company's location or premises?

☐ Is work performed using the company's hardware or software?

☐ Is work required to be done at a specific time of day?

If you answer "yes" to more than one of these questions, then you can be considered an employee and not a consultant.

Q **An author is an individual who holds a copyright for a creative work. Who can be defined as an author?**

A First and foremost, the person who creates the work is deemed as the author. However, two variations may change the issue of authorship. If an employee of a company creates a creative work in the line of duty for the company, the copyright becomes the property of the company. If a creative work is created by an individual for a company, with the scope of the project including transfer of copyrights (through a contract or work-for-hire agreement), then the copyright becomes the property of the hiring body.

Q **To copyright a creative work, don't I have to register it through the U.S. Copyright Office?**

A A creative work is the property of the creator from the day of creation. Simply attaching a copyright signature (Copyright 1997, John Doe) protects the work under "intent to copyright" without officially registering it through the U.S. Copyright Office.

Workshop

The Workshop provides quiz questions to help you solidify your understanding of the material covered and exercises to give you experience in using what you've learned. The quiz answers are provided in Appendix A, "Quiz Answers." Try to understand the quiz answers before you go on to tomorrow's lesson.

Quiz

1. What is the difference between a copyright and a patent?

2. What are the different types of commissioned works defined by the Supreme Court?

3. What are the various factors to consider when deciding what to charge for your services?

4. When you're creating a project budget, how do long- and short-term gains affect your final decisions?

5. If you hire a subcontractor, with what issues do you need to be concerned?

7

6. What are the main parts of a proposal?

7. What are the main parts of a contract or work-for-hire agreement?

8. When you're striving to consult with a particular company, how do you achieve a win-win relationship?

Exercise

Look at the various things that you have created or plan to create. What would make an impressive promotional piece? How would you use it in a demonstration setting? If you plan to pursue professional consulting, begin assembling the resources you need. Begin developing a contact list and promotional items. Take the small steps today to enable you to be a better Web consultant tomorrow.

WEEK 1

In Review

Week 1 showed you the various hats that a Webmaster wears. Indeed, the range of skills and breadth of knowledge is wide. You learned that many institutions have more than one person who creates and maintains a corporate Web site. However, there will almost always be one individual assigned to manage the entire group—the lead Webmaster. Undoubtedly, that person will have many of the skills and knowledge described in the first seven days of this text.

Day 1, "The Webmaster: Jack of All Trades"

Day 1 showed you a quick overview of the various hats that a Webmaster must wear. You learned that the Webmaster is more than just an individual who knows how to program a Web page using the HTML language. Indeed, the tasks that the Webmaster must be able to perform are varied; the Webmaster must be able to competently use the Internet and its vast resources and also be able to manage all the various resources involved in developing today's massive Web sites. Being able to master the technology, technique, and maintenance of a Web site is the core of a Webmaster's responsibility.

In addition to the Webmaster's responsibilities, you also learned from where the Internet has come and where it might be going. You learned that the Web is a natural outgrowth of the Internet but that the conceptualization of it occurred much earlier. In 1965, Ted Nelson helped define the non-proprietary system that would enable communication through hypertext and hypermedia. Not allowing the vision to die, many other individuals made significant contributions to the multiprotocol, universal computer communication scheme. After nearly 30 years, what was conceived finally became a reality.

At the end of the lesson you learned the various Internet services you can use for Internet communications, including the World Wide Web, FTP, Gopher, Telnet, and news. Each of these technologies enables specific communication to occur, and each has its own advantages and disadvantages. Each of these builds upon the other from the early days of e-mail to what we now know and enjoy on the World Wide Web.

Day 2, "The Internet Specialist"

Day 2 began with a look at the real-time Web interpreter called the browser. You looked at the browser's internal and external functioning. Externally looking at the user interface and its work area, you learned how the browser downloads and composites pages on the fly as each element is retrieved from a remote Web server. You also got a behind-the-scenes look at what is happening at the software level when this occurs. Remember that every item retrieved from the Web server is stored on your local machine. You also learned the definition of all the various aspects of the Web browser, including the preferences, plug-ins, scripting, embedded programs, and helper applications.

Day 3, "The Information Design Specialist"

On Day 3, you learned the overall communication process from a global standpoint. When you have something you want to communicate, how do you design and develop a Web site that communicates your message efficiently and effectively? This lesson walked you through the process used to create many well-designed sites and communication tools.

You learned how planning is the biggest key to creating an effective Web site. Looking at the content, audience, development, and delivery systems is key to providing content that is audience centered and can be delivered to their computers. The audience is the most critical aspect of delivering content. As any good presenter knows, you must make the content relevant and interesting to the audience, and to do that you must put yourself in their shoes and look from their vantage point.

After you have analyzed these various elements you then can develop a goal statement, objectives, and abstract for your site. These documents become critical documentation for the choices you made during the analysis. They can be used to bring new people on the development team up to speed, as well as justify your decision-making process to supervisors and overseers.

Designing a site that communicates effectively also includes the visual aspect of the site. In addition, the navigability of your site depends upon the interface you use. Metaphors and interfaces must complement and complete the content provided at your site. A strong correlation between the two will help your audience overcome the navigation of your site to focus on what they really came for: your information. You want to provide the easiest means possible for your audience to get at the information. Many a site is dodged because the audience is not able to find what they are looking for.

When you have planned all the physical attributes of the site, you must make decisions about the layout of your site and how you will arrange all of the files and directories on your server. Developing a scheme for arranging and laying out your files on your Web server is extremely important. Files simply strewn on a server make maintenance more a task of memory than of management.

Day 4, "The Media Designer"

On Day 4, you began to get a feel for the graphics delivered at a Web site and how important they are. You learned the delicate balance between graphics, content, and your audience's opinion of your Web site. A Web site with rich graphics and not much content has very little to say. A site with too few graphics and too much content can ultimately bore the audience to death. There is a definite advantage to creating visually appealing graphics and effectively using them at your site.

Page layout is an important part of designing effective Web pages. In this lesson you learned that there are many elements that contribute to this overall effectiveness. Negative space, positive space, consistency, visual appeal, typefonts, graphics, and multimedia elements all contribute to effective communication via Web pages.

Dealing with fonts is much more than just defining a style tag and letting it go. Various font sizes, styles, and types affect the visual appeal of the page. You learned that the two main types of fonts are defined by whether they have serifs, or small feet and tails. Fonts with serifs are called serif fonts. Fonts without serifs are called sans serif fonts. Serif fonts are generally used for body and small text, whereas sans serif fonts are used for headlines and large bodies of text such as titles and subtitles. Effectively choosing typefonts will directly affect the visual appeal of your page.

In addition to fonts, you also learned how color affects the visual aspect of the page. Many studies have been executed to determine both the aesthetic and psychological effects of colors on personal interpretation. Remember that color can be used symbolically, but transcending cultural boundaries can generate different interpretations because our interpretation of color is based on our experience and not an inherent behavior or existing attribute.

The lesson ended with a look at the two main types of graphics, vector and raster, and some of the various characteristics of each. You also learned the various graphics file formats that can be found on the Web, as well as the major differences between them.

Day 5: "The Technical Designer"

On Day 5, you looked at the various hardware concerns you will have when you connect to the Internet. Looking at the basic networking models, you learned that the entire Internet system is based upon the client/server model.

The biggest concern in developing pages is how fast the pages and information will be delivered to your audience. Their connection to the Internet, as well as your server's connection, determine this speed. You learned that there are three predominant ways in which users can be connected to the Internet. These include direct network connection, dial-up connection, and dial-up access. Direct network connection is the fastest, and dial-up access is the slowest.

Connecting your server to the Internet is also a contributor to the speed at which your pages are provided to your audience. The faster your computer and connection, the faster your pages will be sent out on the Net. In this lesson, you learned several different ways to connect your server to the Internet, including ISDN, T1, frame relay, and Switched Multimegabit Data Service (SMDS), as well as other services such as cable and satellite links. Regardless of the service, you learned that the Internet is based entirely on the TCP/IP protocol.

In this lesson, you also learned the various options you have when you choose a machine, which include either a PC or workstations. You learned the various attributes of each type of machine and how they affect performance.

Day 6, "The Technical Manager"

On Day 6, you learned the management functions that a Webmaster must perform. Managing software and hardware are the two biggest functions, but also involved are the various individuals involved in Webmastering groups. People cannot be managed like software and hardware; people must be supported, coached, and encouraged. Managing people as if they were resources will result in a less effective group.

Day 7, "The Professional Consultant"

On Day 7, you learned the professional consulting side of Webmastering. Many individuals are pursuing their dream of owning their own businesses. Although this sounds like a wonderful career, you learned that there are some negative aspects of consulting. The two biggest involve the resources and the motivation of the individual. The single consultant must manage all aspects of the business, not just the production of Web sites. To do so requires a vast number of skills, some of which the individual might not have. The consultant must acquire skills and resources to equip himself with the necessary business skills to manage the consulting practice.

This lesson also looked at the issue of copyrights and how they are established. The biggest copyright determiner for the consultant is whether or not he is legally considered an employee or a consultant. This lesson noted several questions established by the Supreme Court to decide this issue. Remember that there is not a single rule that determines whether or not you are a consultant or employee.

Throughout this lesson, I presented a basic philosophy of consulting with which I have been successful. Keep in mind that this is not an absolute philosophy. Different circumstances require a different philosophy. However, if you use what is presented in this lesson as a rule of thumb, you will be successful.

Concluding this lesson is a discussion of the various parts of a consultant's proposal. A proposal should contain the major features highlighted in this section. They include an abstract, introduction, description, project plan, and budget.

WEEK
2

At a Glance

This week focuses on the particulars of developing Web pages and coding them in HTML. Undoubtedly, this is what most people think of when they hear the term Webmaster—someone who knows HTML. As you will have already seen, there is much more to the proverbial Webmaster, but HTML programming and utilization of other Web languages and features are important as well.

8

9

10

11

12

13

14

Day 8

Introduction to HTML and Block Tags

As you learned on Day 1, "The Webmaster: Jack of All Trades," the HyperText Markup Language (HTML) is a subset or derivative of Standard Generalized Markup Language (SGML). Created by Tim Berners-Lee in 1989, it was, and still is, based on SGML. For a comprehensive description of SGML, refer to the International Standard ISO 8879 or check the World Wide Web Consortium's Web site at http://www.w3.org.

NEW TERM *SGML* or *Standard Generalized Markup Language* is a system for defining structured documents that can be ported from one machine to another without having to deal with extraneous hardware and software issues.

The idea behind SGML was to use embedded code tags to describe all the elements of a particular document or program. The code tags do not make specific references to elements that are inherent to any machine or platform. Due to this, the file can be offloaded to any other machine, read, and displayed. The SGML language was designed to create portable, independent documents and programs that could outlast any particular machine, operating system, or application.

The Origins of HTML

HTML does not include all of the various elements of the SGML language. It is actually much simpler. It also includes one other significant feature: the capability to utilize hypertext. Basic hypertext environments, such as the Windows Help menu, are not new; most people use them on a day-to-day basis. However, the ability to create our own hypertext environment is powerful and unique.

When HTML was first introduced, it had relatively few tags; the first version had as few as 30 tags that could be used to define a document. When version 2.0 of the HTML language was adopted and introduced, it provided many more tags and attributes that could be used to define and create a viewable document.

Today we are quickly approaching version 3.2 of the HTML language. This book introduces some of the new features in the language—ones that have been added since HTML 2.0. However, at the time of this writing, the specifications for HTML 3.2 have yet to be ratified by the W3C, and some minor things might change later. Currently, Netscape and Explorer support HTML 3.0 extensions. If you are interested in checking out the latest developments in the language, check out Yahoo!'s information at `http://www.yahoo.com/Computers_and_Internet/Software/Data_Formats/HTML/` or go directly to the World Wide Web Consortium at `http://www.w3.org/pub/WWW/`.

SGML

Although SGML sometimes is overshadowed by HTML, it still is in wide use today. It often is used in documents that utilize complex search engines and text manipulation schemes. Often it is associated with large catalogs, digital dictionaries, and encyclopedias in which the capability to utilize the text of the document is extremely important. SGML also can be used in high-end multimedia programs and applications.

The Browser Defines Style

As you begin to pick up the basics of the HTML language, keep in mind that you are creating a semantic definition of a document; it is not a fixed layout. Remember that the actual compositing of text, graphics, and multimedia elements is as much a result of the browser and platform as it is of the HTML code itself. As you have already learned, the platform and browser can drastically affect what is laid out and viewed on a computer screen.

8

Editors

Currently, there are several ways to create HTML documents. Because HTML files are simple ASCII text, you can use any ASCII text editor to generate HTML files. There also are several new commercial tools available that enable you to create Web-based documents from existing documents from Microsoft Word and Adobe PageMaker. Generator applications such as Microsoft FrontPage, Adobe PageMill, and Macromedia Backstage Designer enable you to create entire sites from scratch in a visual fashion rather than by direct coding. The following sections refer to programs such as Microsoft FrontPage and Adobe PageMill as *generators.*

Text-Based Editors

One of the best ways to learn the HTML language is by using a simple text editor. By forcing yourself to enter code manually, you learn much more about the programming style than through the use of an HTML generator application. I often prefer to use a text editor over a generator because I have more control. I suggest using a text editor such as Microsoft Word or Windows Wordpad or Notepad (see Figure 8.1) as you begin learning the language.

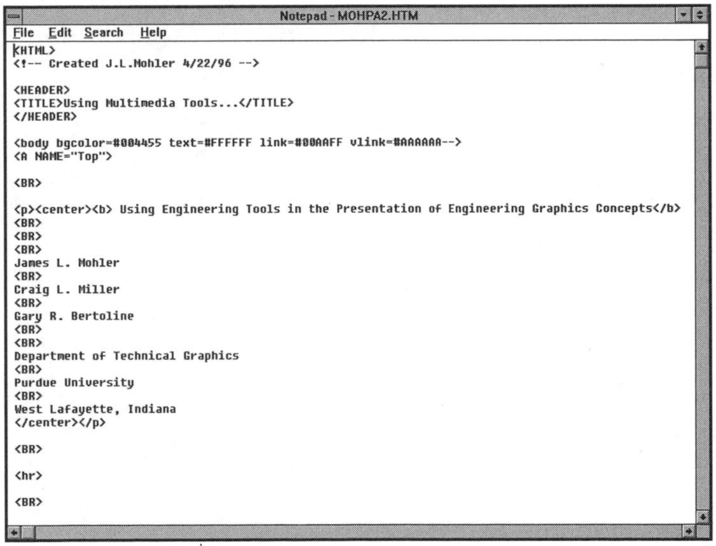


```
<HTML>
<!-- Created J.L.Mohler 4/22/96 -->

<HEADER>
<TITLE>Using Multimedia Tools...</TITLE>
</HEADER>

<body bgcolor=#004455 text=#FFFFFF link=#00AAFF vlink=#AAAAAA-->
<A NAME="Top">

<BR>

<p><center><b> Using Engineering Tools in the Presentation of Engineering Graphics Concepts</b>
<BR>
<BR>
<BR>
James L. Mohler
<BR>
Craig L. Miller
<BR>
Gary R. Bertoline
<BR>
<BR>
Department of Technical Graphics
<BR>
Purdue University
<BR>
West Lafayette, Indiana
</center></p>

<BR>

<hr>

<BR>
```

Figure 8.1.
Using a text editor to pound in the code.

I believe that to be a good Webmaster you must have a very firm knowledge of the HTML language. I am amazed at the number of people who use quick and dirty generator tools and then complain because they cannot fix the problems that generators sometime cause. It is extremely important to have a very good working knowledge of the structure and execution of the HTML. Using a text editor to create your code is the best way to learn the fundamentals of Web page creation. In addition, there are several HTML editors that make entering the HTML code much easier.

WYSIWYG Tools

Over the past year, many applications have been created that enable a person with little knowledge of the HTML language to create HTML pages and Web sites as shown in Figure 8.2. Microsoft's FrontPage application makes managing and creating a Web site a visual rather than code process. However, with all of these tools, knowledge of HTML programming is still required. Often, you'll want to do something that you've seen on the Web but can't get your generator to perform. Maybe it's a special frame setup or form and your generator can't create it. So what do you do?

Figure 8.2.

*Using Microsoft
FrontPage to create
a Web site.*

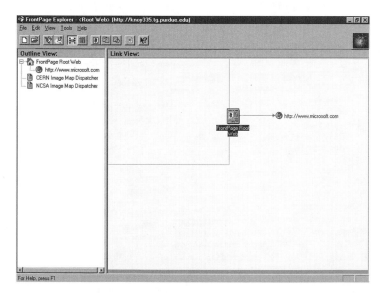

You should make learning the language a prerequisite to buying a code generator such as FrontPage or PageMill. Sure, after you understand how to generate hard code, generators are very handy, but you must first understand the code that the generator creates. The problem with getting a generator and learning HTML from it is that generators often add browser-specific HTML tags or "junk" codes that aren't defined. Often it can be difficult, even for experienced HTML junkies, to decipher HTML code from a generator.

In addition, many of the code generators still have problems creating specific items. Ultimately you will have to learn the language because there are still things that you cannot effectively or efficiently pull off with these programs. Learn the language, you can do anything the language supports. Learn a generator, and all you can do is what the generator supports. This doesn't mean you have to memorize every style tag or attribute, but you should know the basics of HTML code so that you can fix any problems that arise as well as create code structures that some generators don't support.

Tags and Attributes

The HTML language uses primary code words to define different elements within a document. These primary code words are called *tags*. In addition, each tag can have its own settings or parameters, which are called *attributes*. You can identify tags in HTML code by looking for the carrots (< >) that surround them. HTML tags almost always appear in pairs such as <H1>...</H1>.

For example, in Figure 8.3 you see an example of a simple Web page. You can use the heading tag, <H1> (shown in boldface), to create a line of text that says, "Technical Graphics." The tag is actually <H1>. However, notice the words ALIGN=LEFT inserted into the tag. In addition to simply placing the text on the page, the line of text can be left-, right-, or center-justified using the heading tag's ALIGN attribute. The default for alignment is left justification. Here ALIGN=LEFT has been inserted to show you how to use the attribute inside the <H1> tag, although the text would default to ALIGN=LEFT without including this attribute. Therefore, the line of code shows

```
<H1 ALIGN=LEFT>Technical Graphics </H1>
```

Figure 8.3.
*HTML coding
showing tags
and attributes.*

```
<!DOCTYPE "HTML 3.2//EN">
<HTML>
    <HEAD>
        <TITLE>What is Technical Graphics?</TITLE>
    </HEAD>
    <BODY>
        <H1 ALIGN=LEFT> Technical Graphics </H1>
    </BODY>
</HTML>
```

NOTE

Tags and attributes are not case sensitive. It does not matter whether you enter tags in uppercase or lowercase, but you should be consistent. Use either all caps (as in the examples), or all lowercase to make it easier to read.

This is how tags and attributes are used. The attribute ALIGN=LEFT is a setting for the tag <H1>. The attribute is inserted right into the tag. The tag will use the defaults for its attributes if you don't include attributes in the tag.

In reality, the text that is displayed (Technical Graphics) could also be called an attribute of the tag <H1>. Figure 8.4 shows how the page displays in the browser.

Figure 8.4.

Tags and attributes shown using Netscape's Document Source option.

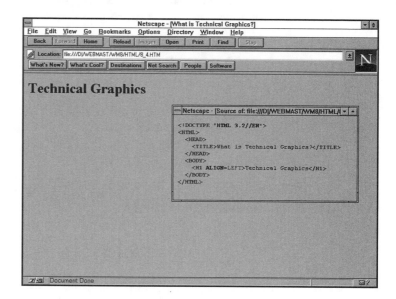

NEW TERM *Tags* are the main or primary HTML code words; *attributes* are settings or optional parameters for those tags.

There are many tags, or code words, in the HTML language. Much like any other programming language, such as BASIC or Pascal, there are many code words so that you can do many different things. In addition, each code word has its own options, or attributes. As you can see in Figure 8.5, there are many different tags, and each tag has specific attributes that can be used with it.

NOTE With a little digging, you will find that for many of the HTML tags there are more attributes than what are presented in this book. The attributes that are omitted here are not supported by Navigator and Explorer, which are the two most popular browsers. Likely you will not want to use them for this reason; however, a comprehensive quick reference is included in Appendix B, "HTML 3.2 Reference."

Figure 8.5.

There are many different tags, each with its own attributes.

```
<!DOCTYPE "HTML 3.2//EN">
<!-- Created J.L.Mohler 11/12/96 -->
    <HTML>
    <HEAD>
        <TITLE>Technical Graphics 217 Lab Assignments</TITLE>
    </HEAD>
        <BODY TEXT="#000000" bgcolor="#FFFFFF" vlink="#FF0000"
        ➥ALINK="#FF0000">
        <HR>
        <IMG SRC="gear.gif" BORDER=0 ALIGN=RIGHT>
        <H4>Department of Technical Graphics</H4>
        <H1>TG 217 Drawing Systems</H1>
        <H3>Lab Assignments</H3>
        <UL>
            <LI><A HREF="index.html">Course Description</A></LI>
            <LI><a HREF="217_lay.html">Weekly Layout </A></LI>
            <LI><a HREF="217_ske.html">Sketching </A></LI>
        </UL>
    </BODY>
    </HTML>
```

NOTE

If you use Navigator 2.0 or later, accessing the Document Source option under the Edit menu will show you a color-coded version of the page currently in the browser. The colors will be different for tags and attributes, enabling you to visually distinguish tags from attributes.

Syntax

Now take a minute to learn about syntax, the basic rules of speech for the HTML language. As an HTML programmer, probably one of the most frustrating things is to program a page and have errors crop up because you typed the wrong character. Searching a page for a single typographical error is a pain, but it is the nature of the beast.

As you learned earlier, each tag can be identified by the carrots that surround it such as <H1> or <LI>. Each tag has both internal attributes, such as the ALIGN=RIGHT option you saw previously, as well as external attributes such as <H1> Technical Graphics </H1>, where Technical Graphics is the external attribute. You must be sure that each tag you enter begins properly and ends properly. Note that the line starts with <H1> and ends with </H1>. Usually the ending tag causes problems—if you forget to add it—but misspellings and unintentional characters will also cause problems. When a page does not appear correctly in a browser, check for typographical errors and tags that are left open.

NOTE

Several of the tags in the HTML language do not need a closing tag such as </H1>. However, you'll find that many require it. To make life simpler, get in the habit of closing every tag. Remembering those that need to be closed and those that can remain open will become difficult. For simplicity's sake, close them all.

In addition to spelling and unintentional characters, realize that the HTML language does not recognize concurrent spaces. A double space (concurrent space) in a line of text will appear in a displayed document as a single space. The same is true of extraneous spacing in a document. The browser will ignore all extraneous spaces in a Web document. In the previous example (Figure 8.5), the browser ignores the indenting at the beginning of the lines as well as between lines of code. They are shown this way in the examples to make them easier to read; however, the browser will ignore the indenting.

Comments

In any programming language, it is customary and recommended to add internal documentation to the code that you crank out. Often, you can use internal documentation to help find certain lines of code as well as to insert special comments or information for people who might be reviewing your HTML code.

The HTML language includes a special tag that enables you to insert comment lines within the HTML files you create. A comment line is a line that is ignored by the browser or other interpreting program. Comment lines are used to insert programmer comments or descriptions of what certain portions of the code do. A comment line begins with <!-- and ends with -->. Figure 8.5 includes a comment line that looks like the following:

```
<!-- Created J.L.Mohler 11/12/96 -->
```

This comment line shows the creator and date. It's always a good idea to include a comment line such as this so that you know the last date the file was modified as well as who created it. You might want to use comment lines throughout the document to help you remember what does what in the code.

8

Resources

There are many different resources on the Web that provide a lot of information on HTML programming. If you would like more information, exercises, and examples on HTML coding beyond what is covered in this book, you might want to check out the following sites:

- [ ] http://members.aol.com/teachemath/class.htm
- [ ] http://www.woodhill.co.uk/html/html.htm
- [ ] http://www.book.uci.edu/Staff/StyleGuide.html
- [ ] http://www.interlink-2000.com/guide-to-publishing-html.html
- [ ] http://www.emerson.emory.edu/services/html/html.html
- [ ] http://www.mcp.com/general/workshop/
- [ ] http://www.sirius.com/~paulus/html30.html

To find more information about HTML, check out the following books from Sams.net Publishing:

- [ ] *Teach Yourself Web Publishing with HTML 3.2 in 14 Days, Professional Reference Edition*, by Laura Lemay
- [ ] *HTML 3.2 and CGI Unleashed, Professional Reference Edition*, by John December and Mark Ginsberg

NOTE

> Don't forget that you have one of the best HTML resources connected right to your computer. If you are having trouble coding a page and you know how you want it to look, surf the Web and find a page that looks like what you are trying to generate. Most browsers enable you to view the source code using the Document Source or Source option. One of the best ways to learn good programming skills is to look at code that has already been created by an experienced programmer.

Basic Structure

Every HTML document has the same general structure—even pages that use complex scripts and multimedia elements. With the advent of HTML 3.2 there have been many tag and attribute additions to the language, but the overall structure is still the same. The primary parts of an HTML document are denoted by the <DOCTYPE>, <HTML>, <HEAD>, and <BODY> tags. Each of these tags is known as a document structure tag. They define and delimit the major portions or sections of the HTML document.

 Document structure tags are the HTML tags that define and delimit the major portions or sections of the HTML document. They are the tags necessary in order for a viewing program to properly interpret the HTML file.

 NOTE

Although version 3.2 of the HTML language has new tags and attributes, keep in mind that the browsers many people are currently using might not support every new or existing feature. Just because the HTML language enables a tag to be used does not mean that all browsers support the new tags. This doesn't mean you can't use these tags, but it does mean that the new tags and attributes won't have any effect when viewed in older browsers. In addition, you must be careful because some of the new tags can cause adverse effects when viewed through an older browser. Again, test your pages using your target audience's browser to be sure the tags are supported.

The <DOCTYPE> Element

The first line that should be included in any HTML document is the <DOCTYPE> tag.

The <DOCTYPE> Tag

The <DOCTYPE> tag specifies what version of HTML is being used and to what governing body and specification the document conforms.

For example, the simplest <DOCTYPE> line can look like

```
<!DOCTYPE "HTML 3.2//EN">
```

This line simply says that the file is an HTML 3.2 file. Another <DOCTYPE> line might look like

```
<!DOCTYPE HTML PUBLIC "-//W3C//DTD HTML 3.2//EN">
```

This line says that the document uses the HTML 3.2 document type definition (DTD) developed by the World Wide Web Consortium.

8

You will find that many people do not use the <DOCTYPE> tag in their HTML pages. In fact, you don't have to use it for the page to load properly. However, it is recommended, even specified as mandatory by the W3C, that you use the <DOCTYPE> tag because many older browsers will check for this line to see whether the file can be displayed properly.

HTML Elements

In order for the browser to open the HTML file, it must be told that the file actually is an HTML file. You can do this within the document by marking the beginning of the file with the <HTML> tag and the end of the file with the </HTML> closing tag. The <HTML> tag marks the beginning of the file, and the </HTML> closing tag marks the end of the file. All HTML files must have these tags to work properly. All other tags, excluding the <DOCTYPE> tag, must reside within the <HTML>...</HTML> tags.

> **The <HTML> Tags**
>
> The <HTML>...</HTML> tags mark the beginning and the end of the HTML file.

The <HTML>...</HTML> section of the document is divided into two different sections. Like most digital files, the first part is called the header or head. This section is marked by the opening and closing <HEAD>...</HEAD> tags. The second part of the HTML section is the body, which holds the actual description of the elements to be shown in the browser work area. The body is marked by the <BODY>...</BODY> tags.

<HEAD> Elements

The header section of an HTML document describes the various characteristics of the document itself. Much like the items on the cover of a book or the heading of a letter, the header section describes several specific attributes of the HTML document.

> **The <HEAD> Tags**
>
> The <HEAD>...</HEAD> tags are used to define specific document parameters and characteristics. Valid tags within the <HEAD>...</HEAD> tags include TITLE, ISINDEX, BASE, STYLE, SCRIPT, META, and LINK.

Probably the most widely used tag in the <HEAD>...</HEAD> section is the <TITLE> tag. This particular tag is required for the document to load properly and is the only one that is displayed in the browser. All other tags specified in the <HEAD>...</HEAD> section are not displayed in the browser's work area.

> **The <TITLE> Tags**
>
> The <TITLE>...</TITLE> tags are used to define the short title line that is displayed in the browser's title bar.

Two things must be noted about the <TITLE> tag. Make sure the length of your title doesn't exceed 60 characters. As with any application, the number of characters that can be displayed in the title bar is limited. Excess characters will cause the title to be truncated.

You also want to make sure that the title line is descriptive of your page. Many Web site search engines use the data contained in the title to conduct searches. Using a title such as My Homepage will mean very little to a search engine that operates this way. Use descriptive titles to describe your pages.

The <TITLE> tag, as well as the other tags that can be used in the header section, must be completely contained within the <HEAD>...</HEAD> tags. Misplaced tags can cause unexpected results.

In addition to the <TITLE> tag, the other tags that can be used in the header section are

- ☐ <ISINDEX>—Used for simple keyword searches.
- ☐ <BASE>—Defines an absolute URL to use for relative URL links.
- ☐ <STYLE>—Established for use with style sheets.
- ☐ <SCRIPT>—Reserved for use with scripting languages.
- ☐ <META>—Used to supply information that cannot be supplied anywhere else in the document.
- ☐ <LINK>—Used to define the independent relationships of the current page with other documents in the Web structure.

NOTE

You will see some of these header tags used in other sections of the book. The only one you need to be concerned with of right now is the <TITLE> tag.

Body Elements

Finally, you come to the meat and potatoes of the HTML document. The second part of the HTML file, which is contained within the `<HTML>...</HTML>` limiters and right after the `</HEAD>` tag, is the `<BODY>...</BODY>` tags. This section houses all of the instructions for laying out the HTML document.

The `<BODY>` Tags

The `<BODY>...</BODY>` section defines the actual instructions for laying out graphics, text, multimedia, and other elements in the browser's work area.

The `<BODY>` tag has several attributes, or settings, for the various items that occur within the body. You use attributes within the `<BODY>` tag to set the background color, to establish a tiling background image, or to set the color of various text elements. The attributes that can be used within the `<BODY>` tag itself include the following:

- [ ] `BGCOLOR="color"`—Defines a background color for your Web document, where *color* is replaced with a hexadecimal color value.

- [ ] `TEXT="color"`—Defines the color of your document's normal text, where *color* is replaced with a hexadecimal color value.

- [ ] `LINK="color"`—Defines the color to be used for links you haven't visited, where *color* is replaced with a hexadecimal color value.

- [ ] `VLINK="color"`—Defines the color to be used for links you have visited, where *color* is replaced with a hexadecimal color value.

- [ ] `ALINK="color"`—Defines the highlight color used when you click on a link, where *color* is replaced with a hexadecimal color value.

- [ ] `BACKGROUND="myimage.gif"`—Defines an image to be tiled across your document's background.

NOTE

An exception to the basic HTML file structure is the use of frames in the Web page. Whenever you use frames in a Web document, the `<FRAMESET>` tag will replace the body section of the document. First, read through the rest of today's lesson and then see Day 12, "Using Frames To Format Pages" for more information on this tag.

Now that you've examined the basic structure of a Web document, look at an example showing them in use. In Figure 8.6, compare the code sample to what is displayed in the browser. Note the first line, which identifies which version of HTML is being used. Note the definition of the start and end of the HTML document using the <HTML>...</HTML> tags. Notice also that the HTML section is divided into the header and body sections. The header section, marked by <HEAD>...</HEAD>, contains a title shown in the title bar, and the body section contains a heading and paragraph of text. In the body, we have also modified some of the characteristics of the document by using some of the body attributes. All HTML documents will conform to this basic structure.

Figure 8.6.

The basic HTML document structure.

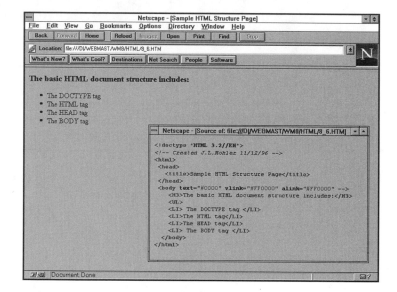

Body Tags

Most of the tags that you will use in your documents will be contained within the <BODY> section of your documents. This makes sense, because all of the data in this section composes what you see in the browser's work area. All of the body elements can be further subdivided based on what they actually enable you to define in the HTML file.

The two types of tags that occur within the body of the HTML file are block tags and text tags. A single document usually will contain an intermixed number of block and text tags. Both can be used simultaneously. The biggest distinguishing characteristic is that block tags cause paragraph breaks to occur around the tagged text whereas text tags do not. The rest of today's lesson looks at the various block tags that you can use in a document. Tomorrow you will look at text tags and how to intermix the two to create interesting pages. You'll see that block tags alone don't give you much in the way of visual appeal or interactivity. Block tags are designed to enable you to create blocks of information on your pages.

Block Tags

 Block tags are HTML tags that enable you to specify the formatting and arrangement of lines or bodies of text or graphics. They are characterized by a preceding and following blank line or space.

As you create Web documents, you will define a semantic definition of elements to be laid out on the page. You'll want to create groups of words through the use of paragraphs, or you might want to generate a list of items on the page. To do these things, you would use a block tag. All the block tags cause text or graphics to be grouped in a certain way. Block elements also create a line break between the block tag and the following element (usually another block element). Figure 8.7 shows an example of block tags being used in the following code. Notice the line breaks between the block tags, which can be seen in the browser. All block tags create a blank line before and after the items being blocked out.

```
<!DOCTYPE "HTML 3.2//EN">
<!-- Created J.L.Mohler 11/12/96 -->
 <HTML>
  <HEAD>
   <TITLE> Technical Graphics 217 Lab Assignments</TITLE>
  </HEAD>
  <BODY>
   <HR>
   <H4>Department of Technical Graphics</H4>
   <H1>TG 217 Drawing Systems</H1>
   <H3>Lab Assignments</H3>
   <P><B>Weekly Lab Assignments</B></P>
   <TABLE BORDER=3>
     ...
     ...
     ...
   </TABLE>
  <P>
  <HR>
  <BR><IMG SRC="jm.gif" BORDER=0 HEIGHT=29 WIDTH=34 ALIGN=RIGHT></P>
  <P>For information contact: <A HREF="mailto:jlmohler@tech.purdue.edu">
  ➥James L. Mohler.</A></P>
 </BODY>
  </HTML>
```

Figure 8.7.

Block elements are used to loosely format a page of text.

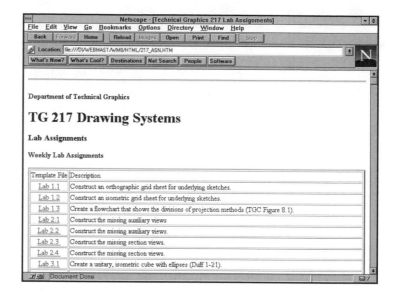

There are many block tags that you can use in a document. Block tags include the following:

- ☐ Headings, which are defined by <H1>...</H1> through <H6>...</H6>
- ☐ Paragraphs, which are defined by <P>...</P>
- ☐ Divisions of text (a special tag used with style sheets), which are defined by <DIV>...</DIV> or <CENTER>...</CENTER>
- ☐ Unordered lists, which are defined by <UL>...</UL>
- ☐ Ordered lists, which are defined by <OL>...</OL>
- ☐ Definition lists, which are defined by <DL>...</DL>
- ☐ Preformatted text blocks, which are defined by <PRE>...</PRE>
- ☐ Quotations, which are defined by <BLOCKQUOTE>...</BLOCKQUOTE>
- ☐ Addresses, which are defined by <ADDRESS>...</ADDRESS>
- ☐ Horizontal rules, which are defined by <HR>
- ☐ Line breaks, which are defined by
- ☐ Interactive forms, which are defined by <FORM>...</FORM>
- ☐ Tables, which are defined by <TABLE>...</TABLE>

Headings

The <HX> tag is one of the most commonly used block tags. This tag is used to represent titles, subtitles, and other headings by providing a single opening and closing tag that can be used rather than having to style the text using multiple text-level tags. The heading tags are often sought out by Web search engines and software robots that automatically compile lists of Web sites and their respective content.

The <HX> Tag

The <HX> tag defines the headings for the HTML document, where *x* can equal a value of 1 to 6. Headings defined by <H1> are rendered in a larger font and are deemed the most important head. As the value of *x* increases, the font size and importance decreases as shown in Figure 8.8.

Figure 8.8.
The use of various headings.

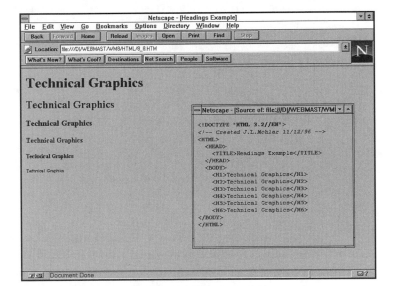

Formatting Paragraphs and Divisions

Text paragraphs in a Web document are the simplest type of block tag that can be used.

The <P> Tag

The <P> tag defines a block of text to be displayed as a paragraph in the Web
document. A blank space is inserted before and after a block paragraph.

The paragraph tag can be used to create multiple paragraphs of information within the Web
page. Within the <P> tag you can use the ALIGN attribute to set the alignment of the text to
left, right, or center justified. The following code is shown in Figure 8.9:

```
<!DOCTYPE "HTML 3.2//EN">
<!-- Created J.L.Mohler 11/12/96 -->
<HTML>
 <HEAD>
  <TITLE>A Procedural Model for Interactive Multimedia Development</TITLE>
 </HEAD>
 <BODY BGCOLOR=#004455 TEXT=#FFFFFF LINK=#00AAFF VLINK=#AAAAAA-->
  <BR>
  <CENTER><B>A Procedural Model for Interactive Multimedia Development</B>
  <BR> James L. Mohler
  <BR> Purdue University
  <BR> West Lafayette, Indiana USA
  </CENTER>
  <BR>
  <HR>
  <BR>
  <CENTER><I><B>Abstract</B></I></CENTER>
  <P ALIGN=RIGHT> This paper discusses a model for ...
  </P>
  <HR>
  <BR>
  <CENTER><I><B>Introduction</B></I></CENTER>
  <P>Interactive multimedia is being heavily ...
  </P>
 </BODY>
</HTML>
```

When you use the <P> tag, you will notice two specific things. As you begin to intermix
graphics and text together, the <P> might not always format the page as you'd like. As you
learned on Day 4, "The Media Designer," differences in fonts can cause the paragraphs of
text to shift across platforms or browsers.

In addition, you will also find it difficult—actually impossible—to indent the first line of the
paragraph with the <P> tag. On Day 10, "Utilizing Graphics and Image Maps," you learn a
method of using small inline images to "fake" an indent with a graphic rather than trying to
achieve it with HTML code.

Figure 8.9.

Using the <P> tag to format paragraphs.

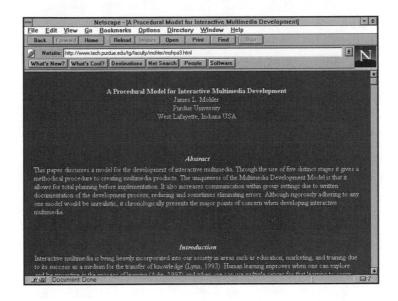

NOTE

A commonly used attribute that is not supported by every browser is the NOWRAP attribute. This disables the word wrapping feature of the <P> tag. Instead of using this tag, you should insert a line break, <BR>. The <BR> tag is discussed in more detail later in this chapter (see the section "Line Breaks").

In addition to the paragraph tag, you also can use the <DIV>...</DIV> tags to define major segments of your document. Some browsers prefer the <DIV> tag over the simple <P> tag.

The <DIV> Tag

The division tag, or <DIV> tag, enables you to define blocks or sections of a document that should all be treated similarly, such as all text of a specific paragraph or section justified left or right.

You can use the <DIV> tag in place of the <P> tag. The <DIV> tag has the same attributes as the <P> tag. For example, you can use the <DIV> tag like this:

```
<DIV ALIGN=LEFT> This is a paragraph of text that goes on, and on,
➥and on....</DIV>
```

A special tag is available for representing the <DIV> tag with the ALIGN=CENTER attribute. The <CENTER> tag can be used in replace of <DIV ALIGN=CENTER>. In essence, they do the same thing. The <CENTER> tag is a shorthand way of representing <DIV ALIGN=CENTER>. If it does the same thing as the <P> tag, why have the <DIV> tag at all? The main reason the <DIV> tag exists is because it gives you another option. It is commonly used with style sheets, which enable you to format many different pages using a set format or "style." Although this is available, it has yet to be widely implemented in Navigator or Explorer.

Lists

The HTML code language supports three various types of lists that you can create in your documents. You have the choice of creating unordered lists, ordered lists, or definition lists. Each uses a different tag and has its own set of attributes. The following list shows the various types of lists and their tags:

- ☐ Unordered lists, which use the <UL>...</UL> tags.
- ☐ Ordered lists, which use the <OL>...</OL> tags.
- ☐ Definition lists, which use the <DL>...</DL> tags.

Figure 8.10 shows an unordered list containing three items. Notice that to define the list, you use the <UL>...</UL> tags. Within the list you see the <LI> tag.

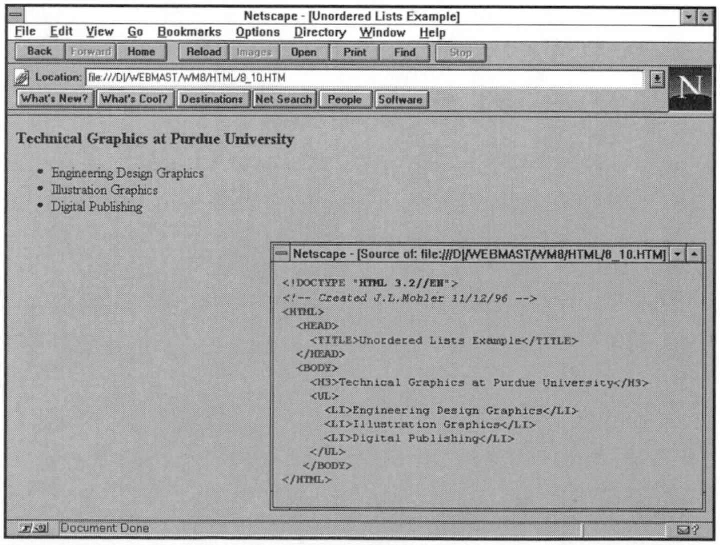

Figure 8.10.

Using unordered lists in a Web document.

The <UL> Tag

The <UL> tag is used to create unordered lists in the HTML language. An unordered list creates a vertically bulleted list on a Web page.

The <LI> Tag

The <LI> tag is used within the <UL>...</UL> tags to define the items that are to be shown in the list. These are called list items.

A list can contain as many list items as you want, but more than five becomes less effective. In addition, you can change the default bullet for the entire list by using the TYPE=DISC, TYPE=SQUARE, or TYPE=CIRCLE with <UL> to make the bullets either discs, squares, or circles. Lists also can be nested. The bullets will automatically change within the nested lists to represent hierarchy, as shown in Figure 8.11. I must note, however, that Internet Explorer always uses a single bullet for all occasions.

Figure 8.11.

Nesting lists.

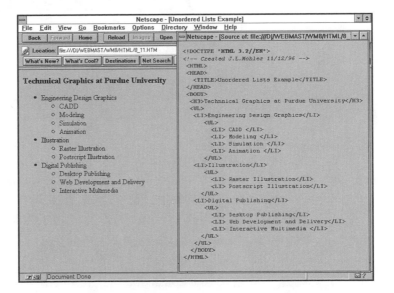

In addition to being able to set the bullet type for an entire list, you can alternatively set it for each list item. Similar to the attribute for the <UL> tag, you can set the bullet type for each list item by using the TYPE=DISC, TYPE=SQUARE, and TYPE=CIRCLE attributes within the <LI> tag.

For example, you could have a list in which each item uses a different bullet, as shown in Figure 8.12. Note that "disc" is the default for the list item unless it is overridden by a setting in the <UL> tag.

Figure 8.12.

Using different bullets for unordered lists.

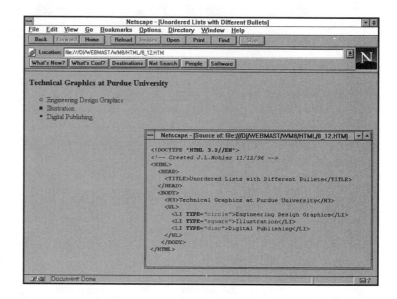

The <OL> Tags

An ordered list, which uses the <OL>...</OL> tags, enables you to create lists that are numerically or alphabetically labeled. By default, ordered lists are numbered.

Similar to the unordered list, the ordered list uses the <LI> tag to define the list items. The list items are defined within the <OL>...</OL> tags. However, with list items in an ordered list, you can set whether you want an alphabetical or numerical listing using the TYPE attribute. With an ordered list, you have the following options:

☐ TYPE="1"—Numerical (1, 2, 3)

☐ TYPE="A"—Uppercase letters (A, B, C)

☐ TYPE="a"—Lowercase letters (a, b, c)

☐ TYPE="I"—Uppercase Roman numerals (I, II, III)

☐ TYPE="i"—Lowercase Roman numerals (i, ii, iii)

Figure 8.13 shows an example of a Web page that uses ordered lists. Notice the difference in the <OL> tags used in each list. Inserting any of the other options for the TYPE attribute will change how the list is labeled. Note that the default for the ordered list is "1" or numerals. Also, note that you can change the number with which the list begins by using the START=*n* attribute, where *n* equals the number with which you want the list to begin.

Figure 8.13.

Using ordered lists in a Web document.

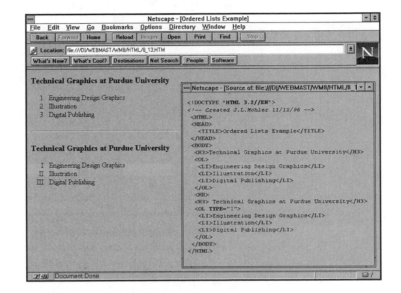

The third type of list is the definition list, which is defined using the <DL>...</DL> tags. These types of lists are used for situations in which you want to present a brief term or series of words and then present further comments on them.

The <DL> Tag

The <DL> tag is used to present a definition list.

Used in conjunction with the <DL> tag are the <DT> and <DD> tags. When the definition list tag was adopted, it was originally designed to present a word and its definition. However, as you'll see shortly, often <DT> and <DD> are used for the term and definition while <DL> is simply used to mark the location of the definition list.

> **The `<DT>` and `<DD>` Tags**
>
> The `<DT>` tag is used within the `<DL>`...`</DL>` tags to define the term that is presented.
>
> The `<DD>` tag is used to present further comment on the term provided within the `<DT>`...`</DT>` tags.

The `<DD>` tag often is used within a `<DT>`...`</DT>` tag set to further comment on the definition. The `<DD>` tag also can be used within a `<DL>`...`</DL>` tag directly. Sound confusing? It's not really. For the most part, programmers at large have taken the command and used it in a way that is more natural to work with. Let's see how it works.

Figure 8.14 shows a definition list that is used as many people interpret it (by definition). Notice that multiple `<DL>` statements were used to achieve a definition list, which means more typing. Also we really don't come out with what we expect in the browser display area. Notice the `<DL>` tag is used for the term, whereas the `<DT>` tag is used for the definition.

Figure 8.14.

The definition list by definition.

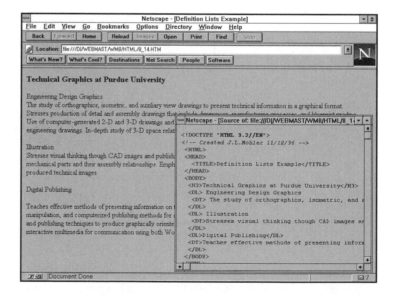

Now note in Figure 8.15 what happens to the list in the browser when you use the `<DT>` and `<DD>` tags for the term and its definition rather than `<DL>` and `<DT>`. You come up with what you really wanted!

Figure 8.15.

The definition list the way it is normally used.

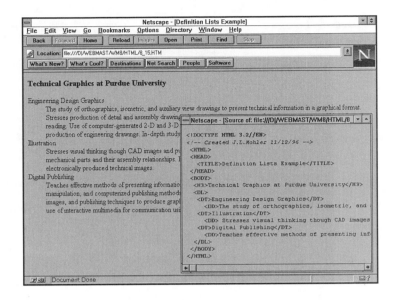

As you conclude your lesson on lists you need to look at two more things. First, with the `<UL>`, `<OL>`, and `<DL>` tags you can use an attribute that applies to any of the three to help reduce the amount of space the list requires for display. You can use the COMPACT attribute with these tags to help reduce the space required for the list. Note, however, that the COMPACT attribute does not work in every browser and that the amount of space that is saved with the COMPACT attribute depends upon the platform and font being used.

The second issue is that with these lists, `<UL>`, `<OL>`, and `<DL>`, you can associate a specific list header with each list. The examples use an `<H3>` tag (a heading) to introduce the list. You could alternatively use the `<LH>` tag right after the opening list tag. In Figure 8.16, you see a modified version of Figure 8.12. Figure 8.16 uses an `<LH>` tag instead of `<H3>` for the list opener. The `<LH>` tag is not always necessary because often you will introduce a list with an opening paragraph or other text block. Also notice the `<BR>` at the end of the `<LH>` line. To get the list to start below the `<LH>` line, you must force a line break with the `<BR>` tag.

NOTE

In addition to the list tags mentioned, there are also two other tags that can be used to create different formats of lists. They are the `<DIR>` and `<MENU>` tags. These tags cause a list to be displayed horizontally across the screen rather than vertically down the screen. The use of these tags is decreasing chiefly because you can now use tables to do the same thing, but you might still see them as you're surfing the Web.

Figure 8.16.

Using the <LH> tag.

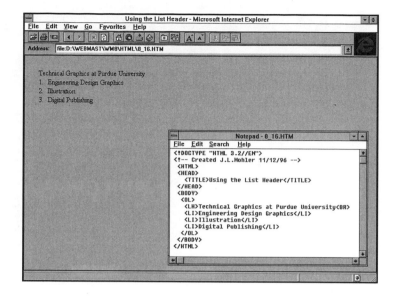

Preformatted Text

As you learned earlier in this chapter, the browser ignores extraneous spaces within a paragraph. Double spaces and, actually, anything more than a single space appear as a single space when the page is loaded in the browser. How can you achieve multiple spaces?

Using preformatted text is advantageous when you want to arrange text with a specific spacing. However, note that using the <PRE>...</PRE> tags displays a monospaced font, which often looks strange compared to the other text on the screen. Figure 8.17 uses the <PRE> tag to insert the department's mission statement into a document using a predefined layout.

The <PRE> Tag

The <PRE> tag enables text to be displayed in the browser work area as it is shown in the ASCII HTML code file itself. The text is displayed using a monospaced—fixed height and width—font.

Figure 8.17.

Using the <PRE> tag to insert preformatted text.

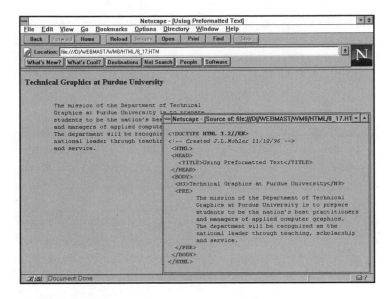

8

Quotations and Addresses

Much like the preformatted text tag, two other tags exist that let you format special items on your page. The first of these is the <BLOCKQUOTE> tag.

The <BLOCKQUOTE> Tag

The <BLOCKQUOTE> tag enables you to format running quotations in your documents. A <BLOCKQUOTE> will automatically indent the margins of the quote to contrast with other body text.

NOTE

One thing you need to be aware of is that you can nest the <BLOCKQUOTE> tag, causing each subsequent quote to be indented further.

Like all block tags, the <BLOCKQUOTE> tag will be offset from other block items with a line space before and after the item as shown in Figure 8.18. However, the <ADDRESS> tag is somewhat special in that it does not offset like other block tags. In addition, the <ADDRESS> tag is an item that is looked for by search engines and software that compile search lists. If you decide to add an address line on your documents, keep this in mind.

The <ADDRESS> Tag

The <ADDRESS> tag enables you to enter an address that is automatically italicized.

Figure 8.18.

The <BLOCKQUOTE> *and* <ADDRESS> *tags.*

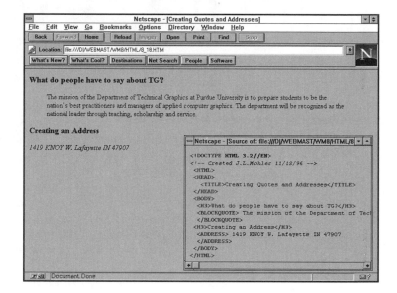

Horizontal Rules

One of the things that will help organize the information on your page into readable sections are horizontal rules, set off by the <HR> tag.

The <HR> Tag

A horizontal rule, or <HR> tag, automatically creates a horizontal line or divider between block elements.

8

The horizontal rule, or <HR> tag, is probably one of the most widely used elements on Web pages. The <HR> tag has many attributes or controls that you can use to define it. These include the following:

- ☐ SIZE=y, where y specifies a thickness in pixels. The default is SIZE=2.

- ☐ WIDTH=x, where x specifies the horizontal width in pixels (WIDTH=20) or as a percentage of the screen (WIDTH=50%). The default is WIDTH=100%.

- ☐ ALIGN=LEFT, ALIGN=CENTER, ALIGN=RIGHT—Determines the alignment of the horizontal rule. The default is ALIGN=CENTER.

- ☐ NOSHADE—Turns off the embossed look of the rule. By default, shading is turned on.

As shown in Figure 8.19, you see multiple, consecutive <HR> tags. Although you would not normally create a page like this, I have done this so that you can see how the attributes affect the rules that are displayed.

Figure 8.19.

Multiple horizontal rules.

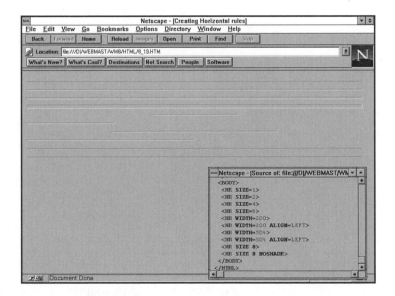

Note that the default width of horizontal rules is 2, the default length (width) is 100%, and the default alignment is center-justified. Adjusting the size changes the thickness of the rule. Changing the width changes the length of the rule, which also shows that the default for the ALIGN attribute defaults to ALIGN=CENTER, or center justification.

As you work with rules, keep in mind that the color of the highlight and shadow colors of the rule will be determined by the background color of the document. Remember that this is set with the BGCOLOR attribute in the <BODY> tag. Also, if you specify a length using the WIDTH attribute, the width will be dependent upon the user's current display setting. It is better to use percentages than a specific number of pixels.

NOTE

One of the things you really haven't learned yet is the size of the user's display. If the user's display is set to a small screen resolution and you define an <HR> length longer than his screen, he will have to horizontally scroll to see all your page. As most will agree, this is not preferred. You must design your pages for the lowest common denominator. Assuming that everyone browsing your page has an 800×600 display or a 1024×768 display is not safe. Most users surf the Net at a 640×480 resolution, which is the lowest common denominator today. It probably will change at some point, but design around today's limitations. Do not design pages, or <HR> rules for that matter, that extend beyond 640 pixels.

Line Breaks

One of the tags that you've probably seen in some of the code in this book is the <BR> or line break tag. This is a very useful tag.

**The
 Tag**

The <BR> tag enables you to insert a line break or "carriage return-line feed" into block elements so that you can force a line break within tags.

You use the <BR> tag to insert line breaks into documents where you want the elements to resume at the next line. Remember Figure 8.16, where it was used with the list header to force the list to start on the next line? Anytime you want an item to be forced to the next line, even if it is in the middle of another block tag, you can insert a line break with the <BR> tag.

Interactive Forms and Tables

The last two block tags probably are some of the most powerful features that you can integrate within your HTML pages. You learn more about these last two tags, the <FORM> and <TABLE> tags, on Day 13, "Using Forms To Gather Data," and Day 11, "Using Tables To Format Pages." The <FORM> tag enables you to create user-enterable fields with which your audience can provide feedback on any number of things. The <TABLE> tag enables you to create a wide variety of structured information using both graphics and text. These tags have a wide variety of options. To explain them well deserves more than a couple of pages.

Summary

Today's lesson focused on defining the basic parts of the HTML language. You have seen that the entire language is composed of tags, the main code words, and attributes, the optional settings for those code words. The entire language can be divided into block tags and text tags. Today's lesson focused on the first of these, block tags, which enable you to format your documents into blocks of information.

As you can see from many of the examples used today, using only block tags can be quite boring; they limit what you can do. With block tags only you have no graphics, no links, and very little style or visual appeal. Block tags are the major arranging tags, ones that let you begin making your information more comprehensible and hierarchical. However, block tags alone do little in the way of interactivity or visual appeal.

Q&A

Q What is the difference between SGML and HTML? How do they differ in the way they are used?

A The HTML language is a simplified derivative of the SGML language. The HTML language is predominantly used on the Web, whereas the SGML language is much broader in use and enables the developer to create products that are text-intensive and allow complex text searches and manipulations. The SGML language was designed to create documents that would outlast any specific application, operating system, or computer. HTML was developed exclusively for Internet-based communication.

Q **What is a code generator? What is the disadvantage of learning how to use only a generator versus learning the HTML code language?**

A A code generator is a visual HTML layout program in which you can create Web pages and sites visually rather than through hard coding a page or site in a text editor. The difference between creating them visually rather than by coding is like the difference between creating cookies from scratch (which I'm no good at) versus using slice-and-bake cookies (a godsend for me).

The disadvantage to learning a generator rather than the language is that many generators do not fully support all the features of the language. When I create slice-and-bake cookies I am limited to the variations that the cookie dough company makes; I never learn to make my own unique variations. However, if I learn to bake cookies from scratch, I can create more unique or elaborate creations. The same is true with generators versus hard coding a page. You will often have difficulty creating things like image maps, frames, or tables—items fundamentally important in Web development. Learn a generator, and you learn only that which the generator can do. Learn the HTML language, and you can do anything the language supports.

Q **What is the difference between a tag and an attribute? How are they used together?**

A Tags are the main code words that are used to define elements in a Web document. An attribute is an optional setting for a tag. Tags can have any number of attributes, or optional settings. An attribute belongs to a tag.

Q **How does a Web browser treat extraneous spaces within a Web document? What about missing spaces?**

A A Web browser will generally ignore extraneous spaces in a document. Spaces that are used to help the programmer read the code, such as indents at the beginning of lines, are ignored outright by the browser. However, missing spaces, such as between attributes or tags, can cause problems when the file is viewed in a browser.

Q **Every HTML code document conforms to the same structure. What are the four main document structure tags of a Web document?**

A The four main elements in all HTML documents are the <DOCTYPE> tag, <HTML> tag, <HEAD> tag, and <BODY> tag. There are two exceptions to this rule: The <DOCTYPE> tag is optional, but is becoming more widely recognized as a needed element for version and ruling body recognition. The <BODY> tag is replaced by the <FRAMESET> tag when the page uses frames.

8

Workshop

The Workshop provides quiz questions to help you solidify your understanding of the material covered and exercises to give you experience in using what you've learned. The quiz answers are provided in Appendix A, "Quiz Answers." Try to understand the quiz answers before you go on to tomorrow's lesson.

Quiz

1. What is a comment? How do you mark it in an HTML file?

2. What are the two main parts that exist between the <HTML>...</HTML> tags? For what are they used?

3. What are the two types of tags that occur within the body section of the HTML document?

4. What are the three types of lists that you can use in a Web document? How do they differ from one another?

5. What is the difference between the <P> tag and the <DIV> tag? What about the difference between the <DIV ALIGN=CENTER> tag and the <CENTER> tag?

6. What special characteristic do the <ADDRESS>, <H1> to <H6>, and <TITLE> tags have in common?

7. What is the problem with designing a Web page that is wider than the audience's display setting?

8. What tag can be used within another block tag to generate a carriage return-line feed?

Exercise

Create a Web page that uses the block elements you've learned. Use a combination of tags and attributes to get a feel for how they work together in the document. Use at least one list, one line break, and a couple of horizontal rules to create a Web document that does one of the following:

☐ Describes your professional strengths and weaknesses

☐ Describes your company or organization

☐ Describes some product or service that your company provides

☐ Describes your family tree

☐ Describes some aspect of your personality

Day 9

Text-Level Tags

As you learned yesterday, the two main types of body tags are block tags and text tags. You saw how block elements can be used to logically arrange bodies and groups of text. But as you saw by the end of the day, using block tags alone presents a very dry Web page with no interactivity or associativity.

Today's lesson focuses on text-level tags that you can use to integrate graphics, text styles, hypertext links, and multimedia elements.

NEW TERM *Text-level tags* are tags that are used to stylize text and add hyperlinks, graphics, and multimedia elements.

Text-level tags enable a developer to provide many of the stylized effects found in Web pages, such as links, graphics, and multimedia elements.

Text-level tags are different from block tags in that they do not add a blank line before and after an element. When you use a text-level element, it does not change the formatting or how the element is arranged. These tags do not cause paragraph breaks to occur. Text-level tags that affect text elements are generally nested inside a block tag or even within another text-level element. However, some browsers cannot recognize nested text-level elements.

In Figure 9.1, a Web page that combines some of the block tags from yesterday and some of the text-level tags discussed today has been loaded into the browser. Can you see any tags that you haven't learned yet? Notice how the text-level tags don't cause paragraph breaks. All text formatting such as bolding, italicizing, or underlining is a result of text-level elements. So is the capability to integrate images, links, and multimedia elements.

Figure 9.1.

Text-level elements are used in conjunction with block elements to create Web pages.

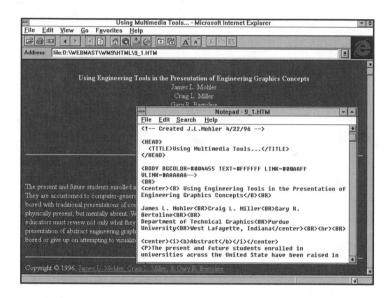

 TIP

As you begin developing your own pages, strive to decide upon all of your block elements first. Define how your information will be laid out and how you will arrange your information so that it effectively can be read on the screen. Then use text-level elements to insert graphics, stylize text, and create links. Define first and then stylize. This will force you to construct the page according to the constraints of the language rather than just doodling or using trial and error.

Physical and Logical Styles

Text-level tags can be divided into three different types of tags: physical styles, logical styles, and other text-level tags. Physical and logical styles affect text styling while the other category enables you to add graphics, links, and multimedia elements.

New Term A *physical style* affects a font style to simply draw attention to the font itself. It communicates no other information through the formatting of the text.

New Term A *logical style* affects a font style to draw attention to the font as well as to communicate some information to the reader.

Before you continue, you should explore this difference. A physical style probably is the most frequently used type of these two styles (physical and logical). For example, suppose you want to italicize a string of text. When you use a logical style to italicize it, the <I> tag, the text will appear italicized when it is viewed in the browser. No matter where you view it, or on what platform, the text will be italic. The italicized text draws attention to only the text itself. However, the idea behind a logical style is that the style not only draws attention to the font but also communicates something else.

For example, maybe you want to not only draw attention, but also have the text communicate something such as a caution or other notable attribute. In this case you could use a logical style such as <EM> for emphasis. When you use a logical style, the rendering of the item is determined by the browser. On one browser it might appear as italic, on another it might appear bold, and on another it might appear as both italic and bold. Logical styles are fluent styles that are rendered based upon the browser and platform. A physical style is a fixed style that will always appear bold, italic, and so on.

Physical Styles

Both physical and logical styles seek to change the characteristics or style of a particular font such as creating bold, italicized, or underlined fonts. However, many people make a distinction due to added meaning behind the logical style.

Physical styles are pretty straightforward. They require both a beginning and ending tag. The following are physical styles:

- [ ] <TT>—Creates teletype or monospaced text
- [ ] <I>—Creates italic style text
- [ ] <B>—Creates bold style text
- [ ] <U>—Creates underline style text
- [ ] <STRIKE>—Creates strikethrough style text
- [ ] <BIG>—Renders the text larger than the surrounding text
- [ ] <SMALL>—Renders the text smaller than the surrounding text
- [ ] <SUB>—Attempts to place the text in subscript style
- [ ] <SUP>—Attempts to place the text in superscript style

Figure 9.2 shows an example of the various physical style tags. Note in the code for this page the intermixing of block tags (`<UL>` and `<LI>`) and text-level tags. This is how you combine these two major types of tags to create Web pages.

Figure 9.2.

Using the various physical style tags.

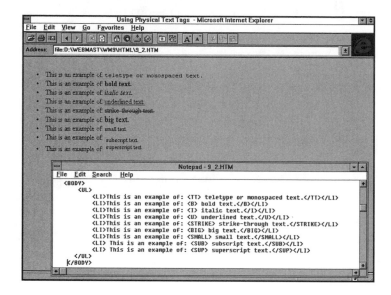

Logical Styles

Logical styles are coded exactly like physical styles, but they are different because they also convey meaning behind how they are formatted. Some people feel there is only a fine line between the physical and logical styles.

The logical styles do more than simply draw attention to a font. They are intended to be used to add communicative value to the text style. You want to emphasize a string of words you deem important. This is a logical style because you are communicating more than simply italicizing text. However, note that the logical style tag creates text that could also be created using the `<I>` physical style. In reality, most people will simply use the tag that first comes to memory instead of sitting there thinking, "Is this a logical or physical style?" You should use whatever comes natural.

Again, using logical styles in your code is much like using physical styles. The following are the logical style tags:

☐ `<EM>`—Renders the font with emphasis

☐ `<STRONG>`—Renders the font with strong emphasis

9

☐ <DFN>—Specifies a defining instance of the stylized text

☐ <CODE>—Renders the font as representing extracted code

☐ <SAMP>—Renders the font as representing output from a program or application

☐ <KBD>—Renders the font as representing text that the reader should enter

☐ <VAR>—Renders the font as representing variables, arguments, commands, or instructions

☐ <CITE>—Renders the font as a citation or reference to another source of information

Using logical styles is much like using physical styles. Again, I have combined these text-level tags with some block level tags so that you can see how they work concurrently (see Figure 9.3). Notice the use of the <UL> and <LI> commands to create the list, and how each list item includes a logical style within it.

Figure 9.3.

Using the various logical style tags.

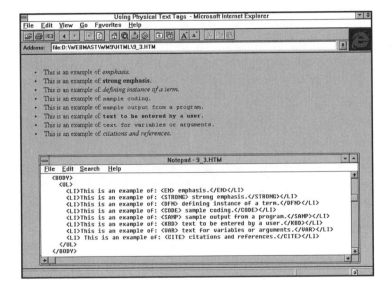

Although I mentioned that there is not much difference between logical and physical styles, you should be aware of one difference between them. Logical styles are somewhat browser-dependent, whereas physical styles are more independent.

When you use a logical style, it tells the browser that the font should be rendered with, for example, emphasis. How the browser actually renders the font is determined by the constructs within the browser. Each browser knows that to place emphasis on a given string of text, it must change the font attributes. One browser might italicize it, whereas another might bold it. It depends on the constructs or predefined attributes set in the browser by the creator of the browser. So when you use a logical style, you can be assured that the font will be rendered differently, but you can't be sure that it will always be italicized or bolded.

With physical styles, however, italic is italic, bold is bold, and so on. Using physical styles sets the font in stone. I prefer to use physical styles instead of logical styles because I don't want somebody else deciding how my pages will look. The logical styles actually are pretty standard, but some browsers can do some funky things with text. Using physical styles guarantees that italic is italic, bold is bold, and so on.

NOTE

> The idea of logical styles is an attempt at crossing cultural, machine, platform, and browser constructs. In theory, it is nice to be able to use a logical style to place emphasis so that it is rendered according to a culture, machine, platform, or browser, but when used, the logical style does not work as well as intended.

A final note about text and text styles before you move on. Because the Web is internationally based, there might be times when you will want to integrate special characters that are used in foreign languages. You also might want to use characters such as the arrows (< >), ampersand (&), or quotations. To do so you must use the special keyboard codes for these characters because they are not recognized by the browser when they are entered in the code. A listing of such characters and their code equivalents can be found in Appendix B, "HTML 3.2 Reference."

Form Elements

You learn about forms in a later chapter. The text-level form elements can be used only with the block-level form tag. You learn the text-level form tags on Day 13, "Using Forms To Gather Data."

Images

Ahhh, the wonderful world of inline images. There are many who wouldn't agree that graphics are wonderful, but this is what makes it all worthwhile for me. I love to work with graphics, so I am biased, but you might agree that without graphics, the Web would be quite boring.

You can do almost anything you want with images on your Web pages. However, as you've learned, you must cautiously integrate graphics so that you don't tax the user's hardware or their patience.

As you learned on Day 10, "Utilizing Graphics and Image Maps," inline images are directly integrated within the document or Web page that is currently loaded into the Web browser. The primary tag for integrating all graphics into a Web page is the <IMG> tag. It is a very important tag.

The <IMG> Tag

The <IMG> tag is used to reference a graphic image file to be included in the display of a Web page.

When you are using graphics on your Web pages you have several options for how you want the graphic to be displayed. Whether you want it aligned left, want a border around it, or if you want a specific amount of space around it, all of these characteristics can be controlled using the <IMG> tag's attributes. They include the following:

- ☐ SRC—Defines the image filename and path to be included in the Web page. This is a required attribute for the <IMG> tag.

- ☐ ALT—Specifies alternative text that should be displayed in nongraphical Web browsers. It also displays the associated text as the graphic being downloaded. Although the ALT attribute is not mandatory, it should be.

- ☐ ALIGN—Controls the alignment of the image in relationship to the text surrounding the image. Valid options are ALIGN=TOP¦MIDDLE¦BOTTOM¦LEFT¦RIGHT.

- ☐ WIDTH—Specifies the intended width of the image in pixels. When this attribute is combined with the HEIGHT attribute, the browser shows a blank box for the image in the browser as the image is loading. If the ALT attribute is also used, the text will display in the blank box.

- ☐ HEIGHT—Specifies the intended height of the image in pixels. When this attribute is combined with the WIDTH attribute, the browser shows a blank box for the image in the browser as the image is loading. If the ALT attribute is also used, the text will display in the blank box.

- ☐ BORDER—Specifies the size of the border for the image. The default is BORDER=2. With BORDER=0 the border is suppressed.

- ☐ HSPACE—Specifies, in pixels, a specific amount of white or negative space to be left on the left and right of the image. The default is a small, non-zero number less than 1.

☐ VSPACE—Specifies, in pixels, a specific amount of white or negative space to be left on the top and bottom of the image. The default is a small, non-zero number.

☐ USEMAP—Specifies that the image be mappable by a client-side image map. This attribute is used in conjunction with the <MAP> tag.

☐ ISMAP—Specifies that the image is an image map. Regions of the image are defined as hypertext links (see Day 10).

☐ LOWSRC—Specifies a low-resolution image to display while the higher, true source image is being downloaded.

Tomorrow's lesson predominantly focuses on the use of the <IMG> tag, but before you move on, take a quick look at the tag in action. Figure 9.4 shows a series of images that have been inserted using the <IMG> tag. Note that specific sizes have been set using the WIDTH and HEIGHT attributes, and that the spacing around the images has been set using the HSPACE and VSPACE attributes. In addition, there are borders around the images.

Figure 9.4.

Using the <IMG> tag to insert images.

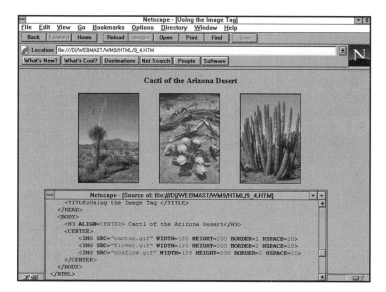

> **NOTE**
>
> A quick note about using the borders option on images: Most of the time you want to click an image that has a border around it because on the Web, most images with borders are hotlinks to another site or page. If you want to use borders on your unlinked inline images, make sure you make them a different color from the identifying link color (normally blue).

Anchors

All images that appear in Web pages would not be possible if the `<IMG>` tag didn't exist. Similarly, note that the hypertext or hypermedia capability would not be possible without the anchor tag, `<A>`. The `<A>` tag enables you to make almost anything a hotlink to the outside world or to another page at your site.

The `<A>` Tag

The `<A>` tag, also known as an anchor, enables objects on a page to be used as hyperlinks. The `<A>` tag can be used with graphics, text, and multimedia elements.

To make the various elements hyperlinks, you must use the attributes of the `<A>` tag. The following attributes can be used with this tag:

- ☐ `NAME`—Used for targeting specific portions of a Web document. Valid entries for the `NAME` attribute are strings such as `part1`, `part2`, and `part3`.
- ☐ `HREF`—Used to specify a URL address that links the item with the site. Clicking the item sends the browser to the URL address specified in the `HREF` attribute.
- ☐ `REL`—Defines the forward relationship of the current page. This is the next page in the site's structure.
- ☐ `REV`—Used to define the backward relationship of the current page.
- ☐ `TITLE`—Used as a title for the linked resource.

Next, look at a few examples using some of the `<A>` tag's attributes. All links inside a document can be considered either internal or external links, in relationship to the current page. The most common type of link is the external link.

External Links

 When the `<A>` tag or anchor uses the `HREF` attribute to define an HTTP address, the link is considered an *external link*. This means that when the user clicks the link it will take him to another site or page.

Figure 9.5 shows the most common use of the `<A>` tag. Notice the `<A>` tag used within the list items. Notice also that the `<A>` tags reference other pages at the site. Presenting a list in this way can be effective, but it is quite simple. Notice that, again, we are combining text-level tags with block tags to create the pages, nesting the text-level tags into the block tags. As a

matter of fact, I already had this page set up with the list block tags. I simply added the text-level elements to it. You will find that this is the most effective way of building the elements on your pages.

Figure 9.5.

The most basic use of the
<A> tag.

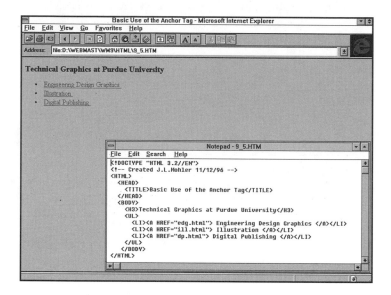

As you learned earlier in this chapter, not only will you want to nest text-level tags into block tags, but you might also want to nest text-level tags into other text-level tags. In Figure 9.6, a series of <IMG> tags are nested into a series of <A> tags to create images that are navigation items. In addition, the anchors, <A>, are nested in the block tags. The code for the page looks like Listing 9.1.

TYPE **Listing 9.1. The code for Figure 9.6.**

```
<!DOCTYPE "HTML 3.2//EN">
<HTML>
  <HEAD>
    <TITLE>Joe's Vacation Hideaway</TITLE>
  </HEAD>
  <BODY BGCOLOR="#FFFFFF" TEXT="#FFFFFF" LINK="#334557">
    <CENTER>
        <IMG SRC="6a.gif" BORDER=0 WIDTH=569 HEIGHT=254>
    </CENTER>
    <HR SIZE=4>
    <CENTER>
        <A HREF="dine.html"><IMG SRC="6b.gif" BORDER=0 HSPACE=30></A>
        <A HREF="shop.html"><IMG SRC="6c.gif" BORDER=0 HSPACE=30></A>
        <A HREF="rec.html"><IMG SRC="6d.gif" BORDER=0 HSPACE=20></A>
        <A HREF="night.html"><IMG SRC="6e.gif" BORDER=0 HSPACE=20></A>
```

```
        </CENTER>
        <HR SIZE=4>
        <CENTER>
            <A HREF="dine.html"> [ Dining ] </A>     
            <A HREF="shop.html"> [ Shopping ] </A>   
            <A HREF="rec.html"> [ Recreation ] </A>   
            <A HREF="night.html"> [ Nightlife ] </A>   
        </CENTER>
    </BODY>
</HTML>
```

Figure 9.6.

Creating hyperlinks with graphics by nesting the <IMG> *tag within the* <A> *tag.*

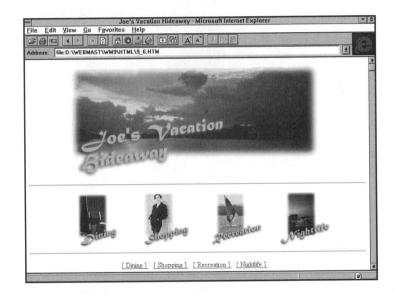

NOTE

In Listing 9.1 note the use of , which inserts a nonbreaking space. Appendix B shows a listing of common HTML representations for special and non-English language characters.

Notice how the page in Figure 9.6 is built. Block-level tags are established first, and then necessary text-level tags are nested into the existing block-level tags. Finally, text-level tags are nested inside other text-level tags. Force yourself to design this way. It will make building your pages much easier.

As you are creating external links, keep in mind that the HREF attribute can be used to link to sites, specific pages, and e-mail addresses. In previous examples you have seen the <A HREF="*XXXX*"> scenario used to link to an external site such as the following:

```
<A HREF="http://www.tech.purdue.edu"> Purdue's School of Technology </A>
```

When you use the <A> tag in this way, the browser will look for a page at the root level of the HTTP server called INDEX.HTML. Whenever you specify a Web address with no page specification, the browser will look for a page called INDEX.HTML. Regardless of the site or anything else, the default page the browser looks for is INDEX.HTML.

NOTE

As you develop sites and pages, keep this tidbit concerning pages named INDEX in the back of your mind. Every major directory of your site should have a page named INDEX.HTML to make your site surfer-friendly. Because the name of Web pages at almost every site changes constantly, it often can be difficult when you go to use a specific Web address that has a page name as part of its destination. Often you'll find that the page has been renamed, making the Web address incorrect (when it ends with a page destination).

For example, suppose you enter a Web address such as http://www.site.com/notsmart/webpage.html into a browser's Web address field. When your browser tries to access it, it says, "Page not available or not found." Unknown to you, the developer at this site changed the name of webpage.html to Webpage.html. The page is there, but your address is not correct because the page name has changed. Remember that Web site addresses are case-sensitive. If the developer has named all pages in all directories using custom names, you have a problem. You cannot access any of the pages at this site.

In another example, the developer of this site is aware of the INDEX.HTML rule. Suppose the address of the site is http://www.site.com/verysmart/index.html. In this scenario, you can enter the site address and your browser will find it. In addition, because the browser automatically looks for INDEX.HTML, you could enter http://www.site.com/verysmart/ and still find the page. Assuming that every directory on this server has an INDEX page, you could enter all of the following and be able to get onto their site:

```
http://www.site.com/verysmart/index.html
http://www.site.com/verysmart/
http://www.site.com/
```

Indeed, using the default page INDEX.HTML is very smart and makes your site surfer-friendly.

Web anchors also can be used to insert e-mail addresses into Web pages. This gives the audience a direct route for sending you e-mail rather than having to write down or digitally copy the address to their mail program. To integrate an e-mail address as a link on your page, enter code similar to the following:

```
<A HREF="mailto:jlmohler@tech.purdue.edu"> Email Professor Mohler. </A>
```

Internal Links

In addition to creating external links, you also can create links within a single page.

NEW TERM   Pages that have links to other sections in the same document are called *internal links*.

For example, suppose you have a very long page and the document has several defined sections. To see the entire document the user must scroll down and not across. It is possible to create a list at the top of the page with the items linked to other sections of the long page. Clicking an item in the list automatically jumps you down the page.

To create an internal link you must create two things. First, you must establish a "jump-to" point in your document. You do this by using the <A> tag with the NAME attribute. For example, somewhere in your document you would create a tag that says

```
<A NAME="jumpto"> This is the text that appears at the jump to point. <A>
```

The second item you must create is the actual link. More than likely at the top of the page you would create a list of link items, one of which would represent the link to your jump-to point. The list item that is linked to your jump-to point would look like the following:

```
...
<LI><A HREF="#jumpto"> Go to jumpto point"
...
```

When the document is viewed in the browser, the line would look like any other hypertext link. However, when a user clicks it, the link would jump farther down the document.

Internal links often are placed at the beginning of major sections of a document. Suppose a document has five major sections that include an abstract, introduction, description, conclusion, and references. You could embed jump-to links in the headings for these elements by using code that looks like this:

```
...
<H3><A NAME="abstract"> Abstract </A></H3>
...
<H3><A NAME="intro"> Introduction </A></H3>
```

```
...
<H3><A NAME="descript"> Description </A></H3>
...
<H3><A NAME="conclude"> Conclusion </A></H3>
...
<H3><A NAME="references"> References </A></H3>
...
```

Then at the top of the document you could create a list of elements that would enable your readers to jump quickly to the various sections of your document. The code for the list might look like this:

```
<OL TYPE="I">
    <LH><B> Table of Contents </B><BR>
    <LI><A HREF="#abstract"> Abstract </A></LI>
    <LI><A HREF="#intro"> Introduction </A></LI>
    <LI><A HREF="#descript"> Description </A></LI>
    <LI><A HREF="#conclude"> Conclusion </A></LI>
    <LI><A HREF="# references"> References </A></LI>
</OL>
```

Using internal links can be effective for pages that are quite long; however, don't overuse them. Many times it becomes difficult for the audience to differentiate between internal and external links because they appear exactly the same in the browser.

Applets and Embedding Sources

Today you have seen the basics of integrating images and links into your page, but you're not finished with these elements yet. Tomorrow's lesson continues the discussion of utilizing graphics.

In addition to graphics and links, multimedia elements also can be integrated into your pages. However, an in-depth discussion of how to do so is not appropriate yet. Before looking at integrating Java applets with the <APPLET> tag or embedding multimedia elements with the <EMBED> tag, you need to look at a few other things first. Tomorrow you learn more about graphics and then continue on with tables, frames, and forms. Then you learn about multimedia objects.

Summary

In today's lesson, you have looked at the various text-level tags provided by the HTML language. You've seen that text-level tags are combined with block-level tags to enable you to create almost anything. It is extremely important that you begin developing pages by establishing the block-level tags, then the text-level tags, and then embedded text-level tags. This will help you organize and arrange your content. Remember: define first, stylize later.

In today's lesson, you also have taken a look at physical versus logical styles. You have also become familiar with the two most powerful tags (in my humble opinion), the <IMG> and <A> tags. These are what give us graphical and hyperlink capability. Now that you have taken a cursory look at the various HTML tags, you continue in tomorrow's lesson to focus on developing graphics for your Web pages.

Q&A

Q What is the difference between a block tag and a text-level tag?

A Block tags are HTML tags that enable you to specify the formatting and arrangement of lines or bodies of text or graphics. They are characterized by a preceding and following blank line or space. Text-level tags are tags that are used to stylize text and add hyperlinks, graphics, and multimedia elements. Text-level tags do not add paragraph breaks to the formatted elements.

Q What is the difference between a physical and logical text style?

A A physical style affects a font style to simply draw attention to the font itself. It communicates no other information through the formatting of the text. A logical style affects a font style to draw attention to the font, as well as communicate some information to the reader.

Q What is the difference between an internal and external link? How does the code for each differ?

A An internal link references a specific section of the current page. An external link references another page or site. The code for an external link uses the HREF attribute to specify a site address or another page. An internal link uses the HREF attribute to specify an anchor name and the NAME attribute to place the anchor point in the document. Internal links require two <A> tags on a single page.

Q Can a text-level tag be nested inside another text-level tag? If yes, give an example.

A Yes. An example is an <IMG> tag nested within an <A> tag to create a hyperlinked graphic on the Web page.

Workshop

The Workshop provides quiz questions to help you solidify your understanding of the material covered and exercises to give you experience in using what you've learned. The answers are provided in Appendix A, "Quiz Answers." Try to understand the quiz answers before you go on to tomorrow's lesson.

Quiz

1. When you are creating Web pages, how should you enter the code? Should you just start entering all tags at once or should you enter one set of tags and then the other? Explain your answer.
2. What two tags can be used to integrate multimedia elements?
3. What are the advantages and disadvantages of using logical text-level tags?
4. What tag do you use to integrate graphics onto a Web page?

Exercise

Create a Web page that describes a particular product or service. Begin with a sketch of the page and how you want it to look. The Web page should include the following:

- ☐ A logo or graphic representing the company that creates the product or provides the service
- ☐ A text description of the product or service
- ☐ A bulleted list of the product's or service's features
- ☐ A graphic showing the product in use or the service being performed
- ☐ An e-mail address for feedback

Day 10

Utilizing Graphics and Image Maps

Now that you've learned most of the tags available for formatting graphics and text in the Web browser, you can begin to look at some of the applied tips and techniques you can use to create your Web pages. As you learned, the predominant image incorporation tag is the `<IMG>` tag. With the wealth of available attributes for this tag, you can do almost anything with a static graphic.

Today's lesson focuses on utilizing images in your pages. More than just throwing an image on a page, you learn how to control their placement to get them just right. To be honest, designing and laying out good-looking pages is an issue of control. After you create a good-looking graphic, you must then be able to use it in a page. If you are familiar with page layout programs such as Adobe PageMaker or QuarkXPress, you'll probably hate the HTML language when it comes to incorporating graphics. If only placement and image control were as slick as it is in these imaging packages, you wouldn't need an entire lesson devoted to integrating graphics and controlling their placement.

Revisiting Imaging Terms

As you get ready to start fiddling with images on Web pages, it's a good idea to revisit the imaging terms because they play an important role in download speed as well as the realism of your graphics. Today's lesson focuses on using Adobe Photoshop to generate your images. You might not have Photoshop, but if you really want to get serious about developing Web graphics, I strongly suggest making the investment. You'll find the myriad of tools in Photoshop makes working in "rasterland" a lot easier, particularly with the newest version (4.0). If you are simply a passive user, maybe purchasing Photoshop isn't what you have in mind. Okay, but you'd love it if you tried it.

NOTE

Just a quick note here. I don't get anything for suggesting that people buy Photoshop—although I should, for as many customers as Adobe gets from my recommendations. I know the tool in and out, and I know of no other raster imaging program that enables you to so easily do the things that it does.

In addition to Adobe Photoshop, there are several shareware tools and programs that you can use to perform basic scaling, dpi, and bit-depth changes. Two of the best are LView Pro (`http://world.std.com/~mmedia/lviewp.html`) and Paint Shop Pro (`http://www.jasc.com`). For more editors and tools check out Appendix C, "Development Tools and Aids."

Know Your dpi

As you learned on Day 4, "The Media Designer," raster images are device dependent, which means that when you begin creating raster images, the dpi is set in relationship to the image's size from the very beginning. Scaling an existing raster image up spreads the dots in it apart, giving you fewer dots per inch. Scaling an existing image down brings the dots closer together, giving you a finer number of dots per inch. When you scale an image down, often data (dots) will be deleted, which can be detrimental to image quality.

Raster images found on the Web need not have a dpi greater than 72, because this is all that can be displayed on a computer monitor. However, if you decide to use a graphic on the Web that was created for some other purpose such as printed media, odds are that the image will have a dpi greater than 72 dpi or an image size that is quite large. To design images for Web distribution, you must use an image editor to decrease the number of dots per inch. Anything over 72 dpi is just hogging bandwidth. You never know, the cyber-police might pull you over

10

for hogging the road! No! Not really! But your audience will be glad you decreased the size when the graphic downloads several minutes quicker.

Know Your Size

Continuing the lesson, you must also be conscious of the physical size of the images you plan to integrate. Remember that image size is simply the physical width and height in pixels. With image placement, the first concern is how you figure out the exact size for your images so that you can insert them at full scale. Then, how do you adjust them so they are the right size? In the section titled "Calculating Image Sizes," you'll do some image adjusting to see how it works.

Know Your Bit Depth

The final image attribute about which you must be concerned is that of bit depth. Remember that bit depth is simply the number of bits allowed to describe the image. The more available bits, the more descriptive the image. The fewer bits, the less descriptive the image.

Because this is a common area of confusion, I would like to interject one more example to help explain bit depth. This is a simple example, but it should get the point across. Imagine that you are given a set of 16 crayons to create an image, and someone else is given a set of 72 crayons to draw the same image. Assume the sketching ability of you and this other person is exactly the same. Whose image will be more representative, the one with 16 different colors or the one with 72 different colors? In theory, the one with 72. This is also how bit depth works: The more bits you can use to describe the image, the more representative or photo-realistic is the image that can be defined with that bit depth. Fewer bits are less descriptive, more bits are more descriptive.

Calculating Image Sizes

Calculating image sizes is relatively easy if you plan your pages. The first step in the process is to know what size the images need to be within your page. The second step is to scale the images to make them the right size.

There are two basic ways of determining the size that your images need to be. The first is to actually lay out all your graphical elements right within your image editor. This is the method I prefer. Let me explain why.

Using a Nonlayered Environment

In some raster editing packages you can create the various elements of your page using a special capability called layers. Layers give you the ability to draw various bitmap elements such as a series of inline images, a banner, or even each individual element on a different layer. Layers are like acetate sheets. Each sheet is transparent until you draw on it. Drawing on layers in a raster editor overcomes a lot of the negative aspects of working with bitmap images.

"What's that guy talking about?" you might ask. Well, look at one of the biggest raster editing problems via an example. Figure 10.1 shows a raster image of a banner you saw on Day 9. Suppose you want to move some of the things around a little. You want to move the text that says "Joe's Vacation Hideaway," so you select it using the wand tool.

Figure 10.1.

Selecting elements to move in a raster image.

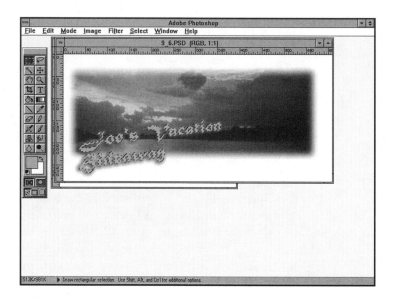

Now drag it to where you want it to be, as shown in Figure 10.2. What happened to the stuff that was behind the text? In flatland, which is a drawing environment without layers, anything that is drawn automatically deletes the pixels behind it. In essence, that which is placed in front deletes that which is behind.

Also notice that the shadow for the text didn't move either. Well, it wasn't selected. Notice how the shadow is a blend between the shadow color and the colors around it. In other words, it is anti-aliased. You could select it so that it would move with the background, but as shown in Figure 10.3, nasty things happen. Remember, we're in flatland!

The problem created is known as an anti-aliasing halo. You learned about anti-aliasing on Day 4. Remember that anti-aliasing is the slight blurring of edges to create smooth edges between raster items. However, this can work against you when you're working in a flatland environment. Notice Figure 10.4; it shows a gray circle on a white background. Notice the blow-up of the edges of the circle. A blend is created between the circle and the background. This is the anti-alias.

10

Figure 10.2.

Dragging the text reveals that the background elements are deleted.

Figure 10.3.

Selecting the shadow with the text and moving it reveals an anti-aliasing problem.

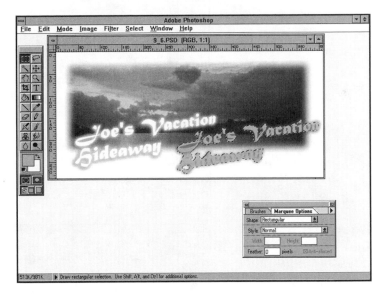

In the second image in Figure 10.4, I took the white circle, copied it, and placed it on a black background. The white garbage floating around the edges of the circle is the anti-alias halo. Because the circle was created on the white background, a fixed anti-alias was created between the gray circle and the white background. When the image was copied and placed on the black background, the fixed anti-alias was copied with it. You need a way to "un-fix" the anti-alias so that, when you paste the circle on the black background, the anti-alias is a blend between black and gray instead of white and gray.

Using a Layered Environment

To solve the anti-aliasing problem, as well as the issue of foreground objects deleting background objects, you need to use layers. Creating your graphics using layers will make your graphic design tasks much easier, as well as much more fun.

Figure 10.4.

A circle created on white, copied, and pasted onto black creates an anti-aliasing problem.

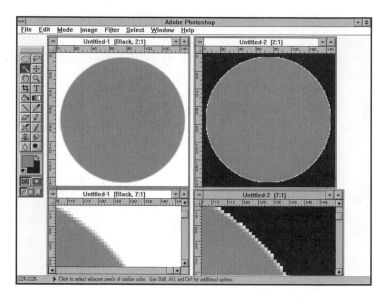

Now do the circle exercise again using layers. Begin by opening a new image with a white background in Photoshop. When you have started a new drawing, open the Layers palette from the Windows | Palettes | Show Layers menu. Click the arrow in the Layers palette to select New Layer, as shown in Figure 10.5. Press OK when a dialog box pops up.

Figure 10.5.

Opening the Layers palette and creating a new layer.

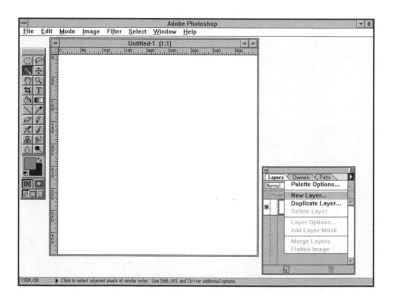

When you click OK you'll see that a layer has been added to the Layers palette, as shown in Figure 10.6. Notice a couple of things in this image. First, you see a small iconic representation of the contents of the layer in the palette. Because both layers are blank, all you see is white. Second, notice the layer that is highlighted, or white. It is the current drawing layer. If you begin to draw right now, whatever you draw will be placed on this layer. You can change the current drawing layer by clicking it. In the Layers palette, you also can turn each individual layer on or off by clicking the small eyeball to the left of the layer's image.

Figure 10.6.

A new layer in the Layers palette.

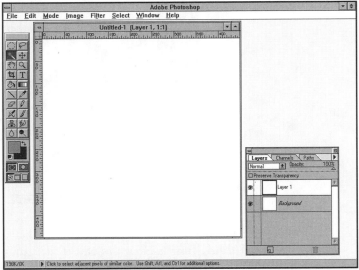

In this palette, also note some of the other controls that are showing. Notice the small drop-down menu and the slider control at the top of the palette. The drop-down menu enables you to create compositing effects between layers. The slider enables you to control the opaqueness of a particular layer. You learn about these a little later. At the bottom of the palette, you see two small icons. You can use the paper icon to add a new layer. It does the same thing that you did earlier by accessing New Layer from the Layers palette's menu. You can use the small trashcan to delete a layer; you simply drag a layer to the trash to delete it. Note that you can also delete layers using the Layers palette's menu.

One final note before you continue: The other layer that is showing in the Layers palette, the background, is somewhat special. This layer cannot be deleted or moved. If you begin to create drawings with several layers, you can change their order simply by clicking and dragging them up or down the layer list. However, the background layer cannot be moved or deleted.

Now on with the show. Remember, we are in the process of creating the gray circle on a white background and then transferring it to a canvas with a black background.

Begin by checking to make sure the new layer you created is the current layer. It should be white. Next, create a circular mask and fill it with gray using the paint bucket as shown in Figure 10.7.

Figure 10.7.

Creating the circle on Layer 1.

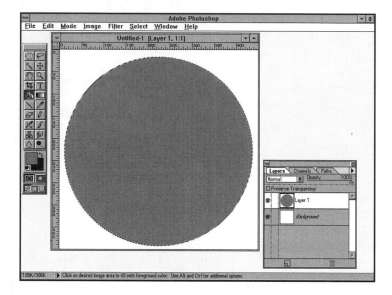

Now notice that the edges have been automatically anti-aliased to make it look smooth, much like the earlier flatland example. Now turn off the background layer by clicking the eyeball for that layer. Notice in Figure 10.8 that the anti-alias created around the circle is not actually a blend between gray and white, but rather a blend between gray and transparency—the gray and white boxes mean that everything surrounding the circle is transparent or no color.

"Why?" you might ask. Well, because the anti-alias is between the gray circle and transparency, you can copy the circle from the layer in this drawing to a new layer in another drawing without an anti-alias halo (see Figure 10.9).

So what does this mean in relationship to Joe's Vacation Hideaway? Take the image from Figure 10.2 and design all of it on layers. Figure 10.10 shows how I actually designed it. Look at the layers that are in this particular image.

Now do the same thing you did a minute ago. Move the text and notice that the background items don't get deleted, and the shadow and highlight for the text also moves without deleting the background. Take a look at Figure 10.11.

Figure 10.8.

The anti-alias is a blend between the gray circle and transparency or no color.

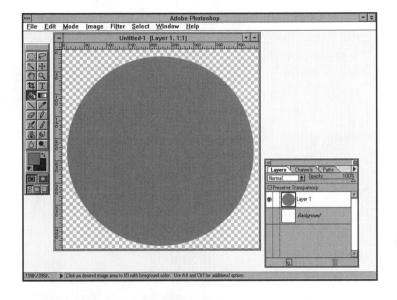

Figure 10.9.

Copying the circle. Hey, no anti-alias halo!

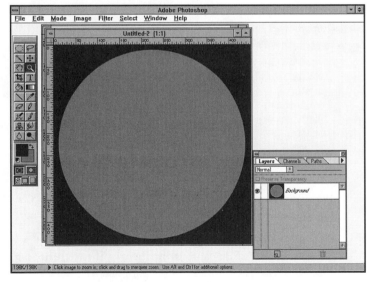

Figure 10.10.

The layers used with Joe's Vacation Hideaway.

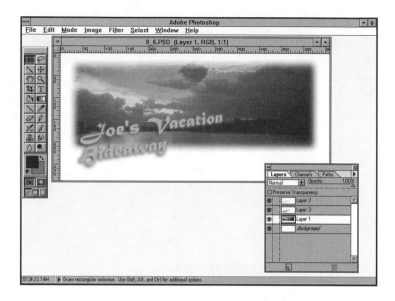

Figure 10.11.

Moving items that are on layers doesn't delete the background and doesn't create an anti-alias halo.

Let me explain the magic. As you saw with the circle example, using layers doesn't create a fixed anti-alias. It also doesn't delete the items behind the objects. Because things are on separate layers, all the parts are kept intact no matter where you move them.

As you can see, Photoshop's layering capability creates a new way to design raster images. Due to its fluidity, I use it to lay out entire pages. If you are not familiar with Photoshop's layering capability I suggest finding a good book on its use. I recommend *Laura Lemay's Web Workshop: Web Graphics and Page Design* (because my co-author and I wrote a lot on using Photoshop specifically, as well as techniques such as the one presented here). You could spend the rest of this book learning about Photoshop alone, but you have more ground to cover than just Photoshop imaging techniques.

How do you size your images if you don't have a layers-capable image editor? One of the best ways to plan your pages is to use grid sketching paper. Using grid paper, you can draw your screen resolution using 1 grid box equal to 10 pixels or something similar. Lay out your screen elements by hand and then count the boxes to calculate what sizes the images need to be.

After you have determined the size for your images, use your image editor to size them. In Photoshop you'll use the Image | Image Size option. This will bring up a dialog box as shown in Figure 10.12. Adjust the width and height of your image, and make sure the Constrain: File Size option is deselected. If it is not, scaling an image down will increase the dpi. When you scale an image, you should notice a decrease in file size.

Figure 10.12.
Sizing images using Photoshop.

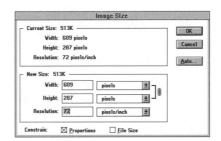

10

One of the nice things about Photoshop is how it blurs images as they are reduced. As in any image editor, reducing the image size too far will result in a blurry blob. However, for Photoshop to resize properly, you must make sure you are currently in a 24-bit mode. Before you resize any image, go to the Mode menu and select RGB Color (24-bit). This gives the editor more colors from which to choose during the blurring process. Blurring a 256-color image looks pretty poor. Again, before you change the size of any image, change the image to high-color, 24-bit, or RGB mode (which are all the same thing) to get the optimum effect.

Inserting Images

The "fun" begins after you have created your images. For me, inserting the images and getting them just the way I want is the part that tries my patience. However, I'll strive to hit the major points of concern in the next few sections to make it a little easier.

Specifying Sizes

As you learned on Day 9, "Text-Level Tags," the <IMG> tag has several attributes that you can use to control the placement and appearance of the images. The first of these are the HEIGHT and WIDTH attributes.

NOTE

> Please note that I find very little use for the HEIGHT and WIDTH attributes. People often use these attributes to scale their graphics instead of scaling them in an image editor. To be honest, you'll save yourself a lot of time, as well as Internet bandwidth, by getting a good image editor and sizing the images before you use them in your Web pages.

Originally, the HEIGHT and WIDTH options were created to enable you to use a single source image for multiple graphics included on a Web page. For example, you could have an image that was 100 pixels by 100 pixels and then use the HEIGHT and WIDTH options to insert it at a smaller size. However, doing this doesn't do much for the way your page looks.

Figure 10.13 shows a graphic inserted into a page at different sizes. Let me build a case against using the HEIGHT and WIDTH attributes to insert graphics any size other then their true size. First, notice that the center graphic has been inserted at its true size. The graphic to the left has its HEIGHT and WIDTH attributes set at half the value. The graphic to the right is set at 150 percent larger. The code for the graphics looks like this:

```
<CENTER>
  <IMG SRC="gear.gif" HEIGHT=90 WIDTH=100 BORDER=0 HSPACE=30>
  <IMG SRC="gear.gif" HEIGHT=180 WIDTH=200 BORDER=0 HSPACE=30>
  <IMG SRC="gear.gif" HEIGHT=270 WIDTH=300 BORDER=0 HSPACE=30>
</CENTER>
```

Figure 10.13.

Using the HEIGHT *and* WIDTH *attributes to size an image is not a good idea.*

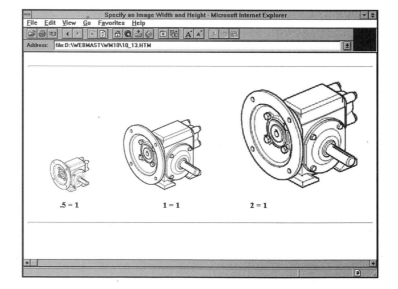

The small image displays OK at a reduced size, although the image is a little ratty and rough. However, using what you know about scaling an image up and down, you should know that you are wasting bandwidth here. In order for the image to be displayed in this way, all the image data must be downloaded, and then the browser must shrink the image on the fly. You would save download time and be able to display a nicer graphic if you sized the image before bringing it into the page.

The image that is displayed 150 percent larger has visible problems. Specifying that the browser scale the graphic up as it is displayed separates the dots in the image. This makes the image appear grainy, and quite frankly, pretty poor. Again, you should size it in a raster program and display it at the true size in the browser.

So what am I saying? Don't use the HEIGHT and WIDTH attributes of the <IMG> tag to enable the browser to size the image. Do the scaling in an image editor and insert the image at its true size. Image editors do a much nicer job of scaling an image, and you won't waste bandwidth. Code your HTML so that it uses the exact or true size of the image in your pages.

Another use of the HEIGHT and WIDTH attributes is to display blank rectangles for images as they are being downloaded, as shown in Figure 10.14. If you specify a HEIGHT and WIDTH, blank rectangles will display as the page is loading. To me, specifying a HEIGHT and WIDTH for an image so that blank rectangles appear during download is a waste of time because I don't like having to write down the image's size. Also, typing it in is just more code to have to enter. You can make your own decision.

Figure 10.14.

Using the HEIGHT *and* WIDTH *attributes reserves blank spots for the images.*

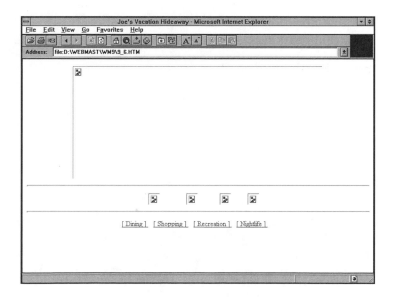

Alignment and Spacing

The attributes for the <IMG> tag that control alignment and spacing are the ALIGN, VSPACE, and HSPACE attributes. You can use the tags together to control the alignment of the image in relationship to the surrounding text; use the ALIGN attribute and the spacing or negative space around the images using VSPACE and HSPACE.

Figure 10.15 shows an example of the ALIGN attribute in action. Note that the image uses ALIGN=LEFT to enable the image to justify left. It also uses the HSPACE attribute to give the graphic a little breathing room. Note that the text automatically flows around the image. Listing 10.1 shows the code for Figure 10.15.

Listing 10.1. The code for Figure 10.15.

```
<!DOCTYPE HTML 2.0//EN>
<!-- Created by J.L.Mohler 11/12/96 -->
 <HTML>
 <HEAD>
   <TITLE> Aligning Images </TITLE>
 </HEAD>
 <BODY BGCOLOR="#FFFFFF" TEXT="#000000">
 <HR WIDTH=50%>
 <BR>
 <H3 ALIGN=CENTER> Technical Graphics at Purdue University </H3>
 <HR>
 <BR>
<P><IMG SRC="purdue.gif" ALIGN=LEFT HSPACE=10> <BR> The mission of the
Department of Technical Graphics at Purdue University is to prepare students
to be the nation's best practitioners and managers of applied computer
graphics. The department will be recognized as the national leader through
teaching, scholarship and service. </P>
 <HR>
 <DL>
   <DT>Engineering Design Graphics</DT>
<DD>The study of orthographics, isometric, and auxiliary view drawings to
present technical information in a graphical format. Stresses production of
detail and assembly drawings that include dimensions, manufacturing processes,
and blueprint reading. Use of computer-generated 2-D and 3-D drawings and
models to stress concepts, applications, and the production of engineering
drawings. In-depth study of 3-D space relationships and solutions to geometric
problems.</DD>
   <DT>Illustration</DT>
<DD>Stresses visual thinking though CAD images and publishing techniques.
Concentrates on drawings that visually represent mechanical parts and their
assembly relationships. Emphasizes the application of color theory to
traditionally and electronically produced technical images. </DD>
   <DT>Digital Publishing</DT>
<DD>Teaches effective methods of presenting information on the printed page,
including composition, use of type, image manipulation, and computerized
publishing methods for camera-ready artwork. Combines technical illustration,
CAD images, and publishing techniques to produce graphically oriented
```

```
documents for business and industry. Focuses on the use of interactive
multimedia for communication using both Word-Wide Web and CD-ROM
distribution media. </DD>
  </DL>
 </BODY>
</HTML>
```

Figure 10.15.

Using the ALIGN *attribute to control an image.*

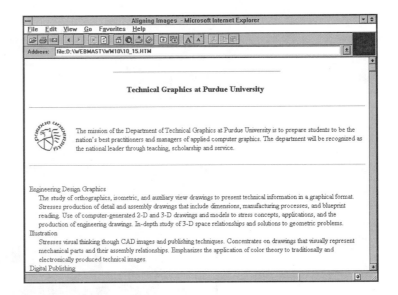

Day 3 highlighted the fact that you must know the resolution of your audience's display screen so that you can design around it. Let me show you why. Figure 10.15 looks nicely formatted because when I designed the image I designed it around an 800×600 screen. But what happens if the audience is viewing the page with a 640×480 screen? Look at Figure 10.16 to learn the answer. Note that the text that was originally flowing around the image must now drop below the image to fit all the text onto the screen. Had I designed around the audience's limitation, the page would have been made to look correct at 640×480. It is extremely important that you do a little research and find out at what screen resolution your audience will typically be viewing. You might want to put the suggested screen resolution right on the Web page. Or, you might want to specify an adjustment parameter or "size gauge" so the audience can adjust its browser to the designed size as shown in Figure 10.17.

Figure 10.16.

Changing the size of the browser window changes how the page is laid out.

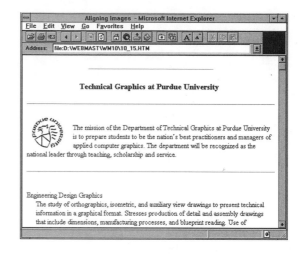

Figure 10.17.

Inserting a size gauge on your page so that the audience can adjust its browser.

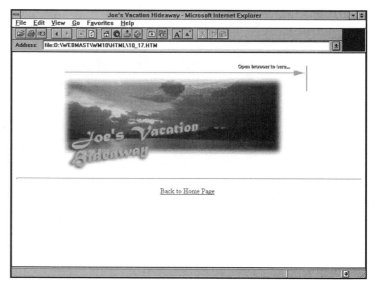

One of the things you will note about the ALIGN attribute is that it is always built in relationship to the surrounding text body. The ALIGN=LEFT setting floats the image to the left margin. The left margin for the text is set as the image's right side so that the text flows smoothly around the image. If there was text before the image, the image would be forced to the next blank line and would proceed from that point.

The following are other values for the ALIGN attribute:

- [ ] ALIGN=TOP—Aligns the top of the image with the top line of the current body of text.

- [ ] ALIGN=MIDDLE—Aligns the middle of the image with the baseline of the current text line. (Note that the baseline is the imaginary line on which the line of text rests.)

- [ ] ALIGN=BOTTOM—Aligns the bottom of the image with the baseline of the current text line.

- [ ] ALIGN=LEFT or ALIGN=RIGHT—Floats the image to the respective margin. The margin is reset to the edge of the image so that text and other elements flow around the image.

The example in Figure 10.15 also uses the HSPACE attribute to enable the graphic to breathe a little. In that example, HSPACE=10, or 10 pixels. This means that five blank pixels were assigned on one side and five on the other. You can use any even or odd number. With both the HSPACE and VSPACE attributes, the value assigned is split and placed on either side of the image.

Borders

One of the other frequently used attributes of the <IMG> tag is the BORDER attribute. This attribute controls the thickness of a border line around the particular image. The default is BORDER=2, and you can suppress the border by using BORDER=0.

Figure 10.18 shows an example of a Web page that uses images with borders. One of the things you need to keep in mind is that, generally, when Web surfers see an image with a blue border they expect or assume that the image is a hyperlink. Web users are conditioned to click an item when they see the notorious blue color. Don't be surprised if you use a different color border to represent a hyperlink and people don't realize it's a hyperlink. On the flip side, using blue borders on images that are not hypertext links can frustrate your audience. Use image borders cautiously.

10

Figure 10.18.

Using borders around your images.

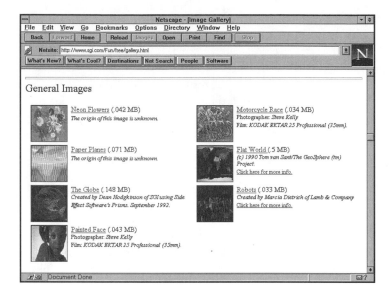

Using the ALT and LOWSRC **Attributes**

The last two image attributes, the ALT and LOWSRC options, give you ways to enable people with nongraphical browsers or slow links to view your Web pages efficiently. The ALT option enables you to specify a title to appear in place of the graphic for nongraphical browsers or when the inline images option is turned off. The LOWSRC attribute, which is not supported by all browsers, enables you to specify a low-quality image for the browser to display when the high-resolution image is being downloaded.

The first of these two attributes is the ALT attribute. As shown in Figure 10.19, the ALT attribute enables you to specify a title to appear in nongraphical browsers. It is also useful if the audience has the inline images option turned off.

To use the ALT attribute, the lines of code for the images need to be modified so they look like this:

```
<IMG SRC="6b.gif" BORDER=0 HSPACE=30 ALT="Dining Image">
<IMG SRC="6c.gif" BORDER=0 HSPACE=30 ALT="Shopping Image">
<IMG SRC="6d.gif" BORDER=0 HSPACE=20 ALT="Recreation Image">
<IMG SRC="6e.gif" BORDER=0 HSPACE=20 ALT="Nightlife Image">
```

NOTE

Make sure that if you use the ALT attribute, the name you want to appear is in quotations. Not all browsers will recognize the entire line if you don't enclose it in quotation marks.

Figure 10.19.

Using the ALT *attribute to specify an image title.*

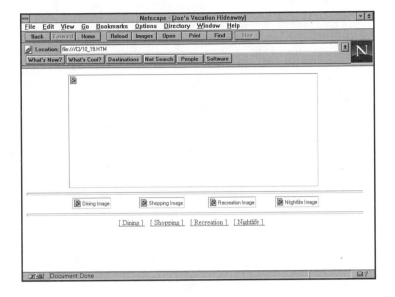

To use the LOWSRC attribute within the previous lines of code, you would add the attribute so that they look like this:

```
<IMG SRC="6b.gif" BORDER=0 HSPACE=30 ALT="Dining Image" LOWSRC="6b_low.gif">
<IMG SRC="6c.gif" BORDER=0 HSPACE=30 ALT="Shopping Image" LOWSRC="6c_low.gif">
<IMG SRC="6d.gif" BORDER=0 HSPACE=20 ALT="Recreation Image" LOWSRC="6d_low.gif">
<IMG SRC="6e.gif" BORDER=0 HSPACE=20 ALT="Nightlife Image" LOWSRC="6e_low.gif">
```

Keep in mind that the whole goal of the LOWSRC attribute is to make the page appear to load quicker. You'll mainly want to use this attribute for images that are quite large. The images displayed in the preceding code are small to begin with, so you probably don't need to use the LOWSRC attribute. You should focus on using the LOWSRC attribute for images that are larger than 30KB. This is where you can make the page look as if it loads quicker. For images smaller than this, just let the original load.

Generating Images

Now that you've gotten intimate with the <IMG> tag and its attributes, it's time to learn how to generate images to use in your pages. Unfortunately, we can't spend a great deal of time dealing with step-by-step methods, but you'll learn many of the technical and aesthetic concerns dealing with graphics in the next few sections.

Creating Thumbnails

A common practice on the Web is to provide small representations of graphics called thumbnails. Thumbnails give the audience the choice of whether it wants to view a larger, more detailed version of your graphic.

NEW TERM A *thumbnail* is a small representation of a larger image. To create them you simply scale an image down to the desired size.

To create a thumbnail, the main thing you need to know is what size the image needs to be so that you can size your images as you learned previously. Again, if you can, lay out your page graphics right in the image editor. At least use grid paper to determine the size that your thumbnails need to be. When you fix your size, use your image editor's sizing command to scale the graphic. Don't forget to put the image into RGB or 24-bit mode before scaling.

Creating Tiles for Backgrounds

One of the <BODY> tag's attributes is the BACKGROUND option, which enables you to specify an image to be tiled across the background of the browser work area. Much like the <IMG> tag's SRC option, the BACKGROUND attribute simply specifies a path and image to be used. This technique is often used in Web pages but can cause problems if you want to utilize other blended or soft images in the foreground. Figure 10.20 shows an example of a tiled browser background.

Figure 10.20.

Using a bitmap for a tiled background.

Be Careful with That Plaid Chip!

When you use the BACKGROUND attribute, you must be careful that the background tile does not overpower or dominate the text and items being displayed in front of the tiles. Throughout the Web you can find pages on which the background that is used overpowers the information being presented, as shown in Figure 10.21.

Figure 10.21.

Be careful using that tie-dye chip as a tiling background!

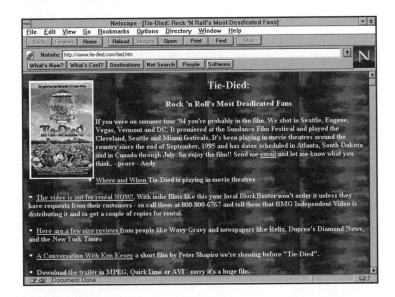

Subtlety Is the Answer

When you are designing bitmaps to be used as background tiles, you must be certain of two things. First, the most effective background tiles are those which are subtle. You want the tiled background to show up, but you don't want it to dominate the rest of the page. Subtlety is the key, as shown in Figure 10.22.

Second, you must make sure that the bitmap will make an effective tile. The horizontal and vertical details must line up as the tile repeats. If these elements don't line up, you'll end up with seams in your background, as shown in Figure 10.23.

Figure 10.22.

Subtle tiles work best for backgrounds.

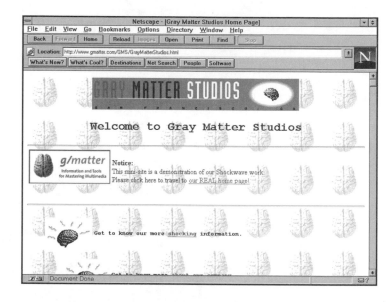

Figure 10.23.

If horizontal and vertical features don't line up in the bitmap, you'll be able to see seams in your background.

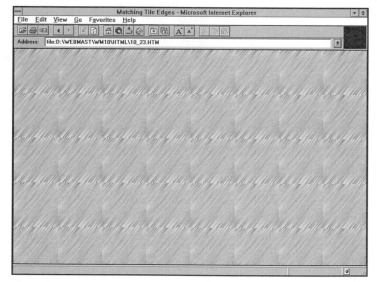

Transparent GIFs

If you decide to use a background tile, or even if you are using a flat color background, you might want to use the transparency feature of the GIF file format for your graphics.

A *transparent GIF file* is a special image in which one color in the image is assigned as transparent. When the image is used in a Web page, the transparent color enables items in the background of the browser to show through.

As shown in Figure 10.24, a transparent bitmap enables the background of the browser to show through the bitmap. This is a pretty effective technique when you are generating bitmaps. As I recommended earlier, if you are using a flat color for your background, you can create nice shadows and blended elements in your graphics. However, you cannot create these blended elements so easily using a tiling image. An alternative is to use transparent GIFs.

Figure 10.24.

Using transparent GIF images.

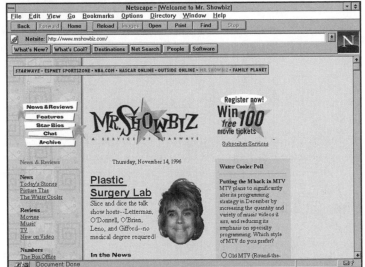

NOTE

To create a transparent GIF in Photoshop 3.0 you will need the special plug-in to be able to save in GIF89a format. You can acquire this filter from Adobe's Web site at `http://www.adobe.com`. In version 4.0 of Photoshop, GIF89a is directly supported in the software.

Now learn how to create a transparent GIF image using Photoshop 3.0. I already have the GIF89a filter installed on my machine. Do the simple circle example so that you'll see the anti-aliasing problem that often occurs with transparent GIF images.

Open a new canvas and create a gray circle in the image. Next, change the mode to 8-bit so that you can save the image in GIF format. Note that if you have the image in RGB mode, the GIF format won't be an option when you go to export the file. Figure 10.25 shows the file to be exported.

Figure 10.25.

The gray circle that will be exported.

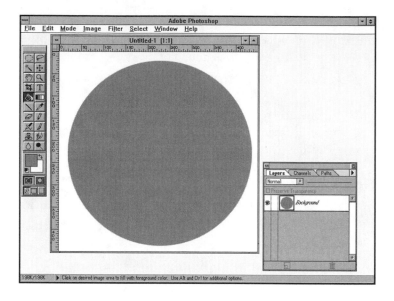

Next, select the File | Export | GIF89a option. The GIF89a Export Options dialog box shown in Figure 10.26 appears. Using the color selector in this dialog box, select the white color as the transparent color and click OK. Give it a filename to finish exporting the file.

Figure 10.26.

The GIF89a Export Options dialog box.

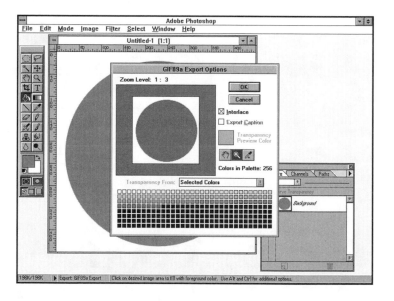

Now create a quick page on which to insert the circle. The coding for the page will look like Listing 10.2.

Listing 10.2. The page for the circle image.

```
<!DOCTYPE "HTML 3.2 //EN">
<HTML>
  <HEAD>
    <TITLE>Using Transparent GIF files </TITLE>
  </HEAD>
  <BODY BGCOLOR="#FFFFFF" TEXT="#000000">
    <CENTER>
        <IMG SRC="circle.gif" BORDER=0>
    </CENTER>
  </BODY>
</HTML>
```

Now look at the circle in the browser as shown in Figure 10.27. Because the browser background is the same color as the canvas on which you created the circle, everything appears to be okay. But what happens if you change the browser background color to black? Look at Figure 10.28.

Figure 10.27.

The transparent circle in the browser.

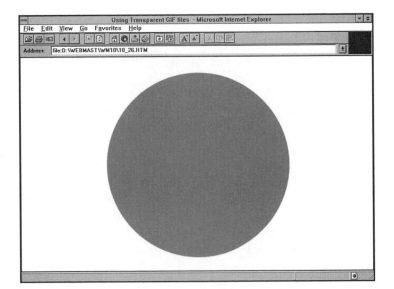

What happened? Notice that the same problem you had before with the fixed anti-alias again causes problems. You get a glorious anti-alias halo. Really there are two specific browser states with which you'll need to be concerned so that you can overcome the problem of anti-alias halo. The browser background determines the method for creating your graphics. The two cases of state are when you use a flat color for the browser background and when you use a tiling image for the browser background.

Figure 10.28.

The circle on a black browser background.

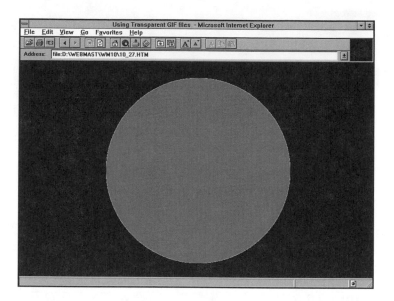

If you are planning to create transparent bitmaps on flat color backgrounds—in other words, if you are using the BGCOLOR option in the <BODY> tag—you simply need to design your graphics on a canvas that is the same color as your BGCOLOR. For example, if you use a blue background in your browser, the canvas on which you design your graphics will also need to be that same blue. If the browser background is yellow, the canvas background is yellow, too.

You might be wondering how you do the color conversion between hex and RGB so you can make sure your canvas is the same color. There are two ways in which you can back calculate from a hex color to an RGB color. The first is to find the hex color you want in the browser and then use the old calculator method in reverse, entering hex values and then changing the calculator mode to decimal to find the decimal equivalent. Or, you can load the color into the browser, capture the screen, and take that image into the image editor so that you can sample the browser color directly. I prefer the image capture method. Regardless of which you use, both will give you the same color results.

The second browser state that affects how you design images occurs when you use a tiling image. In the circle example, if you would have turned off the anti-aliasing when you created the circle you wouldn't have had the halo effect. However, when you turn off anti-aliasing you'll get a very jaggy image as shown in Figure 10.29. You see that as you work with graphics, the larger the image or element, the less apparent the jaggies will be. The smaller the element, the more apparent jaggies will be.

Figure 10.29.

Turning off anti-aliasing fixes the halo but creates a jaggy image.

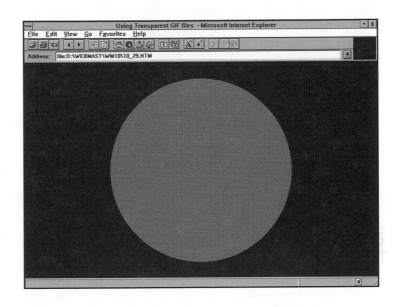

Interlaced GIF, Progressive JPEGs, and PNG

One other graphics technique you will see on the Web is the use of interlaced graphics. Interlacing graphics enables the browser to show a progressive representation of the particular image. Much like focusing a blurry image on a camera, progressive images enable the browser to show a coarse description of the graphic at the beginning of the download. The image then becomes clearer as the rest of it is loaded until it is fully clear at download completion.

When you were exporting the transparent image a few minutes ago, you probably noticed the interlaced option in the Save dialog box. The interlace option in any graphic file format causes the data to be saved non-sequentially. Instead of storing each line of pixels as they appear from top to bottom in the image, interlacing stores every 4th, 8th, or 16th line in that order. So, rather than storing lines 1, 2, 3, and so on, an interlaced file stores line 1, line 8, line 16, and so on. It then repeats at the top of the image with line 2, line 17, and so on. This way, the image can be progressively drawn as the image is downloaded.

One of the newest interlaced formats is the progressive JPEG. Many of the latest imaging applications such as Adobe Photoshop 4.0 support this new rendition of the original JPEG format. When you incorporate a progressive JPEG image, the receiving browser first loads a low-resolution version of the image. It then successively loads higher versions of the image until the final full-resolution image appears. The progressive JPEG is quite impressive, but still, data loss can be a negative because it uses lossy compression.

Before you move on to the next section, one noteworthy occurrence has developed in the world of Web graphics: a new graphics format. This new graphics format has some very distinct advantages over both the JPEG and GIF formats and seeks to better standardize the graphics found on the Web.

The new Portable Network Graphics (PNG) format is a new graphics format that boasts advantages over both the GIF and JPEG formats. The PNG format supports index color up to 256 colors, progressive display, transparency, and lossless compression. It is out to eliminate the use of the GIF format. The biggest problem with the GIF format is that the compression used within it is copyrighted. Many of the Web sites and companies that exclusively use the GIF format could be found under copyright infringement if the company holding the GIF copyright (CompuServe) wanted to pursue it. This is the biggest reason for the introduction of the PNG format.

The PNG format includes several features that make it a threat to the JPEG format as well. The PNG format supports RGB color images up to 48 bits, full masking (beyond the simple transparency setting in the GIF format), and image gamma information for setting color attributes for certain devices. This is a pretty hefty format. It will be interesting to see how quickly this format catches on. The big two (Netscape and Explorer) currently support the new format. In addition, many of the latest image editors enable the developer to generate files in the new format. It appears that GIF and JPEG will be on their way out soon. Keep your eyes on the PNG format.

NOTE

> For more information on the PNG format, check the W3C's information at http://www.w3.org or do a search on PNG at Yahoo! (http://www.yahoo.com).

Using Postscript Graphics

Day 4 briefly presented the issue of using Postscript graphics at your site, and I was purposefully vague. You can integrate vector-based graphics into your pages, but the best way to do so is to convert your graphics to a bitmap format. Let's take a look at the process of converting Postscript images for a moment, because I believe many people would like to use Postscript images that they have created or gotten via clip art.

Rasterizing Postscript Images

The biggest problem with vector graphic conversion (to raster) is that you end up with jaggies—ends that are severely pixelated. However, you can get rid of the jaggies if you convert them correctly. Most vector graphics can be imported or opened into either Macromedia FreeHand or Adobe Illustrator. These two tools are the predominant illustration packages that are used for vector illustration. The first step to being able to utilize vector graphics is the conversion process from vector to raster. Here you learn how to do it in Macromedia FreeHand.

Begin the conversion process by opening the image into the vector program. One of the pluses of Macromedia FreeHand on the PC is that it enables you to export a vector drawing as a TIFF file. The program automatically converts the image to a pixel-based (raster) drawing. However, to make this whole thing work right you must scale the image up to a larger size than you need, as shown in Figure 10.30.

Figure 10.30.

Scaling the image up in the vector program.

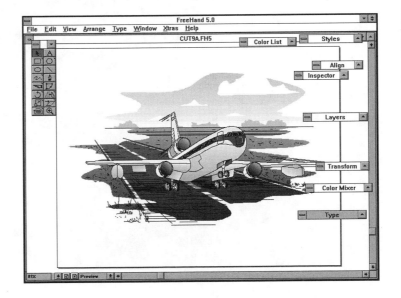

After scaling it up, use the File | Export option and export it as a TIFF image. Now you have a raster image of the drawing, and you can open it into Adobe Photoshop as shown in Figure 10.31.

After you have opened the image into Photoshop the jaggies are quite evident. The first thing you should do is create a new layer. Then select the parts of the image and move them to a new layer by copying and pasting. After the elements are on the new layer you will scale them. The whole reason you scale the image up in the vector program is so that you can scale it back down in the raster package. What happens when you scale the image down in the raster package? The raster editor automatically blurs the edges of the image and, voilá! No more jaggies (see Figure 10.32).

Figure 10.31.
*Opening the rasterized
TIFF image.*

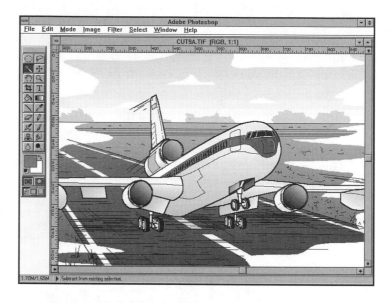

Figure 10.32.
*The finished, scaled,
rasterized vector file.*

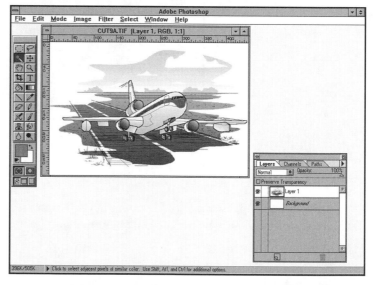

If you do not have access to Macromedia FreeHand to do the TIFF conversion, there are a
couple of other ways to do this conversion.

☐ Convert your raster image to an Adobe Illustrator file and open it directly into
Adobe Photoshop.

☐ Do a screen capture of the vector file as it is open in the vector editor.

10

Working with Image Maps

Undoubtedly, you have by now seen Web pages that have large graphics with multiple links associated to them, as shown in Figure 10.33. Clicking a certain area takes you to one page, and clicking another area takes you somewhere else. Any graphic that functions this way is called an image map. An image map is thus named because the UNIX program that originally enabled it to happen was called "imagemap." However, no matter what horrors you've heard about using image maps, they are really quite easy to create.

Figure 10.33.

An image map used at a Web site.

The basic gist of the image map is that you have a plain image to which you want to create multiple links. Maybe it's a single image with icons that represent various parts of your site or an image that graphically depicts several pages at your site. To use it as an image map, you must define the regions of the image to be linked to various URLs, pages, or files. To define the various regions, simply use coordinate values that describe those regions. These coordinate values are pairs of X,Y coordinates using the upper-left corner of the image as the origin, or 0,0.

In the past, creating image maps was unbearable. Having to calculate the defined regions using an image editor just was not an efficient use of time. Today, however, several shareware tools exist that make it very easy to define the regions for an image map. If you can draw a line, you can create and use an image map.

Originally, image maps required the use of an external program called a Common Gateway Interface (CGI) script, as well as a good relationship with your system administrator. Images that require a CGI script to function are called server-side image maps. The CGI program that they use is actually part of the server software, so you must know where the program resides or at least know someone who does. In any event, server-side scripts use a text file to define the coordinates for the image. When the user clicks the map, the coordinate on which he clicks is sent to the CGI script. The CGI script then looks up the coordinate value in a special file called a Map Definition File located on the server. This is the file that holds all the coordinate values that define the regions for the image map. Associated with the coordinate definitions are URLs that tell the CGI script where to go when the user clicks in the region.

Does it sound complicated? To some degree, working with server-side image maps is difficult. Having to know the location of the CGI script makes the process of using server-side image maps more difficult than it has to be. In most instances today, you can use a different type of image map—a client-side image map. These maps do not use a CGI script, but they do still use a map definition. However, the map definition is embedded right within the HTML file that holds the graphic. This makes image maps a lot easier to use.

Creating Images

Image maps have a tendency to be quite large. Because they hold a lot of information, they often download very slowly. You've probably run into at least one image map that took quite a while to download.

The first step to creating and using an image map is to develop the graphic that you plan to use. As you are creating the graphic, try to keep the file size down. Creating huge images will do nothing but frustrate your users. Most of the image maps I use are GIF images, although you can use JPEG images as well. The biggest issue in using an image map is the file size.

Creating a Client-Side Image Map

After you have created your image, install the Mapedit program onto your computer. Figure 10.34 shows an example of the image used here. Joe has decided that he wants to use an image map for his vacation hideaway. He wants to create four hotlinks, each linked to the appropriate Web page.

When you start the software you will be presented with the dialog box shown in Figure 10.35. For a client-side image map, the software must know where the HTML file is that uses the image. Use the browse button to select your file.

10

Figure 10.34.

*The image for Joe's
Vacation Hideaway.*

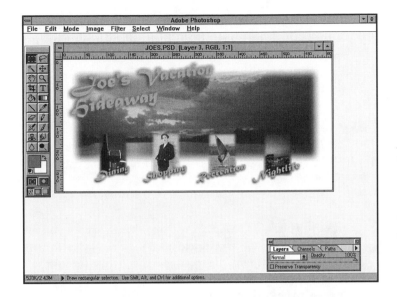

Figure 10.35.

The Mapedit dialog box.

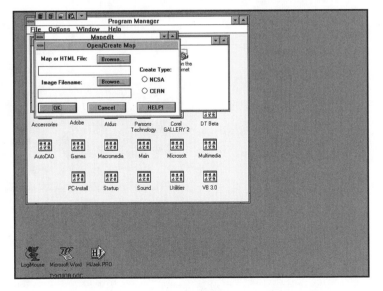

NOTE

For client-side image maps, you'll have to change the drop-down menu at the bottom of the browse dialog box to the HTML Pages *.HTM rather than Map Definition *.MAP. Client-side maps embed the coordinate values right in the HTML files. Server-side maps use an external Map Definition File.

After you have selected the HTML file, Mapedit will show you all of the images that are used in the file. Click the name of the image that you want to be the image map. When you have selected your HTML file and image, click OK in the dialog box. You'll see several radio buttons that are labeled CERN and NCSA, but you don't have to worry about those with client-side maps (see Figure 10.36).

Figure 10.36.

After entering the values, you are ready to begin defining your hotlink areas.

After you click OK, Mapedit will open the image for you to draw upon. Use the buttons at the top of the Mapedit screen to draw squares, circles, rectangles, and lines. In Figure 10.37, I have begun defining the rectangles that define the hotspots in my image. After you make one, you will be presented with a dialog box in which you need to specify a URL address for the spot to be linked to, as well as the alternative text to be displayed in non-graphics browsers.

Figure 10.37.

Defining the rectangles for the hotspots of the image map.

Notice that you have defined the rectangles for your image map, but what if the user clicks on the text for each area that falls outside the region definition? You can add or delete points using the Add Point or Delete Point buttons.

After you define your regions, you need to define the default URL. For example, if your audience clicks outside the defined regions, do you want to take them to another page? Often you'll want to take them to a page that lets them know the background region isn't defined. Other times you'll actually have a page to which the rest of the image is linked. To define the default URL, access the File | Default URL option and enter a URL for the background of the image.

10

After you have defined all your regions and set your default URL, save the file. The coordinate definitions will be automatically saved to your HTML file. The file I generated looks something like Listing 10.3.

Listing 10.3. The HTML for the image map in Mapedit.

```
<!DOCTYPE "HTML 3.2 //EN">
<HTML>
  <HEAD>
    <TITLE>Joe's Vacation Hideaway</TITLE>
  </HEAD>
  <BODY BGCOLOR="#FFFFFF" TEXT="#FFFFFF" LINK="#334557">
    <HR>
    <CENTER>
        <IMG SRC="joes.gif" BORDER="0" USEMAP="#joes">
    </CENTER>
    <HR>
  <MAP NAME="joes">
    <AREA SHAPE="rect" ALT="Dining Establishments" COORDS="74,166,133,257"
    ➥HREF="dine.html">
    <AREA SHAPE="rect" ALT="Places to Shop" COORDS="196,167,254,256"
    ➥HREF="shop.html">
    <AREA SHAPE="rect" ALT="Recreation" COORDS="323,167,383,257"
    ➥HREF="rec.html">
    <AREA SHAPE="rect" ALT="Nightlife" COORDS="451,169,507,256"
    ➥HREF="nitelife.html">
    <AREA SHAPE="default" HREF="nolink.html">
  </MAP>
</BODY>
</HTML>
```

In the code that was added to the HTML file, notice some new tags. Let's take a look at them.

> **The <MAP> and <AREA> Tags**
>
> The <MAP> tag is used to define the parameters for a client-side image map. The <AREA> tag is used inside the <MAP>...</MAP> tags to define the hotspots for the client-side image map.

The <MAP> tag itself has only one attribute, which is required. The NAME attribute specifies a name for the client-side image map. However, the <AREA> tag has several attributes:

☐ SHAPE—Defines the shape of the hotspot being defined. Valid entries include RECT, CIRCLE, POLYGON, and DEFAULT. If you use DEFAULT, it must be the last area defined in the listing.

☐ COORDS—Defines the coordinate values for the area. Valid entries are in the form of X1,Y1,X2,Y2, and so on. Rectangle coordinates are specified by left, top, right, bottom. Circle coordinates are specified by X,Y (center location) and R (radius). Polygon coordinates are specified by successive X and Y values.

☐ HREF—Defines the URL to be linked to the image map's hotspot.

☐ ALT—Defines the text that should be displayed in nongraphical browsers.

☐ NOHREF—Defines a hotspot that does nothing.

Creating a Server-Side Image Map

Creating a server-side map is not significantly different than creating the client-side map until you use it. The problem with server-side image maps is that they cannot be tested until they are uploaded to the server. They also are much more taxing on the server in regards to providing information. However, many browsers do not yet support client-side image maps, so if you want to use one you might have to use a server-side map. Fortunately, the big two, Navigator and Explorer, do support client-side image maps.

To create a server-side map you must first know what type of server your Web site is based upon. It will be either an NCSA server (National Center for Supercomputing Applications) or a CERN (Conseil European pour la Recherche Nucleaire) server. NCSA is the most common. After you know that information, choose the appropriate server in the opening Mapedit dialog box. You also will need to specify a Map Definition File rather than an HTML file to house the coordinate information for the map. When you create a server-side map, the coordinate values are not stored in the HTML file, so you don't already need to have the HTML file built. Proceed and create the regions for your image map as you did before. This time when you save the file, the coordinate information will be stored in the Map Definition File with the name you specified.

After you have generated your Map Definition File, you must then code your page so that it uses the Map Definition File. The HTML code to integrate a server-side map looks like this:

```
<A HREF="/cgi-bin/imagemap/mymap.map"><IMG SRC="../joes.gif" ISMAP></A>
```

Summary

Today you have taken an applied look at using graphics in your Web pages. You've seen both how to calculate your image sizes as well as how to scale your graphic images so that you can insert them into your Web pages at their true size. Keep in mind that you will come out with better results by inserting your images at their true size rather than enabling the browser to do on-the-fly scaling when the pages are loaded.

In today's lesson you also learned how to use the various attributes of the `<IMG>` tag, including the `HEIGHT`, `WIDTH`, `ALIGN`, `VSPACE`, `HSPACE`, `ALT`, and `LOWSRC` attributes. You will use each of these attributes in varying degrees as you create Web pages for yourself and your clients.

Hopefully I have also dispelled the rumor that image maps are for techno-weenies. Client-side image maps are a much better use of network resources as well as much easier to test and utilize. However, because there still are many browsers on user machines that don't recognize client-side image maps, you also learned server-side image maps. As often as is possible, you should try to use client-side image maps because they are more efficient and easier to use.

Q&A

Q What are the three attributes of raster images with which you need to be concerned? Why are they a concern?

A The three attributes of raster images with which you need to be concerned are image resolution, image size, and image bit depth. Each of these attributes affects the speed at which a graphic file downloads.

Q What are the two steps to sizing images for your pages?

A The first step to sizing images is determining the size that the images need to be on your pages. You can either lay out the entire page in an image editor, or you can use grid sketch paper to determine sizes. The second step is to use the image editor to scale the image to the predetermined size found in step one.

Q What are the two biggest problems with a single-layer raster editor?

A The two biggest problems of a single-layer raster editing environment are the deletion of background pixels by foreground pixels and the fixed nature of anti-aliasing that often causes anti-aliasing halos.

Q Before you scale an image, what should you do to the image so that the image colors blur correctly?

A Before scaling an image you must make sure that the image is in the highest bit depth possible. The higher the bit depth, the more colors you have available for the blending that occurs during scaling. When the image is scaled, you can then revert the image back to a lower bit depth.

Q Why shouldn't you use the `HEIGHT` and `WIDTH` attributes to enable the browser to scale an image?

A If you use the `HEIGHT` and `WIDTH` attributes to scale an image down, you enable the browser to scale the image on the fly. This results in data that is unused by the browser, wasting bandwidth. If you use the `HEIGHT` and `WIDTH` attributes to scale an image up, the image will often begin to break apart because the number of dots per

10

inch decreases when the image is scaled up. You should always use an image editor to scale the graphic to the appropriate size before coding it into your Web pages.

Q **How do you create a tiling background in a Web page? What must you be concerned with when doing this?**

A To create a tiling image in a Web page you must first create a small, repeatable graphic to be used. You then use the <BODY> tag's BACKGROUND attribute to specify that the image is to be used as a tiling background. The biggest concern when using tiling backgrounds is that the background should not overpower the foreground text and other elements. Subtlety is the key to effective tiling backgrounds.

Q **What is a transparent GIF image? How is it created?**

A A transparent GIF image is an image in which a specific color in the image is displayed in the browser as transparent color, which reveals anything that is behind it.

Q **What is the trick to using Postscript graphics in your Web pages?**

A The trick to using Postscript graphics in your Web pages is to rasterize the images. Before rasterizing them you must scale them up so that you can then scale them down in the raster editor. Being able to scale them down in the raster editor blurs the image slightly, which gets rid of the jaggies that are characteristic of vector-based drawings.

Q **What is the difference between a server-side image map and a client-side image map?**

A A server-side image uses a CGI script to translate the regional coordinates of the image map. A server-side image map uses the image, and external file called a Map Definition File, and the CGI script to interpret the map coordinates. A client-side image map does not use an external CGI script. The client-side image map uses mapping coordinates that are stored in the HTML code file that uses the image file via the <IMG> tag.

Workshop

The Workshop provides quiz questions to help you solidify your understanding of the material covered and exercises to give you experience in using what you've learned. The quiz answers are provided in Appendix A, "Quiz Answers." Try to understand the quiz answers before you go on to tomorrow's lesson.

Quiz

1. How can layers be used in a raster editing environment?
2. What is anti-aliasing? What is an anti-alias halo?
3. What happens to the image resolution when you change the physical size of the image?
4. What is bit depth? How does it affect raster images?
5. The HEIGHT and WIDTH attributes of the <IMG> tag do two things in Web pages. What are they?
6. How do you control the alignment and spacing of images in Web pages?
7. What do the ALT and LOWSRC attributes do?
8. What are progressive images? Give two examples of formats that can be used.

Exercise

Focus on creating a Web page that uses several images so that you can apply what you have learned today. Create some images of your own as well as utilize some that already exist to practice sizing images and adjusting the image bit depth. Also use the Mapedit program to create at least one client-side image map so you can see how easy it is to utilize them.

10

Day 11

Using Tables To Format Pages

On Day 10, "Utilizing Graphics and Image Maps," you learned several ways in which you can stylize your pages and create something that is visually appealing as well as informative. However, you'll find at times that formatting graphics and text the way you like with the standard block and image tags is difficult. When you look at one of the remaining HTML tags, you'll find that using tables is a very unique way of creating and formatting Web pages. They give you accurate control over how elements appear on the page. They also give you the ability to format your pages in a very consistent manner.

This chapter focuses on using tables to format your pages. Tables were originally designed to house data, but as you surf the Web, you will find ingenious solutions that integrate tables with many of the other tags that are part of the HTML language. Tables also can utilize all of the previous tags you've learned in addition to the table-specific tags. Begin by looking at the basic tags involved in defining a table.

Basic Uses for Tables

Tables have a wide variety of uses in a Web page. They can be used for their original purpose, to present tabular data, or they can be used to help format graphics and entire pages of information. Take a look at the basic tags that are used for an HTML table. In the example, you learn how to create an embossed graphic using a table.

The <TABLE>, <TR>, and <TD> Tags

The <TABLE> tag is used to house all of the data for a particular table in the HTML code. The <TR> tag is used within the <TABLE>...</TABLE> tags to define the rows for the table. The <TD> tag is used within the <TR>...</TR> tags to define the cells within the table row.

The <TABLE>, <TD>, and <TR> tags are the minimum tags required to create a simple table. When you create a table as a developer, you usually begin by defining the first row's data cell and then the items that appear beneath it. Creating tables one column at a time is much easier than trying to develop the entire thing at once. Before you learn the various attributes associated with these tags and see an extensive example, look at the three tags in a very simple example.

Creating Embossed Effects

One of the most basic, yet most effective, uses of a table is to create a simple border for a graphic. As an introduction to the concepts and basic tags involved, begin with a simple exercise. You'll create an embossed graphic as shown in Figure 11.1. You won't have access to the image I used, so you'll have to use one of your own.

To create the image shown in Figure 11.1, enter Listing 11.1.

TYPE   **Listing 11.1. Creating an embossed graphic.**

```
<!DOCTYPE "HTML 3.2 //EN">
<HTML>
  <HEAD>
    <TITLE>Creating an Embossed Image</TITLE>
  </HEAD>
  <BODY>
    <CENTER>
      <TABLE BORDER=14>
```

```
        <TR>
      <TD><IMG SRC="windsurf.gif"></TD>
          </TR>
      </TABLE>
    </CENTER>
  </BODY>
</HTML>
```

Figure 11.1.

Creating an embossed outline graphic using a table.

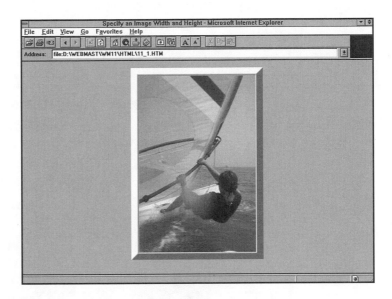

ANALYSIS Notice the relationship between the code and the image in Figure 11.1. In the code, a table is defined with a single row and one data cell. Note that the table's single cell conforms to the size of the graphic that was placed. By default, the data cells of a table will always conform to the size of the object inserted within it. Also notice the border that has been added with the BORDER attribute. This is one of the most common uses of the <TABLE> tag.

Now make it more interesting by adding to the table a second row that contains a title for the graphic, as shown in Figure 11.2. The code for the page looks like Listing 11.2.

TYPE **Listing 11.2. Adding a caption to the embossed graphic.**

```
<!DOCTYPE "HTML 3.2 //EN">
<HTML>
  <HEAD>
    <TITLE> Using Tables </TITLE>
  </HEAD>
  <BODY>
    <CENTER>
```

continues

Listing 11.2. continued

```
<TABLE BORDER=14>
  <TR>
  <TD><IMG SRC="windsurf.gif"></TD>
  </TR>
<TR>
  <TD ALIGN=CENTER>Surfin' USA</TD>
  </TR>
</TABLE>
</CENTER>
</BODY>
</HTML>
```

Figure 11.2.

Adding a title to the graphic.

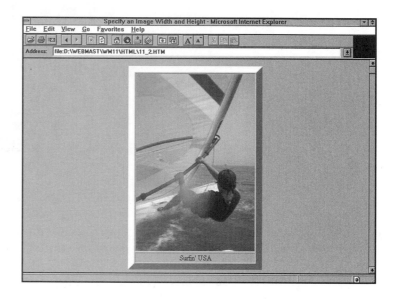

ANALYSIS   As you can see from Listing 11.2, adding an additional <TR> section or table row adds another row to your table. This is how you build the Y dimension (height) of your tables—by adding more rows.

Now add additional columns by adding another <TD> or table data cell to the right of the existing one as shown in Figure 11.3. The added code looks like Listing 11.3.

11

TYPE **Listing 11.3. Adding another graphic and caption.**

```
<!DOCTYPE "HTML 3.2 //EN">
<HTML>
  <HEAD>
    <TITLE>Using Tables</TITLE>
  </HEAD>
  <BODY>
    <CENTER>
      <TABLE BORDER=14>
        <TR>
        <TD><IMG SRC="windsurf.gif"></TD>
        <TD><IMG SRC="windsur2.gif"></TD>
        </TR>
        <TR>
        <TD ALIGN=CENTER>Surfin' USA</TD>
        <TD ALIGN=CENTER>Surfin' USA 2</TD>
        </TR>
      </TABLE>
    </CENTER>
  </BODY>
</HTML>
```

Figure 11.3.

Adding another column to the table.

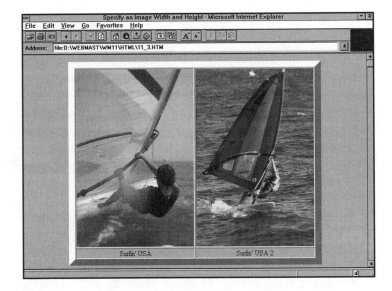

Using the previous examples you can see how tables are built. The <TABLE>...</TABLE> tags mark both the beginning and the end of the table elements. The <TR>...</TR> tags define the rows of the table, and the <TD>...</TD> tags define the cells that define the columns for each row.

Basic Tags and Attributes

As you learned, the <TABLE>...</TABLE> tags define the beginning and end of the table. The <TABLE> tag has several attributes that you can use to set options for the entire table. They include the following:

☐ ALIGN—Enables text to flow around the table much like text flowing around an image. Valid entries for the ALIGN attribute include LEFT and RIGHT.

☐ BORDER—Sets the thickness for the borders of the table boundaries. The default for this attribute is 0, so putting no value makes the borders invisible.

☐ CELLSPACING—Defines the thickness of the cell frames within the table. The default is CELLSPACING=2.

☐ CELLPADDING—Defines how close a cell frame can come to the edges of the object inside the frame. The default is CELLPADDING=1.

☐ WIDTH—Attempts to specify the desired width of the table in either pixels or percentages. However, a value defined with this attribute can be overridden by the values set in other attributes (see the WIDTH attribute of <TR>, <TD>, and <TH> tags later in the chapter).

☐ HEIGHT—Attempts to specify the desired height of the table in either pixels or percentages. However, a value defined with this attribute can be overridden by the values set in other attributes (see the HEIGHT attribute of <TR>, <TD>, and <TH> tags later in the chapter).

As you continue to look at the attributes for rows, cells, and table heads, keep in mind that attributes set for the <TABLE> tag affect the entire table. Attributes set per row, cell, or table head affect only those items.

Row, Cell, and Table Head Attributes

As you learned, the <TR>...</TR> tags define the individual rows for the table, and the <TD>...</TD> tags define the cells for the table. In addition to these two items you also can create a table header cell, which is rendered in boldface text.

11

The `<TH>` Tag

The `<TH>` tag creates a table header cell for the particular row of data cells. The text contained within these cells is rendered in boldface text.

The attributes that can be used with these remaining table tags apply to all three tags, `<TR>`, `<TD>`, and `<TH>`. The following are the attributes for these tags:

- ☐ `ALIGN`—Specifies the alignment of the text or elements within the cell. Valid entries include `ALIGN=LEFT`, `ALIGN=RIGHT`, and `ALIGN=CENTER`. The default is `ALIGN=LEFT`.

- ☐ `VALIGN`—Specifies the vertical alignment of the text or elements within the cell. The default is `VALIGN=MIDDLE`. Valid entries include `VALIGN=TOP`, `VALIGN=MIDDLE`, `VALIGN=BOTTOM`, and `VALIGN=BASELINE`.

The following attributes apply only to the `<TD>` and `<TH>` tags:

- ☐ `WIDTH`—Specifies a width for the element in pixels or as a percentage of the screen. Specifying a width will affect all of the cells in that particular column. Therefore, if multiple cells use the `WIDTH` attribute, the widest cell setting will be used. Note that if the compilation of the cell widths exceeds that specified in the `WIDTH` attribute of the `<TABLE>` tag, the cumulative widths specified per cell will override the `WIDTH` specified in the `<TABLE>` tag.

- ☐ `HEIGHT`—Specifies a height for the cell in pixels or as a percentage of the screen. Specifying a height will affect all of the cells in that particular row. Therefore, if multiple cells use the `HEIGHT` attribute, the tallest cell setting will be used. Note that if the compilation of the cell heights exceeds that specified in the `HEIGHT` attribute of the `<TABLE>` tag, the cumulative heights specified per cell will override the `HEIGHT` specified in the `<TABLE>` tag.

- ☐ `COLSPAN`—Specifies the number of columns that the cell spans.

- ☐ `ROWSPAN`—Specifies the number of rows that the cell spans.

- ☐ `NOWRAP`—Disables the text wrapping feature.

Now that you have looked at the various table tags and attributes, learn how to build a table using them. Because I have an interest in wildlife, you'll be formatting a chart concerning my local wild game. The chart will show my eight local counties and the state of the eight most common game animals. To begin this chart, I'll first lay out the rows and the row header for the counties. The code that I have entered looks something like Listing 11.4.

11

Listing 11.4. Creating the Counties column.

```
<!DOCTYPE "HTML 3.2 //EN">
<HTML>
  <HEAD>
    <TITLE>Central Indiana Wildlife</TITLE>
  </HEAD>
  <BODY>
    <TABLE BORDER=4>
      <TR>
          <TH ALIGN=CENTER>Counties</TH>
      </TR>
      <TR>
        <TD>Boone</TD>
      </TR>
              ...
              ...
              ...
      <TR>
        <TD>Tipton</TD>
      </TR>
      </TABLE>
    </CENTER>
  </BODY>
</HTML>
```

Figure 11.4 shows an example of what this code generates. As you can see, you are going to build the table one column at a time. Now go back and add the second column of data. The code looks like Listing 11.5.

Figure 11.4.

The beginnings of the table.

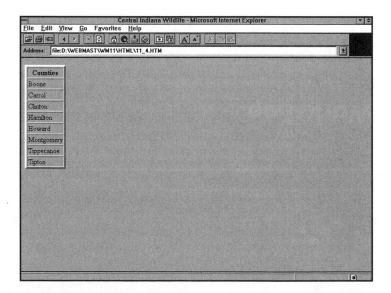

TYPE	**Listing 11.5. Adding the second column.**

```
<!DOCTYPE "HTML 3.2 //EN">
<HTML>
  <HEAD>
    <TITLE>Central Indiana Wildlife</TITLE>
  </HEAD>
  <BODY>
    <TABLE BORDER=4>
      <TR>
    <TH ALIGN=CENTER>Counties</TH>
    <TH ALIGN=CENTER>Squirrel</TH>
      </TR>
      <TR>
        <TD>Boone</TD>
        <TD ALIGN=CENTER>125</TD>
      </TR>
            ...
            ...
            ...
      <TR>
        <TD>Tipton</TD>
        <TD ALIGN=CENTER>101</TD>
      </TR>
      </TABLE>
    </CENTER>
  </BODY>
</HTML>
```

After you have added the second column, the table looks like Figure 11.5. Now go ahead and finish the chart with the rest of the data. After you have entered all the data, the table looks pretty good, as shown in Figure 11.6, but there are a few things that you can do to make it look a little better.

You'll see in the figure that there are a few things that you can do to make your table look a little nicer. First, notice that all the cell borders come pretty close to the edges of the data. The first thing to do is add some space between the text and the data in the cells using the CELLPADDING attribute for the <TABLE> tag. Adding a cell padding of 6 makes the table spread out a little, as shown in Figure 11.7.

Also notice in the chart that there are several cells that don't contain data. The chart will look much better if you insert a blank space in it so that it looks recessed like the rest of the chart. When you are dealing with tables, there are two predominant methods of forcing a blank cell to recess. The first is to use the non-breaking space. To create this character, you must define it using its entity designation of . The second way of achieving this is by using a line break or <BR>. Go ahead and fix these blank cells (see Figure 11.8). You'll find that some browsers do not support special characters, so use the <BR> tag to create the recess.

Figure 11.5.

Adding the second column.

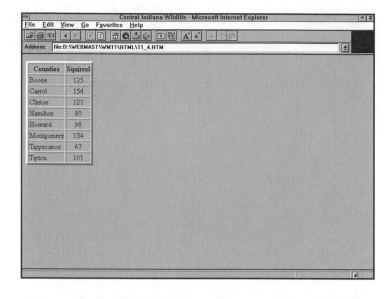

Figure 11.6.

The table after all the data is entered.

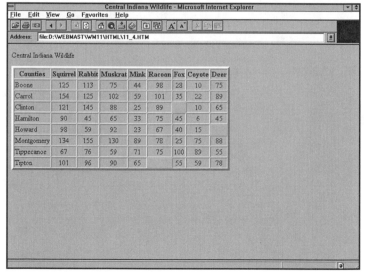

11

Figure 11.7.

Adding some visual space around the data using the CELLPADDING *attribute.*

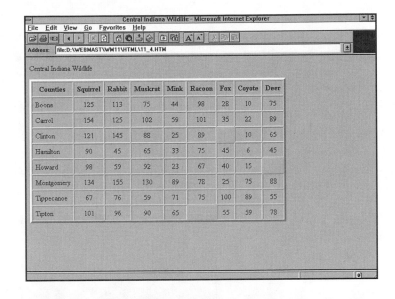

Figure 11.8.

Fixing a blank cell with a special character (*) or a*
 tag.

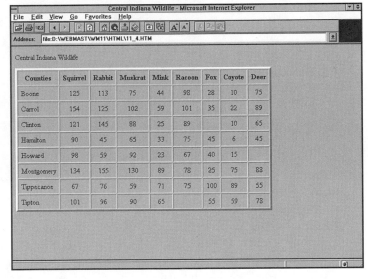

NOTE

Remember that Appendix B, "HTML 3.2 Reference," contains an entire chart of the HTML special characters.

The next thing I would like to do to finish off the table is add some spanning columns and rows. I really want to highlight the difference between what Hoosiers see as "big" game and "small" game. To do this, use two spanning rows as shown in Figure 11.9. Notice the new <TR> section added at the beginning of the chart. This adds a row at the top of the chart. To make these span multiple columns I have used the COLSPAN attribute to make each cell span four columns.

Figure 11.9.

Creating two spanning rows for the various types of game.

Counties	Small Game			Big Game				
	Squirrel	Rabbit	Muskrat	Mink	Racoon	Fox	Coyote	Deer
Boone	125	113	75	44	98	28	10	75
Carrol	154	125	102	59	101	35	22	89
Clinton	121	145	88	25	89		10	65
Hamilton	90	45	65	33	75	45	6	45
Howard	98	59	92	23	67	40	15	
Montgomery	134	155	130	89	78	25	75	88
Tippecanoe	67	76	59	71	75	100	89	55
Tipton	101	96	90	65		55	59	78

If you look closely in Figure 11.9, you'll see that Counties appears to be Small Game, which is not what you really want. To fix this, move the data cell for Counties up to the top row that you created in Figure 11.9, and set its ROWSPAN attribute to 2. Now it will span two rows. Doing this makes up for the "missing" row in the next set of cells. The chart now looks like Figure 11.10. Note that the chart and its title are also centered to make things look a little better.

As you can see, building a chart from ground zero is pretty easy as long as you add things one part at a time. If you just start pounding in the code for a table, you'll probably end up with all sorts of crazy things going on. Begin by entering a single column, and then add the next one, and so on. Finish the chart by adding any other tags, special formatting, or adjustments that you want.

Figure 11.10.
The "finished" chart.

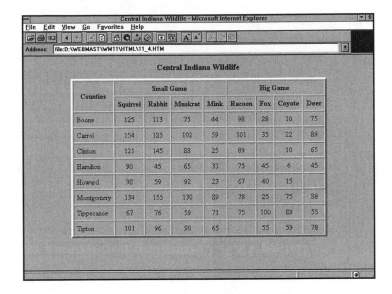

The finished code from Figure 11.10 ended up looking like Listing 11.6.

TYPE **Listing 11.6. The code for Figure 11.10.**

```
<!DOCTYPE "HTML 3.2 //EN">
<HTML>
  <HEAD>
    <TITLE>Central Indiana Wildlife</TITLE>
  </HEAD>
  <BODY>
    <H3 ALIGN=CENTER> Central Indiana Wildlife</H3>
    <CENTER>
    <TABLE BORDER=4  CELLPADDING=6>
      <TR>
        <TH ROWSPAN=2>Counties</TH>
    <TH ALIGN=CENTER COLSPAN=4> Small Game </TH>
    <TH ALIGN=CENTER COLSPAN=4> Big Game </TH>
      </TR>
      <TR>
    <TH ALIGN=CENTER>Squirrel</TH>
    <TH ALIGN=CENTER>Rabbit</TH>
    <TH ALIGN=CENTER>Muskrat</TH>
    <TH ALIGN=CENTER>Mink</TH>
    <TH ALIGN=CENTER>Racoon</TH>
    <TH ALIGN=CENTER>Fox</TH>
    <TH ALIGN=CENTER>Coyote</TH>
    <TH ALIGN=CENTER>Deer</TH>
      </TR>
```

continues

11

Listing 11.6. continued

```
    <TR>
      <TD>Boone</TD>
      <TD ALIGN=CENTER>125</TD>
<TD ALIGN=CENTER>113</TD>
<TD ALIGN=CENTER>75</TD>
<TD ALIGN=CENTER>44</TD>
<TD ALIGN=CENTER>98</TD>
<TD ALIGN=CENTER>28</TD>
<TD ALIGN=CENTER>10</TD>
<TD ALIGN=CENTER>75</TD>
    </TR>
    <TR>
      <TD>Carrol</TD>
      <TD ALIGN=CENTER>154</TD>
<TD ALIGN=CENTER>125</TD>
<TD ALIGN=CENTER>102</TD>
<TD ALIGN=CENTER>59</TD>
<TD ALIGN=CENTER>101</TD>
<TD ALIGN=CENTER>35</TD>
<TD ALIGN=CENTER>22</TD>
<TD ALIGN=CENTER>89</TD>
    </TR>
    <TR>
      <TD>Clinton</TD>
      <TD ALIGN=CENTER>121</TD>
<TD ALIGN=CENTER>145</TD>
<TD ALIGN=CENTER>88</TD>
<TD ALIGN=CENTER>25</TD>
<TD ALIGN=CENTER>89</TD>
<TD ALIGN=CENTER><BR></TD>
<TD ALIGN=CENTER>10</TD>
<TD ALIGN=CENTER>65</TD>
    </TR>
    <TR>
      <TD>Hamilton</TD>
      <TD ALIGN=CENTER>90</TD>
<TD ALIGN=CENTER>45</TD>
<TD ALIGN=CENTER>65</TD>
<TD ALIGN=CENTER>33</TD>
<TD ALIGN=CENTER>75</TD>
<TD ALIGN=CENTER>45</TD>
<TD ALIGN=CENTER>6</TD>
<TD ALIGN=CENTER>45</TD>
    </TR>
    <TR>
      <TD>Howard</TD>
      <TD ALIGN=CENTER>98</TD>
<TD ALIGN=CENTER>59</TD>
<TD ALIGN=CENTER>92</TD>
<TD ALIGN=CENTER>23</TD>
```

```
            <TD ALIGN=CENTER>67</TD>
            <TD ALIGN=CENTER>40</TD>
            <TD ALIGN=CENTER>15</TD>
            <TD ALIGN=CENTER><BR></TD>
              </TR>
              <TR>
                <TD>Montgomery</TD>
                <TD ALIGN=CENTER>134</TD>
            <TD ALIGN=CENTER>155</TD>
            <TD ALIGN=CENTER>130</TD>
            <TD ALIGN=CENTER>89</TD>
            <TD ALIGN=CENTER>78</TD>
            <TD ALIGN=CENTER>25</TD>
            <TD ALIGN=CENTER>75</TD>
            <TD ALIGN=CENTER>88</TD>
              </TR>
              <TR>
                <TD>Tippecanoe</TD>
                <TD ALIGN=CENTER>67</TD>
            <TD ALIGN=CENTER>76</TD>
            <TD ALIGN=CENTER>59</TD>
            <TD ALIGN=CENTER>71</TD>
            <TD ALIGN=CENTER>75</TD>
            <TD ALIGN=CENTER>100</TD>
            <TD ALIGN=CENTER>89</TD>
            <TD ALIGN=CENTER>55</TD>
              </TR>
              <TR>
                <TD>Tipton</TD>
                <TD ALIGN=CENTER>101</TD>
            <TD ALIGN=CENTER>96</TD>
            <TD ALIGN=CENTER>90</TD>
            <TD ALIGN=CENTER>65</TD>
            <TD ALIGN=CENTER><BR></TD>
            <TD ALIGN=CENTER>55</TD>
            <TD ALIGN=CENTER>59</TD>
            <TD ALIGN=CENTER>78</TD>
              </TR>
              </TABLE>
            </CENTER>
          </BODY>
</HTML>
```

Before you leave the chart that you just created, make it a little more interesting by incorporating some graphics into the chart. Incorporating any of the other tags about which you've learned, particularly text-level tags, is quite easy after you have the basic structure of your table. You'll add some graphics so that your chart looks like Figure 11.11. The code is really quite simple. All you have to do is integrate some <IMG> tags into the <TH>, table headers, of the chart. The only thing that is modified is the second row of data cells. You'll also see line breaks in the code that make the graphic appear below the chart text that appears in the cell. The modified chart code looks like Listing 11.7.

Figure 11.11.

Adding graphics to the already formatted chart is quite easy.

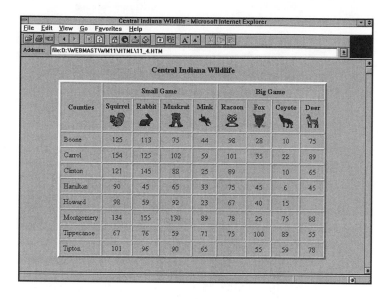

TYPE
Listing 11.7. The code for adding graphics to your table.

```
...
<TR>
    <TH ALIGN=CENTER>Squirrel<BR><IMG SRC="squirrel.gif"></TH>
    <TH ALIGN=CENTER>Rabbit<BR><IMG SRC="rabbit.gif"></TH>
    <TH ALIGN=CENTER>Muskrat<BR><IMG SRC="rat.gif"></TH>
    <TH ALIGN=CENTER>Mink<BR><IMG SRC="mink.gif"></TH>
    <TH ALIGN=CENTER>Racoon<BR><IMG SRC="racoon.gif"></TH>
    <TH ALIGN=CENTER>Fox<BR><IMG SRC="fox.gif"></TH>
    <TH ALIGN=CENTER>Coyote<BR><IMG SRC="coyote.gif"></TH>
    <TH ALIGN=CENTER>Deer<BR><IMG SRC="deer.gif"></TH>
</TR>
...
```

Formatting Pages

Now that you've learned the basics of creating tables, examine some of the other things that you can do with them. As you are working with the HTML language, you'll find that getting graphics and text just the way you want them on the Web page is often difficult. You can use a table to force the text and graphics to conform to the data cells of the table, thus giving you more control and formatting capabilities. Figure 11.12 shows an example of a Web page that uses a table to format the various graphics and text in a very structured way.

Can you see how the table is used to lay out the data inside it? Look at the basic table that is used to lay it out. The code looks like Listing 11.8.

Figure 11.12.

*Laying out a page with a
table.*

TYPE **Listing 11.8. The code for laying out a page with a table.**

```
<!DOCTYPE "HTML 3.2 //EN">
<HTML>
  <HEAD>
    <TITLE>Example Layout</TITLE>
  </HEAD>
  <BODY>
    <TABLE BORDER=6>
      <TR>
        <TD COLSPAN=3 WIDTH=596 HEIGHT=97><H3 ALIGN=CENTER> --BANNER-- </H3>
</TD>
      </TR>
      <TR>
        <TD WIDTH=196 HEIGHT=49><H2 ALIGN=CENTER> Advertisement </H2></TD>
    <TD COLSPAN=2 WIDTH=400 HEIGHT=49><H2 ALIGN=CENTER>Area Banner</H2>
      </TR>
      <TR>
        <TD WIDTH=196 HEIGHT=49><H2 ALIGN=CENTER> Advertisement </H2></TD>
    <TD ROWSPAN=3 WIDTH=256 HEIGHT=404><H2 ALIGN=CENTER> Information </H2></TD>
        <TD ROWSPAN=3 WIDTH=144 HEIGHT=404><H2 ALIGN=CENTER> Subjects </H2>
</TD>
      </TR>
      <TR>
    <TD WIDTH=196 HEIGHT=49><H2 ALIGN=CENTER> Advertisement </H2></TD>
      </TR>
      <TR>
    <TD WIDTH=196 HEIGHT=306><H2 ALIGN=CENTER> Menu </H2></TD>
      </TR>
    </TABLE>
  </BODY>
</HTML>
```

If you turn on all the table borders and look at Listing 11.8 in the browser, you can see how easy it is to make templates that can be used to format pages like this. Figure 11.13 shows how a blank template page would look for the SportsLine page.

Figure 11.13.

A blank template for Figure 11.12.

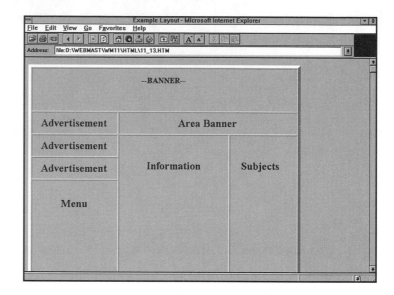

Structuring Data

As you are creating a table to structure your data, make sure that you build the table one column at a time. Developers often begin to create tables by inserting multiple columns at a time as well as various formatting attributes. It gets difficult to tell what's going on when you create the entire table at one time. You'll find that adding one column at a time until the entire table is built is much easier. Then go back and add special formatting such as the ALIGN, COLSPAN, ROWSPAN, and CELLPADDING attributes.

You might also want to use code generators such as FrontPage or PageMill to generate your tables. You probably still will need to add some of the table structure by hard coding, but using a generator will help you create the basic structure very quickly.

NOTE

If you're an experienced Excel user, you might want to look at the Microsoft Assistant for Excel. This add-on application tool will enable you to export your spreadsheets as tabular HTML data. See Appendix C, "Development Tools and Aids," for more details on this and other generator utilities.

11

Structuring Graphics

In addition to structuring a page of graphics and text, you also can integrate other features such as interactive form elements. In Chapter 13, "Using Forms To Gather Data," you learn how to create an interactive form, but keep in mind that those elements can be integrated into other tags as well. Figure 11.14 shows an example of a Web page composed of graphics and interactive form elements.

Figure 11.14.

Almost any other tag can be used with tables.

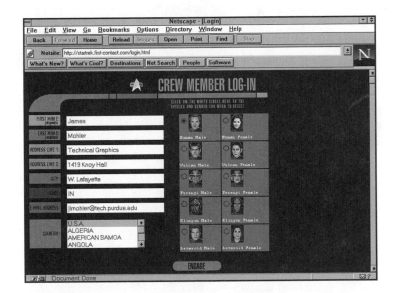

For the developers of Figure 11.14, probably the hardest part of the whole page layout was getting the images the correct sizes. If you want to do something like this, make sure you either sketch it out or lay it out in an image editor. Then simply construct your table around the preformatted graphics. Remember that table data cells always try to size themselves around the contents of the cell. You can partially control this through the CELLPADDING, HEIGHT, and WIDTH attributes. In addition, the cell borders have been turned off to help the look of the page. You can always make the table borders "invisible" to your audience by using the BORDER attribute to turn off the cell borders. If you want to see how this page was created, check out the site at http://startrek.first-contact.com/login.html.

Tips for Creating Successful Tables

Working with tables can be one of the most frustrating things in HTML. However, there are several things you can do to make it a little easier. Begin your tables by doing the following:

☐ Lay out a single column of cells first.

☐ Add subsequent columns of data cells.

☐ Make sure all the columns are inserted before you use text-level tags or other block-level tags.

☐ Insert any block-level tags such as lists or paragraphs that occur within a cell.

☐ Insert any text-level tags that you want to add to format text or to insert graphics.

☐ Create any hyperlinks that you want to appear in the table or document.

☐ Adjust any formatting that applies to the entire table such as justification, height, or width attributes.

Summary

In today's lesson you learned how to use tables to format data and pages. Realistically, you can use tables to format just about anything you want. Most developers use tables to format pages that have many inline graphics and text that must flow consistently and aesthetically together. Tables give you far better control over how text flows around graphics as well as how graphics are placed on the screen.

Q&A

Q What are the four primary tags used to create a table?

A The four primary tags used to create and set up a table are the <TABLE> tag, which defines the constructs for the table, the <TH> tag, which is used to create table heads, the <TR> tag, which defines a table row, and the <TD> tag, which defines a data cell for the row.

Q When you insert items into a data cell, how does the cell react within the table? Can you restrict the cell so that it does not react to items inserted inside it? How?

A When a text or graphic item is inserted into a data cell, the cell expands to the size of the inserted object. However, you can restrict the height or width of a data cell by using the HEIGHT and WIDTH attributes.

Q How do you get a column or a row to extend beyond one data cell?

A To make a table head or data cell extend beyond a single column, use the ROWSPAN attribute. To get a table cell to extend beyond a single column, use the COLSPAN attribute.

11

Q How should you construct your tables? Do you start filling in all the data simultaneously?

A The best way to build a table from scratch is to begin by creating the first column. Then add each additional column, viewing the file in the browser after each column is entered. Then you can add any remaining text-level tags or special formatting to finish the table.

Workshop

The Workshop provides quiz questions to help you solidify your understanding of the material covered and exercises to give you experience in using what you've learned. The quiz answers are provided in Appendix A, "Quiz Answers." Try to understand the quiz answers before you go on to tomorrow's lesson.

Quiz

1. What attribute is used to change the amount of spacing between a cell's contents and its boundaries?

2. Can you predefine the size of a table?

3. How do the HEIGHT and WIDTH attributes used for table data cells affect the HEIGHT and WIDTH attributes used with the <TABLE> tag?

4. How do you insert graphics into a table? What about anchors?

5. How do you make a table appear invisible?

6. How do you get a blank data cell to appear recessed?

Exercise

Create a table similar to the Central Indiana Wildlife chart. If you have no other data on hand, re-create the Central Indiana Wildlife chart. If you use your own data, make sure that the chart has the following:

☐ At least eight pieces of data horizontally and vertically

☐ At least one cell that spans multiple columns

☐ At least one cell that spans multiple rows

☐ At least one data cell with no data (force a recess)

☐ Column headers

Day 12

Using Frames To Format Pages

One of the newest features in the Web world is the support of framed documents. Before the implementation of the <FRAMESET> tag, all documents were known as body documents, or documents that had a body section. Each browser window contained one, and only one, Web page. Today, however, the framing convention, invented by Netscape and now also supported by Explorer, has added a new twist to documents that can be viewed inside a browser.

As you saw on Day 11, "Using Tables To Format Pages," you can create Web documents that are formatted using tables. But as you know, the table must be designed around the audience's display size. If your users view a table that has been designed for a screen size larger than the current setting, they must scroll horizontally to view all of the table. (Note that this is an unwritten cardinal sin. It makes me shudder to think about it.) However, frames can help you overcome this, if you create them correctly. What's worse than scrolling horizontally to see an entire page is having to scroll horizontally three windows in a document to see each of the items displayed in those windows. You'll get into that a little later in this chapter.

Today you'll take a look at how you can use frames in your Web pages. From how they work to creating the programming for them, you'll see that frames can be a good addition to your Web site, but there are some design considerations that you must ponder before cranking out a framed page.

NOTE

> One of the things you must note is that frames are a browser convention. This means they are not included in the "official" HTML tags established by the W3C. Therefore, some browsers still do not support them. The big two, Netscape Navigator and Microsoft Internet Explorer, both support frames. Explorer actually gives you a few more options than does Netscape. If your audience uses one of these two browsers, then you don't necessarily have to be concerned. However, later in this chapter you learn how to use the <FRAMESET> tag to create a Web page that will work in browsers that do and do not support frames.

Working with Frames

So what's the whole point of using frames in your Web pages? Well, predominantly, frames can be used to divide your screen into various windows as shown in Figure 12.1. The windows each contain a single Web page, and the windows actually can be any size you want. However, you must still work within the limitations of your audience's screen size. If you specify a frames page that is too big for the current display, the browser will scale the windows to fit them into the browser work area.

In reality, being able to open multiple pages into a browser is not really anything new. By now, you've probably been to a site that has automatically opened a new browser window to load a document similar to Figure 12.2. In most of the modern operating systems, such as Windows 95 and Windows NT, you can open multiple browser windows that each can contain a different document. For those who have (and can afford) indulgently fast Internet connections, you can even be downloading multiple pages at a time or surfing in two windows at once.

However, frames enable you to do two distinct things. First, a Web page that is divided into frames gives the audience the ability to size the frames as shown in Figure 12.3. After a page is laid out using frames, you can simply drag the frames border to resize the window. This works much the save way as dragging any window in a Windows, Macintosh, or other GUI environment.

Figure 12.1.

Dividing the browser work area into multiple windows using browser frames.

Figure 12.2.

Opening multiple browser windows and documents.

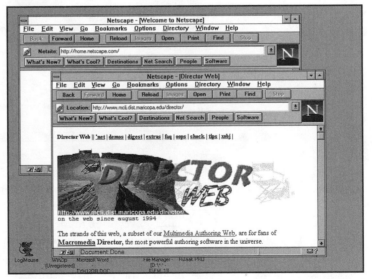

12

The second thing that frames enable is the ability to have one window control the contents that are displayed in another window. For example, you can create a frame that houses a menu for the contents of the site. Clicking on one of the hotlinks in this menu causes the contents of another window to change. Many of the examples on the Web that work this way are graphics related. For example, a site designed to distribute clip art or other graphics images might use a menu down one side of the screen to control what is seen in another window as shown in Figure 12.4.

Figure 12.3.

Sizing the windows established in framed pages.

Figure 12.4.

Using a menu in a frame to control the contents of another frame.

Because each window of a framed Web page houses a separate HTML file, the windows can actually contain anything. Each window is linked to a different Web document, which can contain any of the tags talked about thus far. Figure 12.5 shows an example of a graphics-intense Web page that uses frames. Even though the user can size the frames, keep in mind that the pages you link to the various windows must be designed around the size of the frame. In Figure 12.5, the developer of this page had to design all of the graphics for the window pages so that they would fit into the windows without the audience having to scroll horizontally. Just as with other pages, you'll have to design your graphics and text elements around the size of the area in which the page is displayed.

12

Figure 12.5.

Any tags can be included in the Web documents that appear in the windows.

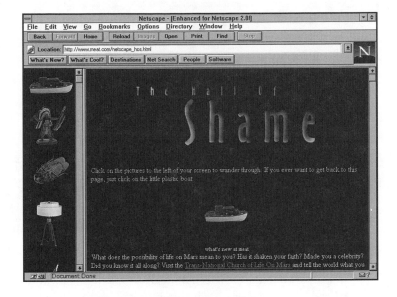

Structure

Up to this point I have said that all HTML documents contain a body section. Well, this statement is partially true. In documents that use frames, the frames section replaces the body of the document. As the browser loads a frame document, the frame document contains only the information to set up the frames and what pages go into those frames. The "body" for a frame document is actually contained in the pages that are inserted into the frames, not in the frame document itself. If you load a Web page that has frames defined, without loading the pages that go into the frames, you have a bunch of blank frames, which aren't worth a whole lot. Keep in mind that the body of a Web page that uses frames is contained in the pages that are loaded in the frames, not in the page that defines or lays out the frames. This will become clearer as you begin entering the code for a frames document.

Defining Frames

The primary tag that is used to create a frame document is the <FRAMESET> tag. As you learned in the preceding section, this tag replaces the normal <BODY>...</BODY> tags found in the HTML document. The document that uses the <FRAMESET> tag (the one that defines the layout of the windows) contains only information relevant to the actual windows or frames. The content for the frames is defined in any number of other HTML files and is stored externally as shown in Figure 12.6.

Figure 12.6.

The content for frames is stored in multiple documents.

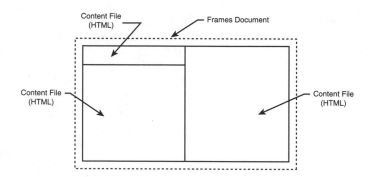

Special Features

One of the special features of a frame document is the capability to open another browser window. This makes two instances or copies of the browser run simultaneously. Using this feature keeps the current document where it is. Typically, choosing a new link replaces the items shown in the browser's work area. Opening a new window leaves the current window where it is—the new window jumps to the specified URL.

Basic Frame Tags and Attributes

As I have mentioned, the primary tag to create frames is the <FRAMESET> tag.

> **The <FRAMESET> Tags**
>
> The <FRAMESET>...</FRAMESET> tags are the containers for the definition of a framed page. The <FRAMESET>...</FRAMESET> tags replace the <BODY>...</BODY> tags in the HTML document.

As I said earlier, the <FRAMESET> tag contains only information about how the screen should be subdivided into windows. Valid attributes for the <FRAMESET> tag include:

- ☐ ROWS—The number and size of row frames that should be created in the browser work area. This attribute splits the screen horizontally. Valid entries include absolute (pixels), relative (wild card characters), or percentages of the screen.

- ☐ COLS—The number and size of column frames that should be created in the browser work area. This attribute splits the screen vertically. Valid entries include absolute (pixels), relative (wild card characters), or percentages of the screen.

12

As you use the <FRAMESET> tag, the ROWS and COLS attributes can use absolute dimensions, relative dimensions, or percentages to define the sizes of the windows that appear in the document. For example, you can specify that a series of frames be created by setting the COLS attribute to 150,150,150,150. These are absolute dimensions. However, specifying absolute dimensions can be detrimental if a user accesses your page at a screen size smaller than you anticipated. In the example, the user's browser would need to have 600 pixels to be able to display your frames as you created them. If users have screens less than 600 pixels, the browser will automatically scale the windows to fit in the user's screen, which can cause problems—horizontal scrolling. A better way of defining frames is by using either the relative or percentage specification. No matter how you define your frames, you have to enable enough extra negative space in the pages shown in the frames for variability in the frame sizes.

The percentage specification is pretty easy to understand. To create a page that defines a series of column frames, each occupying 25 percent of the screen, you would enter COLS=25%,25%,25%,25%. This enables the browser to show the frames, no matter what the display setting. However, as noted, the pages that are shown in these frames must enable enough variability so that the user will never have to scroll horizontally. As you begin designing some pages with frames, you'll look at this a little closer.

If you choose to use the relative dimensioning, understand that it works the same way as percentages. A relative dimension might look like COLS=1*,3*,6*, which is the same as saying 10%,30%,60%. I find in most of my frame pages, as well as ones on the Net, that percentages are used most commonly.

After you have defined the containers for the frames setup, you must then define the contents and other attributes of the frames themselves. This is done using the <FRAME> tag.

The <FRAME> Tag

The <FRAME> tag defines one frame or window in a frames document.

After you have defined a window, you can then use the following attributes to control how it behaves:

- [ ] SRC—The Web page that will appear in the frame.
- [ ] NAME—A name for the individual frame. This attribute is used to enable one frame to control another through a TARGET specification.
- [ ] SCROLLING—Defines whether the frame should have scrollbars. Valid entries for this attribute are SCROLLING=YES (NO or AUTO). The default is AUTO.
- [ ] MARGINWIDTH—The left and right margins for the frame in pixels. This attribute cannot be 0.

☐ MARGINHEIGHT—The top and bottom margins for the frame in pixels. This attribute cannot be 0.

☐ NORESIZE—This disables the ability of the user to size the frame.

Now that you have looked at the various tags, let's see how they actually work. In the remainder of this lesson you'll begin by looking at the basics of creating frames. Then you'll look at how to control one frame with another, as well as how to open new browser windows using frames.

Creating Basic Frames

To begin working with frames, you will start with a very simple example. Let's divide the screen into two columns. This example requires three HTML files. The first is the frames document, which defines how the screen will be laid out. The other two files are the actual documents that are inserted into the frames.

Figure 12.7 shows an example of the frames document. Notice the source code for this file. The <FRAMESET> tag contains the definitions for the frames. You have used the COLS attribute to define two frames that each take up 50 percent of the screen. The code for the content of Frame A and Frame B look like Listings 12.1 and 12.2.

Figure 12.7.

*A simple frames docu-
ment.*

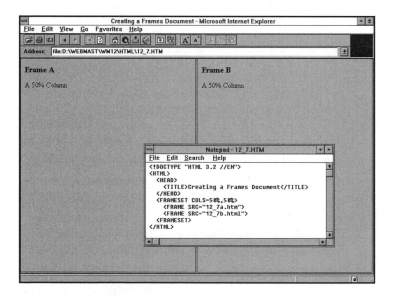

12

TYPE **Listing 12.1. The code for Frame A.**

```
<!DOCTYPE "HTML 3.2 //EN">
<HTML>
  <HEAD>
    <TITLE>Page A </TITLE>
  </HEAD>
  <BODY>
    <H3> Frame A </H3>
    <P> A 50% Column </p>
  </BODY>
</HTML>
```

TYPE **Listing 12.2. The code for Frame B.**

```
<!DOCTYPE "HTML 3.2 //EN">
<HTML>
  <HEAD>
    <TITLE>Page B</TITLE>
  </HEAD>
  <BODY>
    <H3> Frame B </H3>
    <P> A 50% Column </p>
  </BODY>
</HTML>
```

From this example, you can see that any frame setup includes the frames document and an HTML file for each window. Now divide the two columns into two rows, as shown in Figure 12.8. The code for this frames document looks like Listing 12.3.

TYPE **Listing 12.3. Dividing the two columns into rows.**

```
<!DOCTYPE "HTML 3.2 //EN">
<HTML>
  <HEAD>
    <TITLE>Creating a Frames Document</TITLE>
  </HEAD>
  <FRAMESET COLS=50%,50%>
    <FRAMESET ROWS=50%,50%>
      <FRAME SRC="12_7a.htm">
      <FRAME SRC="12_7c.htm">
    </FRAMESET>
    <FRAMESET ROWS=50%,50%>
      <FRAME SRC="12_7b.html">
      <FRAME SRC="12_7d.html">
    </FRAMESET>
  <FRAMESET>
</HTML>
```

12

Figure 12.8.

Dividing the two columns into rows.

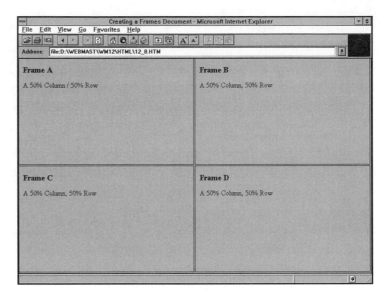

As you can see from this example, you can nest the <FRAMESET> container. In Listing 12.3, the first <FRAMESET> tag defines two columns that are 50 percent of the screen. The second <FRAMESET> tag defines the divisions for the first column—two 50 percent rows. The third <FRAMESET> tag defines the divisions within the second column—again, two 50 percent rows.

NOTE

If you decide that you want to use frames in your pages, make sure that you lay them out on grid paper before you create the pages that go inside the frames. You must create the inserted pages at the size of the frame. Elements that are larger than the frame will require scrolling.

In Listing 12.3, any links to other pages that appear in the windows (that is, links in Page A, B, C, or D) cause the page to be loaded into the respective frame. Figure 12.9 shows the addition of a link to Netscape's Home Page into Page A. However, this creates a fundamental problem if you use the code that you set up previously for the frames.

If you have a clickable link in Page A, when the user clicks on that link, the linked page will automatically load into that window as shown in Figure 12.10. If no other attributes are used for the frame, it will load the page into the frame by default. The problem is that links that occur within your framed pages might not be designed to fit in your frame size. What you really want is to load the externally linked page into a new window.

Figure 12.9.

Putting a clickable link into Page A.

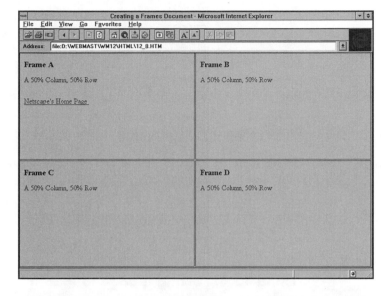

Figure 12.10.

The page is forced to load into the frame.

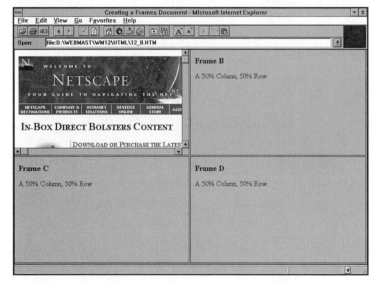

To make a new window open, you need to use the TARGET attribute for the <A> tag. You might say, "Hey, I don't remember seeing that on Day 9," and you would be right. The TARGET attribute usually is used only with frames documents; however, with the _blank option, you also can use it in normal body documents. The TARGET attribute is typically used to enable one frame to update the contents of another frame. You'll learn about this in the next section. However, with the TARGET attribute, there are also several implicit names that you can use.

These implicit names are simply predefined objects that you can reference when using frames documents. Implicit names for targets begin with an underscore and include the following:

☐ _self—Makes the browser update the frame in which the page occurs.

☐ _parent—Makes the browser update the parent of the current frame, assuming one exists.

☐ _top—Makes the browser update the entire browser work area.

☐ _blank—Makes the browser open a new window in which to display the page.

As you can see, there are several predetermined references that you can use as targets for your links. Right now, the one you are concerned with is the _blank setting.

To get your Netscape link to load into a new browser window, you simply need to add a TARGET statement for the page in which the link or <A HREF> occurs. From Listing 12.3, you change the code for Page A so that it includes a target specification as shown in Listing 12.4.

TYPE

Listing 12.4. Forcing a page to load into a new browser window.

```
<!DOCTYPE "HTML 3.2 //EN">
<HTML>
  <HEAD>
    <TITLE>Page A </TITLE>
  </HEAD>
  <BODY>
    <H3> Frame A </H3>
    <P> A 50% Column, 50% Row <BR><BR><BR>
    <A HREF="http://www.netscape.com" TARGET="_blank"> Netscape's Home
    ➡Page </A></p>
  </BODY>
</HTML>
```

Now when the user clicks on the link in Frame A, a new browser window is opened for the document as shown in Figure 12.11.

NOTE

Keep in mind that you can use the TARGET="_blank" attribute in both frames and body documents. However, having every link set this way can frustrate your users. Use it cautiously and only when there is a real need to open a new browser window.

12

Figure 12.11.

Using the
`TARGET="_blank"`
*attribute causes a new
window to be opened.*

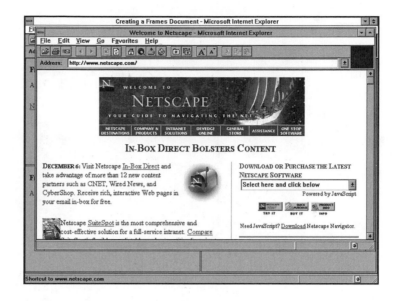

Interaction Between Frames

You've seen how the basics of the frames document works, but now do some things that are a little more complicated. What if you want to have one window controlling another? For example, clicking a link in one page changes the contents of another window. Or, what if you want one frame controlling two other frames? To be able to have one page update another requires the use of frame names and target specifications. If each frame is named, then you can target that frame for updates based on links in other frames.

Controlling One Frame

Begin with an example in which you want to create a menu on the left side of the screen that controls images that are displayed on the right side of the screen. You'll also have a graphic banner at the top that is frozen with no scrollbars and nonmovable frames. Figure 12.12 shows an example of what you will be creating.

To begin setting up this page, the first thing you must do is create the frames document itself. Do this by using the `<FRAMESET>` tag and its ROWS and COLS attributes. However, first you must look at the document to see how the screen needs to be divided. Remember that you can define rows and columns, but the order in which you define them in the code is what determines how the frames will look. To determine how to divide the screen, look at what you want to create and determine whether the columns or rows extend over the entire screen. This will show you whether you need to define the rows or the columns first by using the `<FRAMESET>` tag.

Figure 12.12.

Controlling one frame from inside another frame.

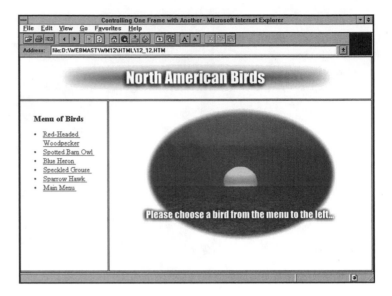

In Figure 12.13, you see two different sets of frames. The code for each of these frame configurations is a little different. Notice that the columns in example A extend over the entire screen. These columns are then divided into smaller segments. In example B, the rows extend over the entire screen and are then divided into smaller segments. In example A you would first define the columns and then the rows by using the <FRAMESET> tag as shown in the following segment:

```
...
<FRAMESET COLS 50%, 50%>
    <FRAMESET ROWS 10%, 90%>
        <FRAME SRC="URL">
    </FRAMESET>
    <FRAME SRC="URL">
</FRAMESET>
...
```

Figure 12.13.

Determining whether to define rows or columns first.

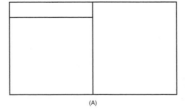 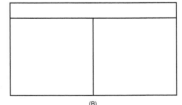

           (A)   (B)

12

This code means that the screen is first divided into two 50% columns. Then the first column is divided into two rows. One is 10% while the other is 90%. The second column is defined by the remaining <FRAME> tag at 100% because there are no rows defined for it.

To create the code for example B, you'd need to define the rows first and then the columns. The code for it would look like this:

```
<FRAMESET COLS 50%, 50%>
    <FRAMESET ROWS 10%, 90%>
        <FRAME SRC="URL">
    </FRAMESET>
    <FRAME SRC="URL">
</FRAMESET>
...
```

Notice that this code defines two 50% columns. The first 50% column is divided into a 10% row and a 90% row. The remaining 50% column is assigned to 100% using the last <FRAME> tag in the code. So you can see that the way in which you define your frames using the COLS and ROWS determines how the final frames document is created.

Looking back at Figure 12.12, notice the rows extend over the entire screen, so you need to define the rows and then the columns. The code for this page looks something like Listing 12.5.

TYPE **Listing 12.5. Controlling one frame with another frame.**

```
<!DOCTYPE "HTML 3.2 //EN">
<HTML>
  <HEAD>
    <TITLE>Controlling One Frame with Another</TITLE>
  </HEAD>
  <FRAMESET ROWS=20%,80%>
      <FRAME SRC="banner.htm">
    <FRAMESET COLS=25%,75%>
      <FRAME SRC="menu.htm">
      <FRAME SRC="screen.htm" NAME="screen">
    </FRAMESET>
  </FRAMESET>
</HTML>
```

In this code you have defined the rows first because they extend over the entire area of the screen. The 20% row is assigned the HTML file called BANNER. It has 100% width. The second row, which is 80%, is further divided into two columns. The 25% column is assigned to the HTML file called MENU, while the 75% column is assigned to the HTML file called SCREEN. Note that you want to be able to choose items in the menu frame and have it update the screen frame. To do this, you must give the screen frame a name, which you can read in the code. Giving a frame a name gives documents in other windows the capability to target the named frame.

12

To see this, look at the code for MENU.HTM. This file shows you how to target frames using anchors. The code for this page looks like Listing 12.6.

TYPE   **Listing 12.6. Creating the menu of birds.**

```
<!DOCTYPE "HTML 3.2 //EN">
<HTML>
  <HEAD>
    <TITLE>Bird Menu</TITLE>
  </HEAD>
  <BODY BGCOLOR="#FFFFFF">
    <UL>
      <LH><H3> Menu of Birds </H3>
      <LI><A HREF="bird1.htm" TARGET="screen"> Red-Headed Woodpecker</A></LI>
          <LI><A HREF="bird2.htm" TARGET="screen"> Spotted Barn Owl </A></LI>
          <LI><A HREF="bird3.htm" TARGET="screen"> Blue Heron </A></LI>
          <LI><A HREF="bird4.htm" TARGET="screen"> Speckled Grouse </A></LI>
          <LI><A HREF="bird5.htm" TARGET="screen"> Sparrow Hawk </A></LI>
          <LI><A HREF="screen.htm" TARGET="screen"> Main Menu </A></LI>
    </UL>
  </BODY>
</HTML>
```

In the anchor tags of this code, you have specified a target. Any time the user clicks on these links, he or she will see the respective document in the frame called screen. Figure 12.14 shows a new screen displayed in the frame called screen. This is how you get one frame to update another frame.

Figure 12.14.

One frame updates another using the TARGET attribute for the anchor tag.

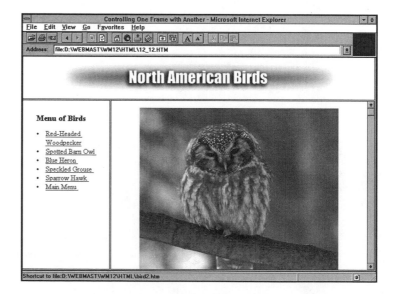

12

Controlling Two Frames

Now that you've seen how to control one frame, look at a way of updating two or more frames based on the interaction with the contents of another frame.

Figure 12.15 shows what you are going to create. Next, you'll need to modify the code so that the menu now controls both the image screen and the text about the particular bird (both frames in the right-hand column). After you understand how it's done, you'll see how easy it really is.

Figure 12.15.

Controlling the content of two frames with a menu from another.

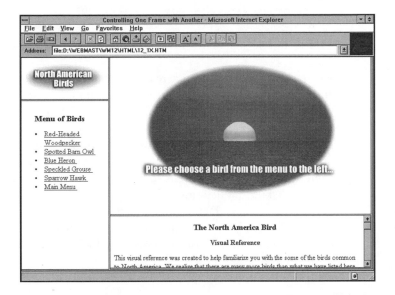

To make this whole thing work, you're going to use something called an indirectly nested frame. In the previous birds example, the frames document alone defines all of the frames and subframes to be arranged on the screen. Because every subframe is defined in the frames document, it would be called *directly nested*. You can actually make references within a frames document to another frames document. This is what you will do to create a document that updates two frames simultaneously. When you have frames documents integrated into other frames documents it is called *indirect nesting*.

NEW TERM A *directly nested* frame is a frame file in which the code for dividing the screen resides in the file itself.

NEW TERM An *indirectly nested* frame is a frame file in which the frame divisions are specified in other HTML files.

The code for the frames document looks something like Listing 12.7.

12

TYPE   **Listing 12.7. Controlling two frames with another frame.**

```
<!DOCTYPE "HTML 3.2 //EN">
<HTML>
  <HEAD>
    <TITLE>Controlling Two Frames with Another</TITLE>
  </HEAD>
  <FRAMESET COLS=25%,75%>
    <FRAMESET ROWS=20%,80%>
      <FRAME SRC="sm_ban.htm">
      <FRAME SRC="menu.htm">
    </FRAMESET>
    <FRAME SRC="split.htm" NAME="split">
  </FRAMESET>
</HTML>
```

Look closely at this code compared to Figure 12.16. You'll see that you have begun by defining two columns, a 25% and a 75% column. You see that the first 25% column is divided into a 20% and an 80% row and that the HTML files associated with them are listed using the <FRAME> tags immediately after. Now look at the next part. This is the important part. Notice that the 75% column is assigned to the file called SPLIT.HTM. Hey, wait a minute! Notice in Figure 12.16 that the column should be divided into two rows, yet you have referenced only an HTML file. Also note that this column is named SPLIT. The reason it looks this way is that the row definitions for that column are in the file called SPLIT.HTM rather than in the code for this document. This is how you get two frames to update simultaneously. You update the indirectly nested frames document (SPLIT.HTM) rather than focusing on the two files that appear in the subdivided frames. Now look inside the file called SPLIT.HTM. The code for it looks like Listing 12.8.

TYPE   **Listing 12.8. Using a split window to define frames.**

```
<!DOCTYPE "HTML 3.2 //EN">
<HTML>
  <HEAD>
    <TITLE>The Split Window</TITLE>
  </HEAD>
  <FRAMESET ROWS=75%,25%>
      <FRAME SRC="s_screen.htm">
      <FRAME SRC="s_text.htm">
  </FRAMESET>
</HTML>
```

Notice that in this file there are definitions for the two rows you saw in the column of the frames document. Through this example, you can see that a frames document can actually be embedded into another frames document. This means that when a user clicks on an option in the menu contained in the main frames document, it updates the 75% column with another frames document, causing both windows to be updated simultaneously. Let's take a look at it graphically.

Figure 12.16 shows how this thing works. Note that the overall file is the master frames document and it has indirectly nested the file called SPLIT.HTM into the right column. SPLIT.HTM contains the row divisions and the <FRAME> references to the content that will appear in the rows in that column. When a user clicks on an item in the menu, the main frames document updates the right side of the screen with a new file called SPLIT2.HTM. SPLIT2.HTM contains the same row divisions as SPLIT1.HTM; however, SPLIT2.HTM references two different HTML files. The code for SPLIT2.HTM looks like Listing 12.9.

Figure 12.16.

Indirectly nested frames.

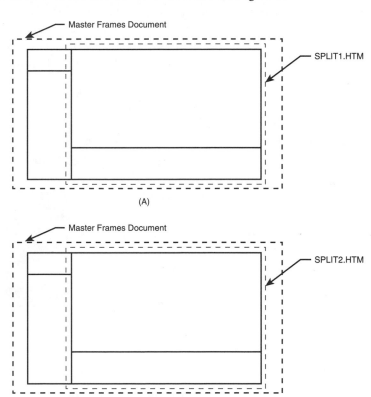

TYPE   **Listing 12.9. The code for** `SPLIT2.HTM`**.**

```
<!DOCTYPE "HTML 3.2 //EN">
<HTML>
  <HEAD>
    <TITLE>Controlling One Frame with Another</TITLE>
  </HEAD>
  <FRAMESET ROWS=75%,25%>
      <FRAME SRC="s_bird2.htm">
      <FRAME SRC="s_text2.htm">
  </FRAMESET>
</HTML>
```

If you replace SPLIT1.HTM in the master frames document with SPLIT2.HTM, as shown in Figure 12.17, clicking on an item in the bird menu would update both the picture of the bird and the text associated with it. Note that for each menu item you have three HTML files: the nested frames document (SPLIT1.HTM, SPLIT2.HTM, SPLIT3.HTM, and so on), the HTML file that contains the image, and the HTML file that contains the text describing the image. Using this technique requires many more HTML files but is extremely effective in Web pages.

Figure 12.17.
Updating both of the frames.

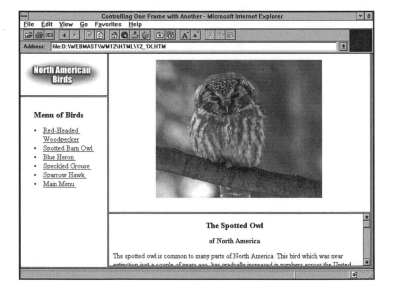

So, why do you have to go through all this to update multiple frames? Well, to be able to have one frame update another, you must use the NAME attribute with the <FRAME> tag and the TARGET attribute with the <A HREF> tag. Note that you can have only one TARGET in the <A HREF> tag, but each frame must have a name. To update multiple windows in any other way would require the ability to assign multiple targets for an <A HREF>, which you cannot do. By using an intermediate frames document, you can enable an <A HREF>'s TARGET to update multiple frames.

Contending with Non-Frame Browsers

To contend with non-frame–capable browsers, you must be aware of the <NOFRAMES> tag.

The <NOFRAMES> Tag

The <NOFRAMES> tag enables the developer to specify an alternative body section within a frames document for browsers that cannot utilize frames.

In all the previous frames examples, if you were to use the <NOFRAMES> tag, which I strongly recommend, it would be inserted into the frames document. To include this in the previous frames document, the code would look like Listing 12.10.

TYPE   **Listing 12.10. Using the <NOFRAMES> tag.**

```
<!DOCTYPE "HTML 3.2 //EN">
<HTML>
  <HEAD>
    <TITLE>Controlling Two Frames with Another</TITLE>
  </HEAD>
  <FRAMESET COLS=25%,75%>
    <FRAMESET ROWS=20%,80%>
      <FRAME SRC="sm_ban.htm">
      <FRAME SRC="menu.htm">
    </FRAMESET>
    <FRAME SRC="split.htm" NAME="split">
  <FRAMESET>
    <NOFRAMES>
      <BODY>
        ...
        Insert alternative body content here for non-frames browsers.
        ...
      </BODY>
    </NOFRAMES>
</HTML>
```

12

Summary

Today you have learned the basics of using frames in your Web documents. By using the basics presented today, you should be able to create a frames document with any configuration. As you have seen, the frames document itself contains nothing but information on how to lay out the frames and what HTML files should be inserted into those frames. You have seen how to update single and multiple frames based on interaction with another frame, as well as how to open new browser windows using implicit targets.

Keep in mind that frames are a browser convention and, therefore, are not supported in all browsers. You should make sure that all frames documents you create have a <NOFRAMES> section so that all browsers can use your pages.

Q&A

Q What is the difference between a directly and indirectly nested frames document?

A A directly nested frames document contains all the subframe divisions within the document. An indirectly nested frames document contains frame definitions in which the subdivisions for some frames are contained within external HTML documents. This enables the user to update multiple frames based on the interaction with another frame.

Q How do I determine whether to define columns first or rows first in my frames document?

A To determine which to define first, you must look at your frame arrangement and see whether you have a single column or row that extends completely across the screen. If you have a column that extends all the way across the screen, you must define your columns first. If you have a row that extends all the way across the screen, you must define your rows first. If no columns or rows extend across the entire screen, you may define either one first.

Q How many HTML files are involved in a simple two-column frames document?

A In a simple frames document with two columns, you have three HTML files: the frames document and the two content files (HTML files) for the two columns.

Q I thought all HTML documents had a body section. Where is the body section of a frames document?

A In a frames document, the body section is replaced with the definition of the frames. In theory, the body section of the frames document is contained in the linked HTML files that are inserted into the frames. In theory, a frames document has multiple body sections, one for each frame.

12

Workshop

The Workshop provides quiz questions to help you solidify your understanding of the material covered and exercises to give you experience in using what you've learned. The quiz answers are provided in Appendix A, "Quiz Answers." Try to understand the quiz answers before you go on to tomorrow's lesson.

Quiz

1. What is the primary tag that contains the information for a frames document?

2. How do you create a frames document that is friendly toward non-frames browsers?

3. How are the TARGET and NAME attributes used in frames documents?

4. What are implicit names and how are they used in a Web document? Why should they be used?

5. As you are designing the content documents that go into your frames, what should your biggest concern be?

Exercise

Create a Web page that uses frames to describe a content area of your choice. Using the North American Birds pages as an example, create a frames page that updates a frame based on interaction with another frame. Make sure you have at least one frame that has nonmoveable borders and no scrollbars.

12

Day 13

Using Forms To Gather Data

To enhance your learning of the various HTML tags and attributes that are available, you need to learn possibly one of the most powerful yet most underrated capabilities of the HTML language: interactive forms. When you began this book you learned about communication. The fact that the sender must send a message is really only part of the communication. For communication to truly occur it must come full circle. There has to be a way for the receiver to send feedback to acknowledge that communication has occurred. Interactive forms enable your audience to send you information.

Have you a need to collect information from your users? Do you want to provide online fill-in forms for your audience, or do you just want to provide a means for them to communicate to you? Regardless of your purpose, interactive forms are the best way to gather this information, as shown in Figure 13.1. Even in its crudest manner, an interactive form enables you to collect information from your audience on just about anything. From fill-in text boxes to drop-down menus, radio buttons, and more complex items, you can make it easy for connected users to provide information and feedback to you.

Figure 13.1.

An example of an interactive form.

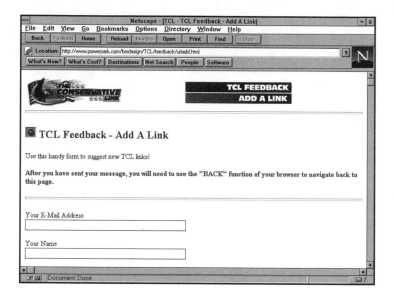

This chapter begins to familiarize you with the various tags and attributes that you can use to create interactive forms. With many examples from cyberspace, you'll examine ways in which to use interactive forms to gather information.

Due to the way in which forms work, this chapter concentrates more on creating effective forms than on all of the technical aspects of formatting the data that is submitted by your users. Like server-side image maps, forms require the use of CGI scripts to be able to format the data that is submitted using a form. With the wide variety of servers and software out there, as well as the myriad of programming languages that you can use to format submitted data, you will not spend a lot of time on platform-, software-, or machine-specific parameters. Undoubtedly, to get forms to work on your particular setup, you'll have to dig into your server-specific items to finish setting them up. There is a lot of information floating around on the Internet concerning the use of interactive forms. Here you'll focus on the specifics of creating these interactive HTML pages. To find more information about the server specifics of interactive forms, check out the following sites, which contain oodles of information on server and script specifics:

- [ ] `http://www.lpage.com/cgi/`
- [ ] `http://netamorphix.com/cgi.html`
- [ ] `http://hoohoo.ncsa.uiuc.edu/cgi/interface.html`
- [ ] `http://www.fln.vcu.edu/cgi/interact.html`
- [ ] `http://www.worldwidemart.com/scripts/`
- [ ] `http://www.eff.org/~erict/Scripts/`
- [ ] `http://www.yahoo.com/Computers/Internet/World_Wide_Web/`

13

Form Tags and Attributes

The easiest way to gather data from your users is through the use of an *interactive form*. The interactive form enables the user to enter data and then press a submit or other similar button to send the data to your server or other location. The server then processes the data and sends it to an appropriate location.

Browsers that support forms enable you as the developer to create an interactive form that can be appropriately viewed on any platform. Most forms utilize drop-down menus, text boxes, buttons, and checkboxes to enable the user to enter data. The HTML form is not platform-specific, which means that these interactive items will resemble those found on the particular platform. For example, checkboxes and drop-down menus in an HTML form will look different when viewed on a PC as compared to a Macintosh. A drop-down menu in an HTML page on the Macintosh will look like other drop-down menus found in the operating system. The HTML form will resemble other interactive elements found on the particular machine as shown in Figure 13.2. For example, the page was displayed in the Windows environment so all buttons and other interactive features will resemble the controls of the Windows environment.

Figure 13.2.

The form draws its elements from the operating system.

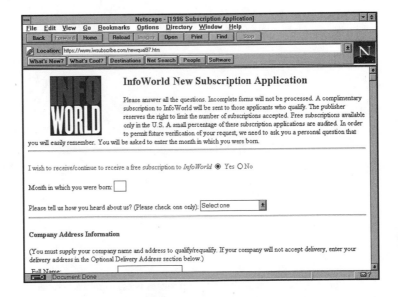

Constructing an interactive form is not much different than constructing any other HTML page. However, interactive forms have three distinct elements: the form header, the input fields, and one or more action buttons or items.

When the input items for an interactive form have been filled in, the user selects one of the action buttons (usually a submit button). The form sends the data to a location such as a script or e-mail address that is defined in the header. If the data is sent to a script, the script formats the data and sends it to an appropriate location such as a text file, e-mail address, or an HTML file as shown in Figure 13.3.

Figure 13.3.
The parts of an interactive form.

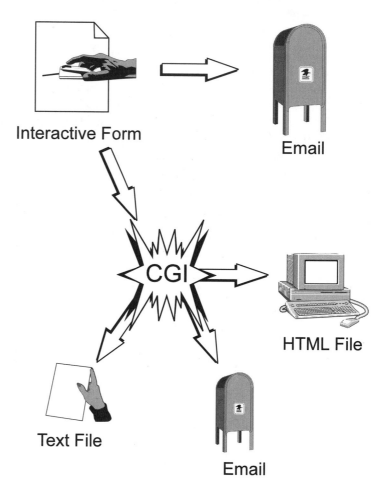

The hardest part of the whole process is establishing the script that processes the data. It is the hardest part because of the wide variety of ways in which it can be accomplished. But before you get into that, learn about the three main items that appear in the form.

13

The Form Header

The main tags that contain the items for a form are the `<FORM>...</FORM>` tags.

> ### The `<FORM>` Tags
>
> The `<FORM>...</FORM>` tags are the containers for the items that compose the form. A form can contain anything except another form and must contain at least one `INPUT`, `SELECT`, or `TEXTAREA` tag.

The `<FORM>...</FORM>` tags provide information that is vital for the form to work properly. When the user submits information via a form, the browser packages the data and sends it to the location found in the `<FORM>` tag. The `<FORM>` tag tells the browser how to package the data. The "packaging" instructions tell where to send the data and how to send the data.

The following is an example of a `<FORM>` tag:

```
<FORM ACTION="mailto:someone@some.place" METHOD="post">...</FORM>
```

This example shows two very important items: the location to which to send the data (`mailto:someone@some.place`) and the method of sending it (`post`). In this example, the raw data is simply being sent to an e-mail address. When the data is sent it will be in a raw or unformatted state.

The following are the valid attributes that can be used with the `<FORM>` tag:

☐ `ACTION`—Specifies the URL to which the data is sent. All forms have an `ACTION` statement. Without it, the data will have no destination. The `ACTION` statement most often will reference to a script location designed by a URL, but it also can be sent to an e-mail address.

☐ `METHOD`—Specifies how the data is sent to the defined location. Valid entries include `GET` and `POST`. The default is `GET`, but you learn both in the section titled "Communication Between the Client and Server."

☐ `ENCTYPE`—Specifies the MIME type of the data to be sent when the `POST` option is used. The MIME type tells the receiving location in what type of file the data is contained.

As you read through this list of attributes the descriptions might be as clear as mud. A little later you learn the differences between the `GET` and `POST` options, as well as how `ENCTYPE` affects the data that is sent. Before looking at these items, look at the HTML tags for the form elements such as text boxes, checkboxes, and drop-down menus.

13

Accepting the Data: Input Fields

All forms contain standard GUI elements that are characteristic of the platform on which the browser is running. The first of these are *input items*.

Input items include a wide range of GUI elements including text boxes, submit and reset buttons, password boxes, checkboxes, radio buttons, and hidden input items. Most of these are created using the <INPUT> tag. Others are created using special tags. Table 13.1 shows the tags that can be used to create input items in a form.

Table 13.1. Typical input controls and their tags.

Type of Input Item	Tag and Attributes
Text Box	`<INPUT TYPE="text"...>`
Password Box	`<INPUT TYPE="password"...>`
Submit Button	`<INPUT TYPE="submit"...>`
Reset Button	`<INPUT TYPE="reset"...>`
Checkbox	`<INPUT TYPE="checkbox"...>`
Radio Button	`<INPUT TYPE="radio"...>`
Hidden Field	`<INPUT TYPE="hidden"...>`
Text Window	`<TEXTAREA>...</TEXTAREA>`
Menu	`<SELECT>...<OPTION>...</SELECT>`

The <INPUT> Tag

The <INPUT> tag is used to define a single field of a form that generally constitutes a single NAME=VALUE pair in the data output of the form.

The <INPUT> tag is used to define all sorts of input items such as text boxes, checkboxes, and radio buttons. Depending on which type of entity you are creating, the attributes for the <INPUT> item will change. The three primary attributes, ones that appear no matter what type of entity you are defining, include the following:

☐ NAME—Defines the label that is associated with the data that is entered in the field. When the data from the form is processed, it will always appear as a NAME=VALUE pair. The NAME attribute of each input item should be unique as well as descriptive. Every <INPUT> tag must have a NAME attribute so that data entered in the field can be identified.

13

☐ VALUE—Defines the default value that should appear in the field. Radio buttons must have a default value. All other <INPUT> types do not require a default value.

☐ TYPE—Defines the type of input entity the item is. Valid entries include TYPE="TEXT", TYPE="SUBMIT", TYPE="RESET", TYPE="PASSWORD", TYPE="CHECKBOX", TYPE="RADIO", and TYPE="HIDDEN".

Now that you've seen the basic attributes, look at the specifics for the different <INPUT> tag types. Note that as the TYPE attribute changes, so do the other valid attributes for the <INPUT> type.

Text and Password Attributes

The first of the values for the TYPE attribute is the "TEXT" option. The TEXT option enables the developer to create a horizontal text box that is by default 20 pixels wide. This simple data entry field enables the user of the form to enter string-based information. For example, the field can be a name field in which the user enters his or her name. By default, the text option does not enable a scrolling text box; however, it will enable the user to type an infinite number of characters.

Using TYPE="PASSWORD" works similar to TYPE="TEXT" except that the entered characters are not displayed on the screen. Instead, asterisks replace the characters in the text box.

The following attributes can be used with the INPUT type set to "TEXT" or "PASSWORD":

☐ MAXLENGTH—Defines the maximum number of characters that the user can enter. It is highly recommended that you use this attribute.

☐ SIZE—Defines the horizontal size of the text box in number of characters.

Submit and Reset Attributes

You use TYPE="SUBMIT" to insert a pushbutton into the form that causes all data entered into the form to be submitted to the URL specified in the form header. Using TYPE="RESET" causes the form to clear all entered fields to their default values. The only attribute that is special when you use these input types is the VALUE attribute. Whatever is placed in the VALUE attribute becomes the name of the button. For example, if you use VALUE="Submit Me" then the words Submit Me will appear on the button.

Checkbox Attributes

The "checkbox" value for the INPUT TYPE creates a checkbox on the form that the user can select or deselect. A checkbox has no value but does require a name. If the user selects the checkbox, the NAME=VALUE pair will appear as NAME=ON in the submitted data. If the checkbox is off, the submitted data will contain no record of the checkbox. You can use the CHECKED attribute to set a checkbox so that it defaults to an ON position.

13

Radio Button Attributes

You use the TYPE="RADIO" attribute for the <INPUT> tag to display a radio button in the form. Generally, there are at least two radio buttons when they are used. By default, one of the radio buttons must be selected at runtime. Data submitted from radio buttons is done so as a group. Grouped radio buttons share a common name and are submitted as a group of information in the submitted data. Radio buttons in a group are distinguished through unique values.

Hidden Attributes

You use the TYPE="HIDDEN" setting to create a hidden input element on the page. Generally, users are not aware of hidden elements unless they examine the contents of your code. The most frequent use of hidden fields is when a single script is meant to process several forms. If this is the case, the script must know which form it is processing. You can use the hidden field to relay information about which form is being processed, and that information then becomes a part of the processed output.

The <TEXTAREA> Tag

With TYPE="TEXT", you cannot create scrolling text fields with the <INPUT> tag, nor can you create a text box that wraps the text within it. To enable this feature you must use a separate form tag—the <TEXTAREA> tag.

> **The <TEXTAREA> Tags**
>
> The <TEXTAREA>...</TEXTAREA> tags enable you to create an adjustable text box for user text entry.

When you are defining a text box for text that would be impractical for the <INPUT> tag, such as an extremely long string of text, there are several ways in which you can define a text box using the <TEXTAREA> tag. The following are the <TEXTAREA> tag attributes:

- ☐ NAME—The label for the NAME portion of the NAME=VALUE pair for the field. The VALUE portion of the <TEXTAREA> will be the text that the user inputs.
- ☐ ROWS—Defines the height of the text area and is a required attribute.
- ☐ COLS—Defines the width of the text area and is a required attribute.
- ☐ WRAP—Defines whether the text wraps around the text area. Valid entries include OFF and PHYSICAL. The default is OFF. Note that when you use the PHYSICAL setting, it generates line break characters in the submitted text.

13

The <SELECT> and <OPTION> Tags

The last two tags used in interactive forms are used together. These two tags enable you to create menus of information from which the user can choose one item. Most often these are displayed as drop-down menus.

The <SELECT> and <OPTION> Tags

The <SELECT> tag establishes the presence of a drop-down menu in the interactive form.

The <OPTION> tag creates the author-defined options that appear in the menu.

You use the following attributes to define the options for the <SELECT> tag:

- ☐ NAME—The label for the NAME portion of the NAME=VALUE pair for the field.
- ☐ SIZE—Defines the number of options that are displayed in the drop-down item. The default is SIZE=1; however, you can set the size to a larger number to display more options in the field. No matter what the SIZE is set to the user can scroll through all the options.
- ☐ MULTIPLE—Enables the user of the form to select more than one item in the menu.

After you have contained the menu using the <SELECT>...</SELECT> tags, you can define the options that will appear in the menu. You can use the following attributes with the <OPTION> tag:

- ☐ SELECTED—Controls whether the item is, by default, selected or not. In a list that uses MULTIPLE, you may use the SELECTED attribute on more than one option.
- ☐ VALUE—Used to define a special value that is used in the NAME=VALUE pair instead of the option's value.

Creating a Form Page

Now create a simple example of a form so you can see how these elements work. Figure 13.4 shows the sample page. Note that some of the simplest tags have been used.

The following is the code for the previous page. Compare the various elements in Figure 13.4 to the code in the page. Note the use of line breaks (
 tags) as well as non-breaking spaces ( ) to get the page to look presentable.

13

Figure 13.4.

Creating a simple interactive form.

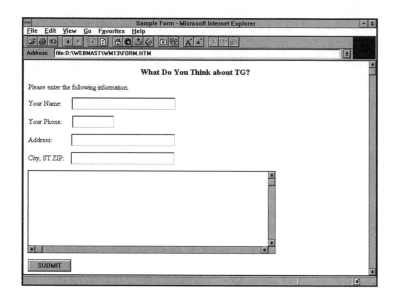

```
<!DOCTYPE "HTML 3.2 //EN">
<HTML>
  <HEAD>
    <TITLE>Sample Form</TITLE>
  </HEAD>
  <BODY BGCOLOR="#FFFFFF" TEXT="#000000">
    <H3 ALIGN=CENTER> What Do You Think about TG? </H3>
    <P> Please enter the following information:
    <FORM ACTION="mailto:shmoe@somewhere.com" METHOD="POST">
    Your Name:     
    <INPUT TYPE="TEXT" NAME="FullName" SIZE="30" MAXLENGTH="30">
    <BR><BR>
    Your Phone:     
    <INPUT TYPE="TEXT" NAME="Phone" SIZE="10" MAXLENGTH="10">
    <BR><BR>
    Address:          
    <INPUT TYPE="TEXT" NAME="Address1" SIZE="30" MAXLENGTH="30">
    <BR><BR>
    City, ST ZIP:   
    <INPUT TYPE="TEXT" NAME="Address2" SIZE="30" MAXLENGTH="30">
    <BR><BR>
    <TEXTAREA NAME="Comments" ROWS=10 COLS=80></TEXTAREA>
    <BR><BR>
    <INPUT TYPE="SUBMIT" VALUE=" SUBMIT "></P>
  </BODY>
</HTML>
```

Sending the Data

As I mentioned earlier in this chapter, when a user submits information from a form, there are two important aspects of the submission: where the form is being sent and how it is being sent. Establishing this information in the form header so that the browser knows what to do with the data is vital. If the form header is missing either of these elements it can do nothing with the data.

Communication Between the Client and Server

To be able to work with forms data, the client machine must package and send the data to a designated server. The data is sent using the HTTP method prescribed in the form header. This transmission will be in the form of either a GET or POST specification in the form header.

The GET method is the default method for transferring normal document requests. Using this method, the data is appended to the URL and sent to the server. However, this can become a problem when the strings of text get quite large. The POST method, on the other hand, is the preferred HTTP method because it sends the data as separate chunks of information rather than appending it to the end of the URL. With the GET method, often the strings will become too long for the server or scripts to handle. The POST method sends small bits of information to the server rather than long strings of information, which makes the data easier to handle.

NOTE

When you use the POST option with an e-mail address, the form often will include the ENCTYPE attribute. This tells the receiving application what type of file the data is and how to open it.

Encoding the Data

As data is sent to the proper location, it is received in matched pairs of information. For example, each field name is accompanied by the value entered for it by the user. An entire string of pairs appears as the output results of a form Web page. It is very important that the name you assign to the various input fields be unique. This makes recognizing the named pairs much easier.

In addition, you must be aware that the values in the generated output will be formatted per certain requirements. First, forms cannot directly deal with the spaces in the values entered in the fields. The spaces that occur between words are replaced with another character, usually the plus sign. In addition, special characters, such as the percent sign (%), pound sign (#), and dollar sign ($), are replaced with their ASCII equivalents. Most non-alphanumeric characters are represented by their hexadecimal ASCII equivalents.

13

Summary

Today's lesson covered the basics of creating form documents. You learned that the three basic parts of a form document are the form header, input elements, and the action statement. All form headers must define a location and method of transferring the data that is submitted by the users. When the data has been entered into a form, the data is sent to the appropriate location using the appropriate action type, which is the HTTP method. Usually, CGI scripts written in various languages are used to help format the NAME=VALUE pairs that are a result of the data entered into a form.

Q&A

Q What two vital elements are included within the form header? Why are they important?

A The two important elements included in the form header are the destination for the submitted data and the HTTP method that is to be used to submit the data. If either is missing, the data cannot be submitted.

Q What are the two locations that you can send form data to? How are they different?

A The two primary locations to which you can send data are a server-side script and an e-mail address. Generally, data that is sent to a script is formatted and output by the script to an author-defined location and file type. Data that is sent to an e-mail address is sent in its raw NAME=VALUE pairs as simply ASCII text.

Q What are the two primary HTTP methods that are used to send forms data? How are they different?

A The two primary HTTP methods that are used to send data are the GET and POST options denoted in the form header. The GET option causes the form data to be attached to the specified URL address. The POST option causes the data to be transferred in smaller, more manageable chunks. The GET option will cause problems with the server due to extremely long entries.

Q What is the primary tag used to create interactive entities on a form's Web page? How do you create a text box versus a radio button using this tag?

A The primary tag that is used to create input items on a form is the <INPUT> tag. To create the various input types, you simply set the TYPE attribute of the tag. Depending on the TYPE you choose, you can use several other attributes that are associated with the given entity.

Workshop

The Workshop provides quiz questions to help you solidify your understanding of the material covered and exercises to give you experience in using what you've learned. The answers are provided in Appendix A, "Quiz Answers." Try to understand the quiz answers before you go on to tomorrow's lesson.

Quiz

1. How is data sent from a form? What format is it in?
2. What important attribute do all the input tags share and why is it important?
3. What two tags enable you to create drop-down menus in an interactive form?
4. How are hidden input elements used in a Web page?

Exercise

Create an interactive form that uses one of each of the input types you have learned. Make sure that you enter all of the needed elements into the form header, as well as the required attributes for the input entities.

13

Day 14

Advanced Web Components

A discussion about Webmastering would not be complete without briefly discussing the wide variety of scripting and multimedia elements on the Web. On Day 4, "The Media Designer," you learned a little about creating various multimedia elements and the things you need to know when you create them. A single chapter is insufficient to describe any of these items in significant detail. Therefore, in today's lesson you'll take a cursory look at each of these technologies, looking at both the advantages and disadvantages of each one. You'll also see examples that typify the current state of the technology in use.

Plug-Ins and Programming

When you started this book, you began making a distinction between items that required the older method of external helper applications as contrasted to the new method of utilizing plug-ins to execute multimedia elements. Similarly, you need to make a distinction between plug-ins and scripting methods as they relate to multimedia elements that appear in Web pages.

NOTE

> You'll probably note that throughout most of today's lesson I refer to pages that use scripting and plug-in elements as multimedia elements. The majority of the languages and plug-in elements are being used to present multimedia elements on Web pages. This is far from what is completely possible in any of the scripting languages or the plug-ins themselves; however, the uses of most of these advanced elements are to present multimedia within Web pages.

Day 1, "The Webmaster: Jack of All Trades," highlighted that in the beginnings of the Web, digital files such as digital movies and sound files could not be opened directly in the browser. These files had to use external applications, which are executed by the browser as specified in the MIME type definitions of the browser. Then plug-ins came along. These browser add-ons gave the browser the capability to open all different types of files, as long as the plug-in had been installed. Then someone with a bright idea thought, "Hey, why not allow additional programming right within the HTML language?" As more of a convention than anything else, today you see many different scripting languages being directly included in Web pages. We've come a long way in five years.

As you surf the Web and find pages that use these advanced elements, it'll often be difficult, simply from looking at the page, to determine which advanced element is being used: Shockwave, JavaScript, or Java. Maybe it's ActiveX that is doing the work. Nonetheless, you will find that many of the scripting languages and plug-ins have very similar capabilities. Often you'll find that the only real differences are minute details that only a computer scientist would acknowledge as "different."

So, how do you tell what's what? How do you know what elements are being used so you can learn from what others have created? Typically, you should look for three things. The three tags used to integrate scripting or plug-in components are the EMBED, APPLET, and SCRIPT tags. As you probably remember, the SCRIPT component actually is an attribute of the <HEAD> tag.

The <EMBED> Tag

The <EMBED> tag enables various objects to be directly linked to HTML pages.

The <EMBED> tag is a kind of catch-all tag. It enables you to integrate many different elements into the Web page. All of the elements that are embedded using the <EMBED> tag are external, meaning that the <EMBED> tag links an external file to the HTML file, much like the <IMG> tag does with images. Items that are integrated using the <EMBED> tag most often require a plug-in for execution. Items that can be embedded include sound files, Shockwave movies, Shockwave images, and VRML files, to name just a few.

The <EMBED> tag has several attributes that you can use to help format these items on the page. The attributes for the <EMBED> tag include:

- ☐ SRC—The source file to be embedded into the HTML file
- ☐ WIDTH—The width of the object being inserted
- ☐ HEIGHT—The height of the object being inserted

Note that you also can use some of the normal <IMG> attributes with some objects and with some browsers. The attributes that can be included are the ALIGN, BORDER, HSPACE, and VSPACE options. You might also specify the <NOEMBED>...</NOEMBED> tags for browsers that do not recognize the <EMBED> tag.

The second of the advanced tags is the <APPLET> tag.

The <APPLET> Tag

The <APPLET> tag is used to integrate Java applications into Web pages.

Valid attributes for the <APPLET> tag include:

- ☐ CODE—The file that contains the compiled Applet subclass in the form of file.class
- ☐ WIDTH—The width of the Java application
- ☐ HEIGHT—The height of the Java application

The last advanced element is the inclusion of embedded scripts within HTML files. These scripts can include JavaScript, ActiveX, and VBScript. To determine whether a scripting language is being used, you must simply look at the header section of the document. In an HTML file that uses scripting, you probably will notice a very large <HEAD> section. Many times the <HEAD> section contains declarations and scripting language controls. At other times, you'll find a <SCRIPT> tag embedded deeper in the document. The <SCRIPT> tag always tells you what type of scripting language is being used.

Scripting languages actually are great if you are familiar with using them. However, you will find that many browsers do not support their use. Some browsers support one and not the other. For example, Microsoft Explorer used to be able to view ActiveX scripting but not JavaScript. Netscape Navigator could view JavaScript but not ActiveX. However, the latest versions of both browsers support the other's scripting languages either directly or through the use of plug-ins. Currently, it appears as if there will be no coordination between Microsoft

14

and Netscape as to supporting all scripting languages. It is likely that both companies will strive to copy the other's technology, although one might appear later than the other. If you decide to use a newer scripting language, make sure that you do not eliminate part of your audience because they are using the wrong viewer or don't have a plug-in. Always do your best to provide the items, such as links to plug-ins or at least a statement telling users what they need to adequately view your page. Doing any less will frustrate the user.

Shockwave

Probably one of the most powerful plug-ins available for the big two browsers is Macromedia's Shockwave plug-in. To understand and use the Shockwave plug-in you must know about Macromedia's products. The three products that you can use for Shockwave are Director, Authorware, and FreeHand. Both Director and Authorware are multimedia authoring environments, but FreeHand is a vector drawing program. Figure 14.1 shows an example of a Shockwave file in a Web page. The page is an interactive puzzle, which is a unique use of this new technology.

Figure 14.1.

A Shockwave movie integrated into a Web page.

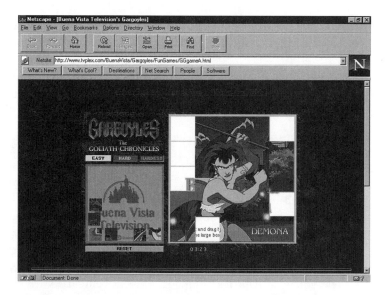

With Shockwave files you can add quite a variety of interactive multimedia elements on the Web. Almost anything that is created in these three programs can be converted and used on the Web, but that isn't always practical. If you have ever worked with these applications, particularly Director and Authorware, you know how big the files can become. A typical multimedia presentation created in Director or Authorware can be anywhere from 1 to 5MB or as much as 650MB, with all the extraneous sound and video files.

14

You have to be realistic about using multimedia elements on the Web. If you'll remember discussions about bandwidth on Day 4, you'll recall that the current state of the Web is not very fast when compared to the huge demands of graphics and multimedia elements. Most users are probably connected using a dial-up connection, and that huge Shockwave movie will take them hours to download. As you surf some of the more common Shockwave sites, you'll see that most movies are at least 50KB, which translates to about one minute to download over a 28.8 Kbps modem. You must very carefully design Shockwave movies if you want to use them in your Web pages. To see more examples of Shockwave movies, check out the following Web sites:

http://www.macromedia.com/

http://www.updatestage.com/

http://www.mcli.dist.maricopa.edu/director/

Regardless of which one of these three applications you are using, you must understand that Shockwave is a plug-in for browsers. It is not what enables you to create Shockwave files. To create Shockwave files from any of these three applications, you must have the application and the appropriate conversion filter for the product. This conversion filter is called Afterburner in all three products. The Afterburner filter converts the appropriate file to one that can be distributed over the Web. The most significant thing that the Afterburner filter does is compress the file. No matter whether you have a multimedia element or a vector image, the Afterburner filter compresses the file so that it can be distributed over the Web. Figure 14.2 shows an example of a Shockwave image created in FreeHand. Note that even vector images are compressed using the Afterburner filter.

Figure 14.2.

A Shockwave image integrated into a Web page.

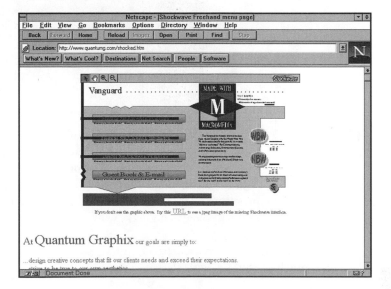

14

After you create Shockwave files, you can integrate them into your Web pages using the <EMBED> tag. Because all three of these elements are visual in nature, you must specify sizes. Make sure that you also include a server MIME type so that your server knows that it can distribute files with the .drw, .apw, and .fhr extensions. Otherwise, the server will not release the requested files to your audience.

Java and JavaScript

Originally created as a consumer electronic language, Java has quickly grabbed hold of much of the Internet programming market. Java itself has some very significant implications when you consider that elements created in Java are designed to run as platform-independent applications. Figure 14.3 shows an example of a Java application.

Figure 14.3.

A Java application used in a Web page.

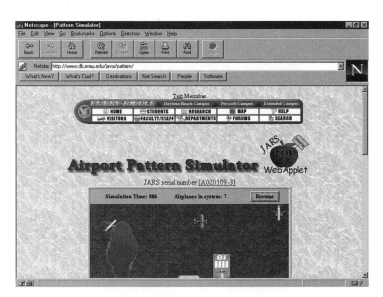

NOTE

When you surf the Web, you'll find that many of the technologies you learn today are in their infancy. Most, if not all, are in the "play" stage, in which designers are doing fun but not necessarily productive things with the technology. That's not to say that there are no productive people using things such as Java. However, most of the sites are testing the technology, and heck, why not have fun while you're doing it?

14

Java applications are designed to be portable. Resembling the C or C++ languages, Java applications are compiled in a *neutral state*, which means they can be ported to many other platforms. This is what makes the Java language so powerful as a development environment. Much like other platform- and software-independent languages, such as SGML and HTML, Java enables programmers to create applications, as shown in Figure 14.4, that can be run on any platform. The small highlighted item in the figure is a Java applet that senses when the cursor is rolled over it.

Figure 14.4.

Java applications are designed to be platform-independent.

One thing I must note is that Java applications will run only on 32-bit environments such as Windows 95 and Windows NT. It can also be run on MacOS 7.5 and UNIX Solaris. If you're planning to get into Java programming, keep this tidbit in mind!

"So what's the difference between Java and JavaScript?" you might ask. The differences are many, but there are many similarities as well. The biggest difference between the two is the way in which they are created and distributed. Java itself requires entering the code, compiling the code, and then making the application available to the server. JavaScript, on the other hand, is actually embedded in the HTML file itself. Using the <SCRIPT> tag, JavaScript code is embedded within the Web document and is interpreted directly by the browser rather than compiled. A Java program must be compiled, and then it is linked to the HTML file through the use of the <APPLET> tag.

14

In addition, JavaScript is also easier to program than its big brother. It adds some conveniences to the actual programming method, making its constructs easier to follow. JavaScript is also applicable to all environments, which includes the Windows 3.*x* and the Macintosh environment. The same is not true of Java.

If it sounds like I am preaching in favor of JavaScript, I must note that there are disadvantages to using JavaScript. First, there have been many security concerns concerning JavaScript. For example, other individuals might be able to peer at certain aspects of your machine, such as your URL history and browser cache. To some, these are security risks. JavaScript is also readily viewable in an accessing browser. This means that if you create a password protection scheme using JavaScript, the user could extract the password from the source code just by reading it.

Although JavaScript does have some disadvantages, I believe its advantages far outweigh its disadvantages. However, you might find that you prefer the security of Java over the easier nature of JavaScript. Fundamentally, anything that can be done in Java can be done in JavaScript and vice versa. To find out more about Java or JavaScript, check out the following sites:

```
http://www.yahoo.com/Computers_and_Internet/Programming_Languages/Java/
```

```
http://www.javaman.com/
```

```
http://www.javaworld.com/
```

```
http://java.sun.com
```

```
http://www.gamelan.com
```

VBScript

As a direct competitor to JavaScript, VBScript also is a powerful Web development scripting language that can be used on the World Wide Web. It was developed in 1995 by Microsoft and is a natural outgrowth of Microsoft's Internet initiative.

Like JavaScript, VBScript is a scripting language that is used directly within a Web page using the <SCRIPT> tag—no <APPLET> or plug-ins required here. However, the biggest difference is that Java and JavaScript are based partially on the C and C++ language, whereas VBScript is based on Visual Basic. Like the stand-alone Visual Basic application programming environment, VBScript shares common elements and constructs, making any successful Visual Basic programmer a successful Web scripter, as well.

Most of the pages that use VBScript use its various controls to enable the user to enter information or do any number of things on the Web, as shown in Figure 14.5. One of the biggest attributes of any scripting language is the capability to execute commands without

14

requesting information from the server. In a plain HTML file, you can insert buttons and controls for the user to navigate through your site. However, when the user clicks on links or other items, the client machine must request information from the server. Every action must pass through the server. With a scripting language, some actions can be executed within the client computer rather than requesting information from the server. This significantly reduces network traffic, as well as speeds up things for the user.

Figure 14.5.

Using VBScript controls.

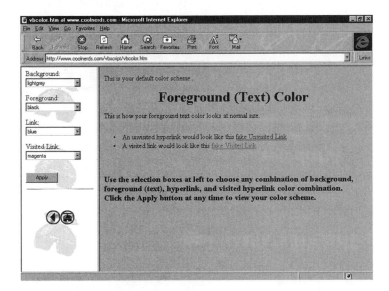

Probably the biggest thing is that VBScript contributes to a Web page is interactive controls. Using many of the standard Visual Basic controls, you can integrate them into your Web pages for use. This enables you to create common interface elements that in many cases are already created. Visual Basic itself comes with many canned buttons, controls, drop-down menus, and so on that can all be implemented by using VBScript, as shown in Figure 14.6.

VBScript also enables you to create Web pages that are relatively intelligent. You can use VBScript to perform data calculations within a Web page, which lets the user come away from your site with more than a passive display of information, as shown in Figure 14.7. There are many sites on the Web that enable you to calculate any number of things, from the cost of a particular car with certain options to the cost of financing a home mortgage through a particular bank. VBScript is very capable in pages that utilize features such as this.

As with JavaScript, there are many security concerns with VBScript. The biggest concern with any scripting language is that it does not open a door for mischievous Web surfers. For the most part, obvious flaws in scripting languages that would enable such things to happen have been disabled or eliminated. VBScript is set up so that it can neither read nor write

14

potentially damaging information to an audience member's hard drive. In reality, none of the scripting languages can physically affect a user's hard drive because they cannot perform write or read operations at the system level.

Figure 14.6.

Utilizing Visual Basic controls.

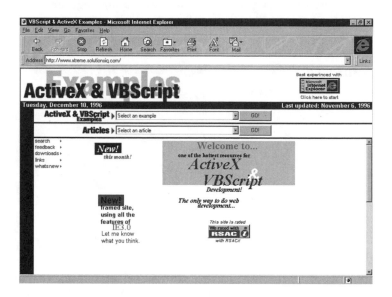

Figure 14.7.

Creating intelligent pages.

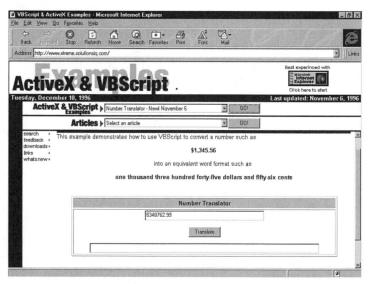

Due to the wide success and ease of use of the Visual Basic programming environment, many individuals have chosen to use VBScript in their Web pages. As a VB user myself, I find that

Visual Basic is much easier to use than JavaScript because I am already familiar with how VB works and the constructs it uses for programming. For more information on VBScript, check out the following sites:

```
http://www.doubleblaze.com
```

```
http://Website.ora.com/devcorner/db-src/
```

ActiveX

VBScript, JavaScript, and Java are all specific scripting languages that can be used within a Web page. ActiveX, however, is more of a standard for including controls in a Web page. All of the applications you see on your desktop every day use a basic set of controls to function. Buttons look similar and often behave similarly because they are derived from the same system-level code representing controls. ActiveX is Microsoft's attempt at making a consistent control system that enables any application, whether it is a local application or one running off the Internet, to use the same control code. The implications of this are quite astounding. Currently, the controls used for the Windows environment are not portable, which means that an application running on another machine cannot use them. Neither can they be used over the Internet. But what if you created a control standard that could be used for any application, including those delivered over the Net? This is Microsoft's goal through the ActiveX standard.

ActiveX is really a standard way of representing the controls that are used by the various scripting languages. As an adaptation of the VBX and OCX control systems used with Visual Basic, as well as the standard controls used with the Windows environment, Microsoft is striving to make transparent the current wall that exists between browsing the Net and working with other applications. ActiveX controls are designed to tear down this wall, making all applications virtual through the use of common control code. By using common control code, applications become distributed across an entire computer system. This enables any online application to use any control that is part of the operating system. It also enables operating systems to be integrated with the browser—the operating system becomes a browser.

So what does this have to do with you? Well, at this point, the ActiveX technology is floundering somewhat, but it is still alive. Currently there are many vendors providing controls for just about everything. However, the stability and reliability of the technology is still unfolding. To find out more about ActiveX technology, check out these sites:

```
http://www.activex.com/
```

```
http://activex.irdu.nus.sg/
```

```
http://www.techWeb.com/activexpress/
```

14

```
http://www.microsoft.com/wwlive/

http://www-math.uni-paderborn.de/~sergiva/activex.html

http://www5.zdnet.com/zdWebcat/content/megasource/activex/activex.html
```

VRML

The last of the advanced Web elements you learn today is Virtual Reality Modeling Language (VRML). VRML (pronounced "ver-mul"), as its name implies, enables a developer to distribute virtual environments over the Web. Do you need to distribute a model of the solar system over the Web? Maybe a new product design or other proposed item needs to be posted for discussion among company officials who are scattered halfway around the world. With VRML, almost anything is possible, as shown in Figure 14.8. The figure shows a three-dimensional world in which the view can look at the objects in any direction or orientation.

Figure 14.8.

Using VRML in Web pages.

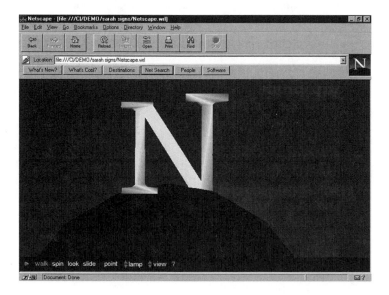

To view VRML documents on the Web, one of the first things you will need is a plug-in to enable you to view these files. There are several plug-ins floating around on the Web, but probably the most notable is Netscape's Live3D. The Live3D plug-in enables you to dabble in these three-dimensional worlds right within your browser. To download the Live3D plug-in, or check out some of the other VRML plug-ins, access

```
http://www.yahoo.com/Computers_and_Internet/Internet/World_Wide_Web/
➥Virtual_Reality_Modeling_Language__VRML_/
```

14

After you have accessed a site that contains a VRML file, it is downloaded to your computer. After it is downloaded, you can move the object around in the three-dimensional computer file, which is pretty cool.

Needless to say, VRML technology is still very young. We really have only begun tapping into what could actually be done with this technology. Probably the most significant limitation of the technology is the current bandwidth issue on the Internet. Because VRML files contain a description of a three-dimensional environment, the size of these files can grow tremendously large. Waiting for them to download can severely test your patience. But more often than not, it's worth the wait.

To find out more about VRML, check out the following sites:

```
http://www.sdsc.edu/vrml/
```

```
http://vrml.wired.com/
```

```
http://www.w3.org.hypertext/WWW/Markup/VRML/
```

Summary

Today you have taken a cursory look at the various advanced Web elements that can be found on the Web. Indeed, you have not even scratched the surface of all the various plug-ins and odds and ends that you can use. One of the most difficult things you'll find as you continue with your career, well beyond this book, is the rate of change and how quickly new Web innovations appear. Undoubtedly, by the time this book hits the press and you get to this closing paragraph, things will have changed yet again. But that's what makes the Web so fascinating—if you get bored with the Web, give it a few days, and something new will be waiting for you!

Q&A

Q What is Java and how is JavaScript different?

A Java is an object-oriented programming language that is used to create platform-independent applications that can be distributed over the Internet. Java programs, called applets, are integrated into Web pages but remain externally linked. They are not directly coded into the HTML code. JavaScript is a simplified rendition of Java that can be used directly in a Web page. The JavaScript code is inserted right within the HTML code and can be viewed by the audience.

14

Q How are JavaScript and VBScript different? Are there similarities?

A Essentially, JavaScript and VBScript are similar in function but different in the way in which they are actually programmed. JavaScript resembles C or C++ programming, but VBScript resembles Visual Basic. Both can be used to integrate controls into a Web page.

Workshop

The Workshop provides quiz questions to help you solidify your understanding of the material covered and exercises to give you experience in using what you've learned. The quiz answers are provided in Appendix A, "Quiz Answers." Try to understand the quiz answers before you go on to tomorrow's lesson.

Quiz

1. What are the three primary tags used to integrate the advanced elements discussed today?
2. What is the difference between a helper application, a plug-in, and a scripting language?
3. Concerning the elements you learned today, what HTML tags are used to integrate each of these elements?

Exercise

Surf the Web and find a Web site that uses each of the different technologies you have learned about today. How is the coding for each different? How are they the same? What tags are used, and how do you know which is which?

14

Week 2

2

In Review

When most people think of the term *Webmaster* they instantly associate it with the HTML language. No book about Webmastering would be complete without a significant portion devoted to developing pages, graphics, and media elements. As you learned in Week 1, being a Webmaster is much more than knowing HTML. However, the first part of this book would be incomplete without a section about programming HTML and creating various elements such as graphics, tables, forms, and frames. The first half of the book focused on knowledge-based information. The second half focused on the application of the HTML language.

Day 8, "Introduction to HTML and Block Tags"

On Day 8, you learned how the HTML language is structured and how to use it. The lesson began by making a distinction between the two main parts of the language: tags and attributes. Remember that tags are the main code words that are used in the HTML language and attributes are optional settings or parameters for those tags. You also learned that most of the tags used in the HTML language require both a beginning and ending tag. Although not all tags require a closing tag, I strongly suggest that you use them. Several of the tags cannot have a closing tag. This is the only time you shouldn't use a closing tag.

On Day 8, you also learned the four basic elements of all HTML documents. These include <!DOCTYPE> (which isn't required but is strongly suggested), the HTML containers, the header, and the body sections. All HTML documents, except for frames documents, use these elements.

To round out the day, you looked at the various block-level tags that are used to format pages. Keep in mind that a block-level tag will always create a blank line before and after the items being formatted. All of the tags introduced on Day 8 are block tags. In most instances, you will begin creating your page by establishing the four main sections (<!DOCTYPE>, <HTML>, <HEAD>, and <BODY>) and then enter the block tags that define the various portions of your document.

Day 9, "Text-Level Tags"

Day 9 continued the lesson of the HTML language by looking at the text-level tags you can use to format text, graphics, and other media elements. Your ability to integrate interactivity and graphics into Web pages is due to the text-level tags.

In this lesson you also learned some of the earliest tags that were available for formatting text. As the lesson stated, there are two main types of text formatting capabilities at the text level: physical and logical styles. Physical styles affect the style of text with no other intended meaning. Logical styles format the text with the intention of implying something such as an emphasized phrase or a line of code the user should enter. Remember that the way in which logical styles are formatted, such as italic or bold, is determined by the browser. Logical styles can vary slightly from one machine to another or from one platform to another. However, physical styles will appear the same across these variables. A physical style of italic will be italic no matter what machine you view it on.

The lesson also covered two of the most powerful tags available in HTML: the <IMG> tag, which is used to incorporate graphics, and the <A> tag, which is used to establish hyperlinks in the document.

Day 10, "Utilizing Graphics and Image Maps"

Because one of the most difficult aspects of building Web pages is using graphics, you spent an entire day looking at how to include graphics on your Web pages. As an expansion of the basic discussion of the <IMG> tag, you took some graphics and used some of the various attributes to make them look several different ways. As you begin building your Web pages, keep in mind the effect the image resolution, image size, and image bit-depth has on the digital file size. You do not need to store more than 72 dpi for Web-based images. Depending on your chosen file format, you can significantly reduce the size of your images by storing them in a 256-color rendition. All three of these variables can drastically affect the size of your graphics, which translates into wait time for the user.

Day 11, "Using Tables To Format Pages"

One of the most fun, as well as most challenging, things to work with in the HTML language are tables. If you are used to tight control over the layout of graphics and text, you'll probably love them. The standard combination of block- and text-level tags doesn't often fit the bill when you are trying to get a consistent look across several pages or browsers. The ALIGN attribute often can cause some pretty strange things to happen globally. When used properly, tables can significantly reduce your amount of frustration when you are laying out your Web pages. As you learned in the lesson, you can create a table template and use it in several of your pages, giving them a consistent look and cutting the amount of time it takes to lay out the page when it is full of graphics and text.

Day 12, "Using Frames To Format Pages"

Following the layout theme presented in the previous lesson, Day 12 presented the abstract notion of having several pages open at once in a single browser window. By dividing up the screen into smaller windows or frames, you can link multiple HTML files to the same browser window. In this lesson, you learned how basic frames work.

A primary document, called a frames document, contains information about how the browser should divide up the screen real estate. The frames document replaces the <BODY> tag with the <FRAMESET> tag and actually contains nothing but frame divisions. The body for frames documents is actually contained in the pages that are linked to each frame, instead of in the frame document itself. In this lesson, you saw several examples of how to open new browser windows, how to control one frame with another, and how to control multiple frames with a single frame. As you begin to use frames, you'll find that controlling several frames with another is very easy.

Day 13, "Using Forms To Gather Data"

As you learned on Day 13, for communication to occur it must come full circle. There must be a way for your audience to send you feedback about your site. There are a wide variety of uses for interactive forms, and almost every site has one. Some collect simple information and others are full-blown online registration schemes. You learned the basics of how to create interactive forms using the various form input elements. You learned that every form has a form header and that the header contains vital information. After the user has entered data into a form, he or she presses a submit button. The browser must know what to do with the collected data, and the form header gives it this information. The header specifies a location to which to send the data as well as how to send it. Often, interactive forms data is sent to an external script for processing, but you can send it to an e-mail address.

Day 14, "Advanced Web Components"

This final lesson looked at the various advanced items and media elements you can use at your site. From Shockwave movies and images to Java applets and the various scripting languages, almost anything you can think of can be done on the Web. The biggest concern you will have when you use these types of elements is whether your audience will be able to view them. For example, Netscape Navigator cannot view ActiveX scripts. Similarly, Microsoft Explorer cannot view Java information. Both these browsers require plug-ins to view media elements such as Shockwave, certain audio elements, and video elements.

APPENDIX

A

Quiz Answers

Day 1, "The Webmaster: Jack of All Trades"

1. HTML, or HyperText Markup Language, is a simplified derivative of the SGML language. HTML is ASCII code that is used to semantically define the various elements that are to be laid out on a Web page. Special software, called a browser, requests Web pages from a Web server and then reads the HTML file to determine how items such as text and graphics should be laid out on the display screen.

2. An HTTP server, or HyperText Transfer Protocol server, is a special computer connected to the Internet that distributes World Wide Web home pages.

3. A Web address uses a word-oriented address called a domain name. A Web site address is characterized by single words separated by periods, such as `www.somesite.com`. The last word is a three-letter extension representing the type of site. For example, `.com` represents a commercial organization, `.edu` represents an educational institution, and `.org` represents a governmental institution. All Web servers begin with `http://`, FTP servers begin with `ftp://`, and Gopher servers begin with `gopher://`.

4. The Mosaic browser was the first truly graphical browser that was distributed for use. It was given away free, which helped establish the Web as a valid and accessible communication tool.

Day 2, "The Internet Specialist"

1. MIME stands for Multipurpose Internet Mail Extension, and it is used to help browsers and other programs recognize files that are distributed over the Internet. The MIME definition tells the program what to do with the file based on its three-letter extension. An extension such as `.GIF` tells a Web browser to open the file with the browser, and an extension of `.ZIP` tells the browser to open a different external application.

2. An intrasite link is a hyperlink that takes a user to another page in the current site. An external link is a link that sends the user to a completely different Web site or page.

3. The browser cache is where elements that are downloaded are temporarily stored. All HTML and associated graphic and media files are stored in the cache. The cache helps reduce the amount of traffic on the Internet by storing elements from a particular site locally rather than having to download them. The browser pulls these elements from the cache on subsequent visits to a site rather than downloading them from the Internet site. If it is not properly maintained, a cache folder can consume massive amounts of hard disk space on the user's computer.

4. An embedded program is a small executable application or file that is embedded into a Web page. When a Web page with embedded elements is accessed, the elements download and then execute. An example of an embedded element is a Java applet, a RealAudio sound segment, or a Shockwave movie.

5. The first page of a Web site is commonly called a home page or a splash page. This page generally is unique and representative of the site's content. Often, a table of contents for the site material is included on this page.

Day 3, "The Information Design Specialist"

1. A site diagram is a map of the pages, files, and directories at a particular site. A site diagram is usually developed to help visualize the entire site as well as help the HTML programmers more efficiently generate Web pages.

2. A metaphor is a storyline or relational construct that is used to help familiarize a site's audience with its navigational structure and setup. A sample metaphor is a book or magazine metaphor, where you navigate the site in the same way you flip the pages of a book.

3. An interface is the point of interaction between the audience and the information, or the user and the computer. An effective interface must utilize the positive elements of human/computer interface design and must allow for feedback to and from both the user and the computer.

4. A license is a fee paid to use a copyrighted item. Licensing fees are generally based on the region of use, the number of replications, and the type of use. A release is a signed document that entitles the requesting individual to use the copyrighted item for a specific purpose. Most releases strictly regulate how the item can be used.

5. The public domain refers to any work that is not protected under copyright (patent or trademark) or media that is not considered a creative work. Items can also be considered public domain if the copyright for the item expires. However, just because items appear on the Internet does not mean that they are public domain. The same copyright laws that apply to traditional media also apply on the Internet. However, copyrights have very little effect internationally.

Day 4, "The Media Designer"

1. The three legs for communication to effectively occur include the tone, visual appeal, and consistency of the Web pages you deliver. Tone mainly deals with the manner in which you present your pages. A site for kids will have a very different tone from a site designed for business professionals. Visual appeal deals with both the quantity and the quality of the graphics you utilize on your pages. A page with poor or few graphics will likely be uninteresting. The final leg is that of consistency. Consistency deals with the number of unchanging elements that appear across your pages. Are navigation items always in the same place? Do you use a common logo or typefont that makes the site look like it was created by one individual focused on one goal or does it look like several individuals with no clear direction? All three of these issues directly affect the communicability of your site.

2. You can implement consistency at a site by using a theme or metaphor, consistently placing navigation items, and using clear informational content and consistent fonts and graphical style.

3. File compression decreases the size of a file by substituting for repetitive data. Internal file compression occurs within a particular graphic file format and affects the actual data in the file. External file compression occurs externally to any given format and does not affect the actual data that is present in the file.

4. Hexadecimal color is a base 16 mathematical representation of a particular color. RGB colors, which most paint packages support, can be converted using a scientific calculator. Convert each R, G, and B value to its hexadecimal equivalent and then combine the three pairs to create the hexadecimal value.

5. Color can affect the interpretation of a Web page both in a physiological and psychological fashion. Colors that are cool or warm appear to recede or come toward you, respectively. Specific colors can also be used to connote or represent certain things.

6. Vector graphics are based on mathematical descriptions. The basic drawing elements include lines, arcs, circles, and squares. Raster-based graphics are drawn a single pixel at a time. The smallest drawing element in raster graphics is the pixel, short for picture element.

7. The three main raster image attributes are image resolution, image size, and image bit-depth. Image resolution describes the number of physical dots per inch (dpi). The image resolution of Web-based documents that are to be displayed only on a computer should be set at 72 dpi. Image size describes the physical width and height of a raster image. Most image size specifications are given in pixel measurements such as 640×480 or 800×600. Image bit-depth describes the physical number of bits that can be used to digitally describe an analog source. The bit-depth of an image describes the number of colors that can be used by the particular image. Common bit-depths include 1-bit, which is black and white, 8-bit, which is 256 colors, and 24-bit, which is 16.7 million colors.

8. The two most widely used Web graphic formats are the GIF and JPEG image formats. The GIF image format supports up to 256 colors (8 bits) and can also support transparency and interlacing. The JPEG format is capable of supporting up to 24-bit images and utilizes lossy compression to decrease file sizes.

9. The biggest concern with any media element being distributed over the Web is the size of the file. Everything on the Web is an issue of bandwidth. The larger the file, the longer it takes to download. Media elements such as video, audio, and graphics can require significant amounts of time to download, which can frustrate users.

Day 5, "The Technical Designer"

1. The two networking models are the client/server model and the peer-to-peer model. The client/server model is the model on which the entire Internet is based. In this networking model, there is a single computer, which is a server responsible for managing all the network traffic. In a peer-to-peer networking model, all the computers on the network take care of managing the network. Peer-to-peer networks are good for smaller networks, and client/server networks are generally quite large. Using the client/server model can be detrimental if the server is not large enough to handle significant network traffic.

2. The main types of connections include ISDN, T1, Frame Relay, SMDS, and cable and satellite links. The biggest difference between these services is the speed at which communication occurs.

3. A LAN, or local area network, is a network that spans a single office or department. A WAN, or wide area network, is a network that spans entire cities or the entire world.

4. A T1 connection is one of the most widely used business Internet connections. This type of connection supports a bandwidth of 1,544 Kbps; however, the monthly cost ranges from $1,000 to $3,000 per month, plus the cost of the leased phone line. Often, a T1 connection can be leased in portions or increments called fractional T1. Fractional T1 is generally divided into multiples of 256 Kbps.

   A T3 connection is much wider and faster than the T1. A T3 line is used only to connect major Internet service providers. T3 lines can support hundreds of LAN networks and boast a 44,736 Kbps bandwidth. T3 forms the Internet backbone's major network connections.

5. Asynchronous communication is communication that occurs without any basis on time. Synchronous communication is modem communication that is based on time. Data that is sent using asynchronous communication must add additional bits to the data being sent so that it can be interpreted on the other end of the line. Because of this, asynchronous communication is slower because of the additional bits added to the data being transferred.

6. An intranet is an internal company web structure that is set up so that employees can share data and information without connecting directly to the Internet.

7. A firewall is special software that protects a corporate network from mischievous and detrimental Internet traffic. A firewall generally enables individuals inside the firewall to see outside the network; however, those outside the network (on the Internet) cannot see in. A firewall usually is interpreted as a means of confining employees; however, it really keeps viruses, hackers, and other troublesome problems out of the corporate network.

8. The three methods of controlling server access are open server access, centralized access, and decentralized access.

Day 6, "The Technical Manager"

1. A revision history document describes all the changes that have been made on a page, series of pages, or a Web site since its conception. The revision history document should include the date, person revising the document, and a description of the changes made to the items.

2. To be effective at time management, you should focus on those things that are not immediate but are important.

3. Communication is the most important aspect of effective consulting.

Day 7, "The Professional Consultant"

1. A copyright protects a creative work. A patent protects an idea. Copyrights are fairly inexpensive, and simply require the attachment of the copyright symbol to be in effect. A patent, however, requires legal proceedings and judicial decisions concerning the validity of the idea. Often a more effective means of protecting an idea is through the use of a non-disclosure statement.

2. Commissioned works include contributions to collective works, audiovisual works, compilations, supplementary works, translations, instructional text, tests, answer material for tests, and atlases.

3. The things you should look at when determining fees include the following:

   ☐ The number of pages

   ☐ The number of graphics on those pages

   ☐ The amount of special programming, such as forms, frames, or scripts

   ☐ Multimedia or other special elements

   ☐ Copyrights

   ☐ Turnaround time

   ☐ Maintenance

4. As you are deciding upon fees you must determine whether there is the possibility of future work. If there is, you might be able to take some short-term loss for the advantage of long-term gain.

5. The biggest concern you should have is that you are ultimately responsible for the work the subcontractor does. You must assure the hiring body of timeliness as well as quality control.

6. The main parts of a proposal include the abstract, introduction, project description, project plan, and project budget.

7. The main parts of a contract are the contracting bodies, length of term, pricing, timeline, description of deliverables, and limitations and scope of the employment.

8. You must approach a possible job by trying to make a win/win situation. If the price is too low for you to make money, you lose and the company wins, and you'll probably end up creating something you (and the company) won't like. If you quote a price that is too high and have no flexibility, the company loses because they cannot pay what you are asking. Again, you lose because you don't get the job. However, if you strive to work out an arrangement that is win for you (you make money) and win for the company (the price is acceptable), you'll find the business arrangement will work out to the advantage of both.

Day 8, "Introduction to HTML and Block Tags"

1. Comments are internal documentation or notes that are included within the actual code of the HTML file. Comments are ignored by the browser. To create a comment line, you mark the line with the `<!-....->` tags.

2. The two main parts within the `<HTML>...</HTML>` tags are the header, marked by the `<HEAD>...</HEAD>` tags, and the body, marked by the `<BODY>...</BODY>` tags. The header is used to describe the attributes of the document, and the body is used to describe the various elements that appear in the work area of the browser.

3. The two main types of tags that occur in the body section are block tags and text-level tags. Block tags are used to create logical blocks of text or graphics. Text-level tags are used to format specific text elements, as well as to incorporate graphics, interactivity, and multimedia elements.

4. The three main types of lists are unordered lists, ordered lists, and definition lists. The unordered list is marked by the `<UL>...</UL>` tags and presents a bulleted list. An ordered list is a sequential list that is marked by the `<OL>...</OL>` tags. The ordered list can use numbers, letters, or Roman numerals. The definition list, marked by `<DL>...</DL>`, can be used to present terms with definitions.

5. There is not much difference between the `<P>` and `<DIV>` tags; they both are used to block out a paragraph of text. However, the `<DIV>` tag can be used with HTML style sheets. There is no difference between the `<DIV ALIGN=CENTER>` tag and the `<CENTER>` tag. The `<CENTER>` tag is a shorthand way of executing the `<DIV ALIGN=CENTER>` tag.

6. The common characteristic among the <ADDRESS>, <H1> to <H6>, and <TITLE> tags is that they are all items at which search engines look when performing a search. Each should be descriptive of the page on which they appear.

7. The problem with designing a Web page that is wider than the audience's display is that the audience will spend more time scrolling than reading or viewing your information. Horizontal scrolling is one of the cardinal sins of Web development.

8. The tag that generates a carriage return-line feed is the <BR> tag. The <BR> tag inserts a paragraph break into the document. It can be used within any other tag.

Day 9, "Text-Level Tags"

1. The best way to code your pages is to insert all your block tags first. Then, insert the text-level tags to be nested within the block-level tags. Then, insert any remaining text-level tags that should be nested within other text-level tags.

2. The two tags that are used to integrate multimedia elements are the <APPLET> and <EMBED> tags.

3. Logical text tags are advantageous because they can enable you to cross cultural boundaries. Emphasized text can be rendered based on the browser. However, because the browser determines how emphasized text is rendered, it might not look the same across browsers, platforms, or machines.

4. The tag that you use to integrate graphics on a Web page is the <IMG> tag.

Day 10, "Utilizing Graphics and Image Maps"

1. Using layers in a raster image editor is like being able to draw on transparent acetate sheets. Each layer is individual, yet the compilation of the layers creates the single image. Using layers helps the developer overcome the two biggest limitations of working in a raster environment. First, because each layer is transparent, any anti-aliasing that occurs is between the object color and transparency, making the anti-alias fluid. Second, layers enable the developer to move sets of pixels around in the image without deleting objects that are behind the object that was moved.

2. Anti-aliasing is blurring the edges of raster objects to make them appear smooth. Anti-aliasing gets rid of jagged edges that naturally appear on pixel-based objects. An anti-alias halo occurs when an object that is created on one background is copied to a new background. The anti-alias that is created when the object is in its original setting appears when the object is moved to the new background.

3. When an image is created there is a fixed relationship between its size and its dpi. Scaling a bitmap graphic up spreads the dots of the image apart, which causes the image to break up or appear grainy. Scaling up a bitmap decreases the density of dots—it decreases the dpi. When you scale down a bitmap image, the dots are forced closer together, which increases the number of dots per inch and makes the smaller image clearer.

4. Bit depth is the physical number of computer bits that can be used to describe a raster image. The higher the bit depth of an image, the more colors that are available and the more photo-realistic the image can be. Common bit depths are 8-bit or 256-colors, and 24-bit or 16.7 million colors.

5. The height and width attributes of the <IMG> tag specify the size at which the image should be displayed in the browser. You can specify that the image be shown larger or smaller than its real size, but this is not recommended. The second thing that the HEIGHT and WIDTH attributes do is define rectangles for the image in the browser. If the user has inline graphics turned off, blank rectangles will appear in the browser's display area.

6. To control the alignment of images in a Web page you use the ALIGN attribute, which aligns the image in relationship to the text surrounding it. To adjust the spacing around an image, use the HSPACE or VSPACE attributes to control horizontal and vertical spacing, respectively. The number specified in these attributes is measured in pixels. Half of the specification is allotted to one side of the image while the other half is allotted to the other side.

7. The ALT attribute controls the text that is displayed in place of the image in non-graphical browsers. The LOWSCR attribute is used to define a low-resolution image that is to be displayed in the browser as the high-resolution image is being downloaded.

8. Progressive images are special images that coarsely display as they are being downloaded. Much like a fuzzy image in a camera that gradually comes into focus, the images become clearer or more defined as the image is downloaded. The image is completely representative of the source image when the entire image is downloaded. Two examples are the interlaced GIF format and the progressive JPEG format.

Day 11, "Using Tables To Format Pages"

1. To change the amount of spacing between a cell's contents and its boundaries you would use the CELLPADDING and CELLSPACING attributes for the <TABLE> tag.

2. You can predefine the size of a table using the <TABLE> tag's HEIGHT and WIDTH attributes. The size is specified in pixels.

3. If the cumulative sizes specified using the <TD> tags exceed that which are specified in the <TABLE> tag, the cumulative sizes will override the settings in the <TABLE> tag.

4. To insert graphics or anchors into a table you insert them into the <TD> lines of the table.

5. To make table borders invisible, set the <TABLE> tag's BORDER attribute to 0.

6. To get a blank data cell to appear recessed in a table, insert either a non-breaking space using its name ( ) or insert a line break, <BR>, into the table's data cell.

Day 12, "Using Frames To Format Pages"

1. The primary tags that are used to contain the frame's information are the <FRAMESET>...</FRAMESET> tags.

2. By integrating a <NOFRAMES> tag at the end of a frames document you can specify body content that will be displayed in non-frames browsers.

3. The NAME attribute is used with the <FRAME> tag to give a frame a name. The TARGET attribute is used with the <A> tag to specify a frame or item to update. The TARGET attribute can specify either an implicit item or the name of a frame.

4. Implicit names are predefined items that you can target for an HTML file. All implicit names begin with an underscore. The primary implicit name that is used is the _blank name, which loads the document into a new browser window.

5. The biggest concern about frame content files is that the HTML file is designed around the size of the targeted frame. If a content file is designed at a size larger than the frame, the user will have to horizontally scroll to see all of the information.

Day 13, "Using Forms To Gather Data"

1. Data that is sent from a form is sent as a series of matched NAME=VALUE pairs. The NAME portion is derived from the name established in the <INPUT> tag's NAME attribute. The VALUE is derived from the text or selection made by the user.

2. All input tags must have a name attribute. The name given to an input field should be unique and identifiable. It is used in the matched pair NAME=VALUE submission from the form.

3. The two tags that enable you to create drop-down menus are the <SELECT> and <OPTION> tags.

4. Hidden input elements usually are used to identify pages that are processed by the same script. The script will use the contents of the hidden field to identify how the output should be processed and where it should be sent.

Day 14, "Advanced Web Components"

1. The three primary tags that are used to integrate the advanced elements discussed are the <EMBED>, <APPLET>, and <SCRIPT> tags.

2. A helper application is an external application that is executed to open a particular file that is downloaded via the Web. The browser associates the application with the file extension through the MIME types definition. A plug-in is an integrated program that adds additional capability to a Web browser so that various files can be viewed within the browser. A scripting language enables a wide variety of elements, native to the language, to be programmed into a Web page. The scripting language's code is entered directly into the HTML code.

3. JavaScript, VBScript, and ActiveX utilize the <SCRIPT> tag. Java applets utilize the <APPLET> tag, and Shockwave files utilize the <EMBED> tag.

HTML 3.2 Reference

This appendix is designed to give you an overview of the tags and attributes presented in the chapters of this book. More than anything it gives you an overview of the language as a whole as well as a useful reference when you are creating code. In an effort to make this appendix useful, the tags have been arranged in the following manner:

- Document structure tags
- Block tags
- Text tags: physical
- Text tags: logical
- Text tags: form elements
- Text tags: other
- Text tags: frames and multimedia

☐ Special characters

☐ Named HTML colors with hexadecimal equivalents

☐ Standard HTML icons

When appropriate, each of the HTML tags includes

☐ The tag name

☐ The tag description

☐ The tag attributes

☐ Tag usage

☐ Tag examples

Document Structure Tags

Document structure tags are the HTML tags that define and delimit the major portions or sections of the HTML document. They are the tags necessary for proper interpretation of the HTML file by a viewing program.

The `<!DOCTYPE>` Tag

The `<!DOCTYPE>` tag specifies the version of HTML that is being used and to what governing body and specification the document conforms.

Attributes

☐ `PUBLIC` or `PRIVATE`—Public file or private file

☐ `HTML 2.0` or `HTML 3.2`—HTML version number

Examples

```
<!DOCTYPE PUBLIC "HTML 3.2//EN">

<!DOCTYPE HTML PUBLIC "-//W3C//DTD HTML 3.2//EN">
```

The `<HTML>` Tag

The `<HTML>`...`</HTML>` tags mark the beginning and the end of the HTML file.

The `<HEAD>` Tag

The `<HEAD>`...`</HEAD>` tags are used to define specific document parameters and characteristics.

The `<BODY>` Tag

The `<BODY>`...`</BODY>` section defines the actual instructions for laying out graphics, text, multimedia, and other elements in the browser's work area.

B

`<BODY>` Attributes

☐ `BGCOLOR="#FFFFFF"`—Defines a background color for your Web document.

☐ `TEXT="#FFFFFF"`—Defines the color of your document's normal text.

☐ `LINK="#FFFFFF"`—Defines the color to be used for links you haven't visited.

☐ `VLINK="#FFFFFF"`—Defines the color to be used for links you have visited.

☐ `ALINK="#FFFFFF"`—Defines the highlight color used when you click a link.

☐ `BACKGROUND="myimage.gif"`—Defines an image to be tiled across your document's background.

Example

```
<BODY BGCOLOR="#FFFFFF" TEXT="#FFFFFF" LINK="#FFFFFF" VLINK="#FFFFFF"
➥ALINK="#FFFFFF" BACKGROUND="myimage.gif">
```

Valid `<HEAD>`...`</HEAD>` Tags

One of the primary sets of tags in the HTML document is the `<HEAD>`...`</HEAD>` tags.

The `<ISINDEX>` Tag

The `<ISINDEX>` tag is used for simple keyword searches.

Usage

```
<ISINDEX "Search Prompt">
```

Example

```
<ISINDEX "Computer Graphic Images">
```

The `<BASE>` Tag

The `<BASE>` tag defines an absolute URL to use for relative URL links. It is the primary document at the particular Web site.

Usage

```
<BASE href="valid.http.site.address">
```

Example

```
<BASE href="http://www.tech.purdue.edu">
```

The `<META>` Tag

The `<META>` tag is used to supply information that cannot be supplied anywhere else in the document, such as a generator name or other pertinent information.

Usage

- [ ] `<META NAME="Name" CONTENT="Name Value or String">`
- [ ] `<META HTTP-EQUIV="Action" CONTENT="Date"`
- [ ] `<META HTTP-EQUIV="Action" CONTENT="X; URL=DOCUMENT.HTML">`

Examples

```
<META NAME="Author" CONTENT="James Mohler">

<META HTTP-EQUIV="Expires" CONTENT="Sat, 30 Sept 1996"

<META HTTP-EQUIV="Refresh" CONTENT="5; URL=SHEET3.HTML">
```

The `<LINK>` Tag

The `<LINK>` tag is used to define independent relationships of the current page with other documents in the Web structure.

Attributes

- [ ] HREF—Specifices a URL or address for the resource.
- [ ] REL—Defines the forward relationship of the document.

☐ REV—Defines the reverse or backward relationship of the document.

☐ TITLE—A title for the linked resource.

Usage

```
<LINK HREF="DOCUMENT.HTML" REL="NEXTPAGE.HTML" REV="PREVIOUSPAGE.HTML"
➥TITLE="CURRENTPAGE.HTML">
```

Example

```
<LINK HREF="jlmohler@tech.purdue.edu" REL="JLM3.HTML" REV="JLM1.HTML"
➥TITLE="JLM2.HTML">
```

Block Tags

Block tags are HTML tags that enable you to specify the formatting and arrangement of lines or bodies of text or graphics. They are characterized by a preceding and following blank line or space. These must be used within the <BODY>...</BODY> sections of the HTML document.

<H1> Through <H6> (HX)

The <HX> tag defines the headings for the HTML document, where *X* can equal a value of 1 to 6. Headings defined by <H1> are rendered in a larger font and are deemed the most important head. As the value of *X* decreases, the font size and importance also decrease.

Attributes

☐ ALIGN—Controls the alignment of the heading. Valid entries are LEFT, CENTER, and RIGHT.

☐ CLEAR—Moves the heading down the page until the margins are clear and do not have elements within them. Valid entries include LEFT, RIGHT, ALL, and PIXELS.

☐ NOWRAP—Prevents the heading from automatically wrapping across the screen.

☐ DINGBAT—Specifies an icon to appear before the heading. See the section titled "Standard HTML Icons" for information on where to see valid entries.

☐ SCR—Specifies an image to appear in front of the heading.

Usage

```
<HX ALIGN=LEFT¦CENTER¦RIGHT CLEAR=LEFT¦RIGHT¦ALL¦PIXELS NOWRAP DINGBAT=&NAME
➥SCR=IMAGE.GIF>
```

Examples

```
<H1> This is a plain old heading </H1>

<H1 SCR=PICTURE.GIF> Jazz it up with an image </H1>

<H1 CLEAR=LEFT NOWRAP> Scoot it down the page and do not wrap the text.</H1>
```

The <P> Tag

The <P> tag defines a block of text to be displayed as a paragraph in the Web document. A blank space is inserted before and after a block paragraph.

Attributes

☐ ALIGN—Controls the alignment of the paragraph. Valid entries are LEFT, CENTER, and RIGHT.

☐ CLEAR—Moves the paragraph down the page until the margins are clear. Valid entries include LEFT, RIGHT, ALL, and PIXELS.

☐ NOWRAP—Prevents the paragraph from automatically wrapping across the screen.

Usage

```
<P ALIGN=LEFT¦CENTER¦RIGHT CLEAR=LEFT¦RIGHT¦ALL¦PIXELS NOWRAP> Displayed
➥text goes here.</P>
```

Examples

```
<P ALIGN=CENTER> This is a sample paragraph that would be center justified.</P>

<P ALIGN=RIGHT CLEAR=50 PIXELS> This is a sample paragraph that would be right
➥justified and scooted down the page until 50 pixels are free.</P>
```

The <DIV> Tag

The division tag, or <DIV> tag, enables you to define blocks or sections of a document that should all be treated similarly, such as all text of a specific paragraph or section justified left or right.

Attributes

☐ ALIGN—Controls the alignment of the division. Valid entries are LEFT, CENTER, and RIGHT.

☐ CLEAR—Moves the division down the page until margins are clear. Valid entries include LEFT, RIGHT, ALL, and PIXELS.

☐ NOWRAP—Prevents the division from automatically wrapping across the screen.

Usage

```
<DIV ALIGN=LEFT¦CENTER¦RIGHT CLEAR=LEFT¦RIGHT¦ALL¦PIXELS NOWRAP> Displayed
➥text goes here.</DIV>
```

Examples

```
<DIV ALIGN=CENTER> This is a sample division that would be center
➥justified.</DIV>
```

```
<DIV ALIGN=RIGHT CLEAR=50 PIXELS> This is a sample division that would be
➥right justified and skooted down the page until 50 pixels are free.</DIV>
```

The <CENTER> Tag

The <CENTER> tag enables you to quickly create a division of text that is center justified. It performs the same function as <DIV ALIGN=CENTER>...</DIV>.

Attributes

☐ CLEAR—Moves the division down the page until all margins are clear. Valid entries include LEFT, RIGHT, ALL, and PIXELS.

☐ NOWRAP—Prevents the division from automatically wrapping across the screen.

Usage

```
<CENTER CLEAR=LEFT¦RIGHT¦ALL¦PIXELS NOWRAP> Displayed text goes here.</CENTER>
```

Examples

```
<CENTER> This is a text division that would be center justified.</CENTER>
```

```
<CENTER CLEAR=50 PIXELS NOWRAP> This is a center justified division of text
➥that would be moved down the page until 50 pixels are free with no automatic
➥wrapping of text.</CENTER>
```

The <UL> Tag

The <UL> tag is used to create unordered lists in the HTML language. An unordered list creates a vertically bulleted list on a Web page.

Attributes

- ALIGN—Controls the alignment of the unordered list. Valid entries are LEFT, CENTER, and RIGHT.

- TYPE—Defines the type of bullet used with the entire list. Valid TYPEs are DISC, CIRCLE, and SQUARE.

- CLEAR—Moves the list down the page until all margins are clear. Valid entries include LEFT, RIGHT, ALL, and PIXELS.

- DINGBAT—Specifies an icon to appear before all the list items. See the section titled "Standard HTML Icons" for information on where to see valid entries.

- SCR—Specifies an image to appear in front of all the list items.

- PLAIN—Does not put any bullets in front of any of the list items.

- COMPACT—Attempts to display the list as compactly as possible.

- WRAP—Wraps the list around a single column before proceeding to the next column. Valid only when used with multiple columns. Valid WRAP values are VERT or HORIZ.

Usage

```
<UL ALIGN=LEFT¦CENTER¦RIGHT TYPE=DISC¦CIRCLE¦SQUARE CLEAR=LEFT¦RIGHT¦ALL¦PIXELS
➥DINGBAT=&NAME SCR=IMAGE.GIF PLAIN COMPACT WRAP=VERT¦HORIZ>...</UL>
```

Examples

- `<UL ALIGN=LEFT TYPE=CIRCLE>...</UL>`—This creates an unordered list, left justified, with circles for all list elements. Note that the `<LI>` tag would be used inside this tag to define the list elements.

- `<UL TYPE=CIRCLE COMPACT>...</UL>`—This creates an unordered list, with circle bullets as compactly as the browser will enable. Note that the `<LI>` tag would be used inside this tag to define the list elements.

- `<UL TYPE=CIRCLE CLEAR=20 PIXELS>...</UL>`—This creates an unordered list with circle bullets. It moves the list down the page until 20 horizontal pixels are free. Note that the `<LI>` tag would be used inside this tag to define the list elements.

The `<OL>` Tag

An ordered list, which uses the `<OL>...</OL>` tags, enables you to create lists that are numerically or alphabetically labeled. By default, ordered lists are numbered.

Attributes

- ☐ TYPE—Establishes the numerical or letter sequence to be used with the ordered list. Valid entries are 1, A, a, I, and i (numerical, uppercase letters, lowercase letters, uppercase Roman numerals, or lowercase Roman numerals).

- ☐ START—Specifies the number with which you want the list to begin.

- ☐ SEQNUM—Also specifies the number with which you want the list to begin (version 3.0 attribute).

- ☐ CLEAR—Moves the list down the page until all margins are clear. Valid entries include LEFT, RIGHT, ALL, and PIXELS.

- ☐ CONTINUE—Specifies the list to continue the sequencing from where the last list left off.

- ☐ COMPACT—Attempts to display the list as compactly as possible.

Usage

```
<OL TYPE=1¦A¦a¦I¦i START=X¦SEQNUM=X CLEAR=LEFT¦RIGHT¦ALL¦PIXELS
➥CONTINUE COMPACT>...<OL>
```

Examples

- ☐ `<OL TYPE=1 START=2>...</OL>`—This creates an ordered list that numerically sequences the list starting with 3. Note that the `<LI>` tag would be used inside this tag to define the list elements.

- ☐ `<OL TYPE=I CONTINUE COMPACT>...</OL>`—This creates an ordered list that is sequenced by uppercase Roman numerals. The list also begins at the number from which the last list left off and the browser will try to display the list as compactly as possible. Note that the `<LI>` tag would be used inside this tag to define the list elements.

The `<LI>` Tag

The `<LI>` tag is used within the `<UL>...</UL>` tags to define the items that are to be shown in the list. These are called list items.

Attributes

- ☐ TYPE—Defines the type of bullet used with the specific list item. Valid types are DISC, CIRCLE, SQUARE, 1, A, a, I, and i but are overridden by a TYPE specified with either the `<UL>...</UL>` or `<OL>...</OL>` tags.

- ☐ VALUE—Changes the current sequencing of the list item in an ordered list.

Usage

Note that the `<LI>` tag is used inside either the `<UL>`...`</UL>` tags or the `<OL>`...`</OL>` tags.

```
...
<LI TYPE=DISC¦CIRCLE¦SQUARE¦1¦A¦a¦I¦i VALUE=X>...</LI>
...
```

Examples

```
<UL>
    <LI TYPE=DISC> List Item 1 </LI>
    <LI    TYPE=DISC> List Item 2 </LI>
    <LI TYPE=SQUARE> List Item 3 </LI>
</UL>

<OL>
    <LI TYPE=CIRCLE VALUE=5> List Item 5 </LI>
    <LI TYPE=SQUARE> List Item 6 </LI>
</OL>
```

The `<DL>` Tag

The `<DL>` tag is used to present a definition list, which presents a list of terms with definitions.

Attributes

☐ CLEAR—Moves the list down the page until all margins are clear. Valid entries include LEFT, RIGHT, ALL, and PIXELS.

☐ COMPACT—Attempts to display the list as compactly as possible.

Usage

```
<DL CLEAR=LEFT¦RIGHT¦ALL¦PIXELS COMPACT>...</DL>
```

Examples

```
<DL>...</DL>
```

```
<DL CLEAR=RIGHT COMPACT>...</DL>
```

The `<DT>` Tag

The `<DT>` tag is used within the `<DL>`...`</DL>` tags to define the term that is presented.

Usage

Note that the <DT> tag is always used within the <DL>...</DL> tags.

```
...
<DT> Term </DT>
...
```

Examples

```
<DL>     HTML
    <DT> Hypertext Markup Language </DT>
</DL>
<DL> SGML
    <DT> Standard Generalized Markup Language </DT>
</DL>
```

The <DD> Tag

The <DD> tag is used to present further comment on the term provided within the <DT>...
</DT> tag.

Usage

Note that the <DD> tag can be used within the <DL>...</DL> tags or the <DT>...</DT> tags.

Examples

```
<DL>
    <DT> HTML
        <DD> Hypertext Markup Language </DD>
  </DT>
    <DT> SGML
        <DD> Standard Generalized Markup Language </DD>
    </DT>
</DL>
```

The <LH> Tag

The list header, or <LH>, tag presents a title or opening line for any of the lists (<UL>, <OL>, or
<DL>).

Usage

A list header must be used directly after the opening statement for a list (<UL>, <OL>, or <DL>)
and before the first list item.

```
...
<LH> This is a List Header
...
```

Example

Use a <BR> tag to make the first list item jump to the next line.

```
<OL>
    <LH> Technical Graphics <BR>
    <LI> Engineering Design Graphics </LI>
    <LI> Illustration </LI>
    <LI> Digital Publishing </LI>
</OL>
```

The <PRE> Tag

The <PRE> tag enables text to be displayed in the browser work area as it is shown in the ASCII HTML code file itself. The text is displayed using a monospaced (fixed height and width) font.

Usage

```
<PRE>
    Text that is formatted in ASCII code.
    Text that is formatted in ASCII code.
    Text that is formatted in ASCII code.
</PRE>
```

Example

```
<PRE>
    Run through the wind,
    Ye large speckled bird
    Put your head in the sand
    How absurd!
</PRE>
```

The <BLOCKQUOTE> Tag

The <BLOCKQUOTE> tag enables you to format running quotations in your documents. A <BLOCKQUOTE> automatically will indent the margins of the quote to contrast with other body text.

Attributes

- ☐ CLEAR—Moves the quote down the page until all margins are clear. Valid entries include LEFT, RIGHT, ALL, and PIXELS.
- ☐ NOWRAP—Prevents the quote from automatically wrapping across the screen.

Usage

`<BLOCKQUOTE CLEAR=LEFT¦RIGHT¦ALL¦PIXELS NOWRAP>`

Example

`<BLOCKQUOTE NOWRAP> This is a quote with no text wrapping </BLOCKQUOTE>`

The \<ADDRESS> Tag

The \<ADDRESS> tag enables you to enter an address that is automatically italicized.

Attributes

- ☐ CLEAR—Moves the address down the page until all margins are clear. Valid entries include LEFT, RIGHT, ALL, and PIXELS.
- ☐ NOWRAP—Prevents the address from automatically wrapping across the screen.

Usage

`<ADDRESS CLEAR=LEFT¦RIGHT¦ALL¦PIXELS NOWRAP> Address Text </ADDRESS>`

Examples

`<ADDRESS CLEAR=LEFT NOWRAP> 9999 Knuckle Sandwich Street, Beard, Indiana`
`➥999999 </ADDRESS>`

`<ADDRESS CLEAR=LEFT NOWRAP> 9999 Knuckle Sandwich Street, <BR> Beard, Indiana`
`➥999999 </ADDRESS>`

The \<HR> Tag

A horizontal rule or \<HR> tag automatically creates a horizontal line or divider between block elements.

Attributes

☐ SIZE=y, where y specifies the thickness in pixels. The default is SIZE=2.

☐ WIDTH=x, where x specifies the horizontal width in pixels (WIDTH=20) or as a percentage of the screen (WIDTH=50%). The default is WIDTH=100%.

☐ ALIGN=LEFT, CENTER, RIGHT—Determines the alignment of the horizontal rule. The default is ALIGN=CENTER.

☐ NOSHADE—Turns off the embossed look of the rule. By default, shading is turned on.

☐ CLEAR—Moves the horizontal rule down the page until all margins are clear. Valid entries include LEFT, RIGHT, ALL, and PIXELS.

☐ SRC—Specifies a custom graphic image to be used for the rule. Valid entries are the filenames of GIF or JPEG images.

Usage

Note that no ending tag is used on horizontal rules.

```
<HR SIZE=Y WIDTH=X ALIGN=LEFT¦CENTER¦RIGHT NOSHADE CLEAR=LEFT¦RIGHT¦ALL¦PIXELS
➥SRC="IMAGE.GIF">
```

Examples

```
<HR WIDTH=50% ALIGN=LEFT>

<HR SIZE 8>

<HR SIZE 8 NOSHADE>
```

The
 Tag

The <BR> tag enables you to insert a line break, or "carriage return-line feed," into block elements so that you can force a line break within tags.

Example

An example of the <BR> tag used in an address line:

```
<ADDRESS CLEAR=LEFT NOWRAP> 9999 Knuckle Sandwich Street, <BR> Beard, Indiana
➥999999 </ADDRESS>
```

The <MAP> Tag

The <MAP> tag is used to define the parameters for a client-side image map.

Attributes

The <MAP> tag itself has only one attribute, which is required. The NAME attribute specifies a name for the client-side image map.

Usage

```
<MAP NAME="mapname">...<MAP>
```

Example

```
<MAP NAME="joe's">...<MAP>
```

B

The <AREA> Tag

The <AREA> tag is used inside the <MAP>...</MAP> tags to define the hotspots for the client-side image map.

Attributes

☐ SHAPE—Defines the shape of the hotspot being defined. Valid entries include RECT, CIRCLE, POLYGON, and DEFAULT. If DEFAULT is used, it must be the last area defined in the listing.

☐ COORDS—Defines the coordinate values for the area. Valid entries are in the form of X1,Y1,X2,Y2, and so on. Rectangle coordinates are specified by left, top, right, bottom. Circle coordinates are specified by X,Y (center location), and radius. Polygon coordinates are specified by successive X and Y values.

☐ HREF—Defines the URL to be linked to the image map's hotspot.

☐ ALT—Defines the text that should be displayed in nongraphical browsers.

☐ NOHREF—Defines a hotspot that does nothing.

Usage

```
<AREA SHAPE="RECT¦CIRCLE¦POLYGON¦DEFAULT" ALT="NAME" COORDS="X1,Y1,X2,Y2,..."
➥HREF="URL">
```

Examples

```
<AREA SHAPE="rect" ALT="Recreation" COORDS="323,167,383,257" HREF="rec.html">

<AREA SHAPE="rect" ALT="Nightlife" COORDS="451,169,507,256"
➥HREF="nitelife.html">

<AREA SHAPE="default" HREF="nolink.html">
```

The <TABLE> Tag

The <TABLE> tag is used to house all of the data for a particular table in the HTML code.

Attributes

☐ ALIGN—Enables text to flow around the table much like text flowing around an image. Valid entries for the ALIGN attribute include LEFT, CENTER, and RIGHT.

☐ BORDER—Sets the thickness for the borders of the table boundaries. The default for this attribute is 0, so not putting any value makes the borders invisible.

☐ CELLSPACING—Defines the thickness of the cell frames within the table. The default is CELLSPACING=2.

☐ CELLPADDING—Defines how close a cell frame can come to the edges of the object inside the frame. The default is CELLPADDING=1.

☐ WIDTH—Specifies the desired width of the table in either pixels or percentages. However, a value defined with this attribute can be overridden by the values set in other attributes (see the WIDTH attributes of <TR>, <TD>, and <TH> following).

☐ HEIGHT—Specifies the desired width of the table in either pixels or percentages. However, a value defined with this attribute can be overridden by the values set in other attributes (see the HEIGHT attributes of <TR>, <TD>, and <TH> following).

Usage

```
<TABLE ALIGN=LEFT¦CENTER¦RIGHT BORDER=2 CELLSPACING=2 CELLPADDING=1
➥WIDTH=X HEIGHT=Y>
```

Examples

```
<TABLE ALIGN= RIGHT BORDER=4 CELLSPACING=4 CELLPADDING=2>...</TABLE>
```

```
<TABLE BORDER=0 CELLSPACING=2 WIDTH=400 HEIGHT=125>...</TABLE>
```

The <TR> Tag

The <TR> tag is used within the <TABLE>...</TABLE> tags to define the rows for the table.

Attributes

☐ ALIGN—Specifies the alignment of the text or elements within the cell. Valid entries include ALIGN=LEFT, RIGHT, or CENTER. The default is ALIGN=LEFT.

☐ VALIGN—Specifies the vertical alignment of the text or elements within the cell. The default is ALIGN=MIDDLE. Valid entries include VALIGN=TOP, MIDDLE, BOTTOM, or BASELINE.

Usage

```
<TR ALIGN=LEFT¦RIGHT¦CENTER VALIGN=TOP¦MIDDLE¦BOTTOM¦BASELINE>
```

Example

```
<TR ALIGN=RIGHT VALIGN=MIDDLE>...</TR>
```

The <TD> Tag

The <TD> tag is used within the <TR>...</TR> tags to define the cells within the table row.

Attributes

☐ ALIGN—Specifies the alignment of the text or elements within the cell. Valid entries include ALIGN=LEFT, RIGHT, or CENTER. The default is ALIGN=LEFT.

☐ VALIGN—Specifies the vertical alignment of the text or elements within the cell. The default is ALIGN=MIDDLE. Valid entries include VALIGN=TOP, MIDDLE, BOTTOM, or BASELINE.

☐ WIDTH—Specifies the width for the element in pixels or as a percentage. Specifying a width will affect all of the cells in the particular column. If multiple cells use the WIDTH attribute, the widest cell setting will be used. Note that if the compilation of the cell widths exceeds the width specified in the WIDTH attribute of the <TABLE> tag, the cumulative widths specified per cell will override the width specified in the <TABLE> tag.

☐ HEIGHT—Specifies a height for the cell in pixels or as a percentage. Specifying a height will affect all of the cells in the particular row. If multiple cells use the HEIGHT attribute, the tallest cell setting will be used. Note that if the compilation of the cell heights exceeds the height specified in the HEIGHT attribute of the <TABLE> tag, the cumulative heights specified per cell will override the HEIGHT specified in the <TABLE> tag.

☐ COLSPAN—Specifies the number of columns that the cell spans.

☐ ROWSPAN—Specifies the number of rows that the cell spans.

☐ NOWRAP—Disables the text wrapping feature.

B

Usage

```
<TD ALIGN=LEFT¦RIGHT¦CENTER VALIGN=TOP¦MIDDLE¦BOTTOM¦BASELINE WIDTH=X HEIGHT=Y
➡COLSPAN=A ROWSPAN=Y NOWRAP>
```

Example

```
<TD ALIGN=CENTER VALIGN=MIDDLE WIDTH=10 HEIGHT=10 NOWRAP> This is the text for
➡the table data cell</TD>
```

The <TH> Tag

The <TH> tag creates a table header cell for the particular row or column of data cells. The text contained in these cells is rendered in boldface text.

Attributes

- [ ] ALIGN—Specifies the alignment of the text or elements within the cell. Valid entries include ALIGN=LEFT, RIGHT, or CENTER. The default is ALIGN=CENTER.

- [ ] VALIGN—Specifies the vertical alignment of the text or elements within the cell. The default is ALIGN=MIDDLE. Valid entries include VALIGN=TOP, MIDDLE, BOTTOM, or BASELINE.

- [ ] WIDTH—Specifies a width for the element in pixels or as a percentage. Specifying a width will affect all of the cells in the particular column. If multiple cells use the WIDTH attribute, the widest cell setting will be used. Note that if the compilation of the cell widths exceeds the width specified in the WIDTH attribute of the <TABLE> tag, the cumulative widths specified per cell will override the width specified in the <TABLE> tag.

- [ ] HEIGHT—Specifies a height for the cell in pixels or as a percentage. Specifying a height will affect all of the cells in the particular row. If multiple cells use the HEIGHT attribute, the tallest cell setting will be used. Note that if the compilation of the cell heights exceeds the height specified in the HEIGHT attribute of the <TABLE> tag, the cumulative heights specified per cell will override the height specified in the <TABLE> tag.

- [ ] COLSPAN—Specifies the number of columns that the cell spans.

- [ ] ROWSPAN—Specifies the number of rows that the cell spans.

- [ ] NOWRAP—Disables the text wrapping feature.

Usage

```
<TH ALIG=LEFT¦RIGHT¦CENTER VALIGN=TOP¦MIDDLE¦BOTTOM¦BASELINE WIDTH=X HEIGHT=Y
➡COLSPAN=A ROWSPAN=Y NOWRAP>
```

Example

```
<TH ALIGN=CENTER VALIGN=MIDDLE COLSPAN=4 ROWSPAN=2>
```

The <FORM> Tag

The <FORM>...</FORM> tags are the containers for the items that compose the form. A form can contain anything except another form and must contain at least one <INPUT>, <SELECT>, or <TEXTAREA> tag.

Attributes

- ☐ ACTION—Specifies the URL to which the data is sent. All forms have an ACTION statement; without it, the data will have no destination. Most often the ACTION statement will reference a script location, but it also can be sent to an e-mail address.
- ☐ METHOD—Specifies how the data is sent to the defined location. Valid entries include GET and POST. The default is GET.
- ☐ ENCTYPE—Specifies the MIME type of the data to be sent when the POST option is used. The MIME type tells the receiving location in what type of file the data is contained.

Usage

```
<FORM ACTION="URL" METHOD="GET"|"POST" ENCTYPE="MIME TYPE/SUBTYPE">
```

Example

```
<FORM ACTION="mailto:someone@some.place" METHOD="POST"
➥ENCTYPE="multipart/form-data">
```

Text Tags: Physical

A *physical style* affects a font style simply to draw attention to the font itself. It communicates no other information through the formatting of the text.

Tags

- ☐ <TT>—Creates teletype or monospaced text.
- ☐ <I>—Creates italic style text.
- ☐ <B>—Creates bold style text.

□ `<U>`—Creates underline style text.

□ `<STRIKE>`—Creates strike-through style text.

□ `<BIG>`—Renders the text larger than the surrounding text.

□ `<SMALL>`—Renders the text smaller than the surrounding text.

□ `<SUB>`—Attempts to place the text in subscript style.

□ `<SUP>`—Attempts to place the text in superscript style.

Examples

```
This is an example of: <TT> teletype or monospaced text.</TT>

This is an example of: <B> bold text.</B>

This is an example of: <I> italic text.</I>

This is an example of: <U> underlined text.</U>
```

Text Tags: Logical

A *logical style* affects a font style to draw attention to the font as well as communicate some information to the reader.

Tags

□ `<EM>`—Renders the font with emphasis.

□ `<STRONG>`—Renders the font with strong emphasis.

□ `<DFN>`—Specifies a defining instance of the enclosed term.

□ `<CODE>`—Renders the font as representing extracted code.

□ `<SAMP>`—Renders the font as representing output from a program or application.

□ `<KBD>`—Renders the font as representing text that the reader should enter.

□ `<VAR>`—Renders the font as representing variables, arguments, commands, or instructions.

□ `<CITE>`—Renders the font as a citation or reference to another source of information.

Examples

```
This is an example of: <EM> emphasis.</EM></LI>

This is an example of: <STRONG> strong emphasis.</STRONG>
```

```
This is an example of: <DFN> defining instance of a term.</DFN>

This is an example of: <CODE> sample coding.</CODE>
```

Text Tags: Form Elements

The following tags and attributes apply to interactive Web forms.

The `<INPUT>` Tag

The `<INPUT>` tag is used to define a single field of a form that generally constitutes a single NAME=VALUE pair in the data output of the form.

Attributes

- ☐ NAME—Defines the label that is associated with the data that is entered in the field. When the data from the form is processed, it will always appear as a NAME=VALUE pair. The NAME attribute of each input item should be unique as well as descriptive. Every `<INPUT>` tag must have a NAME attribute so that data entered in the field can be identified.
- ☐ VALUE—Defines the default value that should appear in the field. Radio buttons must have a default value. All other `<INPUT>` types do not require a default value.
- ☐ TYPE—Defines the type of input entity the item is. Valid entries include TYPE="TEXT", "SUBMIT", "RESET", "PASSWORD", "CHECKBOX", "RADIO", and "HIDDEN".

Note that depending upon the TYPE specified, other attributes can include the following:

- ☐ TYPE="text" or "password"
  - ☐ MAXLENGTH, which defines the maximum number of characters that the user can enter. It is highly recommended that you use this attribute.
  - ☐ SIZE, which defines the horizontal size of the text box in number of characters.
  - ☐ TYPE="submit" or "reset"
  - ☐ VALUE, which defines the text to appear on the button.
- ☐ TYPE="checkbox"
  - ☐ CHECKED, which specifies whether the box is checked by default.
- ☐ TYPE="radio"
  - ☐ CHECKED, which specifies whether the box is checked by default.

B

Usage

```
<INPUT NAME="Name" VALUE="default_value"
➥TYPE="TEXT"¦"SUBMIT"¦"RESET"¦"PASSWORD"¦"CHECKBOX"¦"RADIO"¦"HIDDEN"
```

Examples

```
<INPUT TYPE="TEXT" NAME="Address2" SIZE="30" MAXLENGTH="30">

<INPUT TYPE="SUBMIT" VALUE=" SUBMIT ">
```

The <TEXTAREA> Tag

The <TEXTAREA>...</TEXTAREA> tags enable you to create an adjustable text box for user text entry.

Attributes

☐ NAME—The label for the name portion of the NAME=VALUE pair for the field. The VALUE portion of the <TEXTAREA> will be the text that the user inputs.

☐ ROWS—Defines the height of the text area and is a required attribute.

☐ COLS—Defines the width of the text area and is a required attribute.

☐ WRAP—Defines whether the text wraps around the text area. Valid entries include OFF and PHYSICAL. The default is OFF. Note that when the PHYSICAL setting is used, it generates line break characters in the submitted text.

Usage

```
<TEXTAREA NAME="field_name" ROWS=Y COLS=X WRAP>default text </TEXTAREA>
```

Example

```
<TEXTAREA NAME="Comments" ROWS=40 COLS=80></TEXTAREA>
```

The <SELECT> Tag

The <SELECT> tag establishes the presence of a drop-down menu in the interactive form.

Attributes

- [ ] NAME—The label for the name portion of the NAME=VALUE pair for the field.
- [ ] SIZE—Defines the number of options that are displayed in the drop-down item. The default is SIZE=1. However, setting the SIZE to a larger number causes more options to be displayed in the field.
- [ ] MULTIPLE—Enables the user of the form to select more than one item in the menu.

Usage

```
<SELECT NAME="menu_name" SIZE=1 MULTIPLE>...</SELECT>
```

Examples

```
<SELECT NAME="MyMenu" SIZE=3>...</SELECT>

<SELECT NAME="Another_Menu" SIZE=1 MULTIPLE>...</SELECT>
```

The <OPTION> Tag

The <OPTION> tag creates the author-defined options that appear in the menu.

Attributes

- [ ] SELECTED—Controls whether the item is, by default, selected or not. In a list that uses MULTIPLE, you can use the SELECTED attribute on more than one option.
- [ ] VALUE—Defines a special value that is used in the NAME=VALUE pair instead of the option's value.

Usage

```
<Option SELECTED VALUE="different_value"> Option Name
```

Examples

```
<Option> Apples

<Option SELECTED VALUE="Number_of_Oranges"> Oranges
```

Text Tags: Other

In addition to styling text, you also can insert graphics, create hypertext links, and do other things using text-level tags.

The `<IMG>` Tag

The `<IMG>` tag is used to reference a graphic image file to be included in the display of a Web page.

Attributes

- ☐ SRC—Defines the image filename and path to be included in the Web page. This is a required attribute for the `<IMG>` tag.

- ☐ ALT—Specifies alternative text that should be displayed in nongraphical Web browsers. Although it's not mandatory, it should be used.

- ☐ ALIGN—Controls the alignment of the image in relationship to the text surrounding the image. Valid options are ALIGN=TOP, MIDDLE, BOTTOM, LEFT, or RIGHT.

- ☐ WIDTH—Specifies the intended width of the image in pixels. When this attribute is combined with the HEIGHT attribute, the browser shows a blank box for the image in the browser as the image is loading. If the ALT attribute is also used, the text will display in the blank box.

- ☐ HEIGHT—Specifies the intended height of the image in pixels. When this attribute is combined with the WIDTH attribute, the browser shows a blank box for the image in the browser as the image is loading. If the ALT attribute is also used, the text will display in the blank box.

- ☐ BORDER—Specifies the size of the border for the image. The default is BORDER=2. With BORDER=0 the border is suppressed.

- ☐ HSPACE—Specifies, in pixels, a specific amount of white, or negative, space to be left on the left and right of the image. The default is a small, nonzero number.

- ☐ VSPACE—Specifies, in pixels, a specific amount of white, or negative, space to be left on the top and bottom of the image. The default is a small, nonzero number.

- ☐ USEMAP—Specifies that the image be mappable by a client-side image map. This attribute is used in conjunction with the `<MAP>` tag.

- ☐ ISMAP—Specifies that the image is an image map. Regions of the image are defined as hypertext links (see Day 10, "Utilizing Graphics and Image Maps").

- ☐ LOWSCR—Specifies a low-resolution image to display while the higher, true source image is being downloaded.

Usage

```
<IMG SRC="image.gif" ALT="IMAGE NAME" ALIGN=TOP¦MIDDLE¦BOTTOM¦LEFT¦RIGHT
➥WIDTH=X HEIGHT=Y BORDER=N HSPACE=A VSPACE=B USEMAP¦ISMAP
➥LOWSRC="image_low.gif">
```

Examples

```
<IMG SRC="6b.gif" BORDER=0 HSPACE=30>

<IMG SRC="myimage.gif" BORDER=4 HSPACE=30 VSPACE=20 LOWSRC="l_myimage.gif">

<IMG SRC="joes.gif" BORDER=0 HEIGHT=200 WIDTH=345 USEMAP="#joe's">
```

The \<A\> Tag

The \<A\> tag, also known as an anchor, enables objects on a page to be used as a hyperlink. The \<A\> tag can be used with graphics, text, and multimedia elements.

Attributes

- ☐ NAME—Used for targeting specific portions of a Web document. Valid entries for the NAME attribute are strings such as part1, part2, and part3.
- ☐ HREF—Used to specify a URL address that links the item with the site. Clicking the item sends the browser to the URL address specified here.
- ☐ REL—Defines the forward relationship of the current page.
- ☐ REV—Defines the backward relationship of the current page.
- ☐ TITLE—Used as a title for the linked resource.

Note that the following \<A\> tag attributes are not part of the "official" HTML 3.2 specifications. They are browser conventions. Both Netscape and Explorer support these attributes.

- ☐ TARGET—Specifies the frame or object into which to load the linked resource. Valid entries include a frame name or the following implicit items denoted by the underscore character:
    - ☐ _self—Makes the browser update the frame in which the page occurs.
    - ☐ _parent—Makes the browser update the parent of the current frame, assuming one exists.
    - ☐ _top—Makes the browser update the entire browser work area.
    - ☐ _blank—Makes the browser open a new window in which to display the page.

Usage

```
<A HREF="URL"¦NAME="LINKSPOT" REL="NEXTPAGE.HTML" REV="PREVIOUSPAGE.HTML"
➥TITLE="THISPAGE">
```

Examples

```
<A HREF="www.tech.purdue.edu">...</A>

<A HREF="www.tech.purdue.edu"><IMG SCR="picture.gif"></A>

<A HREF="#profile>...</A>

<A NAME="profile">...</A>

<A HREF="www.tech.purdue.edu" TARGET="_blank">...</A>
```

Text Tags: Frames and Multimedia

To integrate frames and multimedia, you can use the following text-level tags.

The <FRAMESET> Tag

The <FRAMESET>...</FRAMESET> tags are the containers for the definition of a framed page. The <FRAMESET>...</FRAMESET> tags replace the <BODY>...</BODY> tags in the HTML document.

Attributes

☐ ROWS—Defines the number and size of row frames that should be created in the browser work area. Valid entries include absolute (pixels), relative (wild card characters), and percentages of the screen.

☐ COLS—Defines the number and size of column frames that should be created in the browser work area. Valid entries include absolute (pixels), relative (wild card characters), and percentages of the screen.

Usage

```
<FRAMESET ROWS=val1,val2,...valn¦COLS=val1,val2,...valn>...</FRAMESET>
```

Examples

```
<FRAMESET ROWS=25%,50%>...</FRAMESET>

<FRAMESET COLS=25*,50*>...</FRAMESET>

<FRAMESET COLS=100,300>...</FRAMESET>
```

The <FRAME> Tag

The <FRAME> tag defines one frame or window in a frames document.

Attributes

☐ SRC—Defines the Web page that will appear in the frame.

☐ NAME—Defines a name for the individual frame. This attribute is used to enable one frame to control another through a TARGET specification.

☐ SCROLLING—Defines whether the frame should have scrollbars or not. Valid entries for this attribute are SCROLLING=YES, NO, or AUTO. The default is AUTO.

☐ MARGINWIDTH—Defines the left and right margins for the frame in pixels. This attribute cannot be zero.

☐ MARGINHEIGHT—Defines the top and bottom margins for the frame in pixels. This attribute cannot be zero.

☐ NORESIZE—Disables the ability of the user to size the frame.

Usage

```
<FRAME SRC="URL" NAME="frame_name" SCROLLING=YES¦NO¦AUTO MARGINWIDTH=X
➡MARGINHEIGHT=Y NORESIZE>
```

Examples

```
<FRAME SRC="frame1.htm" NAME="frame1" MARGINWIDTH=10 MARGINHEIGHT=10 NORESIZE>

<FRAME SRC="frame3.htm" NAME="frame3">
```

The <APPLET> Tag

The <APPLET> tag is used to integrate Java applications into Web pages.

Attributes

☐ CODE—Specifies the file that contains the compiled Applet subclass in the form of "file.class".

☐ WIDTH—Specifies the width of the Java application.

☐ HEIGHT—Specifies the height of the Java application.

Usage

```
<APPLET CODE="file.class" WIDTH=X HEIGHT=Y>
```

Example

```
<APPLET CODE="myfile.class" WIDTH=250 HEIGHT=71>
```

The <EMBED> Tag

The <EMBED> tag enables various objects to be directly linked to HTML pages.

Attributes

☐ SRC—Specifies the source file to be embedded into the HTML file.

☐ WIDTH—Defines the width of the object being inserted.

☐ HEIGHT—Defines the height of the object being inserted.

Note that you also can use some of the normal <IMG> attributes with some objects and with some browsers. The attributes include the ALIGN, BORDER, HSPACE, and VSPACE options. You also can specify the <NOEMBED>...</NOEMBED> tags for browsers that do not recognize the <EMBED> tag.

Usage

```
<EMBED SRC="PATH_and_FILE" WIDTH=X HEIGHT=X>
```

Example

```
<EMBED SRC="http://www.server.com/example.dwr" WIDTH=220 HEIGHT=73>
```

Special Characters

The chart in Table B.1 shows the special characters that you can use in your Web pages. To use them, insert their character codes into your HTML code.

Table B.1. The ISO-Latin-1 character set.

Character	Numeric Entity	Character Entity	Description
	&#00;-&#08;		Unused
	&#09;		Horizontal tab
	&#10;		Line feed
	&#11; &#31;		Unused
	&#32;		Space
!	&#33;		Exclamation mark
"	&#34;	&quot;	Quotation mark
#	&#35;		Number sign
$	&#36;		Dollar sign
%	&#37;		Percent sign
&	&#38;	&amp;	Ampersand
'	&#39;		Apostrophe
(	&#40;		Left parenthesis
)	&#41;		Right parenthesis
*	&#42;		Asterisk
+	&#43;		Plus sign
,	&#44;		Comma
-	&#45;		Hyphen
.	&#46;		Period (fullstop)
/	&#47;		Solidus (slash)
0–9	0 9		Digits 0-9
:	&#58;		Colon
;	&#59;		Semicolon
<	&#60;	&lt;	Less than
=	&#61;		Equals sign
>	&#62;	&gt;	Greater than
?	&#63;		Question mark
@	&#64;		Commercial "at"
A–Z	A-Z		Letters A-Z
[	&#91;		Left square bracket

B

continues

Table B.1. continued

Character	Numeric Entity	Character Entity	Description
\	&#92;		Reverse solidus (backslash)
]	&#93;		Right square bracket
^	&#94;		Caret
—	&#95;		Horizontal bar
`	&#96;		Grave accent
a–z	a z		Letters a–z
{	&#123;		Left curly brace
|	&#124		Vertical bar
}	&#125;		Right curly brace
~	&#126;		Tilde
	&#127;		Unused
¡	&#161;	&iexcl;	Inverted exclamation
¢	&#162;	&cent;	Cent sign
£	&#163;	&pound;	Pound sterling
¤	&#164;	&curren;	General currency sign
¥	&#165;	&yen;	Yen sign
¦	&#166;	¦ or brkbar;	Broken vertical bar
§	&#167;	&sect;	Section sign
¨	&#168;	&uml;	Umlaut (dieresis)
©	&#169;	&copy;	Copyright
a	&#170;	&ordf;	Feminine ordinal
‹	&#171;	&laquo;	Left angle quote, guillemot left
¬	&#172;	&not;	Not sign
	&#173;	&shy;	Soft hyphen
®	&#174;	&reg;	Registered trademark
¯	&#175;	&hibar;	Macron accent
°	&#176;	&deg;	Degree sign
±	&#177;	&plusmn;	Plus or minus
2	&#178;	&sup2;	Superscript two
3	&#179;	&sup3;	Superscript three

Character	Numeric Entity	Character Entity	Description
´	&#180;	&acute;	Acute accent
µ	&#181;	&micro;	Micro sign
¶	&#182;	&para;	Paragraph sign
·	&#183;	&middot;	Middle dot
¸	&#184;	&cedil;	Cedilla
¹	&#185;	&sup1;	Superscript one
º	&#186;	&ordm;	Masculine ordinal
›	&#187;	&raquo;	Right angle quote, guillemot right
$\frac{1}{4}$	&#188;	&frac14;	Fraction one-fourth
$\frac{1}{2}$	&#189;	&frac12;	Fraction one-half
$\frac{3}{4}$	&#190;	&frac34;	Fraction three-fourths
¿	&#191;	&iquest	Inverted question mark
À	&#192;	&Agrave;	Capital A, grave accent
Á	&#193;	&Aacute;	Capital A, acute accent
Â	&#194;	&Acirc;	Capital A, circumflex accent
Ã	&#195;	&Atilde;	Capital A, tilde
Ä	&#196;	&Auml;	Capital A, dieresis, or umlaut, mark
Å	&#197;	&Aring;	Capital A, ring
Æ	&#198;	&AElig;	Capital AE diphthong (ligature)
Ç	&#199;	&Ccedil;	Capital C, cedilla
È	&#200;	&Egrave;	Capital E, grave accent
É	&#201;	&Eacute;	Capital E, acute accent
Ê	&#202;	&Ecirc;	Capital E, circumflex accent
Ë	&#203;	&Euml;	Capital E, dieresis, or umlaut, mark
Ì	&#204;	&Igrave;	Capital I, grave accent
Í	&#205;	&Iacute;	Capital I, acute accent
Î	&#206;	&Icirc;	Capital I, circumflex accent

continues

Table B.1. continued

Character	Numeric Entity	Character Entity	Description
Ï	&#207;	&Iuml;	Capital I, dieresis, or umlaut, mark
Đ	&#208;	&ETH;	Capital Eth, Icelandic
Ñ	&#209;	&Ntilde;	Capital N, tilde
Ò	&#210;	&Ograve;	Capital O, grave accent
Ó	&#211;	&Oacute;	Capital O, acute accent
Ô	&#212;	&Ocirc;	Capital O, circumflex accent
Õ	&#213;	&Otilde;	Capital O, tilde
Ö	&#214;	&Ouml;	Capital O, dieresis, or umlaut, mark
×	&#215;		Multiply sign
Ø	&#216;	&Oslash;	Capital O, slash
Ù	&#217;	&Ugrave;	Capital U, grave accent
Ú	&#218;	&Uacute;	Capital U, acute accent
Û	&#219;	&Ucirc;	Capital U, circumflex accent
Ü	&#220;	&Uuml;	Capital U, dieresis, or umlaut, mark
Ý	&#221;	&Yacute;	Capital Y, acute accent
þ	&#222;	&THORN;	Capital THORN, Icelandic
β	&#223;	&szlig;	Small sharp s, German (sz ligature)
à	&#224;	&agrave;	Small a, grave accent
á	&#225;	&aacute;	Small a, acute accent
â	&#226;	&acirc;	Small a, circumflex accent
ā	&#227;	&atilde;	Small a, tilde
ä	&#228;	&aauml;	Small a, dieresis, or umlaut, mark
å	&#229;	&aring;	Small a, ring
æ	&#230;	&aelig;	Small ae diphthong (ligature)
ç	&#231;	&ccedil;	Small c, cedilla
è	&#232;	&egrave;	Small e, grave accent
é	&#233;	&eacute;	Small e, acute accent

Character	Numeric Entity	Character Entity	Description
ê	&#234;	&ecirc;	Small e, circumflex accent
ë	&#235;	&euml;	Small e, dieresis, or umlaut, mark
ì	&#236;	&igrave;	Small i, grave accent
í	&#237;	&iacute;	Small i, acute accent
î	&#238;	&icirc;	Small i, circumflex accent
ï	&#239;	&iuml;	Small i, dieresis, or umlaut, mark
ð	&#240;	&eth;	Small eth, Icelandic
ñ	&#241;	&ntilde;	Small n, tilde
ò	&#242;	&ograve;	Small o, grave accent
ó	&#243;	&oacute;	Small o, acute accent
ô	&#244;	&ocirc;	Small o, circumflex accent
õ	&#245;	&otilde;	Small o, tilde
ö	&#246;	&ouml;	Small o, dieresis, or umlaut, mark
÷	&#247;		Division sign
ø	&#248;	&oslash;	Small o, slash
ù	&#249;	&ugrave;	Small u, grave accent
ú	&#250;	&uacute;	Small u, acute accent
û	&#251;	&ucirc;	Small u, circumflex accent
ü	&#252;	&uuml;	Small u, dieresis, or umlaut, mark
ý	&#253;	&yacute;	Small y, acute accent
þ	&#254;	&thorn;	Small thorn, Icelandic
ÿ	&#255;	&yuml;	Small y, dieresis, or umlaut, mark

B

Named HTML Colors with Hexadecimal Equivalents

The following chart lists the most commonly used colors in Web pages. To use them, insert the hexadecimal code into an appropriate location.

Aqua	#00FFFF	Navy	#000080
Black	#000000	Olive	#808000
Blue	#0000FF	Purple	#800080
Fuchsia	#FF00FF	Red	#FF0000
Gray	#808080	Silver	#C0C0C0
Green	#008000	Teal	#008080
Lime	#00FF00	White	#FFFFFF
Maroon	#800000	Yellow	#FFFF00

Standard HTML Icons

To view the current standard HTML icons that you can use and specify in your Web pages, see the World Wide Web Consortium's Web site at http://www.w3.org.

Development Tools and Aids

The following entries show the supplemental files that have been included on the CD-ROM that accompanies this book. Also included is the relative directory in which you can find the files for the program.

Graphics

`\Graphics\Images\Rocket\An_gifs`	Animated GIFs by RocketShop
`\Graphics\Images\Rocket\GIFs`	Static GIFs by RocketShop
`\Graphics\Tools\CompuPic`	CompuPic by Photodex Corp.
`\Graphics\Tools\EZView`	EZViewer32 by Galt Technologies
`\Graphics\Tools\psp41`	PaintShop Pro 4.1 by JASC, Inc.
`\Graphics\Tools\Snagit32`	SnagIt/32 by TechSmith Corporation
`\Graphics\Tools\Thumbs`	ThumbsPlus by Cerious Software
`\Graphics\Tools\Imagegen`	ImageGen by Robert Thievierge

HTML Tools

`\html\ezhtml`	eZ-HTML by DesignTyme
`\html\hotdog3`	HotDog32 by Sausage Software
`\html\htmlnote`	HTML Notepad by Cranial Software

Internet Programming

`\prog\cgi\cgistar`	CGI*Star by WebGenie
`\prog\cgi\libs`	Various CGI libraries
`\prog\cgi\mattcgi`	CGI applets by Matt Wright
`\prog\java\jamba`	Jama by Aimtech Corporation
`\prog\java\jdesign`	JDesignerPro by Bulletproof
`\prog\java\jpad`	Jpad (Pro and Standard) by ModelWorks Software
`\prog\java\jdk`	Java Developer's Kit by Sun Microsystems

Internet Utilities

`\util\winzip`	WinZip 6.2 by Nikko Mak Computing
`\util\adobe`	Adobe Acrobat Reader 3.0 by Adobe Systems
`\util\micrsoft\fpdevkit`	FrontPage 97 Dev Kit by Microsoft
`\util\micrsoft\camcord`	Microsoft Camcorder by Microsoft
`\util\cuteftp`	CuteFTP by GlobalSCAPE, Inc.
`\util\micrsoft\explore`	Internet Explorer 3.01 by Microsoft
`\util\micrsoft\viewers\word`	MS Word 95 viewer by Microsoft
`\util\micrsoft\viewers\excel`	MS Excel 95 viewer by Microsoft
`\util\micrsoft\viewers\powerpnt`	MS PowerPoint 95 viewer by Microsoft

Web Tools

\webtools\webedit	WebEdit by Nesbitt Software
\webtools\webwizard	WEB Wizard by Arta Software Group
\webtools\webwev4b	Web Weaver by Mark McConnell
\webtools\w3e	W3e HTML Editor by NCE/UFRJ
\webtools\mapthis	MapThis! by InContext Systems
\webtools\incon\icspider	Spider 1.2 by InContext Systems
\webtools\incon\webizer	WebAnalyzer by InContext Systems

16-Bit Software and Utilities

\16bit\graphics\images\rocket\an_gifs	Animated GIFs by RocketShop
\16bit\graphics\images\rocket\gifs	Static GIFs by RocketShop
\16bit\graphics\tools\compupic	CompuPic by PhotoDex
\16bit\html\htmlnote\	HTML NotePad by Cranial Software
\16bit\util\adobe\	Adobe Acrobat Reader 3.0 by Adobe Systems
\16bit\util\cuteftp	CuteFTP by GlobalSCAPE, Inc.
\16bit\util\explore	Internet Explorer by Microsoft
\16bit\util\winzip	WinZip by Nikko Mak Computing
\16bit\webtools\webwiz	WEB Wizard by Arta Software Group

Sams

\sams\catalog	Sams Publishing/Sams.net electronic catalogs

APPENDIX

D

Glossary

alignment   The physical arrangement of a body of text.

analog data   Data that is defined by a series of frequency variations.

asynchronous communication   Communication that occurs without any basis on time. Communication is based on the addition of start and stop bits that are added to the transferred data.

Audio Video Interleaved (AVI)   A digital video format that is native to the Windows environment.

balance   Describes how the page elements are arranged visually; comparing one half to another.

bit depth   Defines the physical number of bits that can be used to describe a sample.

bitmap graphics   Graphics in which the smallest drawing element is the pixel or picture element.

block tags   HTML tags that enable you to specify the formatting and arrangement of lines or bodies of text or graphics. They are characterized by a preceding and following blank line or space.

BMP (Windows Bitmap)   Native Windows raster graphic format that supports up to 24-bit color and can use lossless run-length encoding (RLE) compression.

bookmarks   Used in Netscape to give you the ability to save the address of a particular site or page in a menu of the same name.

bridge   Connects two or more similar networks that use the same protocol.

browser cache   A special location, usually a folder or directory, on the user's hard drive where HTML files, graphics, and resource files are stored during the browser work session.

browser software   A software program that enables the user to view Web-based documents. All browsers retrieve semantically described information from remote computers and then composite text, graphics, and multimedia elements on the users' machines.

client/server networking model   Describes a network in which all information is provided and managed by a single computer in the network, called the server.

codec   Stands for Compressor/Decompressor; an algorithm used to expand and compress a digital file.

compression ratio   The ratio of the uncompressed file's size to the compressed file's size. A measurement of the effectiveness of a codec.

digital data   Data that is represented mathematically as a series of zeroes and ones.

dots per inch (dpi)   A measurement used to describe the number of physical, printable dots per square inch of an image.

electronic mail (e-mail)   The ability to send electronic messages and attached files to remote users via the Internet.

eyeflow   The pattern or direction in which your eye flows across a page of information.

favorites   Used in Explorer to enable you to save the address of a particular site or page in a menu of the same name.

file transfer protocol (FTP)   A set of standards for the transmission of files across the Internet.

firewall   A software application that is used to limit or prevent access to network resources. It restricts outsider access while enabling internal users to see the outside world.

gateway   The point of interconnection between two dissimilar networks that handles routing functions and can translate information between the two networks.

Gopher   A menu- and text-based Internet browsing program that can be used to download files and information from remote computers.

Graphics Interchange Format (GIF)   Common Internet graphics format that supports up to 256 colors as well as transparency data.

hexadecimal color   A base-16 mathematical numbering system used to define and describe HTML colors.

hit   When a browser from a remote location requests information from a Web server. Each time a new or different page is loaded from the site, a hit is recorded.

home (splash) page   The main or first page that is loaded from a site. It usually gives the audience an overview of the contents of the site.

horizontal space   The relative width of the letter M in the font.

HTTP server   A Web server. HTTP is an acronym for HyperText Transfer Protocol.

hypermedia   Media-based communications that are not strictly limited to text.

hypertext   Text that is non-sequential or non-linear in nature. The reader is actually able to choose a path to delve deeper into the information.

HyperText Markup Language (HTML)   A Web page language that uses style "tags" to define how text, graphics, and other elements should be arranged on a Web page.

HyperText Transfer Protocol (HTTP)   A set of standards for providing content and media elements on the Web.

image size   The physical height and width dimensions for an image.

information design specialist   An individual who understands the communication process and how to design products that inform, persuade, educate, or entertain efficiently and effectively.

inline graphic   A graphic that is embedded or inserted into a Web page shown in a browser. An inline graphic is displayed without the aid of external viewers or helper applications.

Integrated Services Digital Network (ISDN)   Enables a user to access a digital phone line via dial-up using a codec rather than a modem.

interface   The point of interaction between the computer and the user; it must enable input and output from both parties.

internal links   Pages that have links to other sections of the same document.

Internet Protocol (IP)   A protocol that transfers data using small packets or chunks of data. Data being transferred is broken into packets, sent through the network, and then reassembled on the receiving end.

Internet specialist   An individual who understands what the Internet is, from where it has come, and where it might be going. The Internet specialist also understands how to connect to the Internet and how to utilize it.

intranet   An internal, exclusive, and secure Web server that gives employees and staff inside an institution or company the ability to share information without releasing the information to the Web community at large.

intrasite link   A hotlink that is referenced to other pages within the current Web site or on the current Web server.

Java   An object-oriented programming language used to create executable applications that are commonly distributed over the Internet.

Joint Picture Experts Group (JPEG)   A commonly used graphic format on the Web that supports up to 24-bit color and utilizes lossy compression.

leading   The spacing between multiple lines of text.

letter spacing   The defined spacing between letters.

license   A fee that is paid to use a copyrighted item in another publication.

link, hotlink, or hyperlink   An area on a Web page that, when clicked, takes you to another site or page.

Local-Area Network (LAN)   A computer network that spans a very short distance, such as a network of computers in a single office.

logical style   A text-level tag that affects a font style to draw attention to the font as well as communicate some other information to the reader.

lossless compression   A compression scheme in which a decompressed file creates an exact replica of the original file.

lossy compression   A compression scheme in which certain amounts of data are sacrificed to attain smaller file sizes.

media designer   An individual who understands computer graphics, animation, video, and sound, and can effectively use these media elements to enhance communication.

metaphor   A theme, motif, or storyline that attempts to familiarize the audience with something new using past association.

Motion Pictures Experts Group (MPEG) A digital video format commonly found on the Internet.

Multipurpose Internet Mail Extensions (MIME) A definition scheme that associates a specific file extension with a respective application.

negative space (white space) An area on a page in which no graphical or textual elements appear.

newsgroup An electronic message board on which you can post messages, read messages, and exchange files.

non-transient information Information that changes or becomes outdated on a nine-month to an annual cycle.

peer-to-peer networking model Describes a network in which all computers on the network share equal responsibility for managing and providing information.

physical style A text-level tag that affects a font style to simply draw attention to the font itself. It communicates no other information through the formatting of the text.

PICT A common Macintosh file format that can contain both raster- and vector-based data.

plug-in An add-on program that acts as an interpreter and viewer for multimedia elements distributed over the Web. The plug-in interprets and executes the sound, video, or program to enable the user to listen, watch, or interact with the multimedia element.

point size The overall size of a font measured in points.

Point-to-Point Protocol (PPP) Software that enables both synchronous and asychronous communication to occur via a modem.

Portable Network Graphics (PNG) A newly developed graphics file format designed for Web distribution. It overcomes many of the shortcomings of the GIF and JPEG formats.

positive space An area on a Web page that contains a media element such as text or graphics.

protocol A set of standards that define how data is transmitted and received between computers. A protocol ensures data is transmitted in a defined way so that it can also be received.

public domain Refers to any work that is not protected under copyright (patent or trademark) or media that is not considered a creative work. Items can also be considered public domain if the copyright for the item expires.

QuickTime A digital video format native to the Windows environment.

release A formal agreement that enables an individual to use a copyrighted item at no charge. A release usually defines specific parameters in which the item can be used.

sans serif Fonts without serifs.

saturation The pureness of the color, such as a fluorescent blue compared to a subdued blue.

search engine A Web software mechanism that compares the keyword you enter to words in the HTML files that exist in cyberspace giving you a list of sites that might relate to your keyword.

Serial Line Internet Protocol (SLIP) Software that enables asynchronous communication to occur via a modem.

serif fonts Fonts with serifs.

serifs The small feet and tails that appear on the characters of a font to increase readability.

Standard Generalized Markup Language (SGML) A system for defining structured documents that can be ported from one machine to another without having to deal with extraneous hardware and software issues.

streaming A technology in which data files are sent to the client in chunks. These chunks are playing or executing before the entire file is downloaded.

T1 A type of direct network connection that supports a bandwidth of 1,544 Kbps with monthly cost ranges from $1,000 to $3,000.

T3 A type of direct network connection that supports hundreds of LAN networks and boasts a 44,736 Kbps bandwidth. T3 is also what forms the Internet backbone's major network connections.

Tagged Image File Format (TIFF) A raster graphics file format that can contain up to 64-bit image data and can utilize lossless compression; originally created for high-resolution bitmap images.

TCP/IP The protocol used on the Internet that consists of the Transmission Control Protocol and the Internet Protocol.

technical designer An individual who understands the standards, hardware, and software of a Web network and how to fit them together to make a working site.

technical manager An individual who manages the hardware, software, resources, and people involved in the Web development process.

Telnet An application that enables you to connect to and use a remote computer and its applications.

text-level tags   Tags that are used to stylize text and add hyperlinks, graphics, and multimedia elements.

tone   Refers to the manner in which the Web document is presented to the audience.

transient information   Information that has a short life cycle; it changes or becomes outdated within nine months or less.

typefont   A set of characters with similar attributes, such as similar height, width, and spacing. Examples of typefonts include Arial, Helvetica, and Times.

Uniform Resource Locator (URL)   The specific address of a Web site or Web resource.

value   The lightness or darkness of a particular color, such as a light blue versus a dark blue.

vector graphics   Graphics in which the smallest drawing elements are points, lines, and circles.

weight   The width of the strokes that compose the lines and curves of the letters of a font.

Wide-Area Network (WAN)   A network that includes a wide region, such as networked computers that span an entire city or the entire world.

INDEX

A

A VIACOM SERVICE

The Information SuperLibrary™

 Bookstore

 Search

 What's New

 Reference

 Software

 Newsletter

 Company Overviews

 Yellow Pages

 Internet Starter Kit

 HTML Workshop

 Win a Free T-Shirt!

 Macmillan Computer Publishing

 Site Map

 Talk to Us

CHECK OUT THE BOOKS IN THIS LIBRARY.

You'll find thousands of shareware files and over 1600 computer books designed for both technowizards and technophobes. You can browse through 700 sample chapters, get the latest news on the Net, and find just about anything using our

We're open 24-hours a day, 365 days a year.

You don't need a card.

We don't charge fines.

And you can be as **LOUD** as you want.

MACMILLAN COMPUTER PUBLISHING USA
A VIACOM COMPANY

Technical ┄┄┐
┊
┄┄ Support:

If you need assistance with the information in this book or with a CD/Disk
accompanying the book, please access the Knowledge Base on our Web
site at **http://www.superlibrary.com/general/support**. Our most
Frequently Asked Questions are answered there. If you do not find the
answer to your questions on our Web site, you may contact Macmillan
Technical Support **(317) 581-3833** or e-mail us at **support@mcp.com.**

HTML 3.2 and CGI Unleashed, Professional Reference Edition

—*John December and Mark Ginsburg*

Readers learn the logistics of how to create compelling, information-rich Web pages that grab readers' attention and keep users returning for more. This comprehensive professional instruction and reference guide for the World Wide Web covers all aspects of the development processes, implementation, tools, and programming. The CD-ROM features coverage of planning, analysis, design, HTML implementation, and gateway programming.

Price: $59.99 USA/$84.95 CDN
ISBN: 1-57521-177-7

User level: Accomplished–Expert
1320 pages

Teach Yourself Web Publishing with HTML 3.2 in 14 Days, Professional Reference Edition

—*Laura Lemay*

This is the updated edition of Lemay's previous bestseller, *Teach Yourself Web Publishing with HTML in 14 Days, Premier Edition*. Readers find all the advanced topics and updates, including adding audio, video, and animation to Web page creation. The book explores the use of CGI scripts, tables, HTML 3.2, the Netscape and Internet Explorer extensions, Java applets and JavaScript, and VRML.

Price: $59.99 USA/$84.95 CDN
ISBN: 1-57521-096-7

User level: New–Casual–Accomplished
1,104 pages

Teach Yourself CGI Programming with Perl 5 in a Week, Second Edition

—*Eric Herrmann*

Teach Yourself CGI Programming with Perl 5 in a Week, Second Edition is the follow-up to the bestseller, completely revised and updated to cover Perl 5 in greater detail. It includes complete coverage of Windows CGI and Perl QuickStart to bring the beginning programmer quickly up to speed. It includes detailed instructions for using CGI in a Windows environment. The CD-ROM includes an electronic version of the book, sample source code, and a collection of Perl libraries.

Price: $39.99 USA/$56.95 CDN
ISBN: 1-57521-196-3

User level: Beginning–Intermediate
600 pages

Teach Yourself Java in 21 Days, Professional Reference Edition

—*Laura Lemay and Michael Morrison*

Introducing the first, best, and most detailed guide to developing applications with the hot new Java language from Sun Microsystems. This book provides detailed coverage of the hottest new technology on the World Wide Web and shows readers how to develop applications using the Java language. It includes coverage of how to browse Java applications with Netscape and other popular Web browsers.

Price: $59.99 USA/$84.95 CDN
ISBN: 1-57521-183-1

User level: Casual–Accomplished–Expert
900 pages

Teach Yourself JavaScript in a Week, Second Edition

—Arman Danesh

Teach Yourself JavaScript in a Week, Second Edition is a new edition of the bestselling JavaScript tutorial. It has been revised and updated for the latest version of JavaScript from Netscape and includes detailed coverage of new features such as how to work with Java applets with LiveConnect, writing JavaScript for Microsoft's Internet Explorer, and more! The CD-ROM includes the full version of Netscape Navigator Gold, additional tools, and ready-to-use sample scripts.

Price: $39.99 USA/$56.95 CDN *User level: Beginning–Intermediate*
ISBN: 1-57521-195-5   *600 pages*

Laura Lemay's Web Workshop: Creating Commercial Web Pages

—Laura Lemay and Brian K. Murphy

Filled with sample Web pages, this book shows how to create commercial-grade Web pages using HTML, CGI, and Java. In the classic clear style of Laura Lemay, author of the bestselling *Teach Yourself Java*, it details not only how to create the page, but how to apply proven principles of design that will make the Web page a marketing tool. The CD-ROM includes all the templates in the book, plus HTML editors, graphics software, CGI forms, and more.

Price: $39.99 USA/$56.95 CDN *User level: Accomplished*
ISBN: 1-57521-126-2   *528 pages*

Laura Lemay's Web Workshop: Graphics and Web Page Design

—Laura Lemay, Jon M. Duff, and James L. Mohler

With the number of Web pages increasing daily, only the well-designed will stand out and grab the attention of those browsing the Web. This book illustrates, in classic Laura Lemay style, how to design attractive Web pages that will be visited over and over again. The CD-ROM contains HTML editors, graphics software, and royalty-free graphics and sound files.

Price: $55.00 USA/$77.95 CDN *User level: Accomplished*
ISBN: 1-57521-125-4   *500 pages*

Laura Lemay's Web Workshop: Microsoft FrontPage

—Laura Lemay and Denise Tyler

This is a clear hands-on guide to maintaining Web pages with Microsoft's FrontPage. Written in the clear, conversational style of Laura Lemay, it is packed with many interesting, colorful examples that demonstrate specific tasks of interest to the reader. This book teaches how to maintain Web pages with FrontPage, and the CD-ROM includes all the templates, backgrounds, and materials needed!

Price: $39.99 USA/$56.95 CDN *User level: Casual–Accomplished*
ISBN: 1-57521-149-1   *672 pages*

Add to Your Sams.net Library Today
with the Best Books for Internet Technologies

ISBN	Quantity	Description of Item	Unit Cost	Total Cost
1-57521-177-7		HTML 3.2 & CGI Unleashed, Professional Reference Edition (Book/CD-ROM)	$59.99	
1-57521-096-7		Teach Yourself Web Publishing with HTML 3.2 in 14 Days, Professional Reference Edition (Book/CD-ROM)	$59.99	
1-57521-196-3		Teach Yourself CGI Programming with Perl 5 in a Week, Second Edition (Book/CD-ROM)	$39.99	
1-57521-183-1		Teach Yourself Java in 21 Days, Professional Reference Edition (Book/CD-ROM)	$59.99	
1-57521-195-5		Teach Yourself JavaScript in a Week, Second Edition (Book/CD-ROM)	$39.99	
1-57521-126-2		Laura Lemay's Web Workshop: Creating Commercial Web Pages (Book/CD-ROM)	$39.99	
1-57521-125-4		Laura Lemay's Web Workshop: Graphics and Web Page Design (Book/CD-ROM)	$55.00	
1-57521-149-1		Laura Lemay's Web Workshop: Microsoft FrontPage (Book/CD-ROM)	$39.99	
		Shipping and Handling: See information below.		
		TOTAL		

Shipping and Handling: $4.00 for the first book, and $1.75 for each additional book. If you need to have it NOW, we can ship product to you in 24 hours for an additional charge of approximately $18.00, and you will receive your item overnight or in two days. Overseas shipping and handling adds $2.00. Prices subject to change. Call between 9:00 a.m. and 5:00 p.m. EST for availability and pricing information on latest editions.

201 W. 103rd Street, Indianapolis, Indiana 46290

1-800-428-5331 — Orders   1-800-835-3202 — FAX   1-800-858-7674 — Customer Service

Book ISBN 1-57521-228-5

What's on the CD-ROM

The companion CD-ROM contains software developed by the author, plus an assortment of third-party tools, shareware software, and product demos.

The disc is designed to be explored using an HTML-based Web browser. Using a Web browser program, you can view information concerning products and companies and install programs with a few clicks of the mouse. You must have either a Web browser or another program that recognizes .HTM files in order to preview many of the files included on this CD-ROM.

NOTE This disc was optimized for Microsoft Internet Explorer 3.01; therefore, a 16-bit and 32-bit version of Internet Explorer are included on this CD-ROM for your convenience.

To run the browser program, follow these steps.

Windows 3.1 Installation Instructions

1. Insert the CD-ROM into your CD-ROM drive.
2. From File Manager or Program Manager, choose Run from the File menu.
3. Type *<drive>*\SETUP and press Enter, where *<drive>* corresponds to the drive letter of your CD-ROM. For example, if your CD-ROM is drive D:, type D:\SETUP and press Enter.
4. Double-click the CD-ROM HTML Browser icon in the newly created Program Group to access the home page of the CD-ROM and preview the CD-ROM contents.
5. To review the latest information about the CD-ROM, double-click the icon called About this CD-ROM.

Windows 95 Installation Instructions

1. Insert the CD-ROM into your CD-ROM drive.

2. If Windows 95 is installed on your computer and you have the AutoPlay feature enabled, a Program Group for this book is automatically created whenever you insert the disc into your CD-ROM drive.

3. If Autoplay is not enabled, using Windows Explorer, choose Setup from the CD-ROM drive to create the Program Group for this book.

4. Double-click the CD-ROM HTML Browser icon in the newly created Program Group to access the home page of the CD-ROM and preview the CD-ROM contents.

5. To review the latest information about the CD-ROM, double-click the icon called About this CD-ROM.

NOTE

> For best results, set your monitor to display between 256 and 64,000 colors. A screen resolution of 640×480 pixels is also recommended. If necessary, adjust your monitor settings before using the CD-ROM.